Introduction to Australian Society

A Sociological Perspective

Introduction to Australian Society

A Sociological Perspective

Donald Edgar

Prentice-Hall of Australia Pty Ltd

Prentice-Hall of Australia Pty Ltd, Sydney
Prentice-Hall International Inc, London
Prentice-Hall of Canada Ltd, Toronto
Prentice-Hall of India Private Ltd, New Delhi
Prentice-Hall of Japan Inc, Tokyo
Prentice-Hall of Southeast Asia Pte Ltd, Singapore
Whitehall Books Ltd, Wellington
Prentice-Hall Inc, Englewood Cliffs, New Jersey

Typeset by Abb-Typesetting Pty Ltd,
Collingwood, Vic.
Cover design by Elizabeth Honey
Printed and bound in Australia by
Globe Press Pty. Ltd., Brunswick, Vic.

9 10 89 88 87 86

National Library of Australia
Cataloguing-in-Publication Data

Edgar, Donald Ernest.
  Introduction to Australian society.

  Index
  Bibliography
  ISBN 0 7248 0649 0

  1. Australia—Social conditions. I. Title.

DC 18: 309.1'94'06
DC 19: 994.06'3

Contents

(Each Chapter ends with a comprehensive list of
a. Australian References and b. General
References, relating to the Chapter topics.)

To Patricia, Susan and Lesley

Acknowledgements

It is impossible to acknowledge one's indebtedness for ideas, though the major debt is clearly to my colleagues and to the students I have been privileged to teach over the years.

For practical help the task is easier and there are many who have given generously of their time and care. Typing and duplicating of drafts has been done by Norma Cann, Judy Carr, Jill Gooch, Fay Kolevas, Liza Leigh, Marie Peel and the two ladies from Jentra Secretarial, Veronica Trayford and Jenny Jenkins who handled the overload at rush periods. To them all, my thanks.

Freya Headlam put in many hours searching for latest figures and compiling tables. My thanks to her and to Fleur Spitzer who also helped. Without that support the book's deadline would have been even further over-reached.

My appreciation must also go to Charles Lucas of Prentice-Hall who first suggested the book and to Jillian le Patourel whose gentle urging got the manuscript to a point where it could be edited. Other people I know kindly commented on the manuscript but to mention them might be to divert blame from my own sins of omission and commission.

The book has been fun to write; I hope it is not too dull to read.

Donald Edgar
Melbourne

Sources

The author and publisher have made an effort to trace the source of copyright for material used in this book, however they would be glad to hear of any errors or omissions in the following list.

The Australian statistics are used with the kind permission of the Australian Government Publishing Service and the Australian Bureau of Statistics.

Page 15: W. K. Handcock, *Australia* © Ernest Benn Ltd; Humphrey McQueen, *Australian Politics, a 4th reader*, H. Mayer and H. Nelson (eds), Cheshire, Melbourne, 1976, p.68.

Pages 15-16: Reprinted from Harris, M., *Ockers, Essays on the Bad Old New Australian*, Maximus Books, 1974.

Page 16: Courtesy of Paul Hogan and the Australian Broadcasting Commission; 'Images of Australia' by R. W. Connell, *Quadrant*, March-April, 1968.

Page 18: A. Jacubowicz in *Social Change in Australia*, D. Edgar (ed.), Longman, 1974.

Page 19: Australian Bureau of Statistics, Year Book, 1929; National Population Inquiry reproduced by permission of the Australian Government Publishing Service.

Pages 19-20: Centre for Urban Research and Action.

Page 22: Statistics from L. Aarons, 'Australian Class Structure', *Communist Review*, 192, 1957.

Page 23: Table 1—5, Courtesy of *The Age*.

Page 24: Table 1—6. The Morgan Gallup Poll is conducted by the only Australian member of Gallup International Research Institutes, Inc. No other public opinion poll taken in Australia has this qualification. All Australian results are copyright of the Morgan Gallup Poll.

Page 25: Table 1—8, Courtesy of *The Age*.

Page 42: *Exchange and Power in Social Life*, P. M. Blau, copyright © 1967 John Wiley & Sons. Reprinted by permission of John Wiley & Sons, Inc.

Page 44: T. Parsons, *The Social System*, Free Press, N.Y., 1951.

Page 45: A. W. Gouldner, *The Coming Crisis of Western Sociology*, Heinemann Educational Books, London.

Page 70: By permission of the Australian Government Publishing Service.

Page 72: From Raskall, P., 'Who's Got What in Australia: The Distribution of Wealth' in *Journal of Australian Political Economy*, 1978, No. 2, June.

Page 74: W. F. Connell, *Ruling Class, Ruling Culture*, Cambridge University Press, Cambridge, 1977.

Page 76: Table 3−3, Courtesy of *The Age*.

Page 94-95: Excerpt from *The Social Construction of Reality* by Peter L. Berger and Thomas Luckmann. Copyright © 1966 by Peter L. Berger and Thomas Luckmann. Reprinted by permission of Doubleday & Company Inc.

Page 110: Australian Bureau of Statistics, Census, 1976.

Page 117: E. Shorter, *The Making of the Modern Family*, Collins, London.

Page 122: Table 5−1, from K. Richmond in *Social Change in Australia*, D. Edgar (ed.), Longman, 1974.

Page 123: Table 5−2, from *Families in Australia — a profile*, Family Research Unit, University of New South Wales, 1978.

Page 129: The extract from *The Ascent of Man* by J. Bronowski is reprinted by permission of Angus & Robertson Publishers.

Page 130: 'Brothers and Sisters' from *Judith Wright: Collected Poems* is reprinted by permission of Angus & Robertson Publishers. 'A Spring Song' from *Selected Verse of C. J. Dennis* is reprinted by permission of Angus & Robertson Publishers.

Page 131: From Karl Marx, *The German Ideology*, International Publishing Company.

Page 136: Copyright 1940 and renewed 1968 by W. H. Auden. Reprinted from *Collected Shorter Poems 1927−1957* by W. H. Auden, by permission of Random House, Inc. and Faber and Faber, Limited.

Pages 136 & 137: Wagner, H. R., *Alfred Schutz on Phenomenology and Social Relations*, University of Chicago Press, 1970.

Page 138: Schutz, A., and T. Luckmann, *The Structures of the Life World*, Heinemann Educational Books, London, 1974.

Page 150: Copyright © 1969 by President and Fellows of Harvard College.

Page 162: Melvin L. Kohn and C. Schooler, 'Class, Occupation and Orientation', *American Sociological Review*, Vol. 34, 1969, p.675.

Page 169: S. Harvey in *Social Change in Australia*, D. E. Edgar (ed.), Longman, 1974.

Page 170: A. D. Edwards, *Language in Culture and Class*, Heinemann Educational Books, London, 1976.

Page 185: By permission of the Australian Government Publishing Service.

Page 192: Reprinted from 'School and Society in West Heidelberg' by F. J. Campbell, Melbourne, 1978.

Page 208: Reprinted by permission of Wildwood House Ltd. Copyright © Studs Terkel.

Page 217: Max Weber, *The Theory of Social and Economic Organization*, A. M. Henderson & Talcott Parson, eds. and trans.

Page 222: Table 9−7 reprinted from 'Occupational Prestige in the United States, 1925−1963', *American Journal of Sociology*, 70:3 (Nov. 1964), by permission of the University of Chicago Press.

Page 226: Patrick M. Horan, 'Is Status Attainment Research Atheoretical?', *American Sociological Review*, Vol. 43, 1978, pp.534-41.

Page 231: R. Collins, *Conflict Sociology: Towards an Explanatory Science*, Academic Press, N.Y., 1975.

Page 237: Goldthorpe, J. H. et al, *The Affluent Worker in the Class Structure*, Cambridge University Press, Cambridge, 1969.

Page 240: By permission of the Australian Government Publishing Service.

Pages 253 & 261: P. M. Edgar, *The Politics of the Press*, Sun Books, 1979.

Page 254: Brown A. (comp.), *Australian Media Ownership*, Occasional Media Monograph No. 1, Department of Economics, University of Queensland, 1977.

Page 268: From *Children and Screen Violence*, by Patricia Edgar, published by University of Queensland Press, 1977.

Page 278: From H. A. Bailey and E. Katz, *Ethnic Group Politics*, Merrill Publishing, 1969.

Page 280: Schutz, A., and T. Luckmann, *The Structures of the Life World*, Heinemann Educational Books, London, 1974.

Page 290: F. Mackie in *Social Change in Australia*, D. Edgar (ed.), Longman, 1974; from R. Wild, 'Social Stratification or Statistical Exercises?', *Politics*, Vol. 6, No. 2, pp.169-77.

Page 291: From Martin, J. I., *Migrants Equality and Ideology*, Meredith Memorial Lectures, published by La Trobe University, 1972.

Page 292: Martin, J. I., *The Migrant Presence*, George Allen & Unwin, Australia, 1978.

Page 297: From *Australian Financial Review*, 21 June, 1979.

Page 299: From Head, B. and Patience, A., *From Whitlam to Fraser*, Oxford University Press, Melbourne.

Page 313: *The Weekend Australian*.

Page 321: © Copyright 1979 by Social Policy Corporation.

Preface

Australian sociology has come a long way in the ten years since I taught my first introductory course. Then, there were so few studies based on Australian data that students must, quite understandably, have felt we were pushing an American or British imperialist line. By 1973, when I was asked to write an Australian sociology text, I refused, on pedagogical grounds. It seemed better to produce a new collection that would bring to light the by then growing numbers of research studies accumulating dust on library shelves. This I did in the book of edited readings, *Social Change in Australia*.

In the first chapter of that book I wrote of Australian sociology in terms of 'Paradise lost, sociology regained'. From a narrow empiricist orientation, it seemed to be moving towards a better understanding of power structures, a discovery of culture conflict in everyday life and an acceptance that neutrality on policy issues is impossible and undesirable in any human science. That optimism may have been a little over-weening but it was not misplaced. Sociology in Australia has proved its value since then in an immense output of research on pressing social problems. Still perhaps too obsessed with figures with which to bedazzle politicians, we have now nonetheless a much more comprehensive picture of how Australian society 'works'. Major studies on poverty and inequality, on ethnic affairs, deviance, the media, urban and rural communities have altered the easy acceptance of Australia's traditional myths. There has been a growth, too, in the degree of inter-disciplinary exchange, so that historians, economists, lawyers, philosophers and political scientists contribute jointly to major research efforts.

About the teaching of sociology, too, I am more sanguine, though it is from my dissatisfactions that this book has grown. As Departments of Sociology grow, two things seem to happen. First the competence of expert staff increases and courses in theory, methodology and substantive social areas improve. Parallel with this, however, students often lose track of the central sociological issues. Specialization becomes narrowness. Theory takes on a life of its own as though it were not merely a means to the end of understanding. Theorists are examined in such detail that no-one asks the 'So-what?' questions that should bring people down to earth and to real life sociological issues. The same thing can happen with methodology, though I think the old danger of methods in search of substance has receded. 'Methods' people are no longer just statisticians: they are now fully trained sociologists who insist on thinking theories through before running off with questionnaires or to the computer. Theorists, on the other hand, seem to be obsessed with fine analysis of texts and terrified that someone might ask how it all applies here and now. Neither half-baked philosophy nor a Leavisite concern with the text will do.

Students of sociology must see the wood through the trees. They must be taught to ask the 'So-what?' questions about both theory and research. Above all, they must not be deceived into thinking that sociology is merely a soft, descriptive discipline where 'explanation' is impossible because there are no 'hard facts'. There are hard facts; the goal is explanation of social behaviour and there are techniques for doing it. Endless debates about objective versus subjective sciences, about 'understanding' (*Verstehen*) as a better goal than explanation, about free will and humanistic approaches to the study of society, cannot obscure the fact that we all try to explain social behaviour.

Sociology is, of course, only one of the humanistic sciences. Psychology, law, economics, anthropology, history, philosophy, literature, politics, all try in various ways to understand and explain human behaviour. No one discipline can be 'better' than another because their scope and emphasis differ. Good sociologists will draw on anything to gain insights into their special interests: the impact on human behaviour of social structures and social values. Sociological theories and methods restrict what can be done but give focus to that goal.

Sociology is, in fact, uniquely suited to cultivating what Bierstedt calls 'the liberated mind'. Most people do not understand the vast and universal discrepancy between behaviour and ideal norms, the way society has 'produced' them or the way in which they and their groups 'construct' social reality. What sociology does that other social sciences do less explicitly, is to reveal society 'as part of a human world, made by men, inhabited by men, and, in turn, making men, in an ongoing historical process' (Berger & Luckmann, 1967, p.189).

Sociology can help demote group-based and ethnocentric restraints on action and promote intelligent, less biased views more appropriate in a rapidly changing 'global village'.

The basic facts and principles concerning socialization processes, the social distribution of knowledge and its relation to societal power structures, cultural variations and similarities, and the ubiquitous nature of social change should become part of the intellectual equipment of all who study sociology.

We have also to unteach a lot of 'popular sociology', that often unreliable stock of social knowledge that everyone must have, merely to live in society. We have to demonstrate, not merely advocate, the need for substantiated evidence and rigorous analysis of social data; to show that abstract social theory and observable social facts together contribute to a realistic explanation of social life; to disabuse the 'folk distinction between *theoretical* and *real*' (Edgar, 1970); and to demonstrate the interdependence of logical rules of analysis and methods of investigation without swamping students with methods rather than substance.

Sociology may not be a closed system of thought, but it is not completely open either, and first-year students need to be made aware of its distinct orientation. The unique nature of social, as opposed to natural, science lies in its *Verstehen*, the necessity for subjective understanding as a precursor to scientific explanation. If sociology is the study of people in society and society in people, we cannot leave people out or wish away the idiosyncrasies of their social nature. Sociologists study not simply action, but action into which people read meanings; in fact sociology exists as a study because 'the shared significance of the same kind of social action can alter between collectivities' (Burns, 1969, p.78). Thus, communication processes, the social distribution of knowledge, the distinctions and sources of differing values, attitudes and beliefs in the actions of people need greater emphasis than we give them at present.

Sociology is also uniquely the study of the interdependence between *social* conditions, how each depends on others in the social structure, so that psychological processes should be seen as intervening variables, themselves to be explained in terms of the antecedent social conditions that have produced them. Thus we need to focus on the determinants of social structures as well as the effects of social structure on individual human conduct (Blau, 1969, p.52).

The dilemma posed in writing a textbook is what to include and what to omit. My solution has been to worry less about covering everything than about how to approach what is covered. In line with my firm belief that every course should start with the known, what is familiar, and build outward, I have concentrated upon those aspects of the life-cycle that everyone goes through: the family, education and work. It is expected that other books will be used to supplement what is here presented.

Further, it is assumed that students will not merely read books and attend lectures. Dare I ask how many of our 'introductory' sociology courses involve the actual observation and description of behaviour? How often do we ask students to observe and describe the actions, symbols and behaviour of themselves and others? How often in fact do we ourselves observe human behaviour other than through the blinkers of survey questionnaires? In our haste to stress the theoretical nature of sociology it seems we may have forgotten the basic scientific necessity of describing and observing the social behaviour we claim as our substance. If our aim is subversion (of social falsehoods, not of any political system), to 'shake their confidence in the validity of personal experience' it makes sense only if we start with that experience (Toby, 1961, pp.279—80).

Students should be encouraged to write constantly about their observations of the ways people behave on railway stations, in cafes, buses, theatres, tutorials, at meals and at meetings. They should compare their own with others' ideas and experiences of family life, religion, inequality, work and leisure. Such exercises are a way of stimulating sociological questions: Why do I think and behave the way I do? Why do others (and which others?) disagree? How does behaviour vary in differing situations, with a girlfriend, a group of friends, in the football clubroom or in the lecture theatre? Why do some people change and others resist change? How much power does an individual have in the face of societal pressures?

The consequence of asking such questions must be faced. There will be shock, rejection, even despair as students realize that they cannot take the world for granted. Disenchantment can lead to a demand for social action, involvement or reform. No-one who teaches sociology can maintain the slogan of 'separating *facts* from *values*', a slogan whose substance is 'to suppress values at the expense of facts' (Horowitz, 1965, p.9). Involvement and value judgements should not bother anyone unless he clings to 'the empiricist refusal to view the social sciences as essentially a human enterprise'. Only the pure rationalist expects social behaviour to be consensual and unchanging. Our stand must be for sociology as science, not as rationalization for the status quo. Sociologists must confront a world of conflicting standards—there is no room for the safety of fence-sitting. I would agree with Horowitz that a 'science is judged by how much it gives to the world not by how much it extracts from it' and call to mind that:

> from Montesquieu on, sociology defined itself as a critical activity. The socially relevant purpose of sociology is to achieve an understanding of social behaviour and social institutions which is different from that current among the people through whose conduct the institutions exist, an understanding which is not merely different but new and better. The practice of sociology is *criticism*. It exists to criticize claims about the value of achievement and to question assumptions about the meaning of conduct. It is the business of sociologists to conduct a critical debate with the public about its equipment of social institutions (Burns, 1969, p.79).

Sociology from the first year on should be presented as a humanistic discipline which understands human reality as socially constructed, as a discipline which provides an excellent avenue of approach to what is ultimately a philosophical problem: the relationship between the individual and society.

If an introductory course can offer the best that is available in sociology, and do so in a stimulating, lively manner, it will serve both goals of improving the general education of the majority and of firing the imagination of those few who may go on to study their society through closer research.

It is in that hope that this book has been written. Not to impose a structure on any course, teacher or student; but to bring sociology into focus within the Australian context in an interesting and challenging way. If it causes argument, so much the better.

> No human being is constituted to know the truth, the whole truth, and nothing but the truth; and even the best of men must be content with fragments, with partial glimpses, never the full fruition (William Osler, *The Student Life*).

References

BALDOCK, C. & J. LALLY (1974) *Sociology in Australia and New Zealand*, Greenwood, Westport, Conn.

BERGER, P. & T. LUCKMANN (1966) *The Social Construction of Reality*, Doubleday Anchor, N.Y.

BLAU, P. (1969) 'The Objectives of Sociology' in R. Bierstedt (ed.), *A Design for Sociology: Scope, Objectives, and Methods*, Monograph 9, AAPSS, Philadelphia.

BURNS, T. (1969) 'Comment on Blau's Paper', in R. Bierstedt (ed.), *A Design for Sociology: Scope, Objectives, and Methods*, Monograph 9, AAPSS, Philadelphia.

EDGAR, D. E. (1970) 'Teaching Sociology to First Year Students', in J. Zubrzycki (ed.), *The Teaching of Sociology in Australia and New Zealand*, Cheshire, Melbourne.

EDGAR, D. E. (ed.) (1974) *Social Change in Australia*, Cheshire, Melbourne.

GOULDNER, A. (1968) 'The Sociologist as Partisan: Sociology and the Welfare State', *The American Sociologist*, 3, May.

HOROWITZ, I. L. (1965) *The New Sociology*, Oxford University Press, Oxford.

OSMOND, W. (1972) *The Dilemma of an Australian Sociology*, Monograph No. 2, Arena Publications, Melbourne.

TOBY, J. (1961) 'Denying the Validity of Personal Experience', *American Sociological Review*, 26 (2), pp.279-80.

ZUBRZYCKI, J. (ed.) (1970) *The Teaching of Sociology in Australia and New Zealand*, Cheshire, Melbourne.

Part One

The Study of Society

Chapter 1

Sociological Questions

Theory as a Means of Control

Australian Society?

Examining the Myths
Rural/Urban Australia
Population Characteristics
Class and Inequality
Our Way of Life

1

Some people have described sociological theory as a painful exercise in self-deception and the mystification of ordinary life. But we will hold that it is among the most practical of pursuits because theories offer a way of 'handling' our affairs and of locating ourselves within our society and its history. Certainly much that passes for *theory* in sociology consists only of dressing-up simplistic notions of cause and effect in an attempt to claim for sociology the status of a *science*. But the analysis of social problems demands careful use of theory if it is to have any predictive value or go beyond mere description of what we may observe.

Theory as a Means of Control

People have always tried to 'explain' human existence to themselves. Like other animals, people survive by learning to control their physical environment. Unlike animals however, people gain greater mastery over their environment because they have the capacity to understand it and mould it to suit their own needs. It is the ability to *interpret* what is seen and to *anticipate* the future, that set the human race apart. Habits, learned behaviour and memory are not enough. People can interpret the actions of others, imagine the motivations behind them, and anticipate their likely effects; if they wish, they may act to alter the likely result. In doing this, they are theorizing: putting together past understandings, present situations and future possibilities as a guide to present action.

Unless we have such *theories* about why things happen, we have no control over events or over other people. Since control is essential for survival, the degree of truth or relevance of our *theories* gives us greater or less control over our lives in society.

A common argument concerns the difference between *the natural attitude* of everyday life (the taken-for-granted theories on which ordinary people base their actions) and *the theoretic stance* of the social scientist. The argument goes that through superior ability to 'see through' what others take for granted the social scientist can explain human behaviour in more sophisticated ways than they. We are suspicious of this distinction because much so-called sociological theory is sophisticated in nothing but its language, and because the distinction is based upon an elitist disregard for the complexities of the ordinary person's *theories* about life.

Consider primitive man's forms of magical beliefs. People knew that the sun and moon rose and set each day, that people were born and that they died, that rain, thunder, lightning, flood and fire came at unpredictable times, and that the seasons, stars and planets punctuated time more regularly. But because people could not control these things, they needed a *theory* to explain them away. Strange forces, mystical beings or powers of magic were invoked in various forms by various tribes. Despite the apparent diversity of forms, however, we may observe a common thread running through them: these magical forces were often seen as images of actual people or familiar animals. Since animals and human beings could be controlled (their hunger could be satisfied, their demands met, their anger placated or their energy exhausted) this personification of magical powers gave mankind a form of control over them. He could worship them, pray to them, offer sacrifices to them, build images of them, and put them into temples: in fact, *manage* them more successfully than before. So what looked like primitive forms of religion, uncivilized fetishism or barbaric ritual, were in fact highly sophisticated theories about life which explained events in ways that brought them under control.

This view of theory as *a search for meaning and control* can be explored in relation to the history and development of sociological thought. The aim in this chapter, however, is not to give an exhaustive coverage of classical theorists in sociology, but to give an overview which sets theories within the context of the problems they sought to explain. Every theory of society should be seen as a response to a felt need for meaning and control.

In every epoch there have been competing explanations of social life. It would be wrong to think that one dominant theory always gave way to another in some relentless progress towards *the truth*. There have usually been dominant theories—theories held and advanced by dominant groups within the social structure. However, even at times of massive social control of thought (for example during the church-dominated Middle Ages or the regime of Hitler) other groups have constructed different theories of reality.

Moreover it should be kept in mind that different theories explain different things and that some theories explain more things than others. The *classical* theorists of sociology tried to explain the whole of social *structure*, indicating causes and directions of social change, conflict and stability. Other theorists aim, less broadly, to explain not *why* changes take place but *how* those changes become part of the conscious social *process*. So the aim and scope of any theory must be kept in mind when we evaluate its worth.

The key questions that must be asked of any sociological theory are essentially 'so what?' questions: what is the point?; what is this theory trying to explain?; is it worth explaining?; does it help?; does this theory assist our understanding of, and control over, social life?; does it help to explain social behaviour? The last question may often be forgotten when theory is studied for its own sake. When theorists study other theorists and get carried away with their own word-games it seems even more urgent that we ask 'so what?'. For unless criticisms and counter-criticisms result in a better explanation of social behaviour, the whole relation between theory and practice is lost.

When theorists examine the work of other theorists they ought to ask whether the issues examined, the questions asked and the relationships suggested as explanations of social behaviour are still relevant, still useful, still productive of understanding and control. We would not wish to rule out a scholarly study of social thought; rather we want to sound a warning that textual criticism in itself is not good sociological theorizing unless it relates to the practice of social life.

As a starting point for thinking about the role of theory in the study of sociology, let us state some of the principal considerations that have to be taken into account in putting together theories about society.

The world is physical and therefore limits what humans can do.

Humans are animals with needs (for food, clothing, shelter, and so on). Satisfying our needs requires *work* or labour.

The physical situations into which we are born are different. We therefore face different limitations on our behaviour and develop different forms of adaptation to our environments. The Eskimo and the Australian Aborigine, for example, face different situational limits, thus their forms of labour differ considerably.

People's physical and intellectual powers are different. We are not equal in our personal resources and thus vary in our ability to deal successfully with the environment, to be in control, to labour in order to satisfy our needs.

The capacity of each individual is limited so we must depend upon others for our survival. Our physiological and psychological attributes make us unique in our adaptability and in our ability to satisfy our needs but also restrict what we can do alone. We are thus of necessity—if not by nature—social beings.

Exchange of resources is a central feature of all societies. We exchange food, shelter, money, knowledge, ideas, techniques and skills in order to accomplish our ends. We exchange both our labour power and the products of our labour.

This exchange process involves more or less complex divisions of labour. The most elemental of these divisions is based on sex and the care of children, and revolves around an efficient and sensible allocation of tasks according to who can do them best. Other important factors enter into explaining why and how more complex tasks come to be divided. Indeed it would be true to say that the *division of labour* is one of the central problems of explanation in sociological theory.

Consensus and conflict develop from the division of labour and the processes of exchange that result from the need to share resources. *Consensus* describes the forms of agreement between people, cooperation and mutual interdependence. *Conflict* describes the argument concerning who does what and who gets what in society, the nexus between inequality and domination. Some sociological theories focus more on the *consensus* aspects of the way societies distribute, allocate and coordinate their resources through the division of labour. Other theories take *conflict* as the more basic process and argue that social structures can be explained better in terms of conflicts over power and the clash between vested interest groups than in terms of agreement on values and procedural roles. No adequate theory of society can assert either of these extremes to the exclusion of the other, however, because both consensus and conflict exist in every society.

Structured expectations of who can do what develop as a result of natural

differences of ability and the exchanges that occur as people interact. For example, we expect the baker to be better at making bread than the bricklayer. In a similar way we develop *typifications* about people, places, things and social processes. Patterns of life experience develop and we view the world in terms of concepts and categories to which certain *typical* features belong.

In the normal course of events, most patterns and categories become taken-for-granted. These patterns of *normal* relationships form the basis of a society's institutions, the social structure we accept as the *natural* order of things. This process may be at once desirable and undesirable. We could not function effectively if we questioned closely every process, every category or rule of behaviour. For example, what benefit is there for the average person in knowing how a light switch operates or how a letter gets delivered, as long as it does? It is more usual, and easier, for us not to question people's motives for acting as they do.

There are alternate, often conflicting views of the world, of our pasts, our presents and our futures. *Action* largely depends upon what we have experienced typically in the past, and those old typifications do not always fit the *reality-tests* of present and changing life situations. We learn to typify the world and our fellows through childhood socialization, education, work and life experiences and through our experience of history. Since different individuals and groups come from different pasts and live in different situations, their views of the world and the ways they typify social actions will differ too.

Any adequate theory about society must go beyond simply describing what people take for granted and how people function in everyday life. The aim of theory is to explain why people think and act the way they do; why some views of the world hold sway over alternate world-views; why people conform to, go along with, reject, or rebel against the prevailing social structure and its culture.

Social role theories. Some theories stress the importance of *norms*, agreed-upon rules of conduct which children learn through socialization and adults learn in their various life roles from the *expectations* of others. That is to say, the emphasis now moves from structured expectations about who *can* typically do what to structured expectations about who *should* do what. *Social control* is more easily achieved when people accept, as reasonable, what is expected of them (and adopt the values and rules of behaviour on which the expectations are predicated), than when they do not see the expectations to be legitimate. Theories about social roles therefore rely heavily upon assumptions of agreement, legitimacy, social learning and conformity. They may appear to cast mankind as players acting out set roles in the drama of life.

Free-will theories. This 'theatrical' image gives rise to a set of counter-theories in sociology which place greater emphasis on the *active, interpretive* nature of humankind. Free-will theories reject the notion that people merely play roles and act out internalized, legitimate values and norms; rather, they argue that people constantly interpret situations and make choices on the basis of free will and their own *intentions*. *Socialized man* and *man of free-will* are points of view in the extreme, but, every theoretical view should accommodate at least some aspects of the two extremes. For given that people are born into

7

different situations and are socialized differently, their social interaction will always involve a *negotiation* of meanings so that those with alternate views of the world may reach a common basis for interaction.

Sociological theory must take account of the interaction through which meanings are negotiated (symbolic interaction). Any theory must also accept that there is *no certain outcome* of that interaction. In this sense sociological theory is never likely to be as good at *prediction* as theories in the other sciences. People are not atoms acting in some fixed force-field; they can choose (within limits) and *construct* their own social reality out of the finite reality of the material world. So it would be foolish to expect sociological theories to give total explanations that will 'fit' every situation. All they can hope to do is suggest *probabilities* on the basis of relationships and patterns observable *under certain conditions*. Thus we should expect theories to spell out clearly under what conditions one set of factors will probably lead to a set of results in social behaviour.

Social change is inherent in the human condition. Because different groups and individuals come from different pasts, live in different situations, face different problems of control and have been socialized into different patterns of meaning and behaviour, we cannot expect a static view of society to be adequate. Social interaction, like physical interaction, has no certain outcome. Every social theory, no matter how static its view of human society, must address itself to explaining the sources, rates and effects of change. Notice that we are talking about social and cultural change, not merely about technological changes or biological adaptations to man's environment. As Bronowski (1973, p.48) has pointed out, cultural adaptation leads merely to survival. Even the nomad Lapps who follow the herd and depend upon the reindeer for survival, make a *choice* which can be changed.

Social interaction is not social change. It is important not to confuse structural social change with simple ongoing social interaction or movement. Nisbet (1969) describes the latter as change *within* the system, and the former as change *of* the structure.

He argues that social interaction is incessant and that accepted forms of behaviour and belief are constantly being challenged and negotiated. For example, while monogamy remains the norm in Western societies, new forms of marriage and family living are being tried and tested. But although some people may be alienated from the dominant social system and deviate from its accepted forms, broad social types do persist. Even the potential deadly results of population growth, pollution and over-consumption fail to stir the masses because strong habits, customs, inertia and the taken-for-granted (and the stubbornness of vested interests), operate to maintain the status quo. Rarely is change of the *structure* desired, but it is a task of social theories to explain when and how changes *within* the system develop into changes *of* the system.

Different forms of power develop to set and enforce the means of exchange. The division of labour creates the need for exchange and consequently, the processes of consensus and conflict. Inevitably, questions of needs give rise to questions concerning the ownership of resources or means to satisfy those needs;

the conditions of exchange; the terms of agreements; the fairness or inequity of social arrangements; the vested interests of those with similar needs but unequal resources.

When man was a nomad, a hunter and forager, constantly on the move for survival there was little time to develop new tools, new ideas or new social forms. Around 10 000 years ago however, the pattern changed. In some places man had settled, and had begun to cultivate the land and to domesticate animals. We are told that this was an outgrowth of the end of the last Ice Age, when 'the ground flowered beneath him . . . suddenly, man and plant came together . . . for the bread wheats can only multiply with help; man must harvest the ears and scatter their seeds; and the life of each, man and plant, depends on the other' (Bronowski, 1973, p.64).

In an agricultural community, social rules become more complex. In place of simple nomad laws to punish the theft of a sheep or goat, the rule of law in a settled society is tied to regulating 'matters that affect the community as a whole: access to land, the upkeep and control of water rights, the right to use, turn and turn about, the precious constructions on which the harvest of the seasons depends' (Bronowski, 1973, p.77).

The development of a *surplus* of produce over that which will satisfy immediate needs, however, depends on the invention of machines. In this sense, a machine may be a draught horse or a spindle or a nuclear reactor. The relative ability of different groups to dominate nature through machines creates the power differentials which underlie the conflict running through social history. Bronowski argues that the emergence around 5000 years ago of a new draught animal—the horse—created warfare, the ultimate conflict of power in the negotiation of social exchange. The horse was first used to pull carts and ploughs. Then about 2000 B.C. men discovered how to ride it. This machine was destined for purposes far beyond its original constructive use in allowing the resources of nature to be tapped more readily.

Social processes may transform control by power to control by authority. The use of naked *power* in the interests of particular groups is of course only one way people may control others. The use of sheer force can only be temporary. The attacking horde usually wants what it does not possess, the surplus that comes from productive labour. Seen in that light war is 'a highly planned and cooperative form of theft'. Once all is taken, however, even the conquerers must settle down. They can keep the conquered peoples working as slaves but time and custom change the conquerers' habits. After a time the invader becomes a colonist, a settler, an inhabitant.

In such a process, force or naked power changes to a different form of control, that of *authority*. If people accept demands as just or legitimate the need for constant vigilance against rebellion disappears. If people are taught to accept their place, to conform because they want to rather than because they have to, social control is much easier and less nerve-wracking for those in power.

So every social theory must grapple with questions concerning the processes by which people come to accept the way society is; the way what *is* becomes what *ought* to be; the conditions under which power is transformed to authority; and the social mechanisms by which forms of authority are maintained, challenged or changed.

It is in answer to such questions that theories bring together the search for meaning and control. Not only do individuals and groups look for satisfactory explanations of life and its vagaries so that they can understand and control their day-to-day affairs—they also use those meanings, their theories, to control other people in their own interests. At that point, we say that a social theory has become an *ideology*, a system of meaning used to support the vested interests of those who express it and impose it on other people. It is also at this point that subjective meanings, the myriad thoughts and interpretations of *reality* that individuals hold, become sociological rather than psychological.

Meanings are usually shared. They arise out of a common cultural past and are transmitted to each newcomer through *socialization* into the common frameworks of *normal* behaviour. They are sustained or extended through social interaction where people use signs, gestures and words to indicate their intentions and feelings to one another. In this sense meaning is *inter*-subjective, not merely subjective: it is shared and developed in interaction with others. Without shared life situations, shared needs, shared resources and shared meanings no *social bond* could exist and no joint action would be possible.

This social bond, or rather the various social bonds that develop from our shared pasts, our shared life situations and our shared socialization experiences, naturally work *against* large-scale change, rather than for it. Common definitions of 'objects' (physical, social and abstract) are transmitted through socialization and maintained by the structure of *dominance relations* in society. We are made human *with* other people; we grow out of social conditions and social experience. The image of the individual as a totally free autonomous self, isolated from social facts, desiring to destroy social institutions is naive. Without institutions we would not be human. The more correct and properly political question concerns the *kinds* of institutions. For while institutions are based on shared goals and rules for achieving them, they may operate only in the interests of a few and restrict unnecessarily the behaviour of others. An example we will develop more fully later is the way *bureaucracy* operates. As a system for organizing people to achieve coordinated ends efficiently, a bureaucratic structure may appear to be rational; but too heavy an emphasis on hierarchical authority or on centralized control may create human misery and be inefficient as well. The issues for sociological theory concern the ways certain conditions give rise to certain types of social institutions and the ways these are maintained and changed.

As Nisbet (1969) points out, there is formidable evidence of persistence and fixity in social history, despite revolutions, conflicts and strains. Because they are dedicated to the search for new knowledge, we might logically expect to find that universities, for example, would have changed fairly radically over time. Certainly there are considerable differences between universities like Oxford or Bologna and the less traditional ones like, say, the State Colleges in California. What is taught has also changed with the times. Yet the *how* is strikingly the same. Today's universities are still organized into faculties and colleges; the basic groups are still faculty and students (in recent times joined by 'the administration'); their 'work', still takes the form of subjects, lectures and tutorials; their authority system is still maintained through the passing out of grades, degrees and promotions. Even their conflicts remain of the same nature: in the thirteenth century Bologna students fought for their right to participate in decision-making, and throughout history there have been many clashes between 'town' and 'gown'. It is little wonder, then, that the more broadly-based institutions of church, family, class and community are resistant to change and are fixed in ritual.

Nonetheless some theories take those routines and continuities too far and view social change as a process of steady growth. This view arises from the traditional analogy of society as a biological organism. Just as each part of a plant or animal performs some function essential to the whole organism, so were the parts of a society or of a social institution held to function in relation to the whole. If one part were changed, then the way other parts worked would also change. To an extent the analogy is valid and helpful in explaining social behaviour. For example, if one person on a vehicle assembly line fails to put the bolts in, the car may fall apart, sales fall and jobs go. If no-one takes the lead in small group interaction, tasks may not be completed or the group may cease to meet. But to follow totally or simplistically the growth analogy is to distort history and fly in the face of empirical reality. Change does not take place in an orderly or developmental way; it is more often a response to some form of *crisis* or threat to what has been taken for granted.

Thus famine, flood, earthquake, attack or the gradual build-up of poverty, resentment or disillusionment may precipitate change if they create a *loss of control* over everyday affairs. We use here W. I. Thomas's (1920) definition of crisis as a relationship between human beings precipitated by an inability to cope or to continue in the customary ways of behaving. When the *normal* breaks down, new elements force themselves upon us and threaten to destroy our control over our affairs. They challenge our habits, our customs and our sleepy acceptance of the way things are. In so doing, they wake our attention to the central problems of life—those to do with control over our environment. When attention wakes, thought becomes necessary and the search for new meanings to restore control begins.

Thus when Copernicus and Galileo challenged accepted views of the way man related to the universe, God seemed no longer to be in control. The *theory* of Christianity, the ideology of the Church which held sway, began to be questioned; the search for new explanations was carried forward on a wave of 'positive' science. It was out of such dramatic shifts in ways of viewing the world that new social theories (and eventually sociology) were born.

Theories, then, grow out of circumstances. They are not the products of philosophical abstraction. So when we analyze competing theories, our concern will be for the existential conditions that gave rise to them rather than for the 'sense' they might make of today's world. For any theory we will want to know who was involved and how and why the theory made sense when it originated. We will want to know what the theory sought to explain and whether it was used as an ideology to control the thoughts and actions of others. We must needs be concerned with the historical events and the changes in social structures and social relations that caused changes to the theorizing about human life. It will be vital for us to know how widely any theory was shared and which groups gained satisfactory control because of the explanation it offered. Finally, for any period of change, we shall need to locate the forces at work which shook people free from systems of thought that no longer 'worked'.

Why was it, for example, that Pericles and Luther and Marx and Hitler appealed and were heard when others tried and failed? Ours is not an idiosyncratic, 'great man' view of history: we are arguing that different theories make sense in different circumstances. They answer the questions raised by an awakened search for meaning, and their interpretations offer explanations which put people back in control of their own (and other people's) lives.

Australian Society?

With these basic theoretical issues in mind, we may now consider Australian society as a whole. Our aim will be to pose the relevant questions and to suggest some of the ways in which sociological theory and research may help us to find the answers.

The broadest question concerns whether we have a distinctively 'Australian' culture. How would we go about answering such a question (and does the answer matter anyway, given Australia's minor role in the scheme of world affairs)? Consider our national stereotypes: the digger; the bronzed outback loner; the blonde surfie; the anti-establishment leg-puller who 'cuts down the tall poppies'; the quiet but resourceful Aussie who stands up for his rights but is intensely patriotic. Consider even the mateship myth. How do these images stand up against the facts and figures? Are the facts and figures relevant or meaningful if, no matter what they prove, the cultural myths continue to be believed?

Sociology directs its attention to such issues by insisting on a close relationship between theory and research. Sociologists put ideas and assumptions to the test of empirical observation and critical analysis.

Facts and figures will not tell the whole story because society is more than that. Sociology is the study of social relations and social behaviour: it is the study of social reality as it is consciously experienced by different groups and objectively as it may be seen to affect them. Groups relate to one another in various ways in order to achieve their own interests. And some groups are more successful than others. Sociology must therefore include the study of the ways people feel about society and their position in it. So we may not discuss Australian society, or any other society for that matter, simply in terms of the objective relations between groups, their economic situations or their place in the overall system. We must go further, we must discover why Australian people interpret their places in relation to others as they do and how they feel about it, for that will help explain why they act in ways that may seem to contradict what we objectively know about them.

For example, we may ask why it is that many 'working-class' adults vote

Liberal rather than Labor; why trade unions generally accept the decisions of the Conciliation and Arbitration Commission and work through it; why women accept an inferior role, a limited job range and lower levels of education, even though they have intellectual abilities equal to those of men; why there have been no 'proletarian revolutions' in Australia even though our economic system has always been capitalist; why despite evidence to the contrary, many Australians believe that there is no poverty, no real job shortage, no inequality in our society; why it has been relatively easy for large migrant groups to be absorbed into Australian society without the conflicts and violence that have occurred elsewhere.

The answers are to be found through sociological analysis of the way society operates. We need to examine the pressures that bring people with conflicting interests together in joint action; we need to consider how the outcomes of that joint action are structured or patterned by assumptions about the past and present on the one hand and by the goals of the powerful on the other.

The first step will be to define terms. Journalistic accounts of Australian society take little care to define what they mean by terms such as *working class*, *middle class*, *equality*, *socialist*, *the unions*, *dole-bludger*, *hippie*, *delinquent*, *welfare* and so on. The terms are used as labels to stereotype whole groups of individuals or collections of ideas. *Equality*, for example, may be accepted to mean equal starting points in life, assuming at birth equal wealth, family support and intelligence; or to mean equal opportunity to try, assuming no restrictions on who may go to which schools, try for examinations, study particular subjects or apply for particular jobs; or to mean equal outcomes, assuming that we all learn the basics, we all get our Higher School Certificate, and that we all achieve an equal wage and a house of our own. So it is pointless to argue over whether Australians enjoy equality until we clarify our definition of the word. Only then may we consider the evidence and ask what data might be needed to prove or disprove the existence of that kind of equality.

Similarly, we need to clarify what we understand by *society*. If we mean the national boundaries and all within, that will raise the issue of inter-State rivalries and the question whether we mean to include Aborigines and migrants as part of Australian society. If we accept the 'organic' view of society as a sort of plant (with limbs, branches and leaves all connected to a main trunk) or body (with a heart, lungs and so on, all interconnected and dependent upon one another) we will be faced with other problems.

Since society is made up of many different groups, often cooperating but also conflicting with one another, how will we account for who wins out? Do we picture society in terms of a powerful elite in control of the strings, with a few other groups competing for power, both with the elite and amongst themselves, while the masses drone along with little say? Or do we adopt a *pluralist* model and see Australian society to be a hotch-potch of competing interest groups in an uneasy balance allowing no one 'power elite' to emerge? Do the masses of ordinary 'Aussies' figure much in either model?

Further, how do we explain how society coheres, how it continues over historical time, changes but remains distinctly one 'Australian society'? If our

13

explanation depends on common language, common culture and shared values, we will need to support it with evidence that 'Australians' with British, Greek, Turkish, Italian and Australian-born backgrounds actually do share a common system of cultural values. Further, we shall need to consider whether consensus is necessary if people are to set up social bonds and to work and live together. The factory worker on the shop floor may not agree with the boss's rules or share his values or his interests. Their only point of agreement may be to accept their disagreements for the sake of work in exchange for pay. We may argue that there is no necessary implication of consensus to be drawn from the existence of cooperation and interdependence. In fact Australian history is rich with evidence of conflict between mutually dependent groups.

It may be, however, that people cooperate and maintain social arrangements precisely because they have conflicting interests. If they cannot achieve their goals without 'taking account' of others, they will enter into social arrangements that will decrease the potential for conflict and contribute to the satisfaction of their needs. Those social arrangements (or *structures*) will continue to be accepted so long as they contribute to the satisfaction of the interests of all parties concerned. However, if the balance is upset, if one group may be seen blatantly to exploit another, then conflict will cease to be latent and there will be a demand for change.

Whatever the *theory* or explanation that people accept, it will influence their motives and their social behaviour. If trade unionists see capitalist owners as exploiting their labour (offering low wages or poor conditions), but fail to see that the owners are also constrained by wider political and economic conditions, strike action will be taken for motives of personal gain to union members rather than to change the whole system. Neither will that union bother about pensioners or the unemployed or non-unionized workers because they are not seen to belong to the same interest group. Moreover, so long as the strike is only for better pay or working conditions, the media will not call it 'political'. A 'political strike' is one aimed at gaining control of the State, rather than at solving an issue of mere 'economism'.

On the other hand, people may base their explanations on assumptions which are tied to a belief in the individual, in personal effort and free enterprise. If they do so, their explanations will suggest that failure is the fault of the individual and not a result of how the system operates. These people will assign blame to the loser, not to those who succeed at his expense. Pierre Bourdieu (1977) calls this sort of explanation *symbolic violence*, a method of turning the victim against himself and leaving the power structure intact. The psychology of individual differences (with its partners of I.Q. testing, graded examinations and percentage pass rates) is an example. When schools force classes of children to move together through a fixed curriculum, jump examination hurdles together, leave or repeat if they fail and deny 'drop-outs' the opportunity to 'drop back in' when their interests and circumstances permit, they are committing symbolic violence. It is not the lack of parent help, or teacher ability or unequal opportunities that are blamed; failure is held to rest with the individual. Such an interpretation serves to control entry to the better paid, higher status positions in society, and to ensure that those who do not succeed accept their lower positions without quarrel. According to this sort of explanation it is their own fault, not the system's.

So in explaining how Australia holds together as a *society*, we must consider the patterns of conflict and inter-dependence that give rise to our social roles and institutions, and the ideologies by which those patterns are *explained* by and for people in competing groups.

Examining the Myths

Various images of Australia and Australians are perpetuated in our historical and popular social literature. We are said to be egalitarian, anti-authoritarian and anti-intellectual; our thoughts are held to be shaped by the experience of our rural heritage and the wide-open spaces of life in the outback; we are products of the ethic of mateship among men. We lack a truly cultural elite; we possess a generosity and an openness of spirit; we have a talent for bureaucracy and rely on the State as a sort of milch-cow. Consider the variety of views contained in the following descriptions of the 'typical' Australian. Consider the author, the time and the intent. Consider the nature of the 'proof' that might be needed to support them.

> It is hard to quarrel with men who wish only to be innocently happy (*J. A. Froude*, 1886).

> They wear themselves out in all they do, mistaking the exercise of nervous energy for pleasure . . . The average temper of Australians more and more shows itself either indifferent or hostile to the outer world . . . Everyone is at heart a pessimist (*Francis Adams*, 1893).

> Intolerance of oppression and sympathy for the underdog are among the most attractive features of the Australian character. And yet, is it not possible to exaggerate even these virtues? . . . The passion for equal justice can so easily sour into a grudge against those who enjoy extraordinary gifts, and the aspiration for fraternity can so easily express itself by pulling down those lonely persons who are unable to fraternize with the crowd . . . (*W. K. Hancock*, 1944).

> Australia is a class society in terms of property, a classless society in terms of life-style, and a one-class society in terms of aspirations. All three aspects exist only because of the favourable position Australia has occupied in the imperialist system, so that any analysis of class structure in Australia must begin by placing Australia into the class structure of imperialism and not merely from an analysis of the internal class structure (*Humphrey McQueen*, 1973).

> While Australians have been fiercely competitive in the field of sport with merit being the dominant criterion, in legalized gambling skill has been minimized and chance is the extreme judge. Moreover a sense of fatalism in the Australian national character is a further reflection of this acceptance of chance (*Geoff Caldwell*, 1974).

> Now we are back where we started. Mr Adams, Bob Hawke, Barry Humphries et al have taken advantage of the so-called new nationalism and by cultifying the vestigial gaucheries have made them national virtues once again. Ocker is celebrated. Ocker is phoenix. Ocker is King. Mr Hawke may eschew good manners on television and be praised for it. Teeny bopper interviewers on the media may be

as gauche and blandly ignorant as befits their capacities—but still fill the needs of their audience or readership. The Ugly Australian looks in the mirror and falls in love with his national identity (*Max Harris*, 1974).

Max Harris is a galah, a real twit. He's one of those blokes who uses long words that aren't even used any more, who thinks any bloke is no good if he can't speak with an Oxford accent (and you shouldn't if you haven't been to Oxford). The reason he hates Hoges is that Hoges is, underneath it all, a decent fella. Harris says the true comic Australian is always getting beaten, he never wins. But Hoges has a go at anything, he's a real battler and he never loses. If he runs a lottery he'll win it himself. He's not a loser, and Max Harris doesn't like that (*Paul Hogan*, 1979 on A.B.C. TV).

Connell (1968, in Edgar, 1974, p.40) in reviewing how such images have developed, says:

I think it is best to regard them, rather, as expressions of the author's vision, of the imaginative effort he must make to create a representation of an exceedingly complex and hence ambiguous domain of experience. The reality of what goes on among the millions of people on the Australian continent is immensely different from the reality of ink on paper. To get from one to the other, a writer must select, compress, simplify, distort ... Hancock's account of Australian life was distinguished from the others, before and since, by his understanding of process in history and economics . . . Other books have not had this quality. Grattan, Pringle, Horne, McGregor and company have produced essentially static descriptions, setting out the appearance of Australian society, but not showing how it works.

That comment holds for the psychologically oriented writings of Ronald Conway, whose titles *The Great Australian Stupor* and *Land of the Long Weekend*, capture the imagination and strike familiar chords. However they lack an underlying theory of how society is structured and the sort of empirical evidence that is necessary to support the kinds of assertions he makes.

Rural/Urban Australia

The myth that most Australians lead a tough, lonely but satisfying life in the outback is tenacious but demonstrably untrue. In fact, in 1976, over 70 per cent of Australians lived in major cities and towns (i.e. the 6 capital cities, Canberra, and towns with a population of over 100 000, such as Newcastle, Wollongong, Geelong and the Gold Coast). With the exception of Canberra, all these are on the coast. Table 1−1 illustrates the trend towards life in the cities over the past 70 years. Notice that in that period, the proportion of Australia's population that might be called *urban* has doubled. Proportions also vary from state to state. Victoria and South Australia have above-average capital city concentrations; New South Wales and Western Australia near average; Queensland and Tasmania below average.

The most striking feature of Table 1−1 is the increased capital city concentration in Western Australia. Well below the average in 1906 it is now 'typical'. This 'drift to the cities' would appear even more marked if the table were able to take account of the fact that Canberra has, since the 1920s, drawn off a large number of people who might otherwise have continued to live in State capital cities.

Table 1 – 1   Percentage of population living in capital cities

			1906 %	1976 %
N.S.W.	—	Sydney	35	63
Vic.	—	Melbourne	43	71
Qld.	—	Brisbane	25	47
S.A.	—	Adelaide	46	72
W.A.	—	Perth	21	70
Tas.	—	Hobart	19	41
Total all states (excl. N.T. and A.C.T.)			35	70

(Sources: *Year Book*, 1907, p.58 and 1977–78, pp.100–101)

Over the years the proportion living in rural areas has declined (from 37 per cent in 1921 to 14 per cent in 1976) 'as the major cities and towns have attracted most of the population growth; there have been periods when the rural population has actually declined in numbers. This trend, however, appears to have slowed considerably since 1971' (Year Book 1977–78, p.100). But that is a gross analysis. There have been other trends. In 1971 the proportion of the population living in rural areas was also 14 per cent but by 1976 there had been a slight decrease in the proportion of people living in towns of over one million (i.e. Sydney and Melbourne). Obviously they had not gone to the rural areas. In fact, there was a corresponding increase in towns of population size between 100 000 and 1 000 000 (Brisbane, Adelaide, Perth and Hobart; Wollongong, Newcastle, Geelong and the Gold Coast). There had also been some increase in towns of 50 000 to 100 000. The small towns (under 10 000), however, showed a very slight decrease. Furthermore, the total proportion of the population living in urban centres (i.e. areas of 1000 inhabitants or more) has hardly changed between 1971 and 1976 (85.6 per cent and 85.8 per cent). (*Social Indicators No. 2*, 1978, Table 1.14, p.13)

The figures therefore indicate that growth in the smaller capitals and in the large provincial cities has been at the expense of Sydney and Melbourne. Figures released in *The Age* (5 February 1979, p.3) concerning the residential population of inner-city Melbourne add another dimension to the picture. The population was seen to have dropped from 100 000 in 1947 to 68 000 in 1977. The periods of most rapid decline were between 1961 and 1966 (a drop of 18 per cent), and between 1971 and 1977 (a drop of 11 per cent).

A 1978 attitude poll of residents of New South Wales and Victoria found that between 50 and 60 per cent of Sydney and Melbourne residents would rather live in a smaller city or town, or on the land. Only a minority preferred 'a big city like Sydney or Melbourne'. By contrast, country people were overwhelmingly satisfied with where they lived. Melbourne residents most dissatisfied with big-city life tended to be older, working class, less well educated, and Australian born (*The Age*, 21 September 1978, p.6). So large populations in the big cities do not constitute evidence that Australians are necessarily happy as urban dwellers.

There have been very few systematic analyses of life in Australian cities or of the impact of urban life on Australian social structure. Some notable, recent exceptions include: Stretton, 1970; Spearitt, 1978; McQueen, 1978; Kilmartin and Thorns, 1978. Yet as Jakubowicz (1974, p.329) said, the city is a system of resource allocation that has major effects on our way of life:

> Decisions made about cities, and within them about the allocation of resources, become then political decisions. They are political questions because they reflect the ideological orientations of the power groups within the city. If we remember that over 80 per cent of Australians live in urban settings, the city is then the prime arena for the playing out of the social values of the society, and the stances of the power groups.

If that is so, we will need to find out much more about the urban groups which make the major decisions and about the effects of those decisions on the lives of people in the inner city, the suburbs and even the rural areas. Notice also, however, the other side of the coin. The city is still fed by the country, and most urbanites take it for granted that milk and bread will be delivered, and that supermarket shelves will always be full. Power group decisions could alter that.

Population Characteristics

If we are an urban population, then, what sorts of people live in our cities? May we assume that we are all pretty much the same; that we share common values; that we meet and interact across groups? Who are we? Where do the main groups come from? Are basic demographic changes related to our social structure and social behaviour at different times in history?

Table 1−2   Sex and age distribution of population, 1861−1977[1]

Years[5]	Population in millions[2]			Masculinity ratio[3]	Age Distribution:[4] percentage of population	
	M	F	Total		under 15	65 and over
1861	0.7	0.5	1.2	134	31	1
1881	1.2	1.1	2.3	118	35	3
1901	2.0	1.8	3.8	110	34	4
1911	2.4	2.2	4.6	109	31	4
1921	2.8	2.7	5.5	103	32	4
1933	3.4	3.3	6.6	103	28	6
1947	3.8	3.8	7.6	100	25	8
1954	4.6	4.5	9.1	102	29	8
1961	5.4	5.3	10.6	102	30	9
1966	5.9	5.8	11.7	101	29	9
1971	6.4	6.3	12.7	101	29	8
1976	7.0	7.0	14.0	101	26	9
1977	7.1	7.1	14.2	100		

[1] Sources: *Year Book Australia* (various issues) and *Population and Vital Statistics (Preliminary): December Quarter 1977.*
[2] Figures exclude fullblood Aboriginals before 1961.
[3] Masculinity = number of males per 100 females. Figures exclude fullblood Aboriginals before 1961.
[4] Fullblood Aboriginals excluded before 1966.
[5] Years underlined are Census years.

Notice in Table 1—2 that the proportion of males to females did not become equal in Australia until 1977. Thus the image of Australia as 'a man's country' has some basis in fact. Around 1930, when there were 103 men to every 100 women, the only countries with a higher masculinity ratio than Australia were Argentina (114), Canada (107), the Irish Free State and New Zealand (both 104). The lowest ratios were in Northern Europe (England and Wales, France, Scotland, Poland, Russia) with 92—93 males to every 100 females. Notice, too, the rapid increase in the proportion of old people over the 100 year period.

Where do Australians come from? In the Australian Yearbook of 1929 a sort of 'Australian type' was described apparently ignoring the huge influx of European migrants there had been during the goldrushes and the period of assisted immigration that followed.

The population of Australia is fundamentally British in race and nationality, and furnishes an example of the transplanting of a race into conditions greatly different from those in which it had been developed. The biological and sociological significance of this will ultimately appear in the physical and moral constitution produced by the complete change of climatic and social environment. The new conditions are likely to modify considerably the physical characteristics and the social instincts of the constituents of the population. At present, the characteristics of the Australian population, whether physical, mental, moral or social, are only in the making, and probably a distinct Australian type will not appear until three or four generations more have passed. Even then, it is probable that, with the great extent of territory and differing conditions there will be a number of types varying with locality. At present the Australian is little more than a transplanted Briton, with the essential characteristics of his British forbears, with perhaps some accentuation of the desire for freedom from restraint. The greater opportunity for an open-air life, and the absence of the restricting conventions of older countries may be mainly responsible for this development.

In 1976, a similar statement was being made by the National Population Inquiry (p.17):

Although ethnically more diverse today than 30 years ago, Australians are still predominantly Australian-born and, if British immigrants are included within the same ethnic category, still overwhelmingly of British origin. In most cases the non-British inflow, although substantial in total, has been made up from a great number of very small national groups. In 1971 almost 80% of the the population were Australian-born; over 8% were born in the British Isles, leaving 12% born elsewhere.

Yet that statement is based on figures that reveal Australia to be a truly multi-cultural society. Further, recent governments have agreed that we should end our policy of 'assimilation' and preserve the cultural diversity of our ethnic groups.

As the C.U.R.A. Report on 'Migrants and Education in a Rural Community' (Country Education Project, Victoria, 1979, p.1) states:

Since 1947 when post-war immigration programs commenced some 3.3 million persons have migrated to Australia, producing some two million children. At the time of the 1971 Census 39.6 per cent of Australians were either overseas born or their children; over half of these were of non-English speaking extraction. In the mid

1970s more than one in four Australians could claim to be the product of emigration from non-English speaking countries. United Nations Population Surveys describe Australia in the 1970s as having the largest proportion of overseas born workers of any modern industrialized country outside of the Middle Eastern region. Australia today is very much a multi-cultural and multi-ethnic society.

Table 1—3   Net Immigration by periods: annual averages and percentage distribution

Birthplace	1947—51	1951—61	1961—66	1966—71	1971—73	Total
British	41.4	32.6	54.7	53.9	65.2	45.1
North Europe	7.5	26.3	0.8	4.9	−0.8	11.6
East Europe	37.3	5.0	6.6	13.3	7.6	13.5
South Europe	11.5	33.1	29.4	11.3	−3.5	21.4
Asia	1.6	2.3	5.2	11.2	21.2	5.7
Africa	0.1	0.2	1.5	1.5	2.8	0.9
America	0.5	0.4	1.8	3.8	7.5	1.8
Total Foreign	100.0	100.0	100.0	100.0	100.0	100.0
Annual Average	116 098	83 253	92 051	121 284	56 453	95 249
Australia	−5 728	−5 019	−12 954	−17 056	−21 613	−10 245
NET TOTAL	110 361	78 234	79 097	104 228	38 840	85 004

Does this conclusion really follow? When Melbourne has the second largest Greek population of any city in the world, one must consider also the political positions of those who interpret the bald population figures.

Religious differences have also figured large in Australia's social history, particularly over the issue of secular versus religious education. Since 1972 the issue has become less important and it may be that religion itself as an organizing factor in Australian life has become less important (or takes a different form) than in the past.

Notice in Table 1-4 the waning importance of the Church of England; the gradual increase in the number of Catholics; the recent increase in the number of 'Other non-Christian' (mainly Moslem); the dramatic leaps in 1933 and 1971 in the numbers willing to state 'no religion'.

Clearly, then, Australian society is not homogeneous. We are not all white, Anglo-Saxon Protestants. It is most unlikely therefore that social groups divided by age, sex or ethnic origin will share a common culture. It is even highly unlikely that people from different groups will meet one another at all in communal social relationships.

Class and Inequality

Australia has been described as an *equal society* and sometimes as a *classless society*. Yet if groups live different lives, have different life chances and relate with one another in only limited ways, it is probable that considerable inequalities will develop.

Table 1−4   Religion of population, 1901−1976[1]

	1901 %	1911 %	1921 %	1933[2] %	1947 %	1954 %	1961 %	1966 %	1971 %	1976 %
Christian										
Church of England	40	38	44	39	39	38	35	34	31	28
Catholic[3]	23	22	22	19	21	23	25	26	27	28
Methodist	13	12	12	10	11	11	10	10	9	7
Presbyterian	11	13	12	10	10	10	9	9	8	7
Other Christian[4]	9	11	7	8	7	7	9	9	11	9
Total Christian	96	96	97	86	88	89	88	88	86	79
Non Christian										
Hebrew	*	*	*	*	*	1	1	1	*	*
Other[5]	*	*	*	*	*	*	*	*	*	1
Total non-Christian	1	1	1	*	*	1	1	1	1	1
Indefinite/not classifiable[6]	1	*	*	*	*	*	*	*	*	*
No religion/no denomination	*	*	*	*	*	*	1	1	7	8
No reply/not stated	1	3	2	13	11	10	10	10	6	12
Grand Total	100	100	100	100	100	100	100	100	100	100

* = less than half a per cent.

[1] As described in Census by respondents. Source: *Year Book Australia*, various issues; 1976 figures from ABS 1976 *Census: Characteristics of the Population and Dwellings — Australia*.

[2] In 1933 people were informed for the first time that there was no legal obligation to answer this question. The percentage giving no reply rose dramatically, and there were thus corresponding falls in proportions (though not always numbers) of those adhering to religious denominations.

[3] Comprises people describing themselves as 'Catholic' and 'Roman Catholic'.

[4] Includes (among others) Baptists, Brethren, Churches of Christ, Congregational, Orthodox, Lutheran, 'Protestant', Salvation Army, Seventh Day Adventists.

[5] Includes (among others) Buddhist, Chinese, Confucian, Moslems.

[6] Includes Free Thinkers, no denomination and agnostic.

But, do most Australians believe that they live in a land of equality? According to Wild (1978, p.51), most surveys show that about 80 per cent of people think that there are social classes in Australia; only 13 per cent think there are not. Broom and Jones (1976, pp.63−5) found 98 per cent of their sample quite readily placed themselves in a *class* scheme. However it is hard to know quite what people mean by this. At base it may suggest that people recognize that people are unequal and that Australian society is *stratified*. The factors involved may be simply money or property, but on the other hand they may include educational levels, the social status of occupations, or other forms of status such as housing, dress, life-style or family connections.

Aarons in 1957 argued that Australian society consisted of four major classes. His major criterion for dividing them was the ownership or non-ownership of the means of production. A second criterion comprised the income, living conditions and life-styles that accompanied the basic difference of economic power. He argued that the classes were to be found in the following proportions in Australian society:

Capitalists and big bourgeoisie	1%
Upper middle class (middle and small capitalists, rich farmers, higher professionals and administrators)	10%
Lower middle class (middle and small farmers, small businessmen, lower professionals, middle strata white-collar workers)	30%
Working class (industrial, rural and lower white-collar workers)	58%

On the other hand, an *Age Poll* survey taken in 1977, categorized people according to their own descriptions of themselves as follows:

Upper Middle Class	6%
Middle Class	47%
Lower Middle Class	9%
Working Class	36%

However of those who saw themselves as 'middle class' 36 per cent worked at or were connected with 'blue collar' jobs.

Clearly there is a problem here. It is useful for the sociologist to divide society into classes. But asking people to assign themselves to a particular class may well produce a misleading result if the people asked do not share the sociologist's definitions of what constitute the various classes. Yet this survey of how people see themselves tells us something about Australian society that will need exploring theoretically. For if people define themselves as middle class or working class they are likely to act the part. Sociology does not exclude from its consideration the meanings people hold. For meanings too, are patterned; they vary with each group's life chances and social relationships. The patterns of meanings that people share are what we call *culture*.

But sometimes hard facts speak louder than ideas and there can be no doubt about what Table 1—5 tells us: Australia is an unequal society. Using a definition of poverty adjusted for changes to wages and living costs, Professor Ronald Henderson showed that in 1973, 10.2 per cent of Australian family income units were 'very poor' and 7.7 per cent were 'rather poor'. The most seriously impoverished groups proved to be those on pensions and unemployment benefits.

Notice also that the average weekly earnings at March 1979 were $221.10. It is evident that there is inequality in Australia.

We may now begin to suspect that some of the inequalities we have discovered are *structured* inequalities, and that there are institutional limitations which separate group from group and which reinforce the structure of Australian society. We will investigate these suspicions in later chapters.

For the moment let us simply consider whether the inequalities we have discovered correspond to differences between the ways of life of different groups of Australians.

Table 1−5   Poverty In Australia

Pension type	Weekly pension allowance $	Poverty level $	Amount below poverty level $
Unemployed single person	51.45	69.50	18.05
Unemployed married couple with two children	122.22	130.52	18.30
Unemployed married couple with four children	139.22	167.90	28.68
Single parent with one child	68.20	89.20	21.00
Single parent with two children	80.72	108.10	27.38
Single retired person	53.20	56.10	2.90

(Source: *The Age*, 1 June 1979)

Our Way of Life

Public opinion polls may try to give simple pictures of our way of life by sampling opinions, attitudes and typical behaviour for different groups across the country. What might we make of the cross-cultural comparisons in Table 1−6? Certainly media pundits and advertising men seem to rely heavily on what such figures tell them. But what more would we need to know? Can we even begin to speculate on the reasons for any of the differences shown and do they really tell us much about Australian society?

Our way of life is often stylized as healthy, outdoors and activity-oriented. Yet the facts do not really support such an image. Ischaemic heart disease (to which inactivity, obesity, overeating and drinking, and smoking appear to contribute) is the leading cause of deaths in Australia, accounting for about 30 per cent of all deaths each year since the late 1960s. By contrast, cancer, perhaps the most dreaded disease, accounted for only 19 per cent of all deaths in 1976. (*Deaths, 1976* (ABS) Table 9, pp.12−15; *Social Indicators, No. 2*, 1978, Table 2.4, p.30)

According to mental health researcher Dr Basil Hetzel, speaking in January 1978, Australia's alcohol consumption is now the highest in the English-speaking world. There are an estimated 300 000 alcoholics in Australia—4 per cent of the adult (15+) population. (Ken Stone, addressing a mental health conference, *The Age*, 1 January 1979, p.15) An Australian Bureau of Statistics survey in 1977 found that over 2 per cent of people over 18 reported that they were heavy or very heavy drinkers. It is mainly a male problem—4 per cent of males reported heavy or very heavy drinking, compared with about 0.2 per cent of women. As is usual in such surveys, levels are almost certainly understated. Data on the overall supply of alcohol in Australia would suggest that the incidence of heavy drinking is much higher. ('Heavy' drinking is defined as more than 80 grams of alcohol per day, e.g. one bottle of wine or seven 280 ml beers, or 8−9 nips of spirits.) (*Social Indicators, No. 2*, 1978 (ABS), Table 2.23, p.43)

Table 1 – 6 Australia and the world — how we compare (percentages)

	Aus-tralia	USA	Canada	UK	Other Europe	Latin America	Africa	Far East
Believe in God	80	94	89	76	78	96	95	89
Feel women have equal job opportunities	46	48	44	38	40	55	59	40
Finances main problem facing family	23	40	25	30	18	34	71	40
Very happy personally	37	40	36	38	17	32	18	7
Main national problem?								
a. High cost of living	56	63	60	62	36	41	28	35
b. Unemployment	19	15	15	5	26	11	14	7
Fears and worries for the future								
a. Personal health	19	23	25	23	31	24	33	11
b. Unemployment	13	13	11	13	14	8	5	14
c. Poor living standards	8	20	12	12	13	15	30	36
d. War	11	8	12	8	15	2	2	1
e. Economic instability	9	21	12	8	7	4	1	10
f. Loneliness	6	3	4	6	4	3	1	3
Life better now than 5 years ago	54	33	43	34	40	36	47	30
Life worse than 5 years ago	29	49	30	43	31	31	40	33
If had more money would								
a. Invest in business, farm	27	19	20	15	11	18	44	22
b. Save money	19	33	20	18	22	26	15	26

(Adapted from Gallup International Survey Results, April 1977)

Smoking (closely linked to heart disease and high blood pressure) is also heavy. More than 1 in 3 Australian adults smoke tailor-made cigarettes. Of these, 1 in 4 smokes over a packet a day, and 1 in 40 over two packets (*Social Indicators, No. 2*, Table 2.24, p.44). Death rates for lung cancer and bronchitis reached 7.4 per cent in 1975.

Contrary to myth, leisure activities centre mainly on the home. Table 1-8 shows in a lifetime of 650 000 hours spread over 74 years, how much time we spend in passive ways.

Table 1 – 7 Alcohol consumption for the year 1975/76 (per adult person)

beer:	189 litres, i.e. ½ a litre a day
table wine:	13 litres
fortified wine:	5 litres
spirits:	2 litres (alcohol)

(Source: *Social Indicators, No. 2*, Table 2.22, p. 43)

Table 1−8   How we use our time (average use of 650 000 hours)

Activity	Hours	Percentage
Sleeping	210 000	32 per cent
Going to bed, getting up, getting clean and presentable	80 000	12 per cent
Work	75 000	12 per cent
Eating, drinking	70 000	11 per cent
TV and reading	50 000	8 per cent
Education	29 000	5 per cent
Holidays	25 000	4 per cent
Other	110 000	16 per cent

(Source: *The Age*, June 1978)

One myth suggests that in the absence of horses or dogs, Australians will bet on two flies crawling up a wall. Australians do spend large sums of money on gambling (Caldwell, 1974). A TAB report of 3 August 1978, however, suggested that Victorians may be moving away from gambling towards more active pursuits. What are we to believe? Obviously we need much finer analysis than cultural idiom or gross summaries of statistics allow.

That is what the study of sociology is about. It goes beyond the taken-for-granted, so-called 'common-sense' facts that 'everyone knows' about Australian life. Sociology asks not just for facts and figures, and not just for idle speculation about causes. Sociologists want to specify the *conditions* which give rise to social action. They want to explain both the differences between groups and the structured ways in which groups in Australian society relate to one another. As suggested earlier, we are clearly not a homogeneous, single-culture society; nor are we a society without inequalities and conflicting interest groups.

Indeed, real continuities in the 'Australian national character' may not exist at all. Cultural characteristics arise from the real-life empirical conditions of social structure at a particular point in time. Thus it would be illogical to think of a permanent national character in a changing society. Gerth and Mills (1954) suggest a model of social change which may help us here. For them, social change may take place in the roles, the institutions or the orders comprising a social structure. Furthermore the interconnectedness of the different elements of the structure may evoke both quantitative and qualitative, both micro and macro, changes.

If roles are taken as the unit of change we will need to ask how many people play particular roles and how rapidly are they displaced from them. The shifts from rural to urban work; from production jobs to service jobs; from entrepreneurial to managerial roles; from having a job to being unemployed, might illustrate the point.

If institutions are taken as the unit, we will need to ask how many churches, factories, colleges and political parties exist and what types of institutions are the most dominant. In Australia, the growth of bureaucracies, the decline of small enterprise, the growth of large-scale corporations and the expansion of tertiary educational institutions may be clues to the nature and direction of social change.

Changes to particular institutions may cause entire *institutional orders* to change, as we may see in shifts from laissez faire capitalism to monopoly capitalism or from peace to war. Such shifts involve qualitative as well as quantitative changes. In wartime men are taken out of normal employment and kinship relations, with the result that few husbands, fathers, boyfriends and sons are available; technology fulfils military rather than consumer needs; new rules and regulations operate and the structure of dominance relations changes. As Gerth and Mills (1954, p.403) suggest, 'the great elasticity of modern social structure is indicated by the rapidity with which institutional orders may be recomposed and millions of people accommodated to the recomposition'.

Adjustments are facilitated by the links between institutions, their close interconnectedness in the complex modern division of labour (Durkheim 1964[1933]). But that tells us little about *Australian society*. For that we will need to examine at each historical period 'those institutional orders in which roles are implemented by control over things that require joint activities' (Gerth & Mills, 1954, p.403). For Gerth and Mills these were the economic, the military, and the political orders. Since Australia has never been a world power, the military order has held sway only in very limited periods. However, if we identify the groups who control the means of production and communication, the means of administration and the means of education and social reproduction, we will have some key indicators of the institutional links within the Australian social structure.

So in our study of Australian society the questions we ask will concern institutional interests and control. We will need to consider:

Social areas requiring formal control: for example, work; production; finance; economic policy; state administration; social welfare; trade; transport; communication and education.

The kinds of controls exercised over the less central social activities and institutions: for example, the limits to family autonomy; ethnic group activities; and public demonstrations.

The nature of the groups whose interests and purposes are served by the controls: in particular whose interests dominate and how they are maintained in the central institutions of economics, politics, communication and education.

The groups whose interests are not represented in organized institutional arrangements: for example, minority political groups; ethnic groups; non-unionized labour; the poor; the unemployed; and women.

The social effects of controls on life chances: the structured limits to a share in the resources of wealth, power, knowledge and prestige throughout the life-cycle.

The social effects of controls on the actual distribution of resources: the way that different interest groups receive unequal shares of knowledge, competence and power.

The social effects of controls on cultural concerns: the focus of needs, interests and relevances for different groups and the extent to which their values and motives impel them to be concerned with public or private matters.

The mechanisms by which existing patterns of control are maintained, challenged or changed within Australian society.

We may fruitfully take the last point further. Durkheim suggested that a crucial indicator of social solidarity and its bases would be the *sanctions* that applied and how they operated. Consequently we should examine the nature of the laws and punishments that apply to different groups in society. We should consider how extreme they are and how flexible, and when and where they apply. If offences against public morality are treated more or less seriously, we will need to consider the nature of the offences and the nature of the *public* to which they are offensive. We will need to discover whether exceptions are made within different segments of society and where different standards apply.

A parallel indicator will be in the nature of the *rewards* offered for certain behaviours. We will need to consider whether our society rewards external conformity to its rules or whether it requires actual internal acceptance of the rules: and whether that varies from group to group, from situation to situation. It may be that we reward actual competence (as in skilled work) less than we do the *symbols* of competence (paper qualifications); performance less than moral rightness (as when job interviewers count dress, manners and seriousness of purpose for more than skill or experience).

In summary, we will need to locate those attributes which are given legitimacy and encouraged as indicators of *acceptability* in Australian society. We will also need to identify the kinds of social identities and the groups from which they come whose *respect* is an indicator of the dominant cultural order.

Consider the blockade of the nation's highways by truckdrivers protesting road taxes and freight rates. At first, newspapers and television channels romanticized the action. They referred to the spokesman as 'the new Peter Lalor, King of the Truckies' and to 'a brotherhood of the road' (April 1979). But as soon as the dispute turned to violence and real economic pain began to be felt, the blockade was seen to be illegitimate and social respect was withdrawn.

John Sinclair's study of the press treatment of the 1960s counter-culture shows the process of *respect* working the other way round. At first, long hair, drugs, radical protest and unconventional life-style were seen to be threatening to the social order. Gradually, however, certain features of the counter-culture were *co-opted* or taken over by *respectable* society: wearing jeans, long hair and individual self-expression in themselves posed no threat and could, in fact, be marketed as consumer goods. The issues of control and group interests apply: our explanations for this kind of shift lie in the changes in the social structure and the cultural values which preserve society's dominance relations in whatever form is necessary.

Our focus throughout this book, then, will be less upon specific details of Australian society than upon the sociological questions that need to be asked if we are to understand how our society operates. Answers in the Australian context are not always available, but by asking the questions we may be able to go beyond the journalistic assertions of Australia's image-makers.

Readings and References

a. Australian Society:

AARONS, E. (1957 and 1958) 'Australian Class Structure', *Communist Review*, 192, pp.406-11, and Jan. 1958, pp.37-40.

ADAMS, F. W. L. (1893) *The Australians: a Social Sketch*, Unwin, London.

ALEXANDER, M. (1978) 'Dependency Theory and the Structural Analysis of Australian Society: A World Systems Perspective', *La Trobe Sociology Papers*, No. 41, La Trobe University, Melbourne.

ARNDT, H. W. & A. H. BOXER (eds) (1972) *The Australian Economy*, Cheshire, Melbourne.

BALDOCK, C. V. & J. LALLY (1974) *Sociology in Australia and New Zealand*, Greenwood Press, Westport, Conn.

BALDOCK, C. V. (1978) *Australia and Social Change Theory*, Novak, Sydney.

BELL, R. R. (1973) 'Mateship in Australia: Some Implications for Female−Male Relationships', *La Trobe Sociology Papers*, No. 1. La Trobe University, Melbourne.

BELOT, J. (1978) *Our Curious Home*, Sun Books, Melbourne.

BLAINEY, G. (1966) *The Tyranny of Distance*, Sun Books, Melbourne.

BLOOMFIELD, J. (1974) *The Role, Scope and Development of Recreation in Australia*, Dept. of Tourism & Recreation, Canberra.

BORRIE REPORT (1976) *National Population Inquiry*, AGPS, Canberra.

BROOM, L. & F. LANCASTER-JONES (1976) *Opportunity and attainment in Australia*, Australian National University Press, Canberra.

CALDWELL, G. (1974) 'The Gambling Australian', in Edgar, D. E. (ed.), *Social Change in Australia*, Cheshire, Melbourne, pp.13-28.

CEP (1979) *Migrants and Education in a Rural Community*, Country Education Project.

CONNELL, R. W. (1968 and 1974) 'Images of Australia', *Quadrant*, Vol. 12: pp. 9-19, reprinted in Edgar, D. E. (ed.) *Social Change in Australia*, Cheshire, Melbourne, pp.29-41.

CONNELL, W. F. (1977) *Ruling Class, Ruling Culture*, Cambridge University Press, Cambridge.

CONWAY, R. (1971) *The Great Australian Stupor*, Sun Books, Melbourne.

CONWAY, R. (1978) *Land of the Long Weekend*, Sun Books, Melbourne.

DAVIES, A. F., S. ENCEL & M. J. BERRY (eds) (1977) *Australian Society, A Sociological Introduction*, (3rd ed.), Longman-Cheshire, Melbourne.

DEMPSEY, K. C. (1979) 'To Comfort or to Challenge: The Role of the Church in an Australian Country Town', *La Trobe Sociology Papers*, No. 1. (new series), La Trobe University, Melbourne.

DIXSON, M. (1976) *The Real Matilda, Woman and Identity in Australia 1788−1975*, Penguin, Melbourne.

Drug Problems in Australia—An Intoxicated Society? (1977) Report of the Senate Standing Committee on Social Welfare, AGPS, Canberra.

DUNPHY, D. C. (1971) *Investigators, Social Scientists at Work*, Cheshire, Melbourne.

EDGAR, D. E. (1974) 'Sociology in Australia', in Edgar, D. E. (ed.), *Social Change in Australia*, Cheshire, Melbourne, pp.1-8.

EDGAR, D. E. (1974) 'Reality Construction: Micro Processes and Macro Change', in Edgar, D. E. (ed.), *Social Change in Australia*, Cheshire, Melbourne, pp.669-76.

EMBURY, B. L. & N. PODDER (1972) 'Economic Welfare in Australia' in P. R. Wilson (ed.) *Australian Social Issues of the Seventies*, Butterworth, Sydney, pp. 175-86.

ENCEL, S. (1971) *A Changing Australia*, Australian Broadcasting Commission, Sydney.

FENSHAM, P. J. (1975) 'School and Family Factors Among Commonwealth Secondary Scholarship Winners in Victoria, 1964−71', in D. E. Edgar (ed.), *Sociology of Australian Education*, McGraw-Hill, Sydney.

FROUDE, J. A. (1886) *Oceana, or England and her Colonies*, Longmans.

GOLLAN, R. A. (1978 [1955]) 'Nationalism, the Labor Movement and the Commonwealth, 1880−1900', in G. Greenwood (ed.), *Australia, a Social and Political History*, (rev. ed.) Angus & Robertson, Sydney, pp.145-95.

GREENWOOD, G. (1978 [1955]) *Australia, A Social and Political History*, (rev. ed.) Angus & Robertson, Sydney.

HANCOCK, W. K. (1945) *Australia*, Benn, London.

HARRIS, M. (1974) *Ockers, Essays on the Bad Old New Australia*, Maximus Books, Adelaide.

HENDERSON REPORT: *Poverty in Australia* (1975) AGPS, Canberra.

HETZEL, B. S. (1976) *Health and Australian Society*, (rev. ed.) Penguin, Melbourne.

HORNE, D. (1969) *The Lucky Country, Australia in the Sixties*, Angus & Robertson, Sydney.

HORNE, D. (1976) *Death of the Lucky Country*, Penguin, Melbourne.

JACUBOWICZ, A. (1974) 'The City Game', in Edgar, D. E. (ed.), *Social Change in Australia*, Cheshire, Melbourne, pp.329-43.

KILMARTIN, L. & D. THORNS (1978) *Cities Unlimited*, Allen & Unwin, Sydney.

KING, J. (1978) *Waltzing Materialism*, Harper & Row, Sydney.

Leisure Planning Guide for Local Government, (1977) AGPS, Canberra.

McQUEEN, H. (1973) 'The Suckling Society' in H. Mayer and H. Nelson (eds), *Australian Politics: A Third Reader*, Cheshire, Melbourne.

McQUEEN, H. (1978) *Social Sketches of Australia, 1888−1975*, Penguin Books, Melbourne.

MARTIN, J. I. (1972) 'Quests for Camelot', *ANZJS*, Vol. 8, No. 1, pp.3-17.

MAYER, H. & H. NELSON (eds) (1976) *Australian Politics, A Fourth Reader*, Cheshire, Melbourne.

MÉTIN, A. (1977 [1901]) *Le Socialisme Sans Doctrines*, Felix Alcan, Paris, 1901 (Trans. & ed. R. Ward, Alternative Publishing Co., Sydney, 1977).

OSMOND, W. (1972) *The Dilemma of an Australian Sociologist*, Arena Publications, Melbourne.

PODDER, N. & N. C. KAKWANI (1972) 'The Distribution of Wealth in Australia', *Review of Income and Wealth* 1, pp. 75-92 March.

Population and Australia. First Report of the National Population Inquiry, (1975) Vol. 2, AGPS, Canberra.

Population and Australia, Recent Demographic Trends and Their Implications, (1978) AGPS, Canberra.

ROWSE, T. (1978) *Australian Liberalism and National Character*, Kibble Books, Melbourne.

SAWER, G. (1972) *The Australian and the Law*, (rev. ed.) Penguin, Melbourne.

SINCLAIR, J. (1975) 'Mass Media and the Dialectics of Change: The Melbourne *Herald* and The Counter-Culture in the Late 60's', *ANZJS*, Vol. 11, No. 2, pp.46-9.

Social Indicators, No. 2. (1978) Australian Bureau of Statistics, Canberra.

SPEARITT, P. (1978) *Sydney Since the Twenties*, Hale & Ironmonger, Sydney.

STILLWELL, J. B. (1974) *Australian Urban and Regional Development*, Australia & N.Z. Book Co, Sydney.

STRETTON, H. (1970) *Ideas for Australian Cities*, Orphan Books, Stretton, Adelaide.

SUMMERS, A. (1975) *Damned Whores and God's Police*, Penguin, Melbourne.

The Australian Legend Re-Visited, (1978) Historical Studies, University of Melbourne, Melbourne.

THOMPSON, F. (1971) 'Suburban Living and the Concept of Community', *ANZJS*, Vol. 7, No. 2, pp.23-37.

TURNER, I. (1968) *The Australian Dream*, Sun Books, Melbourne.

WARD, R. (1977) *A Nation for a Continent: The History of Australia, 1901–1975*, Heinemann Educational, Melbourne.

WILD, R. I. (1974) *Bradstow, A Study of Status, Class and Power in a Small Australian Town*, Angus & Robertson, Sydney.

WILD, R. I. (1978) *Social Stratification in Australia*, Allen & Unwin, Sydney.

WILSON, P. R. (ed.) (1972) *Australian Social Issues of the 70's*, Butterworths, Sydney.

WILSON, R. (1976) 'How Fast is Australia Changing?' in H. Mayer & H. Nelson (eds) *Australian Politics: A Fourth Reader*, Cheshire, Melbourne.

ZUBRZYCKI, J. (ed.) (1971) *The Teaching of Sociology in Australia and New Zealand*, Cheshire, Melbourne.

b. General:

BERGER, P. I. (1963) *Invitation to Sociology*, Penguin, U.K.

BOGUSLAW, R. & G. R. VICKERS (1977) *Prologue to Sociology*, Goodyear Publishing, Calif.

BOURDIEU, P. & J. C. PASSERON (1977) *Reproduction in Education, Society and Culture*, Sage, N.Y.

BRONOWSKI, J. (1973) *The Ascent of Man*, BBC, London.

COLLINS, R. (1975) *Conflict Sociology, Toward an Explanatory Science*, Academic Press, N.Y.

DURKHEIM, E. (1964 [1933]) *The Division of Labor in Society*, Free Press, N.Y.

DURKHEIM, E. (1950) *The Rules of Sociological Method*, Free Press, Chicago.

GERTH, H. & C. WRIGHT MILLS (1954) *Character and Social Structure*, Routledge & Kegan Paul, U.K.

GOFFMAN, E. (1959) *The Presentation of Self in Everyday Life*, Doubleday Anchor, N.Y.

LYMAN, S. M. & M. B. SCOTT (1970) *A Sociology of the Absurd*, Appleton, N.Y.

McGEE, P. (1972) *Points of Departure, Basic Concepts in Sociology*, Dryden Press, Illinois.

NISBET, R. (1969) *Social Change and History*, Oxford Univ. Press, Oxford.

STEWART, E. W. & J. A. GLYNN (1971) *Introduction to Sociology*, McGraw-Hill, N.Y.

THOMAS, W. I. & F. ZNANIECKI (1920) *The Polish Peasant in Europe and America*, 5 vols. Badger, Boston.

WRIGHT MILLS, C. (1959) *The Sociological Imagination*, Oxford Univ. Press, N.Y.

See also references at end of Chapter 2.

Chapter 2

Social Theory

2

Philosophers have focused on what *ought* to be. For example, Confucius insisted that Chinese society must not be disturbed, because social relations could only be truly moral and orderly in an unchanging society where tradition was respected. The early teachings of the Church, as reflected by St. Augustine (354–430 A.D.), held that social institutions were only good or bad insofar as they helped humanity towards salvation.

Only when philosophers accepted the need for facts to substantiate opinion, for theory to be based on observation and reason rather than abstract conjecture, could any real study of society emerge. The spirit of humanism had to replace a view of the earth as a vale of tears; the spirit of rationality had to replace the long tradition of spiritual faith; the forces of materialism and practical utilitarianism had to outweigh moralizing dogmatism; and the exploratory urge of science had to locate man and nature at the centre of importance. Only then could social philosophy develop into the modern social sciences of economics, anthropology, sociology and political science. Unlike philosophers, then, social scientists concentrate on what actually exists. When sociology began in the nineteenth century it was a conservative science, a reaction to the excesses of revolution and to the social disruption caused by the expansion of commerce and industry in the western world. Spencer, Comte and Durkheim called for a scientific *positive* study of society that would bring back unity, order and happiness to a chaotic and normless world. In other words, they brought with them for the task, assumptions about what was *good*. They brought with them assumptions about *values*. Modern day claims that sociology is, or assertions that sociology ought to be, a *value-free* science, overlook the implicit value-assumptions which cling to every theorist, irrespective of how carefully objective he or she may set out to be. For every question asked is chosen from the set of possible questions; each method chosen produces data of one sort and omits other data; every conclusion drawn reflects the purposes and moral values of the researcher.

If sociology has always been a value-laden science we may also say something about the nature of those values. The yearning for a lost past of *Gemeinschaft* or close communal bonds, resonates throughout the history of sociology. From Rousseau's romantic view of the child as 'the noble savage' spoiled by civilization, through the functionalism of Malinowski and Radcliffe Brown, through the psycho-analytic theories of Freud, to the newer versions of *humanistic sociology* as found today in the works of Philip Slater (1970), John Nisbet (1970) and Richard Sennett (1974), we may observe a common disillusionment with the mechanical, instrumental links and aspirations of modern society (*Gesellschaft*). The central concern of social theory, it seems, has always been with the place of the individual in the larger scheme of things:

how it is that despite our individuality, despite our personal oddities and our subjective and thus unsharable experience of the world around us, we all seem to behave socially, to orient ourselves to others and to fit in with the social system; how we come to understand others; how we learn the rules that operate in society and come to accept the limits imposed on us by the assertive individuality of others and by their collective presence; how it is that we are still private individuals, capable of our own thoughts, of rejecting the demands of others and capable even of actively working to change the social system.

When men and women could believe that the status quo was ordained by God, or that fate would make useless any attempt to change their lot, such questions were less difficult. In such static societies every other person, every social arrangement, every rule, every encounter, confirmed for the individual his fixed place in the scheme of things. It was only when new ideas and new circumstances began to challenge the accepted meanings and social arrangements, that serious questions began to emerge about why things were as they were and how they might be changed through the exercise of human will. Of course it is an over-simplification to suppose that people have only recently begun to question the social order. Human life has always been subject to change: conquests have brought new influences to bear and groups have always challenged and tried to control one another. Philosophers have theorized about society for thousands of years. However it is only relatively recently that the development of new techniques has made it possible for sociology to emerge as a separate scientific discipline. Instead of speculating from our armchairs we can now gather and analyze facts. We can now test theories by observing their effects in practice, or by comparing societies.

Scientific Method and the Study of Society

Social science aims at explaining social life, but there are varying levels of explanation. The *why* questions about poverty, prejudice, political control, divorce, family processes, deviant behaviour and so on can be answered in many ways. The ways depend not only upon the social scientist's values and biases but also upon the models and research methods that arise from them. The *scientific method* is in itself a value system and its claim to be *objective* or *value-free* will not stand close examination. Nor will the distinction between *pure* and *applied* research do much more than distinguish between the value positions of social scientists.

Science may be better thought of as a method than a specific area of subject matter. Science rests on a common belief with religious faith—that there is an underlying order in nature—but scientists believe that it is possible to understand and explain that order by observing through the senses. *Empirical* observation (i.e., observing the real world through the senses of sight, hearing, touch, taste and smell) allows us to *classify* objects that are like and unlike one another and to observe the *relations* between them. Empirical observations allow us to generalize: all dogs have tails; all societies have families; plants die without water; poverty leads to crime, and so on.

Notice, however, that the last generalization is of a different order of *interpretation* from the first; it implies a regular relationship of causation between *conditions*, a relationship which some people might deny. Yet the notion of *objectivity* in science rests upon an assumption that people agree on the messages that their sense organs send them about the external world and that such messages are independent of our individual wills. Though other people may not agree with us about our thoughts or values, we do agree about the evidence of the senses: we perceive people and objects acting in a way similar to the way others perceive them. Despite the *subjectivity* of our internal thoughts, the agreements we reach with others help us believe in the reality of an external objective world. In short, science begins as the study of whatever we can reach universal agreement about. Since we can only reach agreement if events are repeated and seen to be related in some way, science is the study of relations between events which repeatedly occur under certain conditions. Science states a set of conditional relations, or *if-then* statements—if one event occurs then another event will follow. Such statements may also be *probability statements*: under a given set of conditions it is probable that X will lead to Y. They may sometimes, however, be stated as scientific *laws*, as an invariable association: that X will *always* lead to Y. The scientific model then, may be inappropriate to the study of society. If the object of social science is to explain social behaviour, how analytic or scientific can that explanation be? Firstly, not all the factors affecting social behaviour can be observed via the senses. We can observe people's behaviour but not their thoughts. A car crashing into a shopfront requires more than observation for us to understand it socially. The brakes or steering may have failed; or the driver may have been drunk, playing a prank, trying to commit suicide or seeking vengeance on the shopowner. In other words, social science requires evidence of *motivation* as well as of action. Social science is concerned with meanings, intentions and thoughts, and these things are not so easy to reach agreement about. On the other hand, social causes may not derive from the actions or thoughts of individuals at all. For example, population changes may explain the present decline in some university enrolments in Australia better than any hypothesis about public disenchantment with education, unemployment or political anti-intellectualism. The population-change argument might run like this:
a) the post-war baby boom has now passed through the primary and secondary schools and their enrolments have declined;
b) fewer teachers are therefore needed;
c) consequently the marketability of an arts degree (or a general science degree for that matter) has diminished;
d) and if the number of students matriculating from high schools has declined, it follows that the number who could have enrolled in university courses must also be down.

Durkheim (1950 [1895]) argued that many 'social facts' lie unseen by the ordinary person and can only be discovered by rigorous social-scientific analysis.

Secondly, although social action rests upon agreements between people over definitions and possible courses of action, those very agreements differ from group to group and from society to society. Consequently there are very few universal agreements about which we can generalize to make a science of society. Precisely because social action is based on *meanings*, it will vary as those meanings vary in place, time and situation. In fact, a core question for sociology is why interpretations and meanings vary for groups acting under different conditions. Indeed, a universal science of human behaviour may be impossible simply because those meanings arise from diverse situations. Our very notions of 'reality', the sets of things we have agreed upon and come to take for granted, are culture-bound and rarely absolute. So it may therefore be impossible to reach agreement on scientific laws about conditional relations when the conditions and the events and even the order of association between them vary so much.

Positivism

The sociologist as scientist does not give up hope of discovering patterns in social life and the underlying order of things. This positive hope gave rise to the very word *sociology*. Auguste Comte (1798–1857) coined the term *sociology* in his book *The Positive Philosophy*. He offered an evolutionary view of human beings progressing through three stages in their attempts to understand their own lives. In the first stage (the *theological* stage) people explain events in terms of the direct intervention of supernatural agents. In the next (*metaphysical*) stage people perceive abstract forces as the cause rather than gods or spirits. In the highest stage of human progress (the *positive* stage) people seek laws of explanation in the events themselves. According to Comte, the positive stage is first reached in the less complex sciences of nature such as physics. It would be reached later in the most complex science, that of social physics or sociology. Speaking amidst the turmoil of post-revolutionary France, Comte felt that its time had come. He modelled his method for such a science, the method of *positivism*, on the methods of the natural sciences: the researcher must observe, compare and experiment by comparing normal states with abnormal states. The study of history would provide a backdrop to reveal the true harmony of society. Where previous philosophies had been *negative* and critical of existing social institutions, Comte wanted this new science to be *positive*. He expected that it would identify the true laws by which society should evolve, then diagnose the ills of contemporary institutions, and ultimately prescribe changes that would bring society back into harmony with the underlying process of evolution. Sociology would thus be a positive science working for the good of society.

Obviously such a theory is not value-free. It has a conservative bias aimed at preserving, or at least bringing into balance, the existing social order. Comte pointed up the contrast between *statics*, the study of social order, and *dynamics*, the study of social change. He saw social change as evolution towards greater order and harmony. His model of society was an *organism* which must have order for the smooth functioning of its various interdependent parts.

Metaphorical and Analytic Models

One of the earliest and most persistent models used for sociological explanation is, in fact, based on metaphor rather than scientific analysis. The model is of society as an organism, similar to a plant in biological science, or to the human body with each of its parts related closely to the functions of other parts. Metaphors may be useful in everyday life in that they clarify our understanding of one thing by likening it to another. They do not, however, *explain* behaviour. Consider the oft drawn theatrical metaphor that 'life's a stage'. The analogy is useful to the degree that it allows us to speak of the way a man acts out his roles as 'manager at work', 'father at home' and 'team coach on Saturdays'. It has in fact been annexed by *role theory* as a means of classifying, simplifying and *imaging* the complex forms of observable behaviour. But it describes only by comparison and does not explain either actual behaviour or the existence of *roles*, *expectations* or *statuses*. To provide such explanation we need an *analytic* model which specifies the *conditions* and the *situations* which can be used to *predict outcomes* in social interaction.

Figure 2–1   Aspects of Analytical Explanation

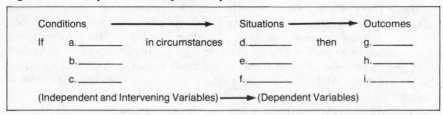

We know that individuals are often not conscious of acting out roles; that they are less calculating, less predictable and more capricious than the metaphor of roles suggests. The metaphor may therefore be misleading because it confuses comparison, contrast and classification (for the sake of *thinking* about possible causes) with true causal explanation. Causal explanation seeks to find regular patterns of co-variation between one variable and another, (see Figure 2–1). There may be limits to the extent to which we can achieve this aim, but social science has claimed to be able to discover the general *laws* underlying social behaviour.

The Organic Metaphor of Society

Yet the basic model of society used by sociologists, economists and political scientists has long been one of metaphor rather than of explanation—the metaphor of society as an organism which develops according to in-built scientific laws. This image of society forces us to consider how theory arises from a social context and how theory leads to forms of control based on values often hidden in metaphor.

Durkheim (1858—1917) writes about society as an organism in *The Rules of the Sociological Method*:

> The first origins of all social processes of any importance should be sought in the internal constitution of the social group . . . the facts of social morphology are of the same nature as physiological phenomena (Durkheim, 1938, pp.112—3).

In other words, he suggests that social structure is the set of relations between organs. These organs are a society's institutions and each must be healthy if the whole is to operate harmoniously. Conflict or disharmony is sickness because it is not the normal state. It is important to note that a moral judgement infuses everything that follows from applying this organic model.

The analogy is misleading and politically dangerous. For one thing, it locates causes in the 'genetic' structure of the organism itself rather than in other, possibly external, conditions. A clear example is the political claim (made by parties of every persuasion throughout our short history) that the evils of Australian society arise from faulty Government policies. In part they do, but Australia is not isolated from the rest of the world; historically it has always depended upon the powers of such forces as European colonial expansion, British capitalism, world trade, foreign investment and other industrialized societies to encourage or prevent development in societies outside their own. Our own tariff laws, taxes, wages and prices certainly affect Australian society from within, but there are other powerful forces at work.

Seeing society as an organism means viewing its institutions as organs which function together to preserve the life of the whole organism. Life depends (in this analogy with the human body) upon each part working in harmony with the rest. But where is the heart of society? Where are its kidneys? Will society as we know it die if the State withers away, or if religion or the family declines, or education takes a new direction?

There is, to be sure, a valuable insight here. Change in one part of society will very likely lead to change in other parts of the social structure. We can and should look for those links between institutions which explain how conditions in one institution produce effects in others. But the organic model may also lead us into dangerous ways of thinking. It may lead us to perceive all conflict as bad, or to regard any change to the status quo as 'sick' or 'deviant' or 'non-functional' because it disturbs a social harmony that we should be trying to preserve. Viewing institutions in this way is also to encourage the preservation of the dominant power relations that gave rise to their legitimacy in the first place and to misunderstand the processes of change.

The organic model is most misleading when it is 'logically extended', that is when the full biological implications of the model are applied to the explanation of social change. In biology, growth means the natural process of development from an organism's underlying genetic code.

The first writers to use the organic growth metaphor to describe society's development were the Greeks. Their concept of growth grew from their expression of *physis*: the essence of growth, the generative power that rested within. Heraclitus believed that society, like a tree or a man, would grow and fade in a predetermined way according to its inner essence—its *physis*. He believed, too, that any deviation from the pre-ordained path was not only unnatural but actually suicidal. Aristotle held that society's natural growth, or *physis*, was to move from the stage of the family, to that of the village, and finally to the stage of the State which is its natural end. As Galt and Smith (1976, p.83) point out, Aristotle's notion that 'the final cause and end of a thing is the best, and to be self-sufficing is the end and the best' began the long-standing logical problem of *functional theory* which confuses the end-product with its cause and 'makes a value judgement that this state of culmination is the best'. This view reappears in present-day notions of 'progress', 'technological development' and 'modernization'.

The idea found one of its most powerful expressions in the work of Herbert Spencer (1820–1903). He wrote at a time when British colonial expansion was subjugating 'inferior natives' all over the world and when the industrial revolution was producing misery and poverty for the rural dispossessed and for the expanding urban population. His theory concerning the 'survival of the fittest' offered a perfect philosophical rationale. By this he meant 'the survival of those in which power of military cooperation is the greatest'. For him the 'destruction or absorption of the smaller ununited societies by the united larger ones, is an inevitable process through which the varieties of men most adapted for social life supplant the less adapted varieties' (Spencer, 1967 [1898], p.78). This idea has had a major impact on social theory, both at the popular and at the formal sociological level.

As we have suggested earlier, every social theory is a means of understanding and controlling social life. Just as the theory of the Divine Right of Kings evolved out of conflicts between feudal barons and made possible the control of all by one, so Spencer's theory of the survival of the fittest served as a justification for subordinating others through colonialism and other kinds of exploitation. It echoes still in our prejudices against 'under-developed' peoples, the poor and the uneducated. It was, in the same period, given a particular biological application in Charles Darwin's *Origin of Species* published in 1859. Indeed Spencer's vision of society evolving through the process of survival of the fittest, became known as 'social Darwinism'. He saw society beginning as 'germs', and then gradually growing into 'social aggregates'. For him the very nature of society (its *physis*) led it to grow larger and more complex. He argued that interference would be to go against nature. Consequently there should be no laws favouring the poor, no health regulations and no compulsory education or taxation of the rich. He believed it inevitable that the 'stern discipline' of civilization would bring 'to early graves the children of diseased parents and single out the low spirited, the intemperate, and the debilitated as the victims of an epidemic' (Spencer, 1967 [1898], p.289). In this way society could be expected to improve.

The fact that such an elite theory could become accepted so widely shows how dominant groups can control cultural ideas (through laws, authority structures, education and the mass media) and how they can institutionalize processes that produce the very effects Spencer claimed were 'natural'. The theory becomes a self-fulfilling prophecy. That part of the analogy which holds that the fittest will survive is true. They do. But the *result* and the *process* are confused with the *cause*. The powerful may happily accept the suggestion that growth and progress are natural and that no interference beyond their own should be allowed. They may legitimately weed out the weak.

Even Marx and Engels treat the transition from primitive societies to capitalism as a natural evolutionary process. They based some of their ideas on the work of Lewis H. Morgan (1818–1881) who saw mankind progressing through the stages of *Savagery*, *Barbarism* and *Civilization*. Their notion—that the internal contradictions of capitalism would inevitably lead to its downfall—also reflects in part the dynamics of 'organism'. In most of these evolutionary theories of social change, the Australian Aborigine represents the most basic stage of mankind's 'infancy'. Arnold Toynbee revived the metaphor in his 'rise and fall' theory of history. And theories of modernization based on the idea that modern societies evolved from primitive societies do the same. (See Rostow (1960).)

These kinds of theories overlook the fact that growth depends upon resources and their distribution; that distribution rests upon unequal power and conflict; that underdevelopment has often resulted from colonial exploitation rather than from some natural inferiority or sickness; and that the tables may turn at any time (as we may now see in the energy crisis which has given the Arab nations new power in the negotiation of their conditions of growth).

Major Theoretical Divisions

Like most branches of Western thought, sociological theories have been *dualistic* rather than *monistic*. Unlike Eastern thought where all reality is reduced to a single principle, where mind and matter, body and spirit are considered to be manifestations of a single substance, Western thought has typically been expressed in terms of contrasts and contradictions. For example, passive and active, male and female, hot and cold, body and mind, spirit and matter, conflict and consensus—are regarded as separates, rather than as complementary principles or forces. The literature of sociology follows similar lines. It does not present a unified view; nor are different theories seen to contribute to, or to complement each other. Rather, theories tend to be presented in contrasting pairs. A classification of theories may read, for example, *conflict* versus *consensus*, or *objective* versus *subjective*, or *normative* versus *interpretive*, or *structural* versus *process*. A brief outline of these contrasts is necessary to an understanding of the following chapters. (See Wallace (1969) for detailed exposition on which this section is partly based.) It is important to note that it is not necessary to adopt any one theoretical position to the exclusion of all others.

Structural Theories

Structural theories proceed on the basis of two assumptions. The first assumption is that society is made up of a number of positions or *statuses* (for example, mother, father, teacher, policeman), more or less fixed in relation to each other. The second assumption is that the way the social actors relate and interact results from the *structure* of the linked statuses. In other words, structural theories try to explain observable social behaviour in terms of the established (*structured*) status positions that a society generates.

Social relationships and social bonds result from *exchange* between status positions in society. Our needs are often satisfied through the services of others. Because people are obliged to repay these services, their mutually dependent relationships will continue. This way of looking at relationships is called *exchange structuralism*. It is based on the notion that society rests on a *norm of reciprocity*, 'a mutually gratifying pattern of exchanging goods and services' (Gouldner, 1960, pp.161–78). Gouldner argues that two special features of this general norm of reciprocity explain much of social behaviour. Firstly, because a gift to someone imposes a sort of duty owed to return the favour, the norm links both past and future events with present behaviour. He suggests that the norm of reciprocity thus creates motives for returning benefits even where someone with greater power might be tempted to exploit a weaker person. In addition, because any exchange creates an expectation of future repayment, the norm of reciprocity encourages social rather than selfish behaviour. It does so because it offers some basis for confidence that if one gives up one's services or valuables, one will, in turn, be repaid. Secondly, Gouldner argues that the norm is very general or 'plastic'. He argues that this helps social stability because one can repay in a variety of ways and is not restricted to a specific role relationship: for example, a favour done by a friend at work may be repaid by service at home.

Durkheim (1964 [1933]) (and, later, Lewis Coser (1956)) argued that no specific contract or formalized exchange can exist unless there exists already a body of norms to regularize such transactions. As Blau (1964) asserts, such a theory of social exchange can only rest upon the existence of some value consensus because people have to agree on what is valuable, what is needed and what is fair. Thibaut and Kelley (1959) reject the notion of one underlying norm of reciprocity and argue that what is seen to be a reward by any individual is a matter for empirical research. In their view, the exercise of control over others (and indeed, the social patterns of interdependence themselves) derives from the sorts of resources different people possess. As Blau insists, exchange between people in order to satisfy their needs is central to much that we observe in society.

> Processes of social attraction, without which associations among men would not occur, give rise to processes of exchange. Unreciprocated exchange leads to the differentiation of power. The exercise of power in collectivities, as judged by social norms of justice, promotes processes of social approval, legitimation, and organization on the one hand, and forces of opposition, conflict, reorganization, and change, on the other. Although there is a strain toward reciprocity in social relations and a strain toward equilibrium in social structures, the same forces that restore balance or equilibrium in one respect are imbalancing or disequilibrating forces in others, which means that the very processes of adjustment create imbalances requiring further adjustments (Blau, 1964, p.7).

The relative emphasis on balance or imbalance leads other structural theories of exchange along different paths.

Functional structuralism stresses the positive side of exchange. Its theorists hold that in order to explain any aspect of society, we must identify its functions (i.e. consequences) for the larger social system of which it is a part. Further, they hold that the consequences of one aspect are causes of other aspects of social behaviour, so that different aspects are *functional* for one another (Merton, 1957, pp.46−7; and Davis, 1959, p.760). It follows then that the wider social system is likely to 'repay' and sustain any part that is functioning properly; but if it ceases to be functional (i.e. becomes *dysfunctional*) it will die out or be eliminated. This is obviously a very broad and non-specific theory. Indeed Merton argues that both functions and dysfunctions may vary widely so they have to be observed empirically rather than predicted (Merton, 1957, pp.19−84). Moreover, we need to distinguish between *manifest functions*—the intended consequences of some social act or custom, and *latent functions*—the unintended and possibly unknown consequences of some persisting social custom which seems at first sight to have no rational purpose for its continuation.

Since, for the functionalist, there are certain functions which must be performed if the society or group or individual is to persist, there are also likely to be *functional alternatives*—alternate ways of achieving the same social consequence. For example, when a factory changes its philosophy of management to accept worker participation, the functions of the boss, the foreman and the production line worker also change; the structure of the factory is different. But there must still be a set of structures to perform such key functions as deciding who will do what, how supplies will be obtained and when tasks will be done. So although we may not see the usual hierarchy of work roles we will find structural alternatives aimed at achieving the same functional effects.

Talcott Parsons (1937) extends this notion of alternatives to suggest that in any society people will be faced with choices among possible means and ends of action. In his early works, he emphasized the voluntary nature of individual choice-making. This perspective has become known as *social actionism* or *social action theory*.

Parsons begins with the simplest form of exchange—interaction between two individuals who perform roles that are mutually dependent on one another. They develop expectations, reward actions that conform and punish those that do not. But their relationship can only be understood within the context of their personality systems and the cultural system of common understandings. Social action thus involves each actor's definition of the situation insofar as it involves his own interests (the *cognitive* element), his desire to maximize pleasure (the *cathetic* element) and his choice between alternatives (the *evaluative* or *normative* element). The actual patterns of interaction form *the social system* at a particular time and place. This system becomes a *society* when it lasts longer than the life-span of those interacting, when it replaces its members biologically and socializes them, and when it meets all its essential functions from within its own resources. There are thus four *functional prerequisites* for any society:

1. *Integration*: it must hold itself together.
2. *Pattern maintenance*: it must develop ways of preserving its pattern of social arrangements.

3. *Goal-attainment*: it must define and achieve its purposes.
4. *Adaptation*: it must adjust to new conditions by developing suitable resources.

This theory of society echoes the early *organic* model of Spencer, Comte and Durkheim. Each part serves a function for the whole; harmony and equilibrium are essential for 'proper' functioning; consensus about values and about what constitutes appropriate means to achieve goals is essential to the maintenance of society. Society then is pictured as an objective 'thing' (i.e., it is *reified*) with an existence of its own beyond the individuals and groups who make it up.

Parsons argued that society generated broad value orientations which guide people when they are making choices. In every situation there are alternate *norms* ('A norm is a verbal description of the concrete course of action . . . regarded as desirable, combined with an injunction to make certain future actions conform to this course' (Parsons, 1949, pp.44−5)). Each *situation* provides the conditions of choice and action. Parsons and Shils (1951) suggest that every need and every role-expectation involves a combination of value-orientations among five *pattern variables*.

> An actor in a situation is confronted by a series of major dilemmas of orientation, a series of choices that the actor must make . . . Specifically, we maintain, the actor must make five specific dichotomous choices before any situation will have a determinate meaning. The five dichotomies which formulate these choice alternatives are called the pattern variables (Parsons & Shils, 1951, p.76).

The five *pattern variables* include:

1. *Affectivity versus Neutrality*, or *Expressiveness versus Instrumentalism*: A task may be approached in one of two ways: either with a good deal of emotional involvement or in an objective fashion where the cost-benefits of action are coldly calculated. The latter will be judged on the value of the extrinsic rewards it produces, but the former may provide personal satisfactions intrinsic to the task.

2. *Self versus Collective Orientation*: An individual may choose to pursue his own interests or to work for the interests of the group as a whole. In theory at least, the dichotomy is demonstrated by the different social orientations of private enterprise and socialism.

3. *Universalism versus Particularism*: A system may be open to entry by all-comers on criteria that apply to all; or it may be closed so that choices are made on the basis of who knows whom. Since our exchanges with others set up close and often emotional bonds or commitments, roles that require more universalistic orientations (such as judges or external examiners) are usually closely watched in case they show favouritism.

4. *Ascription versus Achievement*, or *Quality versus Performance*: An individual orients himself to others according either to the sorts of personal qualities they have (they are pretty or ugly, black or white, wealthy or poor) or to what they can actually do. Ascription is a kind of labelling approach, using categories to assign people certain rights, virtues and defects rather than to judge their status by their objective performance.

5. *Specificity versus Diffuseness*: An individual may relate to others in defined ways through a specific contract (for example in the purchase of a car, the buyer-seller relationship between the individual and the salesman). On the other hand, a relationship may be broader and non-specific (as between, say, husband and wife). The longer a relationship lasts, the more likely it is to become diffuse.

Parsons holds that these broad patterns of value-choices become stable in any society through *socialization* and through *role differentiation and social control mechanisms*.

Socialization is the process by which society's norms and criteria of choice become *internalized* and accepted. In our society, boys are socialized towards toughness and the need to achieve; on the other hand, socialization teaches girls to be emotional and person-oriented.

Role differentiation and social control mechanisms maintain the requirements of particular roles and serve to punish deviations from the accepted. For example, our society requires that doctors be neutral, objective, instrumental and specific in their relationships with their patients. In other words, society expects that doctors and patients will maintain that set of role-orientations whenever they interact. Any breaches of 'professional ethics' may be punished.

We have dwelt at some length on the functional structuralist theoretical stance for two reasons. Firstly, it has been the most dominant approach in American sociology and anthropology and is thus reflected in much of the available social research. Secondly, most of the other approaches to sociological theory are reactions against the value position implicit in functional structuralism. Consequently it is necessary to understand what is being objected to.

Though Parsons' early emphasis on voluntary actions allowed room for the individual to make choices, there was clearly the suggestion of absolute requirements for a workable society. In his later work, these appear as *functional requisites* or *functional imperatives*, suggesting that the individual's range for voluntary action is limited. His theory moves its emphasis from *social action* to the *social system* in which exchanges between social institutions, groups and so on allow little room for voluntary choice or for non-conforming values and behaviour (Parsons, 1951). Thus his functional structural version of exchange moves from the level of reciprocal and unequal exchanges between acting individuals and groups, to an impersonal level where system-wide exchanges structure all life possibilities. As Gouldner protests, this simply takes differences of *power* as given and:

> ignores the fact that such power differences establish a framework in which one party can, and often does, impose himself on another, with resultant conflict between them, even when they do share moral beliefs. Differential power is thus conducive neither to a consensus in moral beliefs and to an attendant complementarity of expectations, nor to a reciprocity or 'mutuality of gratifications'. On two counts, then, great power differences will, by Parsons' own assumptions, impair the self-maintaining equilibrium with which he is concerned (Gouldner, 1970, pp.242–3).

It is the functional stress on the *normative* or consensus, legitimacy-based side of social exchange, that leads to the reservations about the usefulness of this approach. *Interpretive* theories argue for a return to Parsons' earlier voluntarism and emphasize the uncertainty of any outcomes in the negotiation of social reality.

In contrast, *conflict structuralism* focuses on the negative side of the exchange system.

Conflict Theories

Conflict structuralism is a variant of general exchange theory in that it focuses on the structured exchange of acts which are harmful or punitive. Simmel (1955, pp.115–6) pointed out that compromise, which is always a result of exchange processes, is often adopted as a preferable alternative to robbery: a benefit is conferred at the same time as a demand is made. Thus exchange of benefits often helps avoid (or substitutes for) conflict. Such an exchange, however, can only happen where simple desire for something is replaced by an objective notion of 'value'. Each party to the exchange must recognize the value of the objects in question so that giving up a valued object can be compensated for by accepting a substitute of the same value. Of course money is the best example of 'substitutability' of value, and has long been the major basis of exchange in society. (See Parsons, Introduction, Part III: 33*ff*, in Weber, 1964, for a lengthy discussion of the importance of money.)

But *conflict* theory is concerned with more than the mere exchange of injuries between groups and it offers a better explanation of social action, social institutions and social change, than *functional* theories do. Whereas functional theories start from abstract *social needs* to explain how social practices and institutions develop and function to meet those needs, conflict theory asks more basic questions. As Dahrendorf (1958, p.176) puts it:

1. How do conflicting groups arise from the structure of society?
2. What forms can the struggles among such groups assume?
3. How does the conflict among such groups effect a change in the social structures?

He answers that all roles (as points of exchange) centre around the issue of control or dominance. Each role (for example, boss or worker) therefore has both positive and negative control interests. These interests organize themselves into groups (such as political parties, trade unions or employer federations), with their manifest interests usually phrased as clear programs or ideologies. Such interest groups are in constant conflict over the preservation or change of the status quo and its structure of dominance relations; but the actual form of conflict is determined by the *empirical conditions* under which conflict takes place.

All conflict leads to changes in the structure of dominance relations between interest groups. The empirical conditions of social conflict will vary according to the existence of effective situations (group members must be able to communicate, to recruit new members, to have the right to meet and to organize effectively). In any society the *intensity* of conflict will vary according to the presence of effective mechanisms for regulating social conflict (for example, elections rather than civil war; arbitration and conciliation rather than head-on strikes; and courts of law rather than feuds between families). And it is likely to vary also according to the degree of social mobility that is possible. This is so because blocked chances for mobility lead to frustration, tension and greater conflict. (Ben-David, 1963—4, (pp.247—330) and Schumpeter, (1942) present detailed analyses of mobility problems.) Finally the *form* and extent of changes arising from conflict will depend upon the relative power (based on resources) of rulers to stay in power or of rival interest groups to exert pressure, and upon the ability of the conflicting groups to organize effectively. Totalitarian regimes prevent people from moving freely and thereby restrict discussion which might serve to regulate conflict legally. Therefore, any change to a totalitarian regime is likely to be revolutionary.

An ideology of *consensus*, of rational discussion, participation and reasoned sorting out of disagreements can serve to prevent change and may thus (in functionalist terms), be *maladjustive*. Lewis Coser (1956) writes of the social functions of conflict suggesting that every conflict is a sort of transaction and that without legitimate structures to contain social conflict society breaks down. In similar vein, Durkheim (1964 [1933]) argued that the division of labour poses new strains on the normative regulation of society and that the law has to shift from being *repressive* to being something which ensures restitution based on a notion of contract.

Of course it is possible to combine consensus theory and conflict theory. Van den Berghe (1963, pp.695—705) shows that the growth of conflict between groups is usually linked with growing consensus *within* the groups. So consensus may be defined not only in functional terms regarding the norms of a group, but also in terms of dissension with the norms of other groups.

Max Weber (1864—1920) offers the most insightful version of conflict theory. Where Marx and Engels saw group conflict to arise from the economic differences between social classes, Weber (1968 [1922]) insisted that conflict groups develop when there are unequal exchanges or unequal shares of power and prestige, as well as when there are economic differences. He saw society to be constituted of *status groups*, groups of people who associate with one another and who share a sense of equality of status based on participation in a common culture. The term *status groups* is thus roughly interchangeable with *sub-cultures*, but status groups develop first around families and friends and may only then extend to religious, ethnic or educational communities. Their members share a common style of language, manners, tastes in clothing, topics of conversation, opinions, values, preferences in activities and so on. For Weber, a *status group* is an *ideal type* and does not necessarily have distinct boundaries; the actual exclusivity of groups or the degree to which they overlap may only be judged by empirical observation. But since people gain their sense of *identity* from their close associations, status groups develop their own *moral evaluations* about 'them' versus 'us'; consequently they will come to see the rejection or exclusion of 'outsiders' as quite legitimate.

Weber's model of society and of how social change takes place is, therefore, a model expressed in terms of conflict between different status groups. The groups are formed when social interaction produces a similarity of interest among a number of people. Social *bonds* and social *identities* develop out of the web of group affiliations. Each status group works to defend its own *interests* against the interests of rival groups. Social structure arises as some prove to be more successful than others in their conflict over the control of valued resources. The Weber conflict model contrasts markedly, then, with the normative, functional, consensus model in which the needs of the whole society produce norms and institutions that function to meet those needs.

For Weber, the struggle for advantage between status groups revolves round three main *goods* (or, in our terms, *resources*): wealth, power, and prestige. This does not mean that all people desire to maximize their rewards. However it only needs a few to try because power and prestige (and wealth which tends to accompany them) are scarce, and because any effort by a few to grab an unequal share will cause others to struggle (i.e., conflict) to prevent loss of their own control and relative esteem.

As Randall Collins argues (1971, pp.1002—19) identity arises from membership in a group, so group cohesion (based on a common culture and sense of identity) will be 'a key resource in the struggle against others'. Consequently most conflicts will be between status groups rather than within them, and 'the struggle for wealth, power and prestige will be carried out primarily through organizations'.

Thus, institutions do not arise merely from society's needs and the agreed-upon norms which regulate the relations between people. Rather, they are generated by the struggles between status groups as each group tries to impose upon others its own tastes, preferences, sub-cultural values and modes of organizing.

Modern organizations are complex and often contain competing status groups within them. Alliances between groups give the allies greater control over others. Notice how trade unions have increasingly sought to strengthen their influence through the formation of national councils and how the E.E.C. has strengthened the hands of the member countries. Moreover, each status group tries to maintain control by one or both of two methods: by selecting new members of similar status and by convincing people of lower status that they should acknowledge or at least respect the superiority of the group's own culture. Entry to both the medical and the legal professions is successfully controlled by these kinds of tactics. Another example may be the preference given to members of one religious group or another by those who control recruitment to various sections of the Australian public service.

Weber's view of conflict has particularly deep implications for the sociologist's concept of *community*. The functional, consensus notion is that *community* arises from shared values, close interaction and normative regulation. Weber, however, shows that it is conflict over scarce resources between competing status groups that brings people together, first as groups and then as a wider *community*. (Thompson (1972) presents a detailed examination of this view in the Australian context.)

Process Theories

Weber also focused attention on the subjective nature of the process which gives rise to social action and to the identity of individual interests within status groups. As we suggested earlier, no theory worth its salt can exclude the subjective, meaning-based, interpretive side of man's social behaviour. All of the structural theories we have looked at, implicitly or explicitly allow room for the individual, *self-other* relationship on which society is based. So it is largely a matter of relative emphasis that distinguishes theories from one another in this regard. Our sub-headings *Structural Theories* and *Process Theories* may in themselves be misleading if taken too literally. The distinction is merely that some theories highlight the structured patterns of social relations while others focus more closely on the processes of social interaction and on the formation of social groups. So-called *role-theory* falls between these two, partly because processes of interaction develop through playing-at, taking-on and negotiating roles and also because at least one picture of *social structure* is drawn by the structure of roles and their expected behaviour patterns.

For the same reason, the distinction between *micro* and *macro* levels of explanation is arbitrary and may be misleading. *Micro* implies small-scale, possibly *subjective* and focused on the *elements* of social action. But it is out of such social elements that larger social patterns emerge: the *macro-level* grows out of *micro* elements. Blau, for example, argues that *power* is a social creation that emerges from the action of two elements—the attraction of two or more people to interact because they expect some benefit, and their actually engaging in an imbalanced transaction. Likewise, *legitimation* emerges from two elements—applying *universalistic* values to preference choices, and *goal-focused* social interaction. When *power* and *legitimation* are combined they create *authority*. Authority serves as 'an important resource for the stable organization of collective endeavours' and, thus, society (Blau, 1964, p.9).

Verstehen: Weber realized the need for a new definition of social action. He argued that action becomes social when it *takes account* of others, so it therefore has attached to it some *subjective meaning*. There are two levels of subjective meaning: one is the actual meaning to a particular actor; the other is the *ideal* meaning attributed to a hypothetical actor in a hypothetical action situation. And there are four pure types of action:
a) *affectual*: action based on passion, love, hate or devotion;
b) *traditional*: action arising from habit or routine;
c) *wertrational*: irrational action geared to religious or ethical ends which are themselves irrational;
d) *zweckrational*: rationally calculated action which selects the best means by which to achieve ends (as in economics or in complex organizations).

Weber believed that a new methodology for the social sciences was needed in order to explain social action: the methodology of *Verstehen* or subjective understanding. He argued that it was not enough for the social scientist simply to observe objective social behaviour, and to identify norms and objective social relations. He also insisted on the need to get behind the *meanings* and *motivations* that impel people to act in certain ways and to view social processes in terms of meaningful categories of human experience (Truzzi, 1974).

Opponents of Weber's view have argued that we can never properly observe the motivational springs of action. They have also argued that even if we could, it would take our understanding of social action no further than the observation of external patterns of behaviour. In their view, to impute emotions, attitudes and purposes as the explanations of overt behaviour, is to assume that actors are in certain psychological states and that there is some necessary correlation between those states and their observable behaviour. They point out, however, that people's actions do not always reflect their expressed beliefs.

But there are points to be made in Weber's defence. Firstly, Weber was not calling for some sort of subjective and unverifiable introspection. As Schutz later argued, Weber saw social action to be *inter*-subjective rather than private; to be based on common, shared understandings that together constitute social reality. Secondly, Weber's critics with their emphasis on mere objective observation, strike the problem that behaviours which are observably the same may have quite different meanings for the individuals who perform them. Thirdly, *negative* action (the intentional refraining from action) is never observable and may only be explained in terms of the individual's motives and interpretations of the situation giving rise to it. And finally, motives are real in their consequences: it matters not that they may not be observed or even that they may be irrational (Thomas, 1928). For example, it may be demonstrable that a primitive savage's illness is due to some virus, but if the savage believes the illness to have been caused by the gods, then he will act to appease them—and not the unknown virus. Similarly, in seventeenth-century Salem, witchcraft was no figment of the imagination. In that context, for those people, it was an element of social reality. It was and is therefore open to study and social explanation.

The method of *Verstehen*, then, is not introspection. Rather it is a way in which we all make sense of reality: we try to put ourselves in the place of others and to imagine their thoughts, reasons and intentions as they are reflected in their actions. Both Weber and Schutz regard *Verstehen* as *subjective* however, because 'its goal is to find out what the actor means (intends) in his action, not the meaning this action has for the neutral observer or for the actor's partner' (Schutz, 1971).

For Alfred Schutz, this means that sociology has to start with the commonsense knowledge of everyday life rather than with grand theories and abstract concepts. It must identify the motives and goals that lie behind action and the rules of procedure that are based on shared understandings about the world. It must look for social reality as it is experienced by men in everyday life.

Symbolic Interaction

If all social experience is *shared* experience and takes account of the meanings and intentions of others, we must explore the general principles by which people organize their knowledge of the world in their daily lives

Here the principles of symbolic interaction become important. Humans differ from other animals because they are able to use symbols. A symbol can stand in place of an object even when the object itself is not present. For example, when he is at home, a man's physical presence is the *object* 'father' to his children, but the *word* 'father' can symbolize him when he is absent and in fact can symbolize a whole abstract role concept of *every* father. As children grow, they learn that objects exist independently of their own subjective experiences of them. Then they learn to attach a symbol to each object of importance: for example *Mum, Dad, rattle, bottle, bath* and so on. Gradually children learn to think of their *self* as an object too. Once they reach this stage, true symbolic interaction can take place because they have the capacity to interact *with the self* in *reflexive thought*. George Herbert Mead first spelt out the stages of the process in which all children first play at being other people and then take on their roles. In this way children learn about themselves: they learn who they are. They also learn the reasons for the actions of other people.

Children also learn gradually to typify, to categorize, to group and link objects and ideas. In other words, they learn to create mental maps of their worlds which allow new experiences to be understood in contexts that are meaningful to them. Schutz sees symbolic power to grow along with the development of this capacity.

As children, we learn our *typifications* of objects and ideas (and the symbols that stand for them) from others who share a common store of typifications and symbols. When we go on to use those symbols in our communication with others we may therefore expect to be understood. Where we do not share common understandings, symbols or rules of behaviour, we experience the *other* as a stranger. In that case we attempt to *negotiate meaning*, to test for what we might share; we try to agree upon rules for acting towards one another. This general approach is called the *phenomenological* perspective in sociology. Deriving from the work of the philosopher Husserl, it argues that all action is *intentional*, directed at solving some *problem-at-hand* in a particular *situation*.

The phenomenological approach, then, refuses to accept the *objective* observable causes of social behaviour and insists on discovering the *subjective-meaning* basis of each *projected* act. Consequently, phenomenology places the interpreting, active, intentional human being at the centre of its concern and tries to explain how and why different social groups interpret the world in different ways.

The danger here of course is that in focusing exclusively on the acting individual we may overlook the social context which constrains him. This new focus on the active individual, one who negotiates meanings in the process of interacting with others, rightly restores life and humanity to social theory; but it goes too far if it ignores the structural locations within which social relations take place. Just as normative structural theories result in an *over-socialized* view of man, so too, an exaggerated sense of the person's power to alter circumstances may result in an *under-socialized* view of man. Gouldner saw danger in the interactionist theory attempting to explain social conflict within a narrow, internal, pathological framework, rather than as a reflection of wider political and economic contradictions (Gouldner, 1968 and 1971).

And before him, C. Wright Mills in *The Sociological Imagination* (1959) called for sociology to concern itself with the contradictions in which people find themselves, contradictions which stop them from understanding how the world 'out there' has been created, constructed and then taken-for-granted as a thing that cannot be changed.

Bernstein (1971) also insisted that structural relationships do not necessarily imply a static theory but rather set the limits within which interaction can take place by shaping the messages and responses that people can give to one another. But critics of symbolic interactionism and the new phenomenology in social science carefully choose the grounds on which they take issue with Alfred Schutz. They choose to ignore his (and Herbert Blumer's) insistence that symbols, typifications and meanings arise from the wider social context. Schutz and Blumer argue that our knowledge of everyday life is the product of socialization and that most of it arises from pre-existing social arrangements. For example, children learn the symbols they will use in socially approved forms and each child learns only those ideas, skills and ways of behaving and valuing that his family, status group, sub-culture or class has *access* to. The child learns to *know* only a *sector* of the world and what he knows of it varies in clarity depending on how face-to-face his experience of it is and how relevant various experiences are to his own purposes-at-hand. And if we now suppose that 'the child' of the last sentence is female rather than male, we may understand that even sex makes a difference to how the world is experienced and interpreted.

Because *access* to knowledge and skills and even symbols is restricted, both power and conflict are crucial to interpretive theories of social process. When sub-cultural groups gain control over resources such as knowledge, wealth, power and prestige, they may then limit the access of other groups to these resources. The social distribution of knowledge/ignorance, of power/impotence, of competence/incompetence depend on who controls the key institutions and organizations through which those resources pass. Business, schools, churches, professions, unions, elites, even particular families—all limit or open up access. Furthermore, children brought up within a given status group (or as Holzner (1968) calls it, an *epistemic community*) have imposed upon them a set of typifications which have been taken-for-granted by their parents and associates. Their world-view, their self-image and their sense of power are confined by the limits of that group and the way it locates itself in relation to other more or less dominant groups.

We may now turn to some aspects of the social structure of Australian society. Our emphasis will be on *structure* rather than on *cultural meanings*, but this too is an arbitrary distinction. Social institutions (if we accept the conflict model) result from conflict between status groups. Therefore we must examine how various groups in society hold unequal shares of valued resources. This we do in Chapter 3. In Chapter 4 we spell out how the dominant institutions may control our thinking and our way of life. Then in Chapter 5, we look at the Australian family as an example of how taken-for-granted ideas reflect the interests of particular groups and of how the life-cycle leads each of us along different paths depending upon the resources at the disposal of our family as a unit of our wider status group. It seems timely now deliberately to choose to analyze *institutions*: sociology has moved too far away from structural studies and too far towards the individualistic, psychological point of view. That it should have done so is not surprising given the sense of alienation that developed in the 1960s in response to big business, big government and big wars against which the individual felt powerless. A humanistic sociology which stresses the worth of individuals, their individual capacities to act and their power to assert their individuality, is fine as a counter to theories which treat the person as a mere actor playing a role, powerless against stronger social forces. Phenomenology and symbolic interactionism with their insights into how meanings are constantly negotiated and revised and how identity emerges out of that process, rightly restore the person to his or her place in explaining social interaction. So too ethnomethodology usefully restores a sense of the fragility of social norms by showing how our methods of grasping surface rules and tacit understandings vary and change in different ethno-settings. But the welter of naive self-exploration and self-assertion, of attacks on all forms of 'grand theory' and of empirical data-gathering and statistical analysis (wrongly confused with 'empiricism') that followed publication of the Berger and Luckmann 'bible' *The Social Construction of Reality* in 1966, overlooked the basic structural undertones of such theories. For it is fact that much of our social behaviour can be explained in terms of system-produced, institutional effects, almost irrespective of what each individual thinks and does.

The balance, we trust, will be redressed in Part 3 where we treat culture as the pattern of life concerns—the structure of meanings, interests and motivations for different groups in Australian society as they are produced in the family, at school, at work and in the mass media. In line with our conflict-based view of the construction of social realities, our focus will be on the dominant views of more powerful interest groups and on how these operate to reproduce the existing structures of power in Australian society.

Readings and References

ABRAHAM, J. H. (1973) *Origins and Growth of Sociology*, Penguin, U.K.

ARNASON, J., B. BIRCHALL & T. OVEREND (1977) 'Habermas Symposium', *La Trobe Sociology Papers*, No. 42, La Trobe University, Melbourne.

ARON, R. (1965 & 1967) *Main Currents in Sociological Thought*, Vols. 1 and 2, Penguin, U.K.

BEN-DAVID, J. (1963-4) 'Professions in the Class Structure of Present Day Societies', *Current Sociology*, 12, pp.247-330.

BERGER, P. L. & T. LUCKMANN (1966) *The Social Construction of Reality*, Doubleday Anchor, N.Y.

BERNSTEIN, B. (1971) *Class, Codes and Control*, Vol. 1, Routledge & Kegan Paul, London.

BLAU, P. M. (1964) *Exchange and Power in Social Life*, Wiley, N.Y.

BLUMER, H. (1969) *Symbolic Interactionism, Perspective and Method* Prentice-Hall, New Jersey.

BOGUSLAW, R. & G. R. VICKERS (1977) *Prologue to Sociology*, Goodyear Publishing Co., Calif.

BOTTOMORE, T. B. (1971) *Sociology: A Guide to Problems and Literature*, Pantheon, N.Y.

BOTTOMORE, T. (1975) *Marxist Sociology*, Macmillan, London.

BRITTAN, A. (1973) *Meanings and Situations*, Routledge & Kegan Paul, London.

BROADHEAD, R. S. & R. C. RIST (1978) 'Why Social Science Discovered Morality', *Social Policy*, Vol. 9, No. 1, pp.36-40.

BULLOCK, A. & O. STALLYBRASS (eds) (1977) *Fontana Dictionary of Modern Thought*, Fontana/Collins, London.

CAPALDI, N. (ed.) (1968) *The Enlightenment*, Capricorn Books, N.Y.

CARROLL, J. (1977) 'Sceptical Sociology', *La Trobe Sociology Papers*, No. 39, La Trobe University, Melbourne.

COHEN, P. S. (1968) *Modern Social Theory*, Heinemann Educational, London.

COLLINS, R. (1971) 'Functional and Conflict Theories of Educational Stratification', *American Sociological Review*, 36, pp.1002-19.

COLLINS, R. (1974) 'The Empirical Validity of the Conflict Tradition', *Theory and Society*, 1, pp.147-78.

COLLINS, R. (1975) *Conflict Sociology, Toward an Explanatory Science*, Academic Press, N.Y.

COOLEY, C. H. (1964 [1902]) *Human Nature and the Social Order*, Schocken, N.Y.

COSER, L. A. (1956) *The Functions of Social Conflict*, Free Press, N.Y.

COSER, L. A. (1965) *Men of Ideas, a Sociologist's View*, Free Press, N.Y.

COSER, L. A. (1971) *Masters of Sociological Thought*, Harcourt Brace Jovanovich, N.Y.

CUBBON, A. (1976) 'The Social System and the Superadded', *La Trobe Sociology Papers*, No. 20, La Trobe University, Melbourne.

CUZZORT, R. P. & E. W. KING (1976) *Humanity and Modern Thought*, (2nd ed.) Dryden, Ill.

DAHRENDORF, R. (1958) 'Toward a Theory of Social Conflict', *Journal of Conflict Resolution*, 11, p.176.

DAHRENDORF, R. (1959) *Class and Class Conflict in Industrial Society*, Routledge & Kegan Paul, London.

DAVIS, K. (1959) 'The Myth of Functional Analysis', *American Sociological Review*, Vol. 24, pp.757-72.

DENZIN, N. K. (1969) 'Symbolic Interactionism and Ethnomethodology: A Proposed Synthesis', *American Sociological Review*, Vol. 34, pp.922-34.

DIXON, K. (1973) *Sociological Theory, Pretence and Possibility*, Routledge & Kegan Paul, London.

DOUGLAS, J. D. (1971) *American Social Order, Social Rules in a Pluralistic Society*, Free Press, N.Y.

DURKHEIM, E. (1950 [1895]) *The Rules of Sociological Method*, Free Press of Glencoe, N.Y.

DURKHEIM, E. (1964 [1933]) *The Division of Labor in Society*, Free Press, N.Y.

EVANS-PRITCHARD, E. E. (1970) *The Sociology of Comte: An Appreciation*, Manchester University Press, U.K.

FRIEDRICKS, R. W. (1974) 'The Potential Impact of B. F. Skinner Upon American Sociology', *The American Sociologist*, 9, pp.3-8; and 'Reply to Lynch', *The American Sociologist*, 10 (1975), pp.91-2.

GALT, A. H. & L. J. SMITH (1976) *Models and the Study of Social Change*, Schenkman, Cambridge.

GARFINKEL, H. (1967) *Studies in Ethnomethodology*, Prentice-Hall, New Jersey.

GERTH, H. H. & C. WRIGHT MILLS (1958) *From Max Weber: Essays in Sociology*, Oxford University Press, N.Y.

GIDDENS, A. (1973) *The Class Structure of the Advanced Societies*, Hutchinson, London.

GIDDENS, A. (1976) 'Classical Social Theory and the Origins of Modern Sociology', *American Journal of Sociology*, 81 (Jan.), pp.703-29.

GOFFMAN, E. (1959) *The Presentation of Self in Everyday Life*, Doubleday Anchor, N.Y.

GOODE, W. (1960) 'A Theory of Role Strain', *American Sociological Review*, 25, p.194, August.

GOULDNER, A. W. (1959) 'Reciprocity and Autonomy in Functional Theory' in L. Gross (ed.) *Symposium on Sociological Theory*, Row, Petersen & Co., Evanston, Ill.

GOULDNER, A. W. (1960) 'The Norm of Reciprocity: A Preliminary Statement', *American Sociological Review*, April, Vol. 25, pp.161-78.

GOULDNER, A. W. (1970) *The Coming Crisis of Western Sociology*, Basic Books, N.Y.

GROSS, L. (ed.) (1967) *Sociological Theory: Inquiries and Paradigms*, Harper, N.Y.

HAMPSON, N. (1968) *The Enlightenment*, Penguin, U.K.

HEAP, L. & P. A. ROTH (1973) 'On Phenomenological Sociology', *American Sociological Review*, 38, pp.354-67.

HEMPEL, C. G. (1959) 'The Logic of Functional Analysis', in L. Gross (ed.), *Symposium on Sociological Theory*, Row, Peterson & Co., Evanston, Ill., pp.271-310.

HOFSTADTER, R. (1965) *Social Darwinism in American Thought*, Braziller, N.Y.

HOLZNER, B. (1968) *Reality Construction in Society*, Schenkman, Cambridge.

HOMANS, G. C. (1958) 'Human Behaviour as Exchange', *American Journal of Sociology*, 63, pp.597-606.

HOROWITZ, I. L. (ed.) (1967) *The Rise and Fall of Project Camelot: Studies in the Relationship Between Social Science and Politics*, M.I.T. Press, Cambridge, Mass.

HORTON, J. (1966) 'Order and Conflict Theories of Social Problems as Competing Ideologies', *American Journal of Sociology*, 71, pp.701-13.

KUHN, T. S. (1962) *The Structure of Scientific Revolutions*, University of Chicago Press, Chicago.

LEHMANN, T. & T. R. YOUNG (1974) 'From Conflict Theory to Conflict Methodology: An Emerging Paradigm in Sociology', *Sociological Inquiry*, 44, pp.15-28.

LOCKWOOD, D. (1956) 'Some Remarks on "The Social System" ', *British Journal of Sociology*, Vol. 7, pp.134-45.

LOOMIS, C. P. (ed.) (1957) *Ferdinand Toennies, Community and Society*, Harper & Row, N.Y.

LUKES, S. (1974) *Power: A Radical View*, Macmillan, London.

LYNCH, F. R. (1975) 'Is There a Behaviorist Bandwagon?', *The American Sociologist*, 10, pp.84-91.

MEAD, G. H. (1964 [1934]) *On Social Psychology*, A. Strauss (ed.) University of Chicago Press, Chicago.

MERTON, R. K. (1957) *Social Theory and Social Structure*, Free Press, N.Y.

MILLS, C. W. (1956) *The Power Elite*, Oxford University Press, London.

MILLS, C. W. (1959) *The Sociological Imagination*, Oxford University Press, London.

MITCHELL, G. D. (1968) *A Hundred Years of Sociology*, Duckworth, London.

NISBET, R. A. (1966) *The Sociological Tradition*, Basic Books, N.Y.

NISBET, R. A. (1970) *The Social Bond, An Introduction to the Study of Society*, Knopf, N.Y.

NISBET, R. A. (1976) *The Social Philosophers*, Paladin, U.K.

OVEREND, T. (1977) ' "Habermas" Knowledge and Human Interests', *La Trobe Sociology Papers*, No. 35, La Trobe University, Melbourne.

OVEREND, T. & F. LEWINS (1973) 'A Berger and Luckmann Critique', *La Trobe Sociology Papers*, No. 5, La Trobe University, Melbourne.

PARSONS, T. (1937) *The Structure of Social Action*, McGraw-Hill, N.Y.

PARSONS, T. (1949) *Essays in Sociological Theory*, (rev. ed. 1954) Free Press, N.Y.

PARSONS, T. (1951) *The Social System*, Free Press, N.Y.

PARSONS, T. & E. A. SHILS (eds) (1951) *Towards a General Theory of Action*, Harvard University Press, Cambridge, Mass.

PARSONS, T., R. F. BALES, and E. A. SHILS (1953) *Working Papers in the Theory of Action*, Free Press, N.Y.

PELZ, W. (1975) 'Thumbnail Sketches of Pleas for a Wider Understanding of Understanding', *La Trobe Sociology Papers*, No. 13, La Trobe University, Melbourne.

PSATHAS, G. (1973) *Phenomenological Sociology: Issues and Applications*, Wiley, N.Y.

REX, J. (1961) *Key Problems in Sociological Theory*, Routledge & Kegan Paul, London.

ROSE, G. (1978) 'Deciphering Sociological Research: A Perspective on Methodology', *La Trobe Sociology Papers*, No. 46, La Trobe University, Melbourne.

ROSSI, P. (1968) *Francis Bacon: From Magic to Science*, Routledge & Kegan Paul, London.

ROSTOW, W. W. (1960) *The Stages of Economic Growth: a Non-Communist Manifesto*, Cambridge University Press, Cambridge.

RUSSELL, B. (1946) *History of Western Philosophy*, Allen & Unwin Edn. 1974, London.

SCHUMPETER, J. A. (1942) *Capitalism, Socialism and Democracy*, Harper & Row, N.Y.

SCHUTZ, A. (1967 [1932]) *The Phenomenology of the Social World*, Northwestern University Press, I11.

SCHUTZ, A. (1971) 'Concept and Theory: Formation in the Social Sciences', in K. Thompson and J. Tunstall (eds), *Social Perspectives*, Penguin, U.K.

SENNETT, R. (1974) *The Fall of Public Man*, Cambridge University Press, Cambridge.

SIMMELL, G. (1955) *Conflict & the Web of Group Affiliations*, Free Press, N.Y.

SKLAIR, L. (1973) *Organized Knowledge: A Sociological View of Science and Technology*, Paladin, U.K.

SLATER, P. (1970) *The Pursuit of Loneliness, American Culture at the Breaking Point*, Beacon Press, Boston.

SMOLICZ, J. J. (1973) 'Humanistic Sociology: a Review of Concepts and Methods', *La Trobe Sociology Papers*, No. 7, La Trobe University, Melbourne.

SPENCER, H. (1967 [1898]) *The Evolution of Society*, University of Chicago Press. (Selections from *First Principles*, 1898.)

SPENCER, H. (1897) *The Principles of Sociology*, Appleton & Co, N.Y.

THIBAUT, J. W. & H. H. KELLEY (1959) *The Social Psychology of Groups*, Wiley, N.Y.

THOMAS, W. I. (1928) *The Child in America*, Knopf, N.Y.

THOMAS, W. I. & F. ZNANIECKI (1927) *The Polish Peasant in Europe and America*, Knopf, N.Y.

THOMPSON, K. & J. TUNSTALL (1972) *Sociological Perspectives, Selected Readings*, Penguin, U.K.

TRUZZI, M. (ed.) (1974) *Verstehen: Subjective Understanding in the Social Sciences*, Addison-Wesley, U.S.A.

VAN den BERGHE, J. (1963) 'Dialectic and Functionalism: Toward a Theoretical Synthesis', *American Sociological Review*, Oct, pp.695-705.

WAGNER, H. R. (1970) *Alfred Schutz On Phenomenology and Social Relations*, University of Chicago Press, Chicago.

WALLACE, W. L. (ed.) (1969) *Sociological Theory, An Introduction*, Aldine Pub, Chicago, Ill.

WATSON, J. D. (1969) *The Double Helix*, New American Library, N.Y.

WEBER, M. (1958 [1904-5]) *The Protestant Ethic and the Rise of Capitalism*, Scribner, N.Y.

WEBER, M. (1964) *The Theory of Social and Economic Organization*, Free Press Edition, N.Y.

WEBER, M. (1968 [1922]) *Economy and Society*, Bedminister Press, N.Y.

WILLIAMS, R. (1961) *The Long Revolution*, Penguin, U.K.

WILLIAMS, R. (1976) *Keywords, A Vocabulary of Culture and Society*, Fontana, London.

ZEITLIN, M. (1968) *Ideology and the Development of Sociological Theory*, Prentice-Hall, New Jersey.

ZEITLIN, I. (1973) *Rethinking Sociology*, Prentice-Hall, New Jersey.

Part Two

Social Structure: Distributing Life Situations and Life Chances

Introduction

What is Social Structure?

When we talk of *society* we may mean one of two things: either society in general, the way any society of human beings operates, with needs for food, shelter, sex and security being met in different but parallel ways; or a particular society like that of Australia, as was discussed in Chapter One. But as we saw there, it is almost impossible to make any point about 'Australian society' that will stick. We can always say, 'But that only applies to the rich, or to men, or in the city but not in the country, or to Italian migrants but not to Greeks'. Some members of Australian society are 'ockers'—but not all; some are anti-intellectuals, or footy fans, or beer swillers—but not everyone. A catch-phrase like 'The Lucky Country' may capture certain facts and feelings about Australia and its people and yet not ring true when Australian society comes under closer examination.

As soon as we begin to quibble, to ask exactly *who* in Australian society has wealth, jobs, a good education, an 'I'm all right Jack' attitude, access to the law, to government decision-makers or to the stock market, we are thinking sociologically. Sociologists dare not assume that there is one truth, one reality for all Australians, or that there is a set of values and beliefs that we all share, or that all people have equal opportunities. Instead they look for the differences between groups within a society and between different societies in history or in the present-day world. And once those differences have been located they have then to be explained.

Any explanation in terms of social structure is likely to upset those who naively accept the view that every individual makes his own life. To be told that most people marry someone who lives within ten kilometres of their own home arouses cries of anger and dismay: 'We got married because we fell in love'; 'My wife lived in the country and I met her on a business trip'; 'People are not automatons, they have free will and make their own choices'. Similar reactions occur when we point out that today's leaders (whether top business men, academics or politicians) had greater opportunities to succeed because their generation, born during the 1930s and 1940s, was small in size and so the competition was less than it was among those born during the post-war 'baby boom'. Such reactions are also likely if one suggests that the Commonwealth Scholarship scheme introduced by Prime Minister Menzies in 1963 did not help more working-class kids go through university, because middle-class private schools were far superior and their students, rather than the needy, won the scholarships. The standard catch-cries are: 'talent will out'; 'everyone has an equal opportunity'; 'do you want to lower the standards?'.

Such reactions are understandable given the cultural values, beliefs, myths and ideologies that prevail in our society about individual freedom, competition, choice, individual differences in intelligence, working for what you get, and so on. But the people who produce these reactions ignore a crucial fact: society exists before we are born. People are not born into a vacuum to be filled by their own actions. Certainly there is room to move and to exercise control; certainly we have private thoughts, motives and ambitions which influence our actions. Certainly, as Sartre says, it is 'bad faith' to claim that we 'could not say no'. None of our social actions are predetermined in a fixed, hereditary way.

But the society into which we are born has a structure that affects us before we are old enough to have any say. People are already shaped, grouped and related to one another in patterns that have developed over time. As we shall see in Part Two, cultural patterns can maintain some social structures that are no longer useful or that work only in the interests of a few. In any event the social structure exists, and all people *occupy* their places in that structure; it is not created by them.

We can define *social structure*, then, as the way in which people are related to one another through groups and institutions which serve different needs and purposes. The social structure develops out of people's attempts to meet their basic needs. We organize our lives to produce objects that will satisfy those needs. Obviously, since life situations differ, so too will our chances of satisfying needs vary. For example, if I am born an Eskimo I will have a strong need for shelter and warmth. Since wood is unavailable I will have to organize to use the resources that do exists—in this case, ice, and animal skins. That will force me to develop skills in construction, trapping, hunting and curing. And in the group in which I live, certain jobs will be allocated to certain people: if I am a girl my jobs traditionally will differ from those of boys. Survival will depend upon sharing, so the social structure of the family or the group will be very different from those in other environments where there is plenty and where surplus goods can be accumulated. In the extreme, old people whose teeth will no longer cope with the kind of food usually eaten may go out and die in order to avoid being a burden on those who produce.

Notice that the edges rapidly blur between *social structure* (the patterns by which people relate to one another) and *culture* (the rules which say what 'ought to be'). The ideas behind the terms *social structure* and *culture* are closely tied to each other. Culture is the sum of the concerns of people; how they feel about their society and their place in the social structure. Culture involves the *meanings* life has for people in a given social structure. Thus it will usually serve to reproduce that structure because it holds that what *is* (the existing structure of social relationships) is what *ought to be* (the taken-for-granted or insisted-upon boundaries of social interaction).

To bring our examples of social structure closer to home, consider Australia's social structure in the 1780s compared with that of today. For a start, the English settlers denied the validity of the social structure of the Aboriginal tribes around Sydney town. Despite its centuries of adaptation to a land and climate unfamiliar to Europeans, the Aboriginal social structure was seen to be irrelevant. Their way of controlling the land's resources, however, was not enough for Europeans who needed more than fish, wallabies, roots and bark huts to satisfy them. Had the Europeans learned from the culture and social patterns of the Aborigines they may have survived better (as the bones of many an explorer might silently testify), but their needs were not so easily satisfied: they wanted more than survival. The fact that they also had weapons and technological knowledge superior to those of the Aborigines meant that their *power* to enforce their social structure on the old land and its people would prevail.

The first settlers had very different purposes and a vastly different social structure to serve those purposes. Punishment of convicts and settlement of the land were their key goals, but the *resources* available to them for the first outstripped those for the second. They brought with them the structures of the British military, the British legal system and the British class system. However they had to forge a new social system with few women, few families, few agricultural or building skills, no walls (just space) and no prompt logistical support. Inevitably they tried to transfer the structures effective in their homeland to the new situation. They built prison walls; they planted European crops predestined to fail; they reared farm animals doomed to struggle for existence in unaccustomed conditions; they continued to observe quaint, old-world rituals; they stubbornly adhered to rules that worked against efficiency and common sense.

Social relationships were patterned in a brutal way by a social structure which comprised Governor, military personnel, jailers, convicts and a few free settlers. Life chances were distributed by the powerful, with the result that some convicts were condemned to the horror of Norfolk Island or Port Arthur, while others received tickets-of-leave or emancipation. Gradually, however, a new structure emerged.

New situations create new needs. In our infant colony, the lack of resources to meet those new needs forced changes in the way in which life was organized.

The convict who could plough or tend sheep was more useful out of chains than in. A bricklayer or carpenter was a resource not to be destroyed, irrespective of his crime. Men living in such harsh conditions could not forever be denied the comforts of liquor or female company. Needs had to be met, either legally or illegally. In the process, social relations altered and the balance of power changed. Some people gained improved life chances as a new social structure emerged. Evidence of the change may be seen in accounts of the characters and conflicts of our early history: of Francis Greenway, the convict architect; of Captain Bligh and the Rum Rebellion; of the rising power of John Macarthur, as merino wool began to serve the needs of English capitalism; of the emancipists and expanding settlement; of the 'currency lads' and the surprise expressed at how tall, strong and honest were these Australian-born children of convicts; of the long struggle against British Colonial rule; of the rise of the squattocracy and self-government (at least for the property owners). By 1850 the social structure of Australian society had changed significantly.

It is the historian's job to explain how and why such changes took place. It is the sociologist's job to describe and explain how social structures affect the life situations and life chances of groups in Australian society now. The more one understands of history, however, the better one can see both the extent to which old structures and patterns of life concerns have vanished and the extent to which they persist.

Those processes of persistence and change relate basically to how groups with different interests arise and compete for power. Unlike some sociological theories (for example, social systems theory or functionalism) our view of society does not conceive of society's parts fitting together to form one harmonious, logical and purposeful whole. There may be logical relationships between the sort of economy that exists and the sort of family structure, religion and laws that operate. For example, one may easily see the differences between agricultural societies and nomadic tribes reflected in their social structures. But it is dangerous to argue that relationships between institutions or structures reflect consensus, harmony and what is 'natural' or 'functional' in the circumstances without realizing that the links between institutions were forged out of conflict between interest groups competing for a better share of existing resources to satisfy their needs.

It is out of needs (which even if imagined are always real in their existence and consequences) that *interests* arise. Once a need is identified, *purposes* or plans develop. To achieve those purposes new things may become *relevant* and become *resources* that can be used to achieve our ends. Since any resource, whether it be water, food, slaves, money or influential friends, is never *distributed* equally, groups must *organize* themselves to gain access to, and *control* over, resources that will serve their interests. The assumption underlying our theory of society, then, is that control over the *environment* lies at the root of all social interaction. That environment will have natural, technological and human elements. Since individuals vary in their physical strength and their basic mental capacities they are inevitably *dependent upon others* for survival. It is that basic dependence that makes us *inter*-dependent, in other words, social beings. Inter-dependence is, of course, as much a matter of conflict as it is of cooperation. We band together to fight our enemies; we scream at our parents until we learn 'our place'; we selfishly take what we need until stopped by others who need the same. Organization of life into families, tribes, villages, towns, clubs, societies, factories, bureaucracies, governments and nations all result from the *controls sought by conflicting interests to secure shares of those resources seen as relevant to their need-based interests*. It is from these premises that we now look in some detail at social structure as the social distribution of life situations and life chances.

Chapter 3

The Control of Resources

3

One way of describing the social structure of any society is to show who controls which resources. In this chapter we shall document how the simple access to resources is limited from birth. In the next chapter we shall focus on the key groups and institutions which limit that access, and in Chapter 5 we shall look at the ways in which even the most personal choices one is able to make during the life-cycle are structured and limited by the existing social structure.

We will take as our starting point the theories of Karl Marx and Friedrich Engels. As we shall see later there are weaknesses in their views on the growth of capitalism, the inevitability of class struggle and the eventual communalization of societies. But Marx was one of the first to spell out the structural links between a society's *means* of production and the *relations* of production. He argued that in the Middle Ages, the *means* of production (materials, labour and technology) were insufficiently developed to allow for anything beyond individual peasant or craftsman production. In that situation the relations of production could be only personal, between lord and serf or journeyman and master. He argued, however, that those kinds of relations were no longer adequate once the means of production developed. Different sorts of relations had to accompany different means of production.

> We see then: the means of production and of exchange, on whose foundation the bourgeoisie built itself up, were generated in feudal society. At a certain stage in the development of these means of production and of exchange, the conditions under which feudal society produced and exchanged, the feudal organization of agriculture and manufacturing industry, in one word, the feudal relations of property became no longer compatible with the already developed productive forces; they became so many fetters. They had to be burst asunder; they were burst asunder.
>
> Into their place stepped free competition, accompanied by a social and political constitution adapted to it, and by the economical and political sway of the bourgeois class (Marx and Engels, 1973 [1872], p.85).

People organize to ensure their own survival. Depending upon the resources available to them (materials, labour and technology) they will, to a greater or lesser extent, produce objects that satisfy their needs. Where they produce more than they need, that surplus will lead to new social relations through barter or markets or war and conquest. People specialize in what is easiest to produce and exchange their surplus for things they cannot produce. Specialization is, simply, a division of labour. Marx saw specialization to be one of the major determinants of social structure.

> For as soon as the distribution of labour comes into being, each man has a particular, exclusive sphere of activity, which is forced upon him and from which he cannot escape. He is a hunter, a fisherman, a shepherd, or a critical critic, and must remain so if he does not want to lose his means of livelihood; while in communist

society, where nobody has one exclusive sphere of activity but each can become accomplished in any branch he wishes, society regulates the general production and thus makes it possible for me to do one thing today and another tomorrow, to hunt in the morning, fish in the afternoon, rear cattle in the evening, criticize after dinner, just as I have a mind, without ever becoming hunter, fisherman, shepherd or critic. This fixation of social activity, this consolidation of what we ourselves produce into an objective power above us, growing out of our control, thwarting our expectations, bringing to naught our calculations, is one of the chief factors in historical development up till now (Marx and Engels, 1970 [1845–6], p.53).

While Marx yearned for a return to that 'ideal state' where every man could hunt, fish, grow and weave to meet his own needs, that state probably never existed. The natural differences in abilities between people have always given rise to a measure of specialized division of labour. The most basic difference in capacity between men and women—the capacity to bear children—led to a division of labour in which women did not participate equally in heavy physical activities. That, plus the greater value placed on activities like hunting, developed a sexual division of labour that has persisted long beyond its primitive necessity.

As surpluses, specialization of tasks and the division of labour developed, so patterns of control and authority changed. The path from a feudal system to the modern industrialized society of today is a long one, but it developed essentially out of changes in the nature of productive forces and relations of production. Private ownership resulted from specialized surplus. The growth of trade on a wider scale demanded more freedom of movement. The use of money as a means of exchange meant that capital could be accumulated and invested in new ventures. The forging of iron; the invention of the steam and internal combustion engines; and the development of oil and electricity, altered the means of production and thus gave rise to new structures of social relations. Freedom of movement; the rights of burghers to monopolize and exchange specialized commodities; the rise of merchants and other middle men; and the growth of towns and cities beyond walled sanctuaries were all social consequences of technological change.

But for Marx the crucial element in the development of the new mode of production called *capitalism* was the growth of a pool of labour that could be exchanged for wages and other commodities. The workers who provided this labour were no longer masters of the products of their labour. Instead they were forced to sell their labour to the few who owned the means of production. Thus the relations of production under capitalism were no longer relations between individuals, but social relations between two social classes with directly antagonistic interests. Marx and Engels agreed that capitalism offered an extraordinary stimulus to production. However they argued that capitalism also produced its own 'grave-diggers' by creating this new class of exploited industrial workers whose alienation would lead to revolution and the overthrow of the capitalist system. Eventually, by making ownership of the means of production common property, these workers would transform societies and free mankind. But this has not happened. In those countries where there have been 'communist' revolutions, the revolutionaries have largely come from classes other than the industrial proletariat. Nevertheless, Marxism offers some important insights into the relationships between needs, production, the control of resources and the balance of power within a given social structure.

We must avoid reacting emotionally to terms such as 'capitalism' and 'communism'. When they are used in sociology they must be used only as descriptions of different *modes of production,* just as the word 'feudalism' is used. The words are shorthand terms for the complex links between the major *forces* (or *means*) of production and the *relations of production* between those who own and those who work. Pierre Jalée describes a *mode* of production as 'defined both by the level attained by its productive forces, and by the type of relations of production in operation' (Jalée, 1977, p.11).

What then of Australian society? Australia is and has been, since white settlement, a society with a capitalist mode of production.

Wealth, Property, Class

The degree of inequality in a society can be shown by comparing sections of the population on the basis of their relative shares in the distribution and control of resources. Notice I am careful not to say either *groups* or *classes* yet, because both terms have specific sociological meanings. The existence of a 'group' has to be demonstrated; it is not a group if we are only talking about a collection of people lumped together by accident, or for a researcher's convenience. A group must share some sort of common purpose or interest. A *primary group* like the family may be an end in itself. *Secondary groups*, like work groups or school committees, are always means to particular ends—a rational getting-together to pursue shared self-interests. More importantly, the existence of 'classes' must be demonstrated rather than assumed lest we confuse the start and finish of social analysis. A class may be defined in several ways and there is a lot of slippage in the way that the term is used.

Marx's distinction was in strict economic terms between the capitalist class (those who owned the means of production) and the working class (the productive workers who were strictly wage earners but whose labour produced the value and surplus value taken over by the capitalist).

But of course there are also non-productive workers whose labour does not directly produce goods that can be exchanged for surplus value, but who, through banking, merchandising or servicing, help in the accumulation of capital. The service, or tertiary, sector of modern society is the most rapidly growing section of the labour force. It is usually called 'white collar' when compared with 'blue collar' factory workers and other labourers. Notice, though, that even the term immediately raises ideas of differences in status, lifestyle, type of job, educational level and relative income. But for Marx they were not different classes. They may see their interests differently, but they are both still in the position of having to sell their labour power to the owners of capital. Furthermore they are, by definition, not getting *full value* for the work they put in, since full value would mean there would be no profit to use in the further growth of capital.

We may sometimes see white-collar workers referred to as the 'middle class'. But the middle class may also include small shop owners, top managers, business administrators, teachers, academics, and so on. So sociologists (and newspapers) scramble to create new terms for the different income groups. These include: 'lower working class', 'working class', 'lower middle class', 'upper middle class' and 'upper class'. Even more elaborate schemes of *stratification* are built on the geological analogy of layers of rock, with categories like 'upper professional', 'lower professional', 'managerial', ranging down to 'skilled tradesmen', 'service workers', 'unskilled' and 'unemployed'. These are all attempts to describe different sections of a society in terms of relative shares of certain resources, but they slide between share of income, share of wealth, share of social status or esteem and share of power and control over resources. Consequently it is always necessary to query the theoretical and research basis being used for the classification.

There is a further complication in using the term 'class' to describe inequality in society. As soon as we add the word 'social' and speak of 'social classes' we risk a different sort of confusion. A group may be a class in either of two senses:

The members of a group actually share the same social situations, or interact with each other or have similar interests. This is a class *in itself*, meaning that the members have an identifiable place in the social structure. They may be demonstrably a class in say, their economic situation. It is in this sense that we may speak of 'working-class suburbs' or of 'high society'. But while such a class in that sense may be identified, it is not necessarily a class *for itself*. To fit this description the members of the class would have to recognize their own position in the social structure and consciously work together to preserve it or change it. Only in this sense can we speak of *class consciousness*. Indeed, one of the great problems for Marxists and all modern sociologists alike has been to explain why class consciousness does not develop despite clear economic exploitation, and despite the work of trade unions, political groups and parties to bring class awareness to a level of revolutionary activity.

In Chapter 9 we shall examine the various theories that explore this puzzle; for the moment the point is simply that terms such as 'working class' or 'ruling class' should not be used loosely. These terms are analytical tools which do not always match the real world.

Income

In Australia, inequality in terms of income is easy to document. The richest ten per cent of families receive 23.7 per cent of the total income before tax, whereas the poorest ten per cent of families get only 2.13 per cent of total income before tax. That means the rich have incomes giving them more than ten times the purchasing power of the poor (Podder, 1972, p.188). It also means that the top five per cent of households receive more income than the bottom thirty per cent put together.

Broom and Lancaster-Jones (1976) claim that income inequality has been reduced by one-fifth since 1915. Their figures show the top one per cent received 14.6 per cent of total net income in 1915, compared with only 7.9 per cent in 1965. Such figures, however, apply only to male income earners; females were ignored. A study by Lydall (1965, pp.549—69) suggests that since the 1950s the disparity between Australian incomes has widened even though Australian incomes are still more equal than in the other countries studied (except for New Zealand and Sweden). If we consider taxpayers' levels of income we find that in 1971—72, 3.1 per cent earned $10 000 or more, making up 11.3 per cent of total net income, whereas 40 per cent earned less than $3000, making up only 18 per cent of all net income (*Taxation Review Committee*, 1975, p.25). In 1974—75, the average weekly household income for households with children was $280.85. The range was from a low of $121.94 for single-parent homes to $336.18 where there were three or more adults with children (*Household Expenditure Survey*, 1974—75).

The Henderson Commission's figures on poverty in Australia showed that 10.2 per cent of families (i.e. 399 000 household units) were living without adequate incomes (defined by Henderson in 1973 as a couple with two children earning less than $62.70 a week). A further 7.8 per cent (305 000 families) were defined as 'rather poor', earning incomes less than 20 per cent above the poverty line. It is staggering to find that in a rich and supposedly 'equal' Australia close to 20 per cent of all families are living in, or near to, poverty.

As the Henderson inquiry reported, poverty is not just a matter of income distribution.

> Poverty in Australia is inseparable from inequalities firmly entrenched in our social structure. Inequalities of income and wealth reinforce and are reinforced by inequalities of educational provision, health standards and care, housing conditions and employment conditions and prospects. To these must be added the difficulties encountered by poor peoples, not exclusively those with the lowest cash incomes, in gaining knowledge of and access to legal processes (Henderson, 1975).

In other words, there are *systematic* differences in the social distribution of poverty because parts of the social system relate to one another in closely linked ways. If people are born into a poor family, the chances are that they will be less well-fed, be less healthy, go to inferior schools, get lower paid jobs and, in a sense, 'reproduce' their own poverty in the lives of their children.

This is not to say there is no chance of improving one's lot in life. Indeed, one of the strengths of capitalism has been to give most people a better living, or at least the feeling that they are doing better than their parents did. (In Chapter 9, we shall look at the evidence for *mobility*, the improvement of life chances from one generation to the next.)

Poverty is not distributed evenly and certain groups are more at risk than others, as Table 3—1 shows.

Wealth

Wealth is different from *income* and is harder to describe. Wealth includes

Table 3−1   Adult income units by selected disabilities: income in relation to the poverty line (percentages)

Disability	Very poor (below poverty line) %	Rather poor (less than 20% above poverty line) %	Total poor %
Aged males (single)	36.6	13.3	49.9
Aged females (single)	31.0	19.8	50.8
Aged couples	5.0	29.6	34.6
Fatherless families	36.5	12.9	49.4
Motherless families	13.1	4.5	17.6
Large families (4 or more dependent children)	9.4	13.5	22.9
Sick or invalid	21.4	13.8	35.2
Unemployed	16.6	8.2	24.8
All income units	10.2	7.8	18.0

(Source: *Poverty in Australia, Interim Report*, March 1974, p. 9.) (It should be noted that if housing costs are taken into account this picture changes somewhat, e.g. a smaller proportion of old people then fall below the poverty line because many of them own their own housing and do not have to pay a weekly rent.)

owned property in the form of land, housing, bank savings, stock investments, possessions and so on, and can be transmitted from one generation to the next by inheritance. Durkheim, one of the founding fathers of sociology, attacked inheritance in these terms:

> All superiority has its effect on the manner in which contracts are made. If, then, it does not derive from the persons of the individuals, from their social services, it falsifies the moral conditions of exchange. If one class of society is obliged, in order to live, to take any price for its services, while another can abstain from such action thanks to resources at its disposal which, however, are not necessarily due to any social superiority, the second has an unjust advantage over the first at law. In other words, there cannot be rich and poor at birth without there being unjust contracts. This was still more the case when social status itself was hereditary and law sanctioned all sorts of inequalities (Durkheim, 1964 [1933], p.384).

A Royal Commission in Britain in 1972 found that 28 per cent of total wealth was owned by the richest one per cent, 54 per cent by the richest five per cent and 82 per cent was owned by the richest twenty per cent (Atkinson, 1974). This is not much more unequal than Australia. In Britain, despite the advent of the welfare state, the share of the richest groups actually rose between 1911 and 1960. Though the top one per cent lost much of their wealth, it was captured less by the poor or needy than by the next richest nine per cent of the population.

Australian statistics are difficult to find on the distribution of wealth, and are subject to various inaccuracies or omissions. Groenewegen (1972, pp.84−107) says that conservatively 'at the top end of the scale about 11 per cent of the population owns nearly 40 per cent of the wealth while at the other end more than 15 per cent of the population owns less than 5 per cent of the wealth'.

Broom and Lancaster-Jones (1976, p.50) on the other hand calculate that wealth inequality has been reduced by about a fifth between 1915 and 1965 in Australia. They admit that their study may have overestimated the change, since much private wealth never appears in the figures for deceased estates. But even their figures on deceased estates show that 10 per cent of wealth is controlled by the top half of a per cent of the population. In 1977 both Federal and State probate laws were changed to allow direct willing of estates to sons and daughters without the payment of probate. So the 'haves' will continue to enjoy their wealth while the 'have-nots' have lost that remote governmental source of redistribution.

A more recent paper by Raskall (1978) argues that wealth in Australia is becoming less equally distributed because of tax and estate duty laws. Income tax exemptions and concessions on home mortgage interest payments, local government rates, depreciation on fixed assets and imputed rent on owner-occupied dwellings have favoured those who own property. In addition, Australia is one of the few western nations with no capital gains tax.

A major factor in the accumulation of wealth is, of course, inheritance. Whereas in 1938–39 Gift and Estate Duty comprised 2.6 per cent of total net Federal taxation revenue, in 1967–68 it was 1.3 per cent and 0.4 per cent in 1976–77. Several States have abolished, or are moving to abolish, probate duty altogether. And, contrary to the claims of politicians, only some people (those with an estate over $90 000) will benefit from the change.

As Raskall (1978, p.5) points out:

> Wealth endows control over economic resources and their use. Through the ownership of wealth, a person is able to purchase labour power, to appropriate the surplus labour and thus to accumulate further wealth. The wealthy may accumulate wealth in the form of means of production; but they may not. Where they do, they assume the right to withdraw means of production from use. In addition, wealth provides security through knowledge that unexpected expenditure (e.g. through illness) may be met from capital. This security is backed by greater freedom of choice in any activities undertaken. Wealth relaxes any institutional constraint on borrowing funds—'loans' can be obtained from existing capital. Consequently, wealth holders may take advantage of opportunities which others are unable to, because of their inability to borrow. Wealth enables people to overspend current income and finance heavy temporary expenditure—such as housing deposits or education—which serve to increase existing income inequality. In summary, wealth not only provides control over economic resources, but greater choice and control over lifetime activities. As such, despite attempts to define poverty in income terms, wealth is the prime determinant of economic well-being in capitalist society.

It is true, of course, that private home ownership is high in Australia. In 1971 almost 70 per cent of the Australian population had equity in their own home. Moreover 'realty' (property which is not movable or personal) is more evenly distributed than 'personal' wealth, though the top ten per cent still owns 52 per cent of all realty in Australia. But Raskall argues that a better (though indirect) measure of wealth is a person's total assets and liabilities for probate purposes. The fact that these figures miss those whose estates were less than $10 000 (exempt from duty during 1967–72) and those who can avoid estate duty makes them an underestimate. Raskall uses a measure known as the *Gini*

Coefficient of Concentration (ranging from 0 for complete equality of wealth to 1 where all wealth would be held by one person). In 1968–69 the Australian figure was 0.34, compared with 0.47 for India and 0.50 for Mexico where disparities of wealth were more apparent. By 1972, however, the Gini Coefficient of wealth for Australia was 0.702, which means that if two Australians were selected at random, the expected difference in their wealth holdings would be 140 per cent of average wealth (then $10 957), or $15 340. The spread of wealth revealed in this way shows that one per cent of the Australian population owns 22 per cent of personal wealth; the top five per cent own 46 per cent of wealth; the top 10 per cent own almost 60 per cent of Australians' wealth. Put another way, the top five per cent own more than the bottom 90 per cent together, and half of all Australians own less than eight per cent of Australian wealth.

Raskall's figures also show that wealth increases with age, that females own far less at every age level than males, that over 60 per cent of primary producers have wealth-holdings of over $15 000, and that professional men are eight times as likely as male factory workers to belong to the top ten per cent.

Taxation figures (1973–74 *Survey of Income Distribution*) support his analysis. One per cent of Australians receive 45 per cent of the income (from 'interests, rent, dividends, etc.') and ten per cent receive 92 per cent. Individual tax returns, however, show the top one per cent of Australians only *records* 18 per cent of all income from 'gross rents, premiums, dividends, interest, etc.' and the top ten per cent record only 47 per cent. Tax exemptions, family trusts and tax evasion may also favour the wealthy.

It is important not to jump too readily to conclusions from such figures. Our view of social structure as the distribution of life chances suggests that wealth, inheritance and taxation laws help to keep society less equal than the Australian myth of classlessness would have it. But if we stress other figures (average income, home ownership, personal property, etc.) there is still a reality of relative prosperity that may explain something about Australian values and forms of cultural life. If disparities of wealth are less obvious in Australia than in, say, Great Britain or India or the United States, and if the general standard of living is relatively high, then the perceived needs, interests and constraints will have a different impact on social behaviour. A picture of Australians as conservative peasants, owning enough private property to keep them happy, does not alter the structural realities of inequality and power. Such a picture, however, may explain the social relations that exist and the acceptance of life as it is, better than a scenario based on shared values or the 'embourgeoisement' of the working class, or every man's acceptance of authority and his place in the scheme of things.

At present, however, our concern is with the structural distribution of life chances, irrespective of how people feel about their lives. Another useful way of looking at wealth lies in share ownership. In theory, ownership of shares gives one a share of control in the way capital is used. If ownership of the means of production confers power within a capitalist system, we should consider how widely shared is that ownership.

73

Connell (1977, p.41) puts the case for the existence of a minority class which owns the means of production:

On share ownership there is now systematic evidence over a span of twenty years. Wheelwright's study of 102 large companies in 1953 estimated that the top 5% of shareholders held about 53% of the shares. The study of 299 large manufacturing companies in 1962−4 by Wheelwright and Miskelly showed that the top twenty shareholdings in each company accounted for 58% of the shares. A journalist's study of 251 companies in 1972−3 (after the stock exchange obliged listed companies to publish their top 20 shareholders) estimated that the top twenty, making about 4% of shareholders, held about 55% of the shares. The comparisons are not exact, but the orders of magnitude are similar: it is reasonable to conclude that the concentration of ownership has remained much the same over the last two decades.

And Stillwell (1976, p.88) claims that even at the height of the 1967 mining boom, only about 15 per cent of the adult population owned any shares and these owners came mainly from the levels of professionals, business and public service administrators, small businessmen and other white-collar workers. Other writers (e.g. Encel, 1970), give evidence of the key role in finance and renting played by wealthy families such as the Baillieus, Robinsons, Fairfaxes and Knoxes. However, it is companies rather than individuals which monopolize and use capital wealth.

In 1978 the Melbourne *Age* ranked business enterprises owning the largest share of Australia's assets. The assets included capital investments, capital equipment, property and mineral wealth. Table 3−2 shows how these figures destroy the popular belief that manufacturing or mining companies such as Utah or B.H.P. are Australia's wealthiest enterprises.

Table 3−2 Enterprises ranked by assets and turnover

(a) Enterprises ranked by assets ($ million)		(b) Enterprises ranked by turnover ($ million)	
1. C'wealth Bank Corp.	12006	1. B.H.P.	2147
2. Bank of N.S.W.	10654	2. Telecom	1675
3. A.N.Z. Group	9521	3. Woolworths	1238
4. Telecom	6696	4. Aust. Wheat Board	1200
5. National Bank	5610	5. Coles	1133
6. Commercial Bank Aust.	5063	6. Myer	968
7. A.M.P.	4380	7. Conzinc Riotinto	951
8. Commercial Bank Syd.	4004	8. Mitsubishi	931
9. B.H.P.	3504	9. C.S.R.	876
10. State Savings Bank	3217	10. A.M.P.	871

The banks are the dominant owners of Australia's assets. Therefore they are significant controllers of Australian resources, investment and work opportunities. While banks themselves are service industries (as is Telecom, which also ranks high on both assets and turnover) it is the use to which they put their resources that counts. When we consider that majority shareholders in Australian banks may be outside Australia (the A.N.Z. Group and the National are British) and that many of the larger companies are foreign-owned, we must also consider the extent to which any Australian government may control its own economy. The June 1978 decision to drop the planned Federal Resources Tax on foreign investment and to allow less than a 51 per cent Australian ownership in mineral enterprises suggests how strong external economic pressures might be.

The point in looking at figures on income and wealth is not merely to demonstrate social inequalities in Australia. It is to show that unequal distribution of key resources relates to systematic and structured differences in *control*.

Buying power is only one aspect of that control. Newspapers often reflect the middle-class view that working-class families are better off because taxation, housing costs and other expenses leave little for the middle class to spend. It is said that after tax and housing costs are subtracted, families living in working-class suburbs have more money to spend than people in 'upper class' areas. Higher wages, double incomes and lower returns on investment are supposed to account for this move towards equality.

Not considered in this argument, however, is that renting a house denies the future income that might flow from the improved value of a house one owns; that if you can borrow heavily, inflation saves you money; that the middle class invests heavily in education expenses for its children, ensuring greater earning power for them and 'reproducing' inequality in the next generation; and that indirect taxation affects unequal groups unequally.

It is important to understand the difference between *progressive* taxes like income tax and *regressive* taxes like sales tax or value-added tax. The Federal government at present raises about two-thirds of its revenue from 'progressive' income tax (the higher the salary the higher the *rate* of taxation). As Berry shows (in Davies, Encel & Berry, 1977, pp.22 and 38) even income tax only slightly redistributes incomes in Australia. But regressive taxes like sales tax do not work that way; they depend upon the buying patterns followed by social groups. If such taxes are placed on goods bought by lower-income groups, their impact will be to produce greater inequality. Beer, cigarettes and basic foods, if taxed, will become a greater problem for the poor than for the wealthy. And taxes on so-called 'luxury' goods place them further from the reach of the poor.

Another indicator of the way tax laws affect the distribution of wealth in Australia is the share of tax paid by companies compared with the share paid by individual taxpayers. Table 3–3 shows an increasing share is being paid by ordinary taxpayers.

Whereas in 1968–69, personal income tax accounted for 35.2 per cent of total tax revenue, by the 1977–78 financial year it had climbed to 44.9 per cent of the total. During the same period, company tax dropped from 15.3 per cent to 11.8 per cent of the total. Part of the huge rise in government tax revenue (from $6747.9 million in 1968–69 to $26 971.84 million in 1977–78) can be explained merely in terms of inflation. In addition, wages increased by 35 per cent in the Whitlam years of 1973–74. But the selective burden of taxation on individual Australians, a rise of 27.5 per cent in ten years, while company taxes fell by nearly 23 per cent, represents another factor at work in the current social distribution of life chances in Australia.

Table 3–3   Shifts in sources of taxation, 1968–1978

Type of tax	($ million)				
	1968–69	1971–72	1973–74	1975–76	1977–78
Income tax — individuals	2377.41	3764.69	5485.14	9212.65	12122.16
companies	1030.78	1519.66	2013.11	2600.19	3190.11
Excise duties	902.37	1213.06	1554.58	2331.32	2733.49
Liquor taxes	38.81	48.85	58.64	97.74	143.12
Taxes on gambling	106.28	148.16	206.90	339.75	434.22
Taxes on ownership and operation of motor vehicles	227.33	303.42	380.35	550.61	728.52
Other taxes	2064.93	2811.53	4108.44	6190.78	7620.22
Total	6747.91	9809.37	13707.16	21323.04	26971.84

(Source: *The Age*, 1/6/79, based on figures from Australian Bureau of Statistics)

Education

In Chapter 8 we shall look at the role education plays in transmitting social inequality from one generation to the next. Here our intention is merely to show how systematic differences in access to resources such as income relate to *access* to education.

During the 1960s in the United States and Britain, researchers began to notice that economic productivity levels did not relate directly to resources or levels of technology. In addition, personal levels of income often seemed to reflect not only the sort of work done but also the level of education gained. The higher the education, the higher the income; the better the school system and the nation's overall level of education, the greater the productivity and wealth generated. People began to look at education not as a cost to the taxpayer but as an investment in future gains.

Plans for improving 'underdeveloped' countries stressed the role of education as opposed to simple investment in capital equipment or industry. The Cold War mentality, especially after the first Sputnik in 1957, produced a surge of investment in education which has only recently started to decline. Education, particularly vocational education, was seen to be an investment in 'human capital'. In Australia this led to the first direct funding for education by the Menzies government. It took the form of specific science laboratory grants to schools in 1963 and the award of Commonwealth Scholarships to encourage students who could not afford to go to university (Encel, 1971). The Murray Report (1957) and the Martin Report (1965) urged expansion of universities and technical colleges in order to tap the vast resources of hidden talent and to open up higher education for the wider population; all in the cause of economic advancement.

Naturally, the argument was too simplistic. Phillip Foster pointed out the 'vocational school fallacy' as early as 1965. He showed that in African countries the new agricultural schools were less popular because they had to compete against the traditional status of the *academic* primary and secondary schools with their traditional access to the better paid jobs in the public service. In the West manpower planning forecasts proved to be inaccurate and damaging in their effects. There were gluts of high level graduates in particular disciplines because economic trends changed too rapidly for schools or colleges to adjust. There was a growing realization that specific vocational training often made for illiterate, inflexible or narrowly educated people unable to make decisions, adjust to new conditions or retrain easily. The best vocational training was seen by many to be a sound general education. This view was strongly pressed by radical humanists in the late 1960s in their campaign against growth, progress and institutional controls (Holt, 1969; Illich, 1971).

While the aim of the invest-in-education advocates was growth, their catch-cry was 'equality of opportunity'. Since psychology had shown that much more potential talent existed than was being trained, it followed that everyone, regardless of family origins, should be given a chance to develop skills needed in the advancing society. But, of course, a society based on unequal access to the control of resources does not work that way.

If you have no money, children at school are a burden. Hidden costs (uniforms, textbooks, excursions, and so on) work against the children of low-income families staying on at school. Moreover, political influence and parental affluence ensure that middle-class areas get better schools than working-class areas.

Add to this what the *human capital* economists of education failed to see, that families transmit a store of *cultural capital* as well, and we may see how phoney is the 'equal opportunity' debate. While it will be discussed more fully in Chapter 9, we can say now that 'cultural capital' means simply the store of valued cultural goods passed on to children by their families. A wide vocabulary; correct pronunciation; proper grammatical expression; politeness; socially acceptable manners; self-confidence and knowing how to present oneself (e.g. in a job interview); being widely read; and understanding the arts or music all depend upon one's access to parents, relatives, friends and teachers who possess them. They make up the cultural capital that may be passed on from parent to child just as property or money may be inherited. It is often forgotten that these are not 'natural gifts' genetically passed on; they are learned and acquired in the process of growing up and interacting with others (Bourdieu, 1968). Live with those who have them—and want you to have them—and you acquire the same sort of culturally valued capital that gives them their greater control. Live with those who themselves missed out on what the more powerful

77

in society define as desirable qualities (of intellect, behaviour and style) and your chances of gaining control are limited.

Who then in Australian society has access to educational resources? Let us first recognize how huge has been the growth in education as a key institution in the structure of Australian society. Total school enrolments between 1946 and 1975 have very nearly trebled.

Table 3−4   Numbers entering workforce participation age

Year reaching age 15	Numbers ('000)	Difference at each successive age ('000)
1977	255	− 1
1978	252	− 3
1979	247	− 5
1980	237	−10
1981	233	− 4
1982	237	+ 4
1983	239	+ 2
1984	249	+10
1985	248	− 1
1986	263	+15
1987	266	+ 3
1988	251	−15

(Source: Edgar, 1975, p. 9)

Though private school enrolments grew by 173 per cent, the greatest burden was borne by government schools which grew by 273 per cent (Fitzgerald, 1976). Declining birth rates and decreased immigration will bring about a slowing down from now to the turn of the century, but as Table 3−4 shows, there will be 'echo' effects as the children of the baby boom children pass through the system, and retention rates increase as people realize the link between education and job opportunities.

Retention rates, however, show how unequally educational resources are distributed. If we assume that everyone has an equal opportunity from birth and that there is a normal distribution of learning capacity in every group of people, we might predict equal proportions from each group to stay on or leave school at various stages. As Table 3−5 shows, however, that is not the case.

The figures in Table 3−5 tell us quite a lot about different life chances. Students in non-government schools stay on to final year more often than do children in State schools. But that is more true of some States than others. For example private school students in New South Wales stay on less than those in Victoria; and in the Australian Capital Territory those in government schools are almost as likely to stay on to final year as their private school counterparts.

What causes such variations? In the figures, non-government schools include both wealthy independent schools and the poorer Catholic parochial schools. It may be that there are more of the latter in New South Wales. Interstate variations may be based on differences in job opportunities relating to the urban or rural nature of each State's resources. (Is that sufficient to explain

Table 3−5   Retention of students entering secondary school (in per cent) in 1969−70 until cohort in final year 1974, by State and school type

		Entered 1969	School 1970	Year 9 1971	Year 10 1972	Year 11 1973	Final Year 12 1974
N.S.W.	Govt.	100	98.7	85.0	73.4	34.1	29.8
	Non-Govt.		98.6	94.3	88.6	47.2	43.7
Vic.	Govt.	100	100	95.2	81.5	55.9	24.7
	Non-Govt.		97.3	94.9	88.9	79.2	61.0
Qld.	Govt.	—	100	97.7	88.5	33.2	26.5
	Non-Govt.	—	100	99.6	93.6	60.2	51.4
S.A.	Govt.	—	100	96.7	85.4	65.8	26.7
	Non-Govt.	—	100	98.6	96.6	96.2	66.9
W.A.	Govt.	—	100	98.9	88.8	41.9	27.1
	Non-Govt.	—	100	98.1	92.6	65.4	54.1
Tas.	Govt.	100	97.5	92.2	72.0	25.7	19.8
	Non-Govt.	100	96.3	93.4	88.7	48.3	34.4
A.C.T.	Govt.	100	107.0	102.5	96.7	64.2	60.4
	Non-Govt.	100	97.1	97.8	91.8	69.5	65.2

(Source: adapted from Fitzgerald, 1976, pp. 19 and 23)

Table 3−6   Highest level of schooling reached by sex and job prestige, for population not attending school, based on Census 1971

Prestige rank		Never attended		Attended years 1−5		Attended years 1−9		Reached Level 10		Total	
		M%	F%	M%	F%	M%	F%	M%	F%	M%	F%
I.	Upper professional, graziers, lower professional	2.8	1.8	3.7	3.8	6.0	8.7	32.2	41.2	11.1	15.2
II.	Managerial, shop owners, farmers	9.1	5.0	14.3	8.0	13.8	5.0	15.0	4.1	14.0	5.3
III.	Clerical workers, armed services, police	1.3	2.2	4.6	9.6	15.0	42.6	23.5	36.6	14.6	36.2
IV.	Craftsmen	9.8	5.3	17.7	4.2	26.4	2.2	12.3	1.0	21.5	2.2
V.	Shop assistants, operatives, drivers	19.0	33.0	26.9	34.9	21.0	22.2	8.7	8.5	19.5	21.0
VI.	Service workers, miners, farm workers, labourers	58.0	52.8	32.9	39.5	17.9	19.4	8.2	8.5	19.2	20.1

(Source: based on Fitzgerald, 1976, p. 17, Table 2.6)

the Tasmanian figures?) It might be argued that the retention rates in the Australian Capital Territory are high because of the peculiar social class composition of the population in that State.

Table 3—6 reveals how our previous figures on class, employment, wealth and income are reflected systematically in the social distribution of educational resources.

Fitzgerald here uses the Broom and Lancaster-Jones index to show how job prestige and sex relate to one's share of schooling.

It might be argued that if people do not stay on at school, they cannot expect to be lawyers or doctors or skilled tradesmen. The fact is, of course, that if one's parents are poorly educated or working in a low status, less well-paid job, one's own chances of staying on at school are drastically reduced (as Table 3—7 shows). Notice, too, the effects that being female has on one's place in the social structure.

There is no doubt that higher education gives one more marketable skills that will earn more money. Possession of education as a resource helps one gain control of financial resources. Table 3—7 shows median incomes for relative educational qualifications (Fitzgerald, 1976, p.30).

Table 3—7   Median income for full-time workers, by qualifications

	1968—69		1973	
	Males $	Females $	Males $	Females $
Degree	6620)	3210	9210	6790
Non-degree tertiary	5110)		7970	5210
Technician level	4610)	2380	6940	4080
Trade level	3690)		5680	3740
Matriculated or left school at 18*	3780	2370	5450	3750
Left school at 17*	3300	2080	5190	3680
Left school at 16*	3120	1950	4980	3400
Left school at 14 or 15*	3090	1910	4850	3310
Left school at 13 or under*	3010	1880	4700	3210

* No subsequent qualifications

Anyone still doubting that being female was a disadvantage in 1973 needs to ask why females with degrees earn less than their male counterparts. If the answer suggests more females had Arts/Humanities degrees than degrees in Science or Law or Medicine, there are still many 'Why?' questions that require answering. Some of them are suggested in greater detail in Chapter 8 when we discuss the family as socializer.

Unemployment as Lack of Control

There are, of course, many other resources in addition to property, wealth, income and education. Resources such as health, the law, military power and means of communication such as the media, transport and telephones. But they are secondary and most stem from the basic resource that gives one control over one's life and environment—money. If we lived in a simple exchange economy, we would produce some goods and barter them for other goods. Since we live in a capitalist economy that rests on money as a form of exchange, however, it is what we earn for our labour that gives us the chance to control our lives within the social system. In this sense, then, being unemployed is to lose control. In Australia today, unemployment is a factor of increasing importance in the working of the social system.

July 1978 saw the first attempt since World War II to reduce wages. The Master Builders' Association in Melbourne applied to the Arbitration Commission for a $6 per week reduction in building workers' award rates. Their grounds were lack of profitability and they argued that current wage rates were in excess of what could be afforded to keep the building industry viable. Crucially related to this attempt to reduce wages was the over-supply of building tradesmen and labourers due to the general downturn in the housing industry during 1977—78. There is no better illustration of how the control of key resources works within our present social structure.

Employment reflects the relative power of the buyers and sellers of labour. Those who own the means of production buy labour by offering jobs and wages for them. The majority of people must sell their labour by competing for whatever jobs are available so that they can earn enough to stay alive.

In 'good' times when there is an undersupply of labour people easily forget this basic structural arrangement of capitalist societies. Jobs are plentiful, wages higher and working conditions may be bettered. In those conditions, some will see trade unions to be greedy cabals trying to do as little work as possible for the highest possible wage.

The structural relation, however, remains the same: free labour has to bargain for a fair price on the job market. And trade unions exist because an individual worker has less bargaining power than a united group of workers.

The Role of the Unions

In the early nineteenth century a demand by seamen and labourers on ship owners for a wage of four shillings instead of three shillings a day was rejected as unnecessary. Labourers worked up to 60 hours a week for wages such as these. If any worker left his job in protest against bad working conditions he could be imprisoned under the terms of the 1828 Masters and Servants Act, which gave no such amenities as sick leave with pay, superannuation, or worker's compensation. In 1845, after several shows of activity by early unions, that act was made even stricter in its control of 'servants'.

The gold rushes of the 1850s increased the numbers of labourers available, many of whom had seen early trade union demands for better working conditions in England. Unemployment in Victoria in the 1850s led to David Syme's campaign in *The Age* for tariffs on imported goods to protect local industry, and to campaigns by workers against employers. On 21 April 1855 the march of stonemasons working on the first block of the new University of Melbourne led to their being granted an eight-hour day. Coal miners finally won a ten-hour day in 1874. In the same year, W. G. Spence formed the Amalgamated Miners' Association in Victoria to fight for an eight-hour day, better ventilation in the mines, and inspection of machinery to prevent accidents.

Spence also united sheep shearers in 1866 to fight against a cut in shearing rates by pastoralists. When wool prices fell in 1884 and graziers again tried to reduce shearers' wages, the need for unions became even clearer. Depression of prices overseas caused Australian prices to fall by 36 per cent between 1889 and 1894, so wage cuts were called for. Employers wanted to employ non-union labour and the unions felt strong enough to strike. The Seamen's Union refused to load 'black' wool and the great Maritime Strike of 1890 began. Of course the ship owners won: they had more money and could hold out longer; the depression meant that plenty of men would agree to work on the owners' terms; police and soldiers were used to protect 'scab' labourers working in the mines and on the wharves. Further strikes of flour-millers, shearers and miners followed, but it was clear that power lay with the employers and that government support for them would continue.

It was at this point that economics and politics, resources and power, inevitably came together. Industrial action without political support had proved to be worthless and the failure of those strikes removed trade union reluctance to become involved in politics. In 1891 a Labour Electoral League was formed in New South Wales, successfully winning the next election.

The point of this foray into history has been to remind us that having a job, earning a decent living wage and enjoying reasonable working conditions, cannot be taken for granted. They are won and held in a conflict situation between those who own and those who have only their labour to sell. Governments, political parties, the Conciliation and Arbitration Commission, trade unions, employers' organizations—all intervene structurally to modify that conflict (as we shall see in Chapter 9) but the basic conflict remains.

Since 1978, Australia has faced a worsening unemployment situation. Predictions that January 1978 jobless figures of 445 000 would drop significantly were not borne out, and we faced an historical high in the ratio of unemployed to job vacancies, with 23 jobless people for every notified job vacancy. By June 1978, 6.2 per cent of the total workforce was out of work, and by April 1979, the figure was 6.6 per cent, a total of 425 000 out of an estimated labour force of 6 486 000 persons.

In terms of which groups are hardest hit by unemployment the figures are clear. The 15 to 19 year age group comprised only 12 per cent of the labour force, yet they made up 40 per cent of the total unemployed in March 1978. Unskilled manual workers had 60 unemployed for each job vacant, and 28 per cent of the unemployed were from clerical and administrative occupations. Rural workers, especially the young, are among the hardest hit (Edgar, 1979) and the unskilled and semi-skilled blue-collar workers are rapidly being joined by white-collar workers.

As Figure 3—1 shows, the increase in unemployment is not new. There have been peaks in 1952, 1961, and 1972. However, the present rise is dramatic.

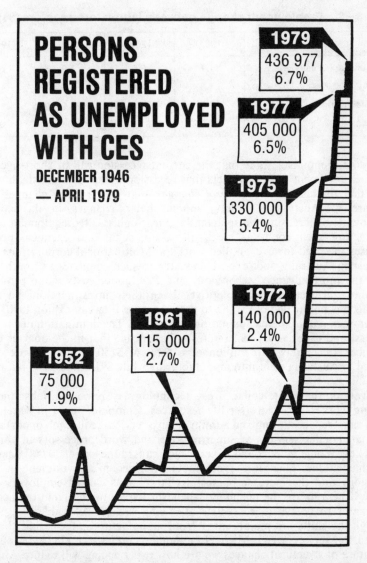

PERSONS REGISTERED AS UNEMPLOYED WITH CES
DECEMBER 1946 — APRIL 1979

1979 436 977 6.7%

1977 405 000 6.5%

1975 330 000 5.4%

1972 140 000 2.4%

1961 115 000 2.7%

1952 75 000 1.9%

The figures in Table 3—8 indicate that jobs have fallen away in both primary industry and in manufacturing, but that manufacturing has been on the decline since the 1960s. Although the absolute number of people employed increased between 1963—64 and 1973—74, employment in manufacturing grew at an annual rate of only 1.9 per cent compared with 2.8 per cent for all other sectors. Its share of total jobs dropped from 28 to 23 per cent, while the tertiary (service) industry sector grew from 61 to 69 per cent.

Table 3—8   Employment change between labour force sectors (%)

Sector	1961	1966	1971	1976
Agriculture, Forestry, etc.	11.1	9.6	7.9	6.3
Mining	1.3	1.2	1.5	1.2
Manufacturing	27.6	27.6	24.2	21.7
Services	60.0	61.6	66.6	70.8

Some economists argue that the current recession will be short-lived, and that unemployment merely reflects that recession. Other economists, however, argue that the change is *structural change*—that is, it reflects changes in the structure of Australian society, in particular changes in its economy. Technology is increasingly displacing labour. Sophisticated equipment used to manufacture such goods as steel, glass, oil, sugar and chemical products decreases the need for even skilled workers. Multinational corporations refuse to invest in Australia and 'export' industry to such countries as South Korea where the most advanced technology and low labour costs make production even more efficient and competitive. Even their investment in Australian minerals has not helped our trade to grow because they can exploit tariff walls, company tax requirements and national subsidies. The domination of capital by overseas, and especially U.S., interests, has meant that in the quarter ending December 1977, only $10 million of a total of $150 million private capital invested in Australia went into manufacturing while $91 million was put mainly into mining.

Even in the white-collar area, technology is removing jobs and thus reducing workers' control over life resources. Computers used in warehouses, banks, finance, accounting and administrative services reduce job opportunities. Automated teller services at supermarkets and word processors in company offices have a huge impact and have already caused the loss of 20 000 typist jobs in Sydney alone. One of the offshoots of Telecom's investment in future technology and the increase in postal charges, has caused employers to tell office workers to use the telephone whenever its use might avoid the necessity for a letter to be typed, so typists are being sacked. As Table 3—9 shows, although the shifts are mainly away from manufacturing, technology has also affected the service areas. Michael Gallagher in *The Age* (24/7/78) suggests 'the nature of structural changes we are now experiencing will reduce Australia to a supplier of raw materials and a consumer of processed goods . . . a quarry and a dump'. We shall look more closely at the effects of unemployment in

Chapter 9. For the moment, we want to stress the *systemic* nature of forces affecting Australia's social structure.

Table 3−9 Employment patterns by industry sector

Sector and Industry	Employed Wage and Salary Earners ('000)				
	June 1971	June 1974	October 1977	Change June '71 to June '74	Change June '74 to Oct. '77
Manufacturing	1298.9	1331.4	1142.8	+ 32.5	−188.6
Mining and Quarrying	75.4	76.8	78.2	+ 1.4	+ 1.4
Electricity, Gas, Water and Sanitary Services	98.7	99.6	103.2	+ 0.9	+ 3.6
Building & Construction	395.9	404.8	354.0	+ 8.9	− 50.8
Tertiary	2539.5	2878.9	3024.5	+339.4	+145.6
Total	4422.2	4806.5	4716.9	+384.3	− 89.6

(Source: Department of Employment and Industrial Relations)

No student of society can be content with simple-minded attacks on the trade unions, or on the government's policy of beating inflation in preference to creating jobs. Nor can we look for answers only within Australia in terms of its internal conflicts between employers and employed, politicians and bureaucrats, voters and elected governments. Systemic links exist between Australia and the outside world and it is likely that government, external trade and foreign policies are of greater significance than anything done inside the country.

This chapter has shown some of the broad issues that underlie an analysis of social structure. We have suggested that certain needs must be met for us to survive; that resources are distributed unequally to meet those needs; that structured social relations develop according to how those resources are controlled and people's needs are met. We have suggested that the patterns of ownership and control of key resources, such as property, wealth and income, must be understood before one can grasp the notion of social structure. In particular, we have used access to a living wage (and its reverse, unemployment) as critical illustrations of the way control over resources affects one's 'place' in the social structure of Australia.

In the next chapter, we shall consider how the broad control of resources is reflected in the central institutions that constitute the pattern of Australian society. It is through institutions that our chances are delimited and through them that the nature of our social relations with other groups and individuals is styled.

Readings and References

a. *Australian Society:*

BEDGGOOD, D. (1974) 'Power and Welfare in New Zealand: Notes on the Political Economy of the Welfare State', *ANZJS*, 10, pp.104-11.

BORRIE REPORT (1976) *National Population Inquiry*, AGPS, Canberra.

BROOM, L. & F. LANCASTER-JONES (1969) 'Father-to-son mobility: Australia in comparative perspective', *American Journal of Sociology*, 74 (Jan.), pp.369-73.

BROOM, L. & F. LANCASTER-JONES (1976) *Opportunity and Attainment in Australia*, ANU Press, Canberra.

BROOM, L. & P. SELZNICK (1977) *Sociology*, (6th ed.), Harper International, N.Y.

CONNELL, R. W. (1977) *Ruling Class, Ruling Culture*, Cambridge University Press, Cambridge.

CRAWFORD REPORT (1979) *Study Group on Structural Adjustment*, AGPS, Canberra.

DAVIES, A. F. (1967) *Images of Class: An Australian Study*, Sydney University Press, Sydney.

DAVIES, A. F., S. ENCEL & M. J. BERRY (eds) (1977) *Australian Society: A Sociological Introduction*, (3rd ed.), Longman-Cheshire, Melbourne.

EDGAR, D. E. (1975) 'Preparing Teachers for Change', *La Trobe Sociology Papers*, No. 32, La Trobe University, Melbourne.

EDGAR, D. E. (1979) 'School-Work Transition in Rural Areas', paper for Office of Youth Affairs, Canberra.

EMBURY, B. L. & N. PODDER (1975) 'Economic Welfare in Australia', in P. R. Wilson (ed.), *Australian Social Issues of the 70's*, Butterworths, Sydney, pp.175-86.

ENCEL, S. (1970) *Equality and Authority: A Study of Class, Status and Power in Australia*, Cheshire, Melbourne.

ENCEL, S. (1971) *A Changing Australia*, ABC, Sydney.

FENSHAM, P. J. (1975) 'School and Family Factors Among Commonwealth Secondary Scholarship Winners in Victoria, 1964—1971', in Edgar, D. E. (ed.), *Sociology of Australian Education*, McGraw-Hill, Sydney, pp.26-40.

FITZGERALD, R. (1976) *Poverty and Education in Australia*, Fifth Main Report of the Commission of Inquiry Into Poverty, AGPS, Canberra.

GOLLAN, R. A. (1978 [1955]) 'Nationalism, the Labor Movement and the Commonwealth, 1880—1900', in G. Greenwood (ed.), *Australia, a Social and Political History*, (rev. ed.) Angus & Robertson, Sydney.

GROENEWEGAN, P. D. (1972) 'Consumer Capitalism', in Playford, J. & D. Kirsner (eds), *Australian Capitalism, Towards a Socialist Critique*, Pelican, Melbourne.

GRUEN, F. H. (ed.) (1978) *Surveys of Australian Economics*, Allen & Unwin, Sydney.

HEADLAM, F. (1978) 'Unemployment Benefits and Work Motivation, an

Annotated Bibliography and Review of Some Recent Research', *Bibliographies in Social Research*, No. 4, La Trobe University, Melbourne.

HENDERSON REPORT (1975) *Poverty in Australia*, First Main Report, April, AGPS, Canberra.

HOUSEHOLD EXPENDITURE SURVEY, (1974-75) *Bulletin*, 6 July 1977.

Household Expenditure Survey (1974-9) Australian Bureau of Statistics, Canberra.

INDYCK, M. S. (1974) 'Establishment and Nouveau Capitalist: Power and Conflict in Big Business', *ANZJS*, Vol. 10, pp.128-34.

LIFFMAN, M. (1978) *Power for the Poor*, Allen & Unwin, Sydney.

LYDALL, H. F. (1965) 'The Dispersion of Employment Income in Australia', *Economic Record*, Vol. 41; pp.549-69.

MARTIN, R. M. (1975) *Trade Unions in Australia*, Penguin, Melbourne.

MARTIN REPORT (1965) *Tertiary Education in Australia*, AGPS, Canberra.

MÉTIN, A. (1977 [1901]) *Le Socialisme sans Doctrines*, Félix Alcan, Paris, 1901, (Trans. ed. by R. Ward, Alternative Publishing Co., Sydney, 1977).

MURPHY, D. J. (ed.) (1975) *Labor in Politics: the State Labor Parties in Australia, 1880–1920*, University of Queensland Press, Brisbane.

MURRAY REPORT (1957) *Report of the Committee on Australian Universities*, AGPS, Canberra.

PERKINS, J. O. N. (1978) *Crisis-Point in Australian Economic Policy*, Macmillan, Melbourne.

PODDER, N. & N. C. KAKWANI, 'The Distribution of Wealth in Australia', *Review of Income and Wealth*, No. 1, pp.75-92, March.

RASKALL, P. (1978) 'Who's Got What in Australia: the Distribution of Wealth', *The Journal of Australian Political Economy*, No. 2, June.

Social Indicators, No. 2 (1978) Australian Bureau of Statistics, Canberra.

STILLWELL, F. (1976) *Who Gets What?*, A.I.P.S., Hodder & Stoughton, Sydney.

Taxation Review Committee, Full Report (1975) AGPS, Canberra.

TERNOWETSKY, G. W. (1979) 'Income Security and Attitudes of the Poor: A Restricted Cross-Lagged Test of Causality and Change' *La Trobe Sociology Papers, No. 5*, (new series), La Trobe University, Melbourne.

WHEELWRIGHT, E. L. (1957) *Ownership and Control of Australian Companies*, Law Book Co., Sydney.

WILD, R. I. (1978) *Social Stratification in Australia*, Allen & Unwin, Sydney.

b. General:

ATKINSON, A. B. (1974) *Unequal Shares: Wealth in Britain*, Penguin, U.K.

BENDIX, R. & S. M. LIPSET (eds) (1966) *Class, Status and Power*, (2nd ed.) Free Press, N.Y.

BENNIS, W. G. (1968) 'Beyond Bureaucracy', in W. G. Bennis and P. E. Slater, *The Temporary Society*, Harper & Row, N.Y., pp.53-76.

BETEILLE, A. (1977) *Inequality Among Men*, Basil Blackwell, Oxford.

BLAU, P. M. & W. SCOTT (1962) *Formal Organizations: A Comparative Approach*, Chandler, San Francisco.

BOTTOMORE, T. B. & M. RUBEL (eds) (1956) *Karl Marx: Selected Writings in Sociology and Social Philosophy*, McGraw-Hill, N.Y.

BOURDIEU, P. (1968) 'Outline of a Theory of Art Perception', *International Social Science Journal*, 19 (3), pp.589-612.

CAPLOW, T. (1964) *Principles of Organization*, Harcourt Brace Jovanovich, N.Y.

COSER, L. (1956) *The Functions of Social Conflict*, Routledge & Kegan Paul, U.K.

DAHRENDORF, R. (1959) *Class and Class Conflict in Industrial Society*, Stanford University Press, Calif.

DAVIS, K. & W. MOORE (1945) 'Some Principles of Stratification', *American Sociological Review*, 10, pp.242-9.

DORNHOFF, G. W. (1967) *Who Rules America?* Prentice-Hall, New Jersey.

DOUGLAS, J. D. (1971) *American Social Order: Social Rules in a Pluralist Society*, Collier-Macmillan, U.K.

DURKHEIM, E. (1964 [1933]) *The Division of Labor in Society*, Free Press, N.Y.

EISENSTADT, S. N. (1968) *Max Weber, On Charisma and Institution Building*, University of Chicago Press, Chicago.

ETZIONI, A. (1969) *A Sociological Reader in Complex Organizations*, Free Press, N.Y.

FOSTER, P. J. (1965) 'The Vocational School Fallacy in Development Planning' in C. A. Anderson and M. J. Bowman, *Education & Economic Development*, Aldine, Chicago, pp.142-66.

GALBRAITH, J. K. (1967) *The New Industrial State*, Houghton Mifflin, Boston.

GIDDENS, A. (1973) *The Class Structure of the Advanced Societies*, Hutchinson, London.

HODGE, R. W., D. J. TREIMAN & P. H. ROSSI (1966) 'A comparative study of occupational prestige', in Bendix, R. & S. M. Lipset, *Class, Status and Power*, Free Press, N.Y. pp.309-21.

HOLT, J. (1969) *How Children Fail*, Penguin, U.K.

ILLICH, I. (1971) *Deschooling Society*, Harper and Row, N.Y.

JALÉE, P. (1977) *How Capitalism Works*, Monthly Review Press, N.Y.

KAHL, A. (1957) *The American Class Structure*, Holt Rinehart & Winston, N.Y.

KASPER, W. (1976) *Issues in Economic Policy*, Macmillan, U.K.

MARCH, J. G. (ed.) (1965) *Handbook of Organizations*, Rand McNally, Chicago.

MARX, K. & F. ENGELS (1970 [1845-6]) *The German Ideology*, International Publishers, N.Y.

MARX, K. & F. ENGELS (1973 [1872]) *The Communist Manifesto*, Penguin, U.K.

MILLER, S. M. (1978) 'The Recapitalization of Capital', *Social Policy*, Vol. 9, No. 3, pp.5-13.

MILLS, C. WRIGHT (1956) *The Power Elite*, Oxford University Press, N.Y.

PARSONS, T. (1977) *The Evolution of Societies*, Prentice-Hall, New Jersey.

SENNETT, R. (1974) *The Fall of Public Man*, Cambridge University Press, Cambridge.
THOMPSON, J. D. (1967) *Organizations in Action*, McGraw-Hill, N.Y.
WEBER, M. (1952 [1904]) *The Protestant Ethic and the Rise of Capitalism*, Allen & Unwin, London.

Chapter 4

Institutional Limitations

4

The main concern of sociology is social organization. Social life is organized life, and even anarchy is a way of organizing human affairs. As we shall see in Part Three when we explore Australian culture, the individual self plays an active part in interpreting how life should proceed. Even the 'self', though, is a product of how life is organized in families, schools, work and other institutions. These patterns of social organization are called the *social structure*. While we may emphasize the limits that structure imposes on different groups, we must also acknowledge that we become thinking, wilful, active, free human beings only in and through those social institutions that constrain us. A dangerous trend in modern society is for people to fail to understand the institutional processes by which they are controlled. A romantic assertion of self, and a denial of our social embeddedness, may lead not to freedom, but rather to the powerlessness of isolation. And if there are others more cynically and socially aware, that is a condition over which they may exercise unchecked control. On the other hand, knowledge of the forces of social structure should lead not to an alienated despair but rather to insights into the ways groups may organize and restructure to meet different social goals.

What then do we mean by an *institution*? An institution is a set of social relations that have been accepted over time as legitimate ways of controlling and ordering social action in a particular field. In this sense an institution may be a group or organization or practice which endures and has continuing significance. All of the following are institutions: Christmas; Easter; the Melbourne Cup; the Liberal Party; the trade unions; Sydney Grammar; parliamentary democracy; the public service; the family; Aussie-rules football; and free enterprise.

Let us consider the characteristics they may have in common. Broom and Selznick (1977, pp.222—4) suggest that institutions develop where a set of practices, habits or norms

(a) serve broad rather than narrow interests but are preserved by those who have a stake in them;

(b) become valued for their own sake or charged with meaning, rather than merely being useful for some technical purpose (such as a formal organization); or

(c) take on a permanent, stable form with a fixed and distinctive character, often drawing from a particular social base.

This definition highlights the processes by which loose, informal social practices become institutionalized; it emphasizes *social integration* but overlooks the possibility of underlying power struggles. Broom and Selznick suggest that 'the key phrase is *socially integrating*'. According to them, the two main elements of institutionalization ((b) and (c) above) 'contribute to group solidarity'. They overlook the fact that institutions may develop and survive because powerful vested interests succeed in imposing their views or asserting their control over a section of social life. As Randall Collins (1975, p.41) says:

> structural theory and power theory mesh at crucial points, since organizational structure refers in large part to the network of attempted controls among . . . members . . . Organizations and stratification are the explanatory core of the field (of Sociology).

The American sociologist Lester Ward (1841–1913) saw social institutions such as law, marriage and religion as means by which people improved their control over nature. He argued that while they might have developed gradually and unconsciously, institutions came about because people sought an efficient means of achieving their own interests. Some groups achieved institutional control and in so doing were able to meet their interests more successfully than others. Consequently, a society's institutions would reflect the interests of the dominant groups. Ward therefore argued that sociology should be applied to allow everyone to realize his full potential through deliberate social re-organization.

Where the controls defining institutional boundaries have been thoroughly accepted, we say that *power* has become *authority*, that is accepted as *legitimate* by those who are subject to it. Too often, however, the notion of authority obscures the continuing struggle for power. Rather than carry out the tasks imposed by others (from the top in bureaucracies and from below in voluntary associations), people may subvert official control. Professions (like medicine, law and engineering) reserve the powers to control entry, practice and performance. In spite of 'professionalization' (a particular example of institutionalization) however, they are often threatened by client complaints or rival groups such as nurses, chiropractors and legal aid officers trying to institutionalize their own vested interests in the scheme of things.

The best evidence for a power-related view of institutions is to be found in the social bases from which their members are drawn. That is relatively easy to establish for institutions like private schools, business clubs and trade unions. It becomes less easy, however, when we examine institutions like 'education' and 'the family'. Therefore we should avoid using the term 'institution' in a concrete way: it is a conceptual term having many different concrete expressions in the wider social structure. Further, social organization includes social classes, formal organizations, status groups, work groups, voluntary associations and informal networks—and these may cut across the broader, analytically defined, institutions. Thus, for example, we will find it difficult to talk of *the Australian family* as a homogeneous institution because work, status, religion, ethnicity and so on make for multiple family types and styles.

Another aspect of an institution which is not developed in the Broom and Selznick definition concerns the emotional bonding involved in what they call *group solidarity*. Durkheim in *The Elementary Forms of the Religious Life* (1912) demonstrated the power of the emotional bonds to which we attach moral ideals. Attack 'the family' and see how many people spring excitedly to its defence. Attack someone's religious beliefs, throw scorn on going to the football, or refuse to stand up for 'God Save the Queen' and you will touch some very sensitive nerves. In other words, an institution is not just the outcome of dispassionate power conflicts, or negotiation, or mere mechanical exchange processes. Our interests determine what is relevant and thus important to us. Our social actions are directed towards satisfying needs and serving interests, and the bonds we share with others who help us meet those ends become highly value-charged. That may explain why people defend rituals, resist change and criticize new norms of behaviour, even when the old institutional practices seem to have lost their original purpose.

The Process of Institutionalization

Human behaviour quickly takes on patterns because the same needs recur and actions must be repeated to serve those needs. Repetition leads to habit, making life easier because we no longer have to think consciously through all the steps of a problem. When these habits are shared and taken for granted by others, and we come to expect that a person of type *A* will act in type *A* ways, we are entering the process of institutionalization. For we can *typify* (Schutz 1967 [1932], Berger and Luckmann 1966) members of a social group in terms of their typical actions. Another way of saying this is that typical persons in habitual circumstances or situations will *probably* act according to our expectations —they will act out a *role*. At first, we might observe an individual's behaviour and come to see that it is habitual and thus typical of this individual. Later, when we observe others doing similar things in similar situations, we generalize beyond the individuals and conclude that their actions are *typical* of people in that position (or *status*). Thus, once we realize that our own father is not the only one who habitually or typically goes to work, controls the money, disciplines severely, or plays rough games, we have identified a *typification* of the 'father role' which in general makes life easier to understand. We categorize everything in this way as we learn (through socialization) to invest the world with meaning. Dogs bite, girls cry, boys push, police put people in gaol.

As Berger and Luckmann (following Schutz) suggest, once such experiences have taken on a shared quality with other people, once they have gained a 'history' through repetition, and are understood as having an existence beyond the particular girls, fathers or policemen who embody them, they take on a reality of their own and are taken for granted as 'objective' fact. They are *internalized* into the child's consciousness as part of its general equipment for competent life performance. The taken-for-granted is seen as legitimate so long as it meets the reality tests of life and goes unchallenged by any conflicting world-view. As we shall see in Chapter 7, *language* is the main mechanism by which such typifications are conveyed and learned, the language itself predetermining certain rules and lines of thought.

It is in this sense that institutions act as *controls* on social conduct.

The children must be "taught to behave" and, once taught must be "kept in line". So, of course, must the adults. The more conduct is institutionalized, the more predictable and thus the more controlled it becomes. If socialization into the institutions has been effective, outright coercive measures can be applied economically and selectively. Most of the time, conduct will occur "spontaneously" within the institutionally set channels. The more, on the level of meaning, conduct is taken for granted, the more possible alternatives to the institutional "programs" will recede, and the more predictable and controlled conduct will be. (Berger and Luckmann, 1966, p.62).

Berger and Luckmann (1966, p.65) call this set of shared, accepted and often taken-for-granted knowledge, *recipe knowledge*. They claim that every institution has its own body of recipe knowledge which it transmits to each new generation, 'that is, knowledge that supplies the institutionally appropriate rules of conduct'. As a result, challenges to knowledge, to the 'everyday rules' (Douglas, 1971) will be seen as challenges to *reality*, to the accepted world views that become sedimented in habit, ritual and tradition. The institutional order clearly reflects how the power to define reality is distributed and imposed through organized social life. In this sense institutions and other forms of social organization exhibit inequalities which may have arisen from natural differences in resources or abilities but which have become accepted as part of the social order. Thus we may pose the following questions when we seek to analyze the institutions within any society:

Under what conditions has this institution developed?
What is the *recipe knowledge* of this institution?
What are the everyday rules, habits, rituals and traditions attached to it and which it imposes?
Whose interests are served and whose needs are met by the view of reality which the institution promotes?
Which groups of people are actively involved in, peripherally affected by, or unconcerned about the operation of the institution?

The last question is crucial to our understanding of social structure and its reproduction through culture. Not all institutions are relevant or important to all groups. For example, what happens in universities may not interest a farm labourer unless his son or daughter wants to attend one. His share in recipe knowledge, the rules about higher education, is likely to be severely limited. If no-one asks him, he will have no need to know. The institutional rules of schooling apply to everyone, but their effects may be very different depending upon our other statuses or places in the social structure. What Holzner (1968) calls *relevance structures* determine our share, and each group's share, in the total stock of knowledge. So, for example, if our paths never cross with those of wharf labourers, factory workers or garbage men, their concerns and institutional networks will not concern us and their power struggles will not affect our view of *reality*. It will be likely that our typifications of them will be very vague because our 'need to know' is so limited. In Schutz's terms (1967 [1932]) they are *anonymous* typifications, not based on face-to-face understanding. It is even possible that our actions might be based on as little as *stereotypifications*—stereotypes which distort the truth by hiding a complex reality. (In Chapter 11 our concern will be with the way the mass media may structure our anonymous stereotypes and prevent our better understanding by maintaining the social segregation of groups whose institutional linkages never meet.)

It follows, therefore, that social structure is a function of the knowledge that groups have of the institutional order. Lack of knowledge means lack of power to influence what happens. Other resources like money, property or strength can only be brought to bear if problems are known and seen to be relevant.

Australian society is so segmented, so institutionally differentiated, that the realities of interlocking institutional power may rarely be apparent to a large proportion of the population. For example, it may be difficult to see the relationship between political institutions and economic institutions; educational processes and the economic and moral values that produce them; and social inequalities and the institutional arrangements that might rectify them. It is not easy to see the links between areas of control. Instead of classes, instead of strong political parties, instead even of status groups, we have segregated clusters of cultural groups (or, as Holzner calls them, *epistemic communities*), whose relevance structures rarely coincide. Certainly the institutions of government are pervasive and much of our life is channelled through the institutional rules of bureaucracies, both public and private. Yet, for example, the life situations of socialites may rarely intersect with those of factory workers; or public servants with migrant women; or pensioners with academics. We need to consider how many commonly accepted sets of 'rules of everyday life' there are and to what extent the world views of different groups are parallel. It is glib to talk of 'migrants' as a group or of 'the Australian way of life' without examining the assumptions that lie behind such typifications.

The point is that whether or not people share a common view of the world, and whether or not they actually meet one another socially, their lives are structured by an institutional order that they may not understand. Their acceptance of the status quo acknowledges either their own lack of power (governments do things for us) or their acceptance of institutionalized inequalities as legitimate (the teacher orders, the pupil obeys, the boss has a right to control life at work, etc.).

Life-Cycle Choice Points

The life-cycle of any human being contains a number of choice points. Different individuals, however, because of their different characteristics have different ranges of options from which to choose.

Some characteristics are *ascribed*. Sex, race, religion, minority or majority group membership, economic advantage or disadvantage are ascribed. They are dependent on the chance of birth but society assigns value judgements to them. Rights, virtues, faults and status accompany the characteristics over which the newborn had no say. What follows, for example, from being born a girl? It used to be pink clothes, the right to cry a lot, soft toys, limited games, 'feminine' role models and expectations, time spent more with mother than with father, earlier intellectual development yet fewer school options, less higher-education and restricted job opportunities, less likelihood of inheriting money or being set up in business, marriage to a 'bread-winner' male, bearing children, suburban living, late career start, and lowered earning capacity.

What role expectations and life chances follow from being born black in Australia? Or having non-English speaking parents? Or being born Catholic rather than Protestant? 'Feminism' has taken on new meanings and traditional institutional structures of the family, work and education have been affected. But to what extent have the others been affected? Australia may not be a 'lucky country' for all the groups in it.

Other characteristics, for example educational attainment, are said to be *achieved*. Note, however, that achieved characteristics are closely linked to ascribed ones. It is possible for one not to live up to one's ascribed status; but more importantly one's ascribed characteristics may prevent one from achieving anything beyond the status those characteristics carry with them.

The width of the range of options open to an individual gives us a guide to the institutional limits on attainment that operate within a given society.

Let us consider some of the choice points and the choices that have to be made. Immediately after birth the baby may or may not go to a health centre for regular check-ups, and may or may not be treated by a doctor whenever illness occurs or is suspected. But baby care centres are located closer to the homes of some Australians than to those of others. And not all families have health insurance.

The young child may or may not go to kindergarten. Much depends on whether the parents can afford the fees and on whether places are available. Children who have no access to pre-school education may develop, both socially and intellectually, at a slower rate than children who have such access and may already be lagging behind at the time they reach primary school (Edgar, 1973).

Children may be sent to a state primary school or to a private school with better facilities or to an impoverished parochial school. Upon leaving primary school they may enrol in a private secondary school or in an academically-oriented high school or in a school which has no academic orientation. They choose the subjects that they will study, and whatever choice they make will have important consequences for their futures. High-school graduates may choose to go to university or to a technical college or to work or not to work.

Young adults may choose to marry early, late or not at all. Those who marry may choose to have children early, late or not at all. They may choose to buy a house, rent a flat or to have no permanent shelter at all.

Thereafter people face yet further choices in their working, social and domestic lives. However, it will now be apparent that many of these ostensibly free choices will be made in an environment shaped by bureaucratic rules, government officials and the availability or unavailability of economic and human resources.

There is no comprehensive map of the patterns of institutional constraints on life-cycle choice points for the Australian community. Jean Martin (1978) has mapped the inadequacy of organizational responses to migrant needs, in education, health care and work; Wild (1974) and Oxley (1974) have both described the limits to inter-group social contact in smaller country towns; Tatz (1979) has analyzed the broad mistreatment of Aborigine peoples: but no-one has yet taken a segment of the Australian population—such as working-class families in an inner suburb, or single-parents in a country town, or middle-aged executives—and traced how Australia's institutional structure helps or hinders, touches or stands aside from their lives at those common choice-points where everyone must decide a path to follow. Until that is done, we shall have only broad theories rather than specific conditions related to specific consequences for particular groups in particular situations.

The closest that Australian sociology has come to mapping the institutional networks of a social group is in regard to the so-called 'upper class'. Encel (1970) showed that interlocking family networks are very strong at this level, the leaders of Australian business being drawn from fifty-six family groups. They attended elite private schools (over 70 per cent), elite universities (Cambridge nine per cent, Oxford seven per cent), were Protestants (100 per cent) and were members of wealthy private clubs such as The Melbourne, Athenaeum, Sydney Golf and Australian. As our figures on Australian wealth indicate, a very small percentage of the population holds a huge proportion of wealth in property and shareholdings. Yet even here we cannot be sure that ownership of resources and common educational and social backgrounds mean that they actually work together as a class, or even interact with each other very much. Resources and membership of the same institutions may create the potential, but we need evidence of actual meetings, joint decision-making or consensus before we can claim that there is deliberate collusion. Australia's 'upper class' is not united; indeed our pastoral history created a rural elite whose interests often directly conflicted with those of urban business groups. Yet pastoral companies own significant shares in mining, banking, insurance and manufacturing companies and there is evidence of shared interests and actual social interaction. Connell (1977) details the high levels of conflict within the 'ruling class' between 1968 and 1972 concerning foreign takeovers of Australian assets. Details of the crash of Associated Securities Limited in 1979 revealed the close connections between banking (the Royal Bank of Scotland), transport (Ansett), the stock exchange (Sir Cecil Looker) and pastoral politicians (Sir Henry Bolte). Methodologically we need detailed case studies to show who knows whom, who makes decisions on what, whose interests are being served in decision-making and non-decision-making (Lukes 1974), and on the degree to which they share common value assumptions and support agreed courses of action.

The rural elites offer another example of institutional linkages. Though they too can hardly be said to be united (the larger graziers supporting the Liberal Party while the smaller farmers support the Country Party), Australia's history has produced strong institutionalized rural-political networks. Squatters held sway in our early Legislative Councils and in Victoria voting in the upper house required the ownership of property until 1950. Electoral boundaries were drawn to give disproportionate weight to rural votes, and strong lobbies such as the National Farmers Union, the Australian Wool and Meat Producers Federation and the Australian Woolgrowers and Graziers Council still ensure protection for rural produce. In March 1979 the New South Wales Government moved to amend electoral laws to ensure city voters were not disadvantaged by the weighting given to rural electorates. Pastoral families such as the Baillieus, Maple-Browns and Faithfuls (see Encel, 1970, pp.378−89 and Wild, 1974) have close links with business families and are large shareholders in companies like B.H.P., Tooths Brewery, Yarra Falls woollen mills and the M.L.C. Assurance Company. Encel describes the Fairbairn family (Encel, 1970, pp.304−5) and the Baillieus (Encel, 1970, pp.379−81) to show the close family, business and political linkages which constitute an Australian 'upper class'. With growing government influence on economic activities such men are increasingly to be found in parliament, on advisory bodies and on the boards of public corporations such as Qantas and TAA. In relation to other groups in the population, this group's share of potential power and its actual influence on political and economic decision-making is disproportionate to its size.

Running parallel to the power of the 'establishment' is the power of unions and other workers. Unions in Australia have become highly bureaucratized. They are now able to exact concessions from employers and to gain for their members a privileged institutional position over non-unionized workers and especially women struggling to gain equality in the labour market. When workers' claims are institutionalized through unions, they legitimate the social structure of Australian capitalism and limit the life chances of those not within trade union structures. Wild argues that the manual working class has been incorporated very solidly within the capitalist structure in Australia through our complex system of arbitration and compulsory national wage-fixing. Instead of a revolutionary attitude based on class consciousness, 'Australian workers comply with the bureaucratic authority structure of liberal democracy as part of their pragmatic acceptance of their position in the capitalist order' (Wild, 1978, p.61). Trade unions focus on economism (getting a bigger share of the economic cake) rather than political action; their actions are controlled by bureaucratic internal rules, the authority of the Trades Hall Council, the A.C.T.U., and the laws applying to the Arbitration and Conciliation Commission. Wage rises have been awarded half-yearly (since 1978) and these decisions are generally accepted. Wildcat strikes sometimes occur, but rarely with violence, and the result is always a negotiated settlement either through worker-employer channels or via the bureaucracy of compulsory wage-fixing and conciliation hearings. The power of such institutionalized channels for resolving conflict rests in the legitimacy accorded them by those on both sides.

The Bureaucratization of Institutions

Work and the division of labour are key determinants of social structure and, therefore, also of the nature of our institutions. We shall discuss work and its effects in Chapter 9, but for the moment we need to consider work in relation to other institutions. Where work is at the simple subsistence level, productive relations centre on who does what and the way food, shelter and clothing will be divided. Authority relations may determine that a bigger share goes to chiefs, or men, or the overlord, but the organizational demands will be slight.

Once a surplus of any kind occurs, however, or new products emerge, or new markets for exchange open up, a whole new set of institutionalized arrangements becomes necessary. Rules develop for collection, transport, marketing, exchange, payment and consumption and the structure becomes more complex. The basic commercial and financial institutions of the simple market give way to new institutions of production. The family or village as the unit of production changes to a more highly organized form of production involving new ways of handling manpower and produces a new and separate role for people—their *occupational role*. No longer artisan/farmer/manager combined, the person becomes a unit with a specialized task, part of a complex network of tasks and duties. Because no one person may perform all the tasks required, each separate work task must be linked and coordinated with others to produce the final product. The process of coordinating separate tasks for collective ends is known as *rationalization* and makes for a *rational bureaucratic* form of organization.

Rational coordination brings people together in ways vastly more complex than the ties of kinship or the obligations of feudal fealty demand. It involves contracts made between individuals and organizations. It involves, too, a gradual shift from contracts freely negotiated to contracts bound by institutionalized rules and perhaps governmental laws which insist on standards to be met. Legislation establishing the basic wage, weekly hours of work, safety rules, tea-breaks, overtime awards, working conditions, severance payments, sick pay and holidays protects individuals from the possible vagaries of employers. It also highlights the conflict basis of institutional change as new institutions (for example, trade unions, employers' federations, arbitration courts and so on) emerge to handle new social needs.

Within the actual environment of work, personal relationships give way to bureaucratic rules which allow for rational coordination, efficient production and easy replacement of individual people occupying positions in the hierarchy. Weber (in Eisenstadt, 1964) considered the rise of bureaucracy to be at the one time the most beneficial and the most dangerous trend of the modern industrial age; he feared 'the iron cage' of conformity and the dehumanization that could result from it.

Weber saw modern institutions to have arisen from the forces of rationality unleashed by the new science and philosophy of *Enlightenment. Traditional* authority, and thus the legitimacy of social institutions, had been based on personal loyalty, obedience and custom. Traditional institutions, therefore, were characterized by loose, ad hoc decision-making, unsystematic and capricious rules, unspecified areas of competence, an insecure hold on office and particularistic favouritism based on the leader's pleasure. Weber saw this to be *non-rational* in the sense that it was an inefficient structure for achieving its goals. In contrast, modern organizations were increasingly based on *rational-legal* authority which emphasized clear rules, clear lines of command, competence and clear coordination of functions to achieve the institution's purpose.

Such a *bureaucratic* institutional framework made possible the efficient functioning of a highly complex division of labour and was a notable achievement of the modern age. Weber argued that at the same time, however, it held within it the dangers of alienation common to all institutions, regardless of whether they were in the economic order. Institutions set limits to man's freedom, creativity and personal responsibility and, while the new rationality opened up many possibilities, in bureaucracies it could develop into an 'iron cage'. In consequence he called for a struggle against 'order' for the sake of 'order'; an opposition 'to this machinery in order to keep a portion of mankind free from this parcelling-out of the soul, from this supreme mastery of the bureaucratic way of life'. (See Mayer, 1943, pp.127–8, and Broom and Selznick, 1977, p.208).

Since the rationalization of human conduct creates the conditions necessary for a systematized and hierarchical division of labour, Weber held that the rational state precedes capitalism and is not dependent upon it. As we shall see later on, this was important to his theory of social classes, which he saw partly in Marx's property-owner/propertyless terms, and partly to be increasingly diversified into multiple levels. He believed bureaucracy to be the link between rational efficient organization and the worker's alienated, powerless state—for in a bureaucracy the worker was separated not only from the products of his own labour but also from control of the means of administration and the means of war. That is why Weber explored so closely the links between religious institutions and forms of economic structure, as he did in *The Protestant Ethic and the Rise of Capitalism* (1904/30).

Weber observed a third form of authority giving legitimacy to social institutions: *charismatic* authority. While in some senses this is another pre-bureaucratic, traditional way of structuring social relationships, Weber saw charisma as playing a crucial role in all institutional change. He rejected Marx's view that change emanated from the basic contradictions within a social system, because he saw historical events and empirical conditions of time, place and circumstance to have vital impacts on social behaviour.

He believed institutions to be in constant tension insofar as they served human needs under changing conditions. Social control depended upon acceptance of the legitimacy of traditional institutions. But the charismatic individual is more than just a new authority: he is 'set apart from ordinary men and treated as endowed with supernatural, superhuman, or at least specifically exceptional qualities' (Weber, in Eisenstadt, 1968, p.xviii). Thus pure charisma and the followers' sense of duty to the leader constitute the very antithesis of traditional morality and of the accepted ways of organizing social relations. The charismatic leader tends to challenge, and even destroy, the status quo with its accepted social framework.

For Weber, charismatic groups or sects or political parties are more important than individual leaders and their appeal comes 'in times of psychic, physical, economic, ethical, religious, political distress' (Weber, in Eisenstadt, 1968, p.xxiii). In other words, when existing institutions are under threat or are weak, they are no longer seen to be meaningful or to provide order or control. Weber argues that charismatic appeal lies in the leader's supposed connection to some central feature of man's existence, such as the central institutions of politics or religion. Eisenstadt holds that whenever *routines* are broken or disturbed charismatic symbols are present (as they are in the rites of passage between one stage of life and another). The 'central' social institutions are those 'concerned with maintaining order and providing some meaningful symbolic and institutional order' (Shils, 1965, pp.199–213). Since institutional norms are never fully accepted 'the relative claims of various charismatic individuals or groups create contradictory or alternative routes for the desire for order' (Shils, 1965, pp.199–213).

As various new organizations and institutions develop to achieve their goals they enter into exchange with other institutions. There is an exchange not only of goods but also of ideas, goals and standards of 'normal' behaviour. If the new group can offer a better set of goals, or a more efficient, more meaningful way of achieving goals, it gains an advantage in social exchange. Weber believed that in this way the Protestant Ethic was central to the rise of capitalism. The Protestant Ethic had the advantage of strongly emphasizing individualism, activism and responsibility; it also emphasized a direct relation of the individual to God, with no mediating priests or ritualistic organizations and therefore encouraged an openness capable of continuous redefinition. In historical conditions where the social, cultural and political orders were only loosely linked, structural and value characteristics combined to allow ideas to influence actual behaviour in a markedly productive way: the rise of capitalism.

Even the charismatic leader must slow down and settle in if he wishes to survive and maintain the new order. As Bronowski (1973, p.86) puts it:

> Horse or tank, Genghis Khan or Hitler or Stalin, it can only feed on the labour of other men . . . civilization is made by settled people.

Weber says charismatic power must always return to everyday life and he calls the process of making the new order permanent the *routinization of charisma*. It may not be too unkind to see the rise and fall of the Whitlam Labor Government as such a process, though the succeeding leader with his new institutional order did not have quite the same charismatic appeal or starting point. As Aron (1967, Vol. 2, p.245) puts it, the charismatic leader or group must assure continuity and the means of succession. The Dalai Lamas of Tibet were chosen by search for evidence of a prior life; the Popes by election; the Kings by the Doctrine of Divine Right. Whatever the ritual, individual charismatic qualities must be transferred to some orderly institutional framework and this is a step in the routinization of charisma. It is not necessarily a decline since a new, more rational order is being built; at charismatic points in history there is greater scope for rationality to answer the basic problems of the day and those with the best answers fill the void. But Weber saw a danger in the extension of 'substantive rationality' (*Wert-rationalität*, rationality in the realm of meaning and values) because this could limit freedom far beyond the needs of ordinary functional rationality (*Zweck-rationalität*). For example, a bureaucracy could go too far in routinizing and dehumanizing life. An associated side of this routinization of charisma Weber saw to be a disenchantment with the world (*Entzauberung der Welt*), a demystification and secularization of life as substantive rationality was extended. He believed bureaucracies blocked the emergence of gifted or charismatic individuals and felt the relationship between the centre (the key institutions of meaning and authority) and those on the periphery would eventually be devalued because people had too much access to them, could see through them, and cynically would ask, 'Is that all there is?'.

His fears have been echoed many times since, not the least concerning authority and institutions in Australia. Eisenstadt (1968), Zijderveld (1971), Douglas (1971), Slater (1970), and Sennett (1974), all point to the displacement of loyalties and attention from public institutions to private, face-to-face relations and activities. Sennett (1974) deplores 'The Fall of Public Man' and calls for a return to ritual, to shared values and activities, to public excitement and an end to private disenchantment. Perhaps Slater's book *The Pursuit of Loneliness* overdramatizes the situation, but social change is difficult to pursue where individuals are powerless to act alone.

We need to examine closely the forms of authority and rationality that pervade Australian institutions and consider the ways they limit the creative expression of individual and group responsibility. We need to consider whether the rational-legal forms have reached the point where they serve only the narrow interests and goals of our dominant groups. We need to consider whether the organizational and administrative constraints go beyond the functional for that area of social need.

Bureaucratic organizations separate not only task from task and role from role, they also separate work institutions from other institutions such as home, school and community and allow those institutions to pursue their separate interests in apparently unconnected ways. Thus economic processes may seem to be separated from areas of political decision-making, and work to be separated from non-work or leisure. Veblen's (1925) concern with the 'leisure class' becomes of wider interest now that leisure or non-work is a large part of everyone's life and now that the time allocated to work may be further reduced. This trend gives us a chance to watch the actual formation of new institutions. As yet the guidelines for the institutionalization of leisure are not clear though the growth of Leagues Clubs in New South Wales, discotheques, and local and overseas tourism may be part of the process.

In Australia our origins in colonial government control, our vast distances and our tendency to favour centralization to cope with the problems that arose, have made us one of the most highly bureaucratized nations in the world. Parsons (1977, p.179) claims that bureaucratization developed primarily in governments, and Australia has been a highly governed society from the start. The most rapid area of expansion has been in white-collar employment and now nearly 30 per cent of the male workforce is employed by government. The skills demanded in administration, accounting, the law and so on require further education and so the further bureaucratization of schools and universities. In this light the key to Australian institutions may lie in the easy legitimation of the authority of the State and its bureaucracy. A ready acceptance of authority may make for a docile populace but it also leads to one lacking in initiative, drive and originality. The result has been a contradiction for Australian free enterprise capitalism: the State has been expected to provide too much and in so doing has had to interfere with the freedom of the private sector. Conservative governments have been forced to redress the balance by returning to a 're-capitalization of capital' (Miller 1978, pp.5—13) that is, by reducing public works and encouraging expansion of the private sector by reducing taxation on corporations.

Separate and specialized work roles create a differentiation of Australian institutional networks and life-styles. The white-collar middle-class person rarely contacts the blue-collar manual worker because institutionally, both at work and at home, their lives are organized separately. Because work and leisure, home, school, church and state exist in separate institutions whose linkages are not immediately apparent, many people fail to see the links that closely connect the different institutional spheres. For this reason we shall now look more closely at the most universal of human institutions, the family. The family is the crucible of our thoughts and actions; the place where our world views, our concepts of the 'real world' and its social structure are forged. It is an institution most private and most separate; yet, as we shall see, the very form and character of the family as an institution are shaped by its location in a wider set of social institutions. And its 'function' is not restricted to a privatized refuge from the world.

Readings and References

ARON, R. (1965 and 1967) *Main Currents in Sociological Thought*, Vols. 1 & 2, Penguin, U.K.

BANTON, M. (1965) *Roles: An Introduction to the Study of Social Relations*, Basic Books, N.Y.

BARNES, B. (1977) *Interests and the Growth of Knowledge*, Routledge & Kegan Paul, U.K.

BENEDICT, R. (1946) *Patterns of Culture*, Penguin Books, Baltimore.

BERGER, P. L. & T. LUCKMANN (1966) *The Social Construction of Reality*, Doubleday Anchor, N.Y.

BLAU, P. M. (ed.) (1976) *Approaches to the Study of Social Structure*, Open Books, London.

BRONOWSKI, J. (1973) *The Ascent of Man*, BBC, London.

BROOM, L. & P. SELZNICK (1977) *Sociology: a text with adapted readings*, (6th ed.) Harper & Row, N.Y.

CICOUREL, A. V. (1969) 'Basic and Normative Rules in the Negotiation of Status and Role', in D. Sudnow (ed.) *Studies in Interaction*, Free Press, N.Y.; and in H. P. Dreitzel (ed.) (1970), *Recent Sociology No. 2*, Macmillan, U.K., pp.4-45.

COLEMAN, J. S. (1961) *The Adolescent Society*, Free Press, N.Y.

COLLINS, R. (1975) *Conflict Sociology, Toward an Explanatory Science*, Academic Press, N.Y.

CONNELL, R. W. (1977) *Ruling Class, Ruling Culture*, Cambridge University Press, Cambridge.

COSER, L. (1964) *The Functions of Social Conflict*, Free Press, N.Y.

COY, P. (1975) 'The Migrant Passenger Ship as a Total Institution', *La Trobe Sociology Papers*, No. 18, La Trobe University, Melbourne.

DOUGLAS, J. D. (1971) *American Social Order, Social Rules in a Pluralistic Society*, Free Press, N.Y.

DOWNS, J. F. (1975) *Cultures in Crisis*, Glencoe Press, Calif.

DUNCAN, H. D. (1962) *Communication and Social Order*, Oxford University Press, N.Y.

DURKHEIM, E. (1954 [1912]) *The Elementary Forms of the Religious Life: A Study in Religious Sociology*, Free Press, N.Y.

EDGAR, P. M. *et al* (1973) *Under 5 in Australia*, Heinemann, Melbourne.

EDWARDS, A. D. (1976) *Language in Culture and Class*, Heinemann, Melbourne.

EISENSTADT, S. N. (1968) 'Charisma and Institution Building: Max Weber and Modern Sociology', Intro. in S. N. Eisenstadt (ed.), *Max Weber on Charisma and Institution Building*, University of Chicago Press, Chicago.

ENCEL, S. (1970) *Equality and Authority, Study of Class Status and Authority in Australia*, Cheshire, Melbourne.

GROSS, N., W. S. MASON & A. W. McEACHERN (1964) *Explorations in Role Analysis*, Wiley, N.Y.

HALL, T. (1959) *The Silent Language*, Doubleday, N.Y.

HAMILTON, P. (1974) *Knowledge and Social Structure*, Routledge & Kegan Paul, U.K.

HENRY, J. (1963) *Culture Against Man*, Random House, N.Y.

HOLZNER, B. (1968) *Reality Construction in Society*, Schenkman.

HOMANS, G. C. (1950) *The Human Group*, Harcourt Brace Jovanovich, N.Y.

ISRAEL, J. (1971) *Alienation, from Marx to Modern Sociology*, Allyn & Bacon, Boston.

KLUCKHOHN, C. (1962) *Culture and Behavior*, Free Press, N.Y.

KROEBER A. L. & TALCOTT PARSONS (1958) 'The concept of culture and of social system', *American Sociological Review*, 23 (Oct.), pp.582-3.

LINTON, R. (1936) *The Study of Man*, Appleton, N.Y.

LUKES, S. (1974) *Power: A Radical View*, Macmillan, London.

MALINOWSKI, B. (1944) *A Scientific Theory of Culture*, University of North Carolina Press, Nth Carolina.

MARTIN, J. I. (1978) *The Migrant Presence*, Allen & Unwin, Sydney.

MAYER, H. (1964) *The Press in Australia*, Lansdowne, Melbourne.

MERTON, R. K. (1968) *Social Theory and Social Structure*, Free Press, N.Y.

MILLER, S. M. (1978) 'The Recapitalization of Capitalism', *Social Policy*, 9 (3), pp.5-13.

MILLS, C. W. (1940) 'Situated Actions and Vocabularies of Motive', *American Sociological Review*, vol. 5, no. 6, pp.904-13.

NEUWIRTH, G. (1969) 'A Weberian Outline of a Theory of Community: its Application to the "Dark Ghetto" ', *British Journal of Sociology*, 20, pp.148-63.

OXLEY, H. G. (1974) *Mateship in Local Organization*, University of Queensland Press, Brisbane.

PARSONS, T. (1966) *Societies: Evolutionary and Comparative Perspectives*, Prentice-Hall, New Jersey.

POLLNER, M. (1975) 'The Very Coinage of Your Brain: the Anatomy of Reality Disjunctures', *Philosophy and Social Science*, 5, pp.411-30.

SAPIR, E. (1924) 'Culture, genuine and spurious', *American Journal of Sociology*, 29 (Jan.), pp.401-29.

SAPIR, E. (1935) 'Symbolism', in *Encyclopaedia of Social Sciences*, Vol. 14, Macmillan, N.Y., pp.492-5.

SCHUTZ, A. (1967 [1932]) *The Phenomenology of the Social World* (transl. G. Walsh & F. Lehnert), Northwestern University Press, Ill.

SENNETT, R. (1974) *The Fall of Public Man*, Cambridge University Press, Cambridge.

SEPPILLI, T. & G. C. ABBOZZO (1974) *Conceptual Scheme of a Theory of Culture*, Perugia, Italy.

SHILS, E. A. (1965) 'Charisma, Order and Status', *American Sociological Review*, 30, pp.199-213.

SHILS, E. A. (1975) *Center and periphery: essays in macrosociology*, Chicago University Press, Chicago.

SLATER, P. (1970) *The Pursuit of Loneliness*, Beacon Press, Boston.

SMUCKER, M. J. & A. C. ZIJDERVELD (1970) 'Structure and Meaning: Implications for Social Change', *British Journal of Sociology*, 21, pp.375-89.

TATZ, C. M. (1979) *Race relations in Australia*, University of New England, Armidale, N.S.W.

THOMAS, W. I. (1928) *The Child in America*, Knopf, N.Y.
VALENTINE, C. A. (1968) *Culture and Poverty*, University of Chicago Press, Chicago.
VEBLEN, T. (1970 [1899]) *The Theory of the Leisure Class*, Unwin, London.
WAGNER, H. R. (1970) *Alfred Schutz On Phenomenology and Social Relations*, University of Chicago Press, Chicago.
WEBER, M. (1947 [1922]) *The Theory of Social and Economic Organization*, Oxford University Press, N.Y.
WEBER, M. (1958 [1904-5]) *The Protestant Ethic and the Rise of Capitalism*, Scribner, N.Y.
WEBER, M. (1964) *The Theory of Social and Economic Organization*, Free Press Edition, N.Y.
WHORF, B. J. (1956) *Language, Thought and Reality*, Wiley, N.Y.
WILD, R. A. (1974) *Bradstow*, Angus & Robertson, Sydney.
WILD, R. A. (1978) *Social Stratification in Australia*, Allen & Unwin, Sydney.
WILLIAMS, R. (1960) *Culture and Society, 1780—1950*, Doubleday, N.Y.
ZIJDERVELD, A. C. (1971) *The Abstract Society*, Doubleday Anchor, N.Y.

Chapter 5

The Family as an Institution

Function or Conflict?

Male Roles and the Division of Labour

Female Roles in the Family Institution

Women and Work

5

The basic social unit, at least in terms of the individual's social experience, is the family. Although the family can be organized in different ways, its core is the *family of procreation*. It consists of parents and children residing together. It is the basic sexual unit in which reproduction occurs; the basic child-rearing unit; and the basic economic unit in which consumption takes place.

In Australia, at the 1976 Census, the marital status of the population was:

Never married	6 155 754
Now married	6 207 957
Permanently separated	243 690
Divorced	217 424
Widowed	673 108
Not stated	50 625

The average Australian family has 2.2 children. Over a third of families have two children. Of all Australian families, 1 660 300 were two-parent families in 1976, while 164 800 or 9 per cent were one-parent families. One-parent families average only 1.9 children; most such lone parents have only one child. Of all Australian children, one in every thirteen lives in a one-parent family. Of them, 88 per cent live with the mother alone and 12 per cent with a lone father.

As soon as such figures begin to categorize families, the chances of describing *the family*, or even *the Australian family* diminish. Obviously the patterns of relationships, the economic circumstances and the roles to be taken will vary enormously from family to family, even without considering the further ethnic or cultural differences in values and forms of behaviour. In 1978 the Family Research Unit study revealed a median male income for two-parent families of $160 per week, compared with $141 for male lone parents and only $46 per week for female lone parents. Whereas only one per cent of all Australian families have to live in other than a house or a flat (for example, a caravan or shared room), one in every five one-parent families board or lodge with others and only a third are buying their own homes. On the other hand nearly three quarters of *intact* two-parent families are buying their own homes. While nearly half of all Australian mothers are now in the workforce, at least part-time, lone mothers tend to be in one of two extreme positions: either unemployed or in full-time work. More Australian-born parents than those from overseas are likely to be alone; about 70 per cent of those in one-parent families left school before they were 16, compared with 65 per cent of mothers and 57 per cent of fathers in two-parent families. Men in transport and trades occupations are more likely to be alone than men in professional or adminis-trative positions.

Even these few bald figures illustrate the complex links between the family and education, work, income and ethnicity, and enable us to guess at (or, better, hypothesize about) those conditions within the family structure that affect a child's life chances and view of the world. The unequal distribution of resources strongly affects the family as an economic unit and as a source of cultural capital.

The institution of the family certainly exists in every society. While we often tend to think of the small nuclear family as the normal one there are actually enormous variations in the normal kinship patterns and family structures to be found in different societies. The normal pattern of family structure within a society reflects the division of labour within that society.

In some societies, like that of the Eskimos of north-west Greenland, social structure is synonymous with kinship: although some hunting bands include outsiders, most communities are composed of related families. In such societies the extended family is the norm. Extended families are those where children, after marriage, bring their spouses to live with their parents. Rules of descent, which define authority relations and rules of property inheritance, vary between *patrilineal* extended families (composed of parents, their sons and the sons' wives and children) and *matrilineal* extended families (where the males, after marriage go to live with their wives and the wives' parents). Descent in a patrilineal system is traced through males only, whereas in a matrilineal system it is traced through the females. Even in matrilineal systems, however, authority may reside in males; usually the mother's elder brother acts as head of the kin group.

In the United States, as in Australia, we trace descent *bilaterally* through males and females, with both paternal and maternal kin groups being equally important to the child. We term both father's and mother's siblings 'aunts' and 'uncles', their children our 'cousins', but we do not usually attach any importance to blood relationships more distant than those of second cousin. These differences in kinship networks are important in explaining the inheritance of wealth and the individual's location or sense of place within the social structure.

Function or Conflict?

Sociologists often write of the *functions* of the family. Fears about the declining functions of the family at times suggest the decline, death or disintegration of the family itself as the basic unit of society. We will consider what that might mean.

A functionalist approach explains society by identifying the major institutions that exist and the functions or ends that they serve. Clearly political institutions (the State, monarchy, parliament, political parties and pressure groups) serve political ends; the churches serve religious ends; educational institutions teach children, train specialists and expand the store of knowledge. This is not entirely a waste of words or necessarily self-evident. For example, the British monarchy no longer serves the ends of rule, control, or religious leadership that it once did. A functional argument, however, would suggest that once the original purpose or reason had gone, the institution that grew to meet those needs or interests would itself disappear. The argument obviously does not hold in the case of the British monarchy. Neither is it easy to define when a change in structure is more aptly described as the disappearance or death of an institution. For example, slavery as an institution has disappeared but its functions of cheap labour, enforced relocation and colonization live on in other forms (Smucker & Zijderveld, 1970).

The functions of any institution are not necessarily exclusive to it. Consider the generally accepted functions of the family:

the regulation of sexual behaviour and reproduction;
the socialization of children;
the protection of children (and the old);
emotional support and affection for its members;
health and well-being of its members;
the main consumption unit for society's products.

Clearly, many other institutions do the same kinds of things. In primitive societies, almost all of the functions of society (religious, economic, political and emotional) are carried out by the family and kin group. In our own society, however, many specialized functions are now performed by institutions such as the school, the church or government agency. In particular, baby care centres, hospitals, kindergartens and schools contribute to a different and perhaps declining role in child care.

The problem with talking of *functions*, however, lies in the assumption that institutions were established with the *purpose* of performing the function they now happen to perform.

A further problem is the implicit notion that if things are *functional* then they must by definition meet needs well, and they must be in harmony with other needs and other institutions. This notion denies the possibility of conflict and fails to consider whose needs the institution is functioning to meet. If on the other hand we perceive institutions to arise from conflict, from the struggles between groups to meet their needs, new insights may emerge.

For example, the law serves to regulate conflict. It is in this sense that Lewis Coser (1956) writes of *the functions of conflict*. An Australian institution specially designed to handle conflict is the Conciliation and Arbitration Commission. Here disputes between employers and employees are processed within strict rules of negotiation. But it may only work when both sides accept the rules. Strikes do not disappear simply because the Commission exists. Trade unionists have increasingly challenged rules which require wage rises to be justified but which do not require price rises to be justified. The failure of the Prices Justification Tribunal to control prices effectively should lead us to seek to identify the power bases of the dominant institutions and in whose interests they operate. Consider when a strike might rightly be called *a political strike*; and why the distinction is made at all. Since all strikes are disputes over control (of profits, wages, labour power, time, authority) they are all political in a sense. If government policies clearly favour employers by keeping wages low, then every union demand represents a challenge to the government and to the status quo it seeks to maintain. In contexts like these we may identify the inter-connections between our institutions and the groups whose interests they serve.

The family also serves to regulate *social conflict*. For example, a child's fight with the boy next door or a parent's bad day at work will find its way into the family for resolution of one kind or another. Poverty, unemployment, serious illness and death all impinge directly on intra-family relationships.

Of course these are heavy burdens for any single institution to bear and societies have increasingly set up other institutions to share the load. Our public services offer assistance to the unemployed and social welfare to those in trouble. Governments, however, often resist tackling an issue such as child care, claiming that it is the family's task. In so doing, they do not acknowledge that a segmented labour market without adequate child-care facilities perpetuates the sexual stratification of work.

The Spanish sociologist, Castells (1977, 1978) also suggests that the family's function as the main consumption unit for the products of the society is being taken over in part by the State. He refers to recent trends in the use of State resources as *collective consumption*. Included among the resources which the State may control and distribute are housing, transport, welfare, health services and education. Because the State may distribute such resources unequally and because different groups have different needs for help, Castells argues that the collective consumption process has been politicized. He further argues that today's urban crises reflect the politics behind the distribution of State resources. If the State's resources are limited by the amount of capital it may take out of the private sphere to finance public works, it will need to make decisions concerning the kinds of services it will provide. It may need to decide between housing and central office buildings; freeways and local services; big hospitals and local health-care centres. But whatever its decision, its total contribution to collective consumption is limited by the capital it may remove from the private sector. Public services are therefore likely to decline as governments seek to limit the growth of public spending.

The mere discussion of functions is also inadequate when we come to consider the very complex links between institutions. To do that we will need to examine conflicts of interest and negotiations of power. We began this part of the discussion by focusing on the oft expressed fears that the family as the basic unit of society might be in decline. If Castells is right about the State's wishes to limit the growth of collective consumption, then the private sphere of home and family is unlikely to receive new State benefits. It is particularly unlikely to receive any benefits which might interfere with the structural interests of business and free enterprise capital. If that is so we may expect the family as an institution to be put under greater strains: its traditional role of 'buffer zone' between the individual and the wider social structure will be threatened. In particular, we may expect such a trend to affect disadvantaged social groups more than others for whom the social structure provides better life chances.

The trend towards what is known as the detached nuclear family and away from extended kin groups has allowed greater freedom of movement for the family group but has created greater isolation and emotional stress for parents and children. This burden has fallen particularly on women. Women's former usefulness in the social network of kin group and community has given way to a pattern of total economic dependence and suburban isolation. Childbashing was not so possible when others constantly shared in a baby's welfare. Divorce or death of a spouse was similarly buffered by the support afforded by the extended family. Such advantages, however, might have been qualified by the strains of living with in-laws and of being subject to group-determined rules about property and the work to be done.

Moreover, recent research suggests that in Western societies the notion that the extended family used to be much stronger may have shaky foundations. Hareven (1977) claims that because of increased life expectancy, the reduced hazards of childbirth and the more rigid patterns of timing in modern society (relating for example to school attendance, home-leaving, marriage, having children, and compulsory retirement) there may be more three-generation families now than existed in the past. Rather than reducing 'stability' in family life, such factors increase uniformity even if they place heavy demands on a unit which now needs greater flexibility than ever before.

Also contrary to romantic myth and the historically misinformed theories of people such as Marion Levy, industrialization did not necessarily produce the nuclear family. Wrigley (1977) suggests that the Westen European pattern, even before industrialization, was quite unlike that of other traditional societies. Wrigley points out that late marriage for women and the typical pattern of separate and small conjugal households may have helped the process of urban industrialization, rather than followed it. They may have helped too, rather than merely resulted from, the growth of an ethic of individualism and private self-exploration during the period of the Enlightenment. It is suggested that even before industrialization the family had a special importance as a privileged institution, and that the father had an even more privileged position as the monitor of what Davis (1977) calls *the family's store and reputation.*

Male Roles and the Division of Labour

There is a tendency these days to forget that the male is still generally regarded as the dominant partner in marriage. Despite changing norms and modified sex roles, a wife still takes her husband's name; the man's work and income are still of major significance; and his social relations still set the central pattern for his family.

This dominance is a historical consequence of the traditional centrality of work, property and class in Western societies. Women came to occupy an inferior position, and laws concerning marriage progressively enshrined that inequality. In the early Christian era marriage was a private matter of mutual consent, but as time passed both Church and State increasingly interfered. At first, man and woman simply declared that they took each other as husband and wife (*verba de praesenti*), but in the Middle Ages it became customary to do this at the door of the church (*in facie ecclesiae*). No priest was involved, but the ecclesiastical courts later functioned to settle disputes. This public declaration ensured the validity of marital status and the legitimacy of children.

In 1563 the Roman Catholic Council of Trent legislated to make the presence of a priest and two witnesses at the marriage ceremony compulsory. Since England had broken with Rome in 1534 this new procedure did not affect English law, and marriage in England continued for two centuries to comprise the church door declaration and publication of banns (or obtaining a licence). The frequency of clandestine marriages led to the passing in 1753 of Lord Hardwicke's Act. This Act made it compulsory to publish banns and then to celebrate marriage in the presence of an episcopally ordained priest and two witnesses, according to proper Church of England rites. Only Jews and Quakers were exempt. We may see that the institution of marriage only gradually emerged from what had previously been the secular institution of the family.

The main reason for codifying what had been a private matter seems to have been economic. Secret marriages could be denied by either party and therefore give rise to disputes about property. The consequences of rights to property given by the laws relating to inheritance also made it convenient for further laws to be passed which made parental consent a condition of valid marriage. Since the propertied classes saw dynastic alliances as of vital concern they regulated the economic consequences of marriage tightly.

Upon marriage the husband acquired the right to manage his wife's freehold land, while all she got was the right to dower (that is, a life interest in only one-third of his freehold lands of inheritance) and the right to maintenance (which was lost if she committed adultery or deserted) (Finlay, 1979).

In the nineteenth century, war, colonial opportunities and assisted migration had taken so many men away from England that nearly one-third of women aged 20 to 44 had to remain spinsters. The earlier novels of Jane Austen reflect elegantly the brutal fact that, for women without independent means, any husband was better than none. Even the quaintness today of yesterday's 'breach of promise' suits shows the economic and social vulnerability of women. For the status of marriage conferred legal rights as well as obligations.

The most rigid form of codifying the norms or rules of any institution is the law. The law acts as a constraint which has the full strength of society's sanctions behind it. Thus changes in family law both reflect and produce changes in the norms and sanctions of the society. In Australia the most significant alteration has been the *Family Law Act* (1975) and the creation of the *Family Court of Australia*. There were a number of social circumstances that made the new law not only necessary but also acceptable. Evidence of changing social relations included the increased rate of Australian divorce (from 2.7 per 1000 in 1921–25 to 9.61 in 1946–50, to below 7 in 1956–65 and to a high of over 12 since 1972); the decline in the actual number of births, and a rise in ex-nuptial births; the earlier mean age at which Australians were marrying (27 for males and 24 for females in 1921–25, down to 23.7 for males and 21.2 for females in 1976); the more tolerant attitude towards premarital sexual relations; and the increasing tendency for single mothers to keep their children. Such changes meant that the life of a marriage was potentially longer and the chances for breakdown greater.

Though the law moves slowly it invariably reflects changing normative patterns within a society's institutional structure. Although in 1866 the law defined marriage as the *union for life of one man and one woman to the exclusion of all others*, it never really meant that (divorce having been introduced in law in 1857). What actually happens should not be confused with *the essence* or ideal. As Finlay (1979, p.116) puts it, 'The modern attitude, by contrast, sees in the enforcement of a marriage relationship which has ceased to be one except in name a positive detriment to the very institution and concept of marriage itself'.

Thus the law has shifted towards the notion of *irretrievable breakdown* as the single ground for divorce. Divorce in itself was always easier (indeed even necessary) for the wealthy. The need for a male heir, to whom property could be passed on, made illegitimacy an issue of importance to the wealthy, but irrelevant to the poor. As the English middle classes became economically and politically more powerful after the 1832 Reform Act, however, divorce was more widely practised and a Divorce Act was passed in 1857. Until then a man could divorce his wife for adultery, but a woman could divorce her husband only if adultery were aggravated by bigamy, incest, cruelty or desertion. The male's advantage was partly removed in 1926 (but not in Victoria until 1961). New Zealand and some Australian states led the way in introducing insanity as a ground for divorce, and gradually the law came to recognize other causes of breakdown. In 1963 the House of Lords removed the requirement of proof of intent in cases based on cruelty, and in 1969 the Divorce Reform Act substituted irretrievable breakdown as the sole ground for divorce.

In Australia the situation was chaotic because each of the six states had its own system of family law. Section 51 of the Australian Constitution had mentioned marriage, divorce and custody as matters on which the Commonwealth might legislate but the Commonwealth did not use its legislative powers until the passage of the 1959 Matrimonial Causes Act and the 1961 Marriage Act. These consolidated the laws and offered fourteen grounds for divorce. However State courts continued to deal with these matters under vested powers. Disagreement over legitimacy and property rights led to a concerted review of family law by the Labor Government in 1972, and the new *Family Law Act* (1975) put a stop to investigations of fault. Adultery and cruelty as grounds were abolished; new rules regulated maintenance, property and custody of children; and new procedures removed divorce from the crime-associated magistrates courts and into the more specialized and more humane setting of the Family Court. Irretrievable breakdown now constitutes the sole ground for divorce in Australia.

Female Roles in the Family Institution

We have suggested that the dominant position of men with regard to the family's economic position (and to its status and relative power in the social structure), has been understated. By contrast, the image of the mother as the exclusive, natural, loving deliverer of child care, has been promoted with rather more enthusiasm in recent times than ever before in the past.

Philippe Aries shocked people when he first argued that in traditional society *maternal indifference* was more characteristic than *motherly love*

(Aries, 1962). Edward Shorter (1975) goes further to claim that the first signs of 'modern' maternal love that Aries found in noble and upper bourgeois groups in the sixteenth and seventeenth centuries, did not reach the consciousness of the European masses until the early nineteenth century.

> Good mothering is an invention of modernization . . . Mothers in villages and small towns across the continent from Cornwall to Lettland seldom departed from traditional—often hideously hurtful—infant hygiene and child-rearing practices . . . Nor did these mothers often (some say 'never') see their infants as human beings with the same capacities for joy and pain as they themselves . . . These millions of traditional mothers were not monsters. They had merely failed the 'sacrifice' test. If they lacked an articulate sense of maternal love, it was because they were forced by material circumstances and community attitudes to subordinate infant welfare to other objectives, such as keeping the farm going or helping their husbands weave cloth (Shorter, 1975, pp.170—1).

Yet we still find researchers arguing (on the basis of assumptions about basic innate capacities to love and nurture) that women's role must be tied to the rearing of children and that the family is essentially an institution where women must perform their essential function of mothering.

Alice Rossi asserts strongly that the mother is, and should continue to be, the most important parent figure. She bases her views on a *biosocial* argument that biological factors shape the parameters within which learning takes place. She argues against functional theories of the family which accept age and sex as the focal points of the division of labour between men and women, and between parents and children. She argues also against newer theories of the family, which emphasize an egalitarian ideology to the near exclusion of innate sex differences. Instead she insists on 'the central biological fact that the core function of any family system is human continuity, through reproduction and child-rearing' (Rossi, 1977; p.2).

Rossi holds that both the *sexual script* (social rules and norms governing the behaviour of men and women in their sexual, mating relationship to each other) and the *parenting script* (those rules and norms governing the birth and rearing of children) are linked through this underlying physiological basis. She rejects an overly cultural determinist view (the *nurture* or socialization view) in favour of one which integrates *nature* with varying social conditions. Although she is fully aware that her evolutionary framework leaves her open to radical attack, Rossi nevertheless offers us another view of the constraints within which social behaviour develops.

Rossi's starting point is that *Homo sapiens* evolved only 40 000 years ago, that industrial societies have existed only for two hundred years and that over 90 per cent of human history has been spent in hunting and gathering societies. Rossi (1964) holds that we, though living in a technological world, 'are still genetically equipped only with an ancient mammalian primate heritage that evolved largely through adaptations appropriate to much earlier times'. Though a sexual division of labour developed, women contributed half or more of basic food staples through their productive labour and were not restricted to child-bearing and child-rearing. More crucial, says Rossi, was the selective development in men of muscle strength and visual acuity for hunting, and in women of other qualities useful for rearing children and gathering food. Where earlier evolutionists emphasized male superiority and ignored the possible effects of hormones on male behaviour, endocrinology suggests that social experience can affect hormonal secretion in an interactive way. Thus male rhesus monkeys who suffer defeat and diminished status in their group show a drop in testosterone secretion, which can be reversed by exposure to a female monkey. This, suggests Rossi, indicates that androgens and oestrogens are not 'male' or 'female' hormones inducing aggressiveness or eroticism; they are present in both males and females to an extent which both shapes and is shaped by social circumstances. Yet, she argues, a basic sexual difference makes women respond to children and vice versa in ways that men are physiologically incapable of. Consequently, mother-child contact will be crucial for 'proper' development, and parenting is likely to be more difficult where the social *script* prescribes equal efforts on the part of the male.

In Chapter 8 we shall examine other evidence bearing on the way that early childhood socialization may influence the development of male and female roles. For the moment, however, there are other tests which might be applied to Rossi's argument. Notice that at one point she uses her evidence to support the claim that biology determines behaviour, but at another to suggest that social conditions affect biology. If the latter view is correct, of course, we might ask why the necessity to insist on mothers doing the early child-rearing. If, on the other hand, *parenting scripts* are physiologically based, we shall need to account for the fact that different societies often have different *parenting scripts*. We should then probably go further to identify the nature of the effects of different *scripts* on the socialization of children. Finally, consider Rossi's claim that little or no cultural variation can be found in the physical proximity and closeness of the mother and the infant in the early months following birth. We shall need to ask why from this it necessarily follows that an egalitarian ideology in fact involves profound difficulties when applied to child-rearing. (See also the *Berkeley Journal of Sociology*, Vol. XXII, 1977−8 for the feminist debate which followed Rossi's controversial article.)

Anthropological evidence demonstrates why it is wrong to confuse biological roles with sociological roles. For example, a *father* may be a *genitor* responsible for conception, yet need not be a *pater*, the person who raises and rears the child as a father. The Nuer in the Sudan designated females as paters; the Tallensi in the Nile Basin had *deputed genitors* to beget children on behalf of old married men. The Nayar, a matrilineal society in nineteenth-century India, had their women 'married' at 13. They were then 'divorced', lived with a brother and were visited by lovers. If a child was born it lived in the home with the brother (though he was usually absent) and sister who reared it, but one of the lovers (not necessarily the genitor) offered to *be* the father and thereby to legitimize the child.

In other words, social fatherhood is separable from biological fatherhood, and both the sexual script and the parenting script vary accordingly. Genealogy recognizes social parenthood, not necessarily biological parenthood. What seemed to be crucial in the anthropological studies we have referred to was the *legitimacy principle* (Malinowski) whereby no child was allowed to be born out of wedlock. Marriage was always necessary for legitimate birth, even among the Nayar where one lover accepted responsibility for the child. Malinowski argued that sex might be free but that motherhood or fatherhood never is.

Notice the serious theoretical issues involved here. The legitimacy principle ensures that every child is put into some defined system of social relations; it is not left to die or grow up 'outside' society. Such jural relations designate a sociological father and mother. The 'father' may be a female or several persons, but the role makes that person legally responsible for the conduct of the child. Malinowski's definition of the universal institution of the family, then, boils down to a set of social relations defining the rights and obligations of the child via those made legally responsible for its conduct.

This is an analytic definition, not a concrete one. It tells us what the family is supposed to do but not what it is or what it looks like. In this sort of definition, the institution of the family is not what exists but is rather a set of interlocking norms that are widely believed in and conformed to, that is, the *script* defining social parenthood.

What problems might arise with a definition like Malinowski's? It implies, of course, that illegitimacy is disapproved of in every society. Yet the rate of illegitimacy in some societies (for example, Barbados 70 per cent; Haiti 67–85 per cent) demonstrates that this is not true. William Goode (1960) cites the incidence of shotgun marriages in rural England, the 'capture males' tradition in Sweden and the high illegitimacy rates in rural and black urban America, but believes such behaviours do not deny the existence of norms supporting the legitimacy principle. His interviews (later discounted because they were mostly with middle-class respondents) show that people continue to consider sexual activity outside of marriage to be deviant: females are always punished for becoming pregnant outside marriage; illegitimate unions are less stable than legal marriages; people prefer to live in legal unions; and most adults eventually do marry—or, if they divorce, remarry—rather than stay single. Goode therefore concludes that in spite of high illegitimacy rates, the legitimacy principle holds true as the basis of the family institution. His explanation for 'deviant' relationships is that there has been a breakdown in some economic circumstances of the system of social controls governing the marriage 'market'. Control by parents in the form of courtship or chaperonage breaks down in the lower classes; the economic capacity to buy a man by dowry has gone; and many men do not have stable occupations. Thus many non-legal unions are formed because women cannot strike the desirable bargain for a stable marriage.

Such an argument is clearly based on a Western middle-class view of the norms that should govern marriage. Even Rodman's (1963) *value stretch* criticism of Goode (which holds that the lower classes cannot live with guilt and thus adopt other norms which validate their behaviour) assumes that one set of overriding norms should apply to marriage.

There are also problems if we consider the recent increase in the number of single mothers who choose to keep and rear their children. The single mother is also the sociological father in that she is legally responsible for the child. In this circumstance the analytic definition of the family as an institution by which the rights of the child are defined might still hold. However we still have to ask whether the single mother and her illegitimate child fit a norm of parenthood. The child is still, under the law, defined as illegitimate even though it can be legitimized by the subsequent marriage of its parents (Marriage Act, 1961, Australia). Moreover, under British common law an illegitimate child 'was a stranger in law not only to his father but to his mother and all other 'relatives': hence he had no legal right to maintenance or other benefit deriving from the status of parent and child' (Cretney, quoted in Finlay, 1979; p.305). It was not until 1969 that the English Family Law Reform Act made it possible for illegitimate children to inherit property. Though the social stigma still persists, Australian income tax laws provide benefits for de facto spouses, and all Australian states have now enacted *status of children* legislation which equalizes the legal position of children born in wedlock or outside it. The Royal Commission on Human Relationships (AGPS 1977, Vol. 4, paras 125–130), while suggesting that the law should be cautious in moving to impose legal obligations on de facto partners, strongly supports the children of such unions:

> *130.* In regard to the children of de facto relationships, we are clearly of the view that their rights and status should be the same as those of children of a marriage and that questions of custody, access and maintenance should be determined in the same way as in the case of children of a marriage.

It appears then, that despite wide variation in and changing definitions of the *sexual script*, one of the constant elements in the *parenting script* is that of taking responsibility for the child.

Yet we still tend to see the institution of the family as being quite separate from the institution of work. As a result changing norms about mothering and fathering have not yet been matched by norms and procedures that free women from their traditional (though not very old) home-bound roles.

Women and Work

If institutional norms in our society tend to create a division between men as income earners and women as home-makers, what consequences follow?

A detailed analysis of the pressures placed by old norms about marriage and the family on newly-married couples in today's new circumstances, is provided by Lyn Richards' *Having Families*. Here one may read the words of couples, but especially of women, who feel trapped by their own acceptance of marriage as 'getting set up', 'settling down', and being 'empty without children'. Here too, one may read the self-doubts of women about their competence to act as 'a good mum' and 'a good manager', and still remain 'individuals' in their own right. Chief among their problems are isolation from others and ignorance of the fact that others share their self-doubts and 'unacceptable' feelings of frustration.

This is a cogent demonstration of an institution at work—the normative rules of expected and acceptable behaviour have become so embedded that they are taken-for-granted, seen as real, stubborn social facts. In general, as Lyn Richards says, it is pointless to decry institutional rules. It is pointless because we are social only to the extent that we share understandings, and that we interact on the basis of what can be taken-for-granted about 'everyone'. But as circumstances change, new institutional norms arise creating confusion and conflict between norms that define what 'should' be done. In the context of such stresses the family stands amazingly solid. It survives as society's basic unit despite change. However, changes clearly produce conflict, and the family institution (as defined by the analytic set of widely believed norms) comes under pressure.

In Australia those pressures are not altogether new. For example, the middle-class norm that mothers should not work has not been widely practised, especially among the working class and particularly since World War 2. Neither do unemployment figures accurately reflect the number of women who wish to work since many do not bother to register because of their poor chances of finding jobs. The contrast between the myths and the facts of women's work throughout Western history is shown in Mary J. Beard's *Women as Force in History*, and about women in Australian history in Miriam Dixson's *The Real Matilda*. But some figures may give the current picture more concisely. Australia's male-dominated tradition may be seen in the way that we have lagged behind other developed countries in providing jobs for women. Whereas in 1961 only 18.7 per cent of married Australian women were in the workforce, the figures for the United States were 31 per cent, for Great Britain 32 per cent and for France 31 per cent (see Richmond, 1974). Table 5—1 shows the increasing rate of female participation in the Australian workforce, a fact which inevitably has changed the nature of the family as an institution.

Table 5—2, however, qualifies the roles of women in the workforce. Where mothers are employed at all, they tend to be employed in particular sorts of jobs. They are most likely to be found in jobs that do not require high levels of education, professional qualifications or scientific or technical skills, and in jobs where working hours allow them to fit in with the schedules of children. These sorts of jobs are, of course, lower in status and lower in income.

Furthermore, 80.7 per cent of women in the workforce have no training, compared with 67.6 per cent of males. In 1970 when all apprenticeships were open to either sex, only 2.4 per cent of apprentices were females (Torsh, cited in Dixson, 1976, p.39). And Bettina Cass (1976) found that only 16 per cent of all Australian academics were women. Of these, 64 per cent occupied junior positions; only 20 per cent of Readers and one per cent of Professors were female.

Trade unions have also been less than even-handed in relation to women in the workforce. During the late 1970s they have scrambled to put on a new face, but as late as 1974 A.C.T.U. President Hawke was more concerned with social services than with pressing for equal pay for women. It was only on 2 May 1974 that the Commonwealth Conciliation and Arbitration Commission extended the adult minimum wage to women.

But the issue is no longer whether married women *should* work: nearly half of them do, at least part time. It is rather why other institutions (such as business, trade unions, the public service and the education system) lag behind or refuse to adjust. New pressures for flexitime, both at work and in schools,

Table 5–1 Women in the workforce 1901–1971[1]

Census	(1) Women aged 15–64	(2)	(3) Workforce	(4)	(5)	(6)	(7)	(8)	(9)	(10)
	Total	Married	Total men and women	Women	Married women	% Women at work	Female workforce as % of total workforce	Married female workforce as % female workforce	Married female workforce as % total workforce	%Married women at work
	('000)	('000)	('000)	('000)	('000)					
1901	1 074	546	1 615	330	[2]	30.7	20.5	[2]	[2]	[2]
1911	1 355	702	1 922	386	43[3]	28.5	20.1	11.1	2.2	6.1
1921	1 706	958	2 237	455	42[3]	26.7	20.3	9.2	1.9	4.4
1933	2 153	1 220	2 744	599	66[3]	27.8	21.8	11.0	2.4	5.4
1947	2 523	1 646	3 196	717	142[3]	28.4	22.4	19.8	4.4	8.6
1954	2 776	1 904	3 702	845	258	30.5	22.8	30.5	7.0	13.6
1961	3 135	2 166	4 225	1 059	406	33.8	25.1	38.3	9.6	18.7
1966	3 505	2 385	4 857	1 435	686	40.9	29.5	47.8	14.1	28.8
1971[4]	4 559	2 928	5 305	1 689	958	37.0	31.8	56.7	18.1	32.7

[1] Comparability from census to census is reduced by the number of changes in the definition of the workforce.
[2] Not available.
[3] Includes women who are separated, but excludes widows and divorcees.
[4] 1971 Census figures are available as sample estimates only for a very small number of tabulations. Figures for the total population do not exclude those aged 65 and over. Consequently estimated percentages in columns 6 and 10 are lower than the corrected figures.
Sources: *1961 Census, 1966 Census Population and Housing*, vol. 2, pt. 4, *1971 Census: Sample Estimates*.
Source: K. Richmond, in Edgar, 1974; p. 269, Table 1.

Table 5–2 Occupational classification[1] of employed parents in one-parent and two-parent families.

Occupation	One-parent Families		Two-parent Families	
	Male	Female	Male	Female
Professional	6.1%*	12.0%	13.6%	13.8%
Administrative	6.2%*	3.5%	12.6%	3.2%
Clerical	7.2%	28.6%	6.4%	24.1%
Sales	6.0%*	10.5%	5.0%	13.3%
Farmers, miners	2.7%*	0.8%*	3.1%	1.5%*
Transport	13.7%	4.2%	8.2%	2.6%
Tradesmen	48.8%	11.4%	41.0%	17.0%
Service Industries	4.0%*	24.0%	4.6%	19.2%
Armed Services	0.2%*	0.0%*	1.0%	0.0%*
Non-response	5.1%*	5.1%	4.5%	5.4%
TOTAL	100.0%	100.0%	100.0%	100.0%

[1] This is the standard occupational classification used by the Australian Bureau of Statistics. It does not imply a ranking of occupations.
*Standard error is greater than 30% of the entire estimate.
  Source: *Families in Australia — a Profile*, Family Research Unit, Univ. of N.S.W., 1978, p. 59, Table 26.

may be signs of an adjustment, but social norms change slowly. The media, for example, continue to promote the ideal image of women as the *Women's Weekly* mum, good at cleaning, washing, cooking and looking lovely for dad when he gets home from work (see Sampson and Edgar in Edgar, 1975, chs 18 and 19).

The different State laws on equal opportunities and the reluctance of employers to provide child-care facilities also serve to show how institutions outside the family continue to reinforce old norms about the sexual division of labour. And if the presence of mothers in the workforce is seen to be a threat to the family as it is generally defined, we may see other institutions lending it new support. Lyn Richards (1978, p.183) cites as evidence the sorts of advice provided by a male-dominated medical profession and even the recent promotion of the benefits of natural breastfeeding.

Other institutions, then, may serve to shape and limit the institution of the family. The forces operating on the family well illustrate the concept of *institutional limitations* and demonstrate how closely connected are the various institutions in the social structure. It is too easy to think of the family as separate from the institutions of work, the law, religion and the wider community. When we conceive of the family only in terms of the *nuclear* unit of husband, wife, children and their relationships, we overlook the fact that it is fused within the broader social structure. And when we do, we limit our own understanding and our options for change because we will not ask the kinds of questions to challenge what is taken-for-granted. Questions concerning:

the necessity for the nuclear family rather than the extended family;

the necessity for women in the mothering role rather than men;

the effects of the structure of the family on living patterns and social interaction;

the property rights and legal provisions that bind families and restrict their influence;

the possibility of different male-female, child-parent relationships (like, for example, in the Israeli kibbutz or in the homosexual family);

the way the family reflects, reinforces and reproduces existing authority patterns, dominance relations and the sharing of power.

When we examine the family in the light of these questions, however, we may see how well it is accommodated within our view of the social structure as the distribution of life chances according to who controls needed resources (wealth, money and knowledge) and according to how life-cycle choice points are restricted by key institutions and groups.

Readings and References

a. Australian Society:

BRYSON, L. (1975) 'Husband and Wife Interaction in the Australian Family: a Critical Review of the Literature' in J. Mercer, (ed.) *The Other Half, Women in Australian Society*, Penguin, Melbourne.
BUDDIN, T. (1978) 'Counsellors, Lawyers and Custody Disputes in the Family Courts', *Aust. J. Social Issues*, Vol. 13, No. 3, pp.216-31.
CASS, B. (1976) 'Women at University, Part 1: Family and Class Background', *Refractory Girl*, 10, pp.6-11, 13-19, March.
CURA (1978) *But I Wouldn't Want My Wife to Work Here*, Centre for Urban Research and Action, Victoria.
DAY, L. H. (1964) 'Patterns of divorce in Australia and the United States', *American Sociological Review*, 29, (Aug.), pp.509-22.
DIXSON, M. (1976) *The Real Matilda*, Penguin, Melbourne.
ENCEL, S., MACKENZIE & M. TABBUTT (1974) *Women and Society*, Cheshire, Melbourne.
ENGLISH, B. A., R. J. KING & S. S. SMITH (1979) *Families in Australia—A Profile*, Family Research Unit, University of N.S.W.
FINLAY, H. A. (1979) *Family Law in Australia*, Butterworth, Sydney.
HARPER, J. & L. RICHARDS (1979) *Mothering and Working Mothers*, Penguin, Melbourne.
KRUPINSKI, J. & A. STOLLER (eds) (1974) *The Family in Australia*, Pergamon Press, Sydney.
MERCER, J. (ed.) (1975) *The Other Half, Women in Australian Society*, Penguin, Melbourne.
O'CONNOR, P. (1976) 'Nuclear Versus Extended Households: Stockton, Calif., 1880', *ANZJS*, Vol. 12, No. 1, pp.68-72.
RICHARDS, L. (1978) *Having Families*, Penguin, Melbourne.
RICHMOND, K. (1974) 'The Workforce Participation of Married Women in Australia', in Edgar, D.E. (ed.), *Social Change in Australia*, Cheshire, Melbourne, pp.267-305.
RYAN, E. & A. CONLON (1975) *Gentle Invaders: Australian Women at Work, 1788–1974*, Nelson, Melbourne.
The Australian Family, Research Bulletin, Family Research Unit, Univ. of N.S.W. (1973).
WITTICH, E. (1976) 'Getting Behind the Mystique of Social Institutions: Marriage', *La Trobe Sociology Papers*, No. 31, La Trobe University, Melbourne.

b. General:

ARIES, P. (1962) *Centuries of Childhood: A Social History of Family Life*, Jonathon Cape, London.
ARONOFF, J. & W. D. CRANO (1975) 'A re-examination of the cross-cultural principles of task segregation and sex-role differentiation in the family', *American Sociological Review*, 40, (Feb), pp.12-20.

BEARD, M. J. (1971) *Women as Force in History*, Collier Macmillan, London.

BELL, N. W. & E. F. VOGEL (1968) *A Modern Introduction to the Family* (2nd ed.), Free Press, N.Y.

BLOOD, R. O. Jr. & D. M. WOLFE (1960) *Husbands and Wives: The Dynamics of Married Living*, Macmillan, N.Y.

BOTT, E. (1957) *Family and Social Network*, Tavistock, London.

BRONOWSKI, J. (1973) *The Ascent of Man*, BBC, London.

BURGESS, E. W., H. J. LOCKE & M. M. THOMES (1963) *The Family: From Institution to Companionship* (3rd ed.), American Book Company, N.Y.

CASTELLS, M. (1977) *The Urban Question: a Marxist Approach*, (Trans. by A. Sheridan), Edward Arnold, London.

CASTELLS, M. (1978) *City, Class and Power*, Macmillan, London.

CHRISTENSEN, H. T. (ed.) (1964) *Handbook of Marriage and the Family*, Rand McNally, Chicago.

CORBIN, M. (ed.) (1978) *The Couple*, Penguin.

COSER, L. A. (1956) *The Functions of Social Conflict*, Free Press, N.Y.

DAVIS, N. Z. (1977) 'Ghosts, Kin and Progeny: Some Features of Family Life in Early Modern France', *Daedalus*, Spring, pp.87-114.

DOUGLAS, J. D. (1970) *Understanding Everyday Life*, Aldine, Chicago.

DREITZEL, H. P. (1973) *Recent Sociology, No. 5, Childhood and Socialization*, Collier Macmillan, London.

DURKHEIM, E. (1964 [1893]) *The Division of Labor in Society*, Free Press, N.Y.

GOODE, W. (1960) 'Illegitimacy in the Carribean Social Structure', *American Sociological Review*, 25, pp.21-30.

GOSLIN, D. (ed.) (1969) *Handbook of Socialization Theory and Research*, Rand McNally, Chicago.

HAREVEN, T. K. (1977) 'Family Time and Historical Time', *Daedalus*, Spring, pp.57-86.

HILL, R. & R. KONIG (eds) (1970) *Families in East and West*, Mounton, Paris.

KEESING, R. M. (1975 [1935]) *Kin Groups and Social Structure*, Holt, Rinehart & Winston, U.S.A.

LEVY, M. J. (1949) *The Family Revolution in Modern China*, Atheneum, N.Y.

LIDZ, T. (1963) *The Family and Human Adaptation*, International University Press, N.Y.

MALINOWSKI, B. (1944) *A Scientific Theory of Culture*, University of North Carolina Press, Nth Carolina.

MURDOCK, G. P. (1935) *Our Primitive Contemporaries*, Macmillan, N.Y.

MURDOCK, G. P. & J. W. M. WHITING (1951) 'Cultural determination of parental attitudes: The relationship between the social structure, particularly family structure, and behaviour', in M. J. E. Senn (ed.), *Problems of Infancy and Childhood*, Macy Foundation, N.Y.

NIMKOFF, M. F. & R. MIDDLETON (1960) 'Type of family and type of economy', *American Journal of Sociology*, 66 (Nov), pp.215-25.

PARSONS, T. (1964) 'Age and Sex in the Social Structure of the United States', in T. Parsons, *Essays in Sociological Theory*, Free Press, N.Y., pp.89-103.

PARSONS, T. & R. F. BALES (1955) *Family, Socialization and Interaction Process*, Free Press, Glencoe, Ill.

POSTER, M. (1978) *Critical Theory of the Family*, Pluto Press, N.Y.

RAPOPORT, R., V. T. RAPOPORT & J. M. BUMSTEAD (1978) *Working Couples*, Harper, N.Y.

RODMAN, H. (1963) 'The Lower Class Value Stretch', *Social Forces*, Vol. 42, pp.205-15.

ROSSI, A. (1964) 'Equality between the sexes: An immodest proposal', *Daedalus*, 93 (Spring), pp.607-52.

ROSSI, A. S. (1977) 'A Biosocial Perspective on Parenting', *Daedalus*, Spring, pp.1-32.

SAFILIOS-ROTHSCHILD, C. (1970) 'The study of family power-structure: A review 1960–1969', *Journal of Marriage and the Family*, 31 (May), pp.539-52.

SCHORR, A. L. & P. MOEN (1979) 'The Single Parent and Public Policy', *Social Policy*, Vol. 9, No. 5, pp.15-21.

SHORTER, E. (1975) *The Making of the Modern Family*, Fontana/Collins, London.

SKOLNICK, A. S. & J. H. SKOLNICK (1971) *The Family in Transition*, Little Brown, Boston.

SMUCKER, M. J. & A. C. ZIJDERVELD (1970) 'Structure and Meaning: Implications for Social Change', *British Journal of Sociology*, 21, pp.375-89.

WINCH, R. F. & G. P. SPANIER (eds) (1974) *Selected Studies in Marriage and the Family* (4th ed.), Holt, Rinehart & Winston, N.Y.

YOUNG, M. & P. WILLMOTT (1957) *Family and Kinship in East London*, Routledge & Kegan Paul, U.K.

See also reference lists at end of Chapter 7.

Part Three

Culture as Life Concerns: Reproducing the Social Structure

Introduction:

What Is 'Culture'?

When people speak about 'the Australian way of life' they assume a common culture that is shared by Australians and marks them off from other cultures. As we have seen, Australian society does not offer the same resources, the same chances, the same limits to everyone. So how can we suppose any common culture exists? Just what is a 'culture' and why do we need this term as well as the terms 'society' and 'social structure'?

Culture refers to shared meanings, the *ideas* that result from man's actions in the world. Action comes first. Meanings are the *products of action*. They are products in the sense that man's efforts to control nature (his labour) leave their mark. Artifacts, not mere bones, are the physical marks a culture leaves behind.

> The basic devices of the nimble-fingered mind lie about, unregarded, in any village anywhere in the world ... the needle, the awl, the pot, the brazier, the spade, the nail and the screw, the bellows, the string, the knot, the loom, the harness, the hook, the button, the shoe ... The richness comes from the interplay of inventions; a culture is a multiplier of ideas, in which each new device quickens and enlarges the power of the rest. (Bronowski, 1973, pp.73−4)

But ideas are also products in the sense that they come from *inter*-action, from social action where the actors *share* some meanings. Only when ideas are shared can joint action take place and a society develop. So culture rests on the *communication of meaning*, on a shared interpretation of the physical realities and practical necessities of life. We can accomplish this because we can use *symbols* to stand in place of objects that are not immediately present. It is our capacity to use symbols that makes it possible to *transmit* meanings. Symbols link together the past, the present and the future in a way that gives us more *control* over our shared lives. While culture arises from our past actions, our history and our heritage, culture also conditions further action and limits its range. Culture is the filter through which we see and understand our current reality.

Consider, for example, the meaning of culture for the types of people portrayed in the following extracts. Judith Wright captures vividly the desolate and faded hopes of the outback farmer:

> The polished parlour grew distrait and haunted
> where Millie, Lucy, John each night at ten
> wound the gilt clock that leaked the year away.
> The pianola — oh, listen to the mockingbird —
> wavers on Sundays and has lost a note.
> The wrinkled ewes snatch pansies through the fence
> and stare with shallow eyes into the garden
> where Lucy shrivels waiting for a word,
> and Millie's cameos loosen round her throat.
> The bush comes near, the ranges grow immense.
>
> (Judith Wright, 'Brother and Sisters')

Is that image of apeing English gardens, of middle-class trappings in an alien bush, any more 'real' or typical of Australian culture than C. J. Dennis's inner-city 'larrikin', the Sentimental Bloke?

> Me, that 'as done me stretch fer stoushin' Johns,
>   An' spens me leisure gittin' on the shick,
> An' 'arf me nights down there, in Little Lons.,
>   Wiv Ginger Mick,
> Jist 'eadin' 'em, an' doin' in me guilt,
>   Tough luck! I s'pose it's 'ow a man is built.
> It's 'ow Gawd builds a bloke; but don't it 'urt
>   When 'e gits yearnin's fer this 'igher life,
> On these Spring mornin's, watchin' some sweet skirt —
>   Some fucher wife —
> Go sailin' by, an' turnin' on 'is phiz
>   The glarssy eye — fer bein' wot 'e is.
>
> (C. J. Dennis, 'A Spring Song', in *The Songs of the Sentimental Bloke*, Cornstalk Publishing Co., Sydney, 1929, pp.21–2)

Culture meets us in myriad masks but for those involved the mask is reality. Culture arises from action in and on the world. It consists of patterns of shared ideas, of rules, expectations and motives. Thus a culture gives meaning to group life and serves to support and maintain the social structure.

In that sense, a culture is an organized, shared, and hence meaningful, *interpretation of reality*. None of us has much control over the picture of reality we each develop, because culture is *learned*. It is transmitted by those who precede us according to how their actions have made meaning of their world. Children acquire the culture through socialization. It is imposed on them, they are controlled by it and learn (more or less) to accept it as *legitimate*. As a result, our culture tends to be taken-for-granted because it is embedded in our everyday actions, our 'normal' lives. We should beware, however, of thinking of culture as a *thing*, of reifying it and acting as though culture 'causes' action. For without continued social interaction a culture ceases to exist; without regular use a language as a symbol system dies. A culture does not 'do' anything. It can only be observed in the regular, typical behaviour of a people.

Just as the organized patterns of social structure reflect the outcome of conflict, so too *the* culture is a product of conflict between competing symbols, controlling ideas and competing definitions of reality. It should be at once apparent then, that we cannot continue to speak of *the culture* of a society. Only in a completely closed, tight-knit community is it likely that ideas will be so shared that a unitary notion of culture will hold. Even then, cultural ideas will reflect the *dominance* of one group over another: men over women, priests over men, kings over priests. Karl Marx's (*German Ideology*, p.61) famous dictum: 'The ideas of the ruling class are in every epoch the ruling ideas' need not be limited to capitalist society. Since labour is always a necessity (for some at least) if mankind is to survive, our role in the division of labour will give us a picture of our place in the world. If we are in control, we will feel control; if we are controlled by others our ideas about them and about ourselves in relation to them will reflect their power.

> The production of ideas, of conceptions, of consciousness, is at first directly interwoven with the material activity and the material intercourse of men, the language of real life . . . The same applies to mental production as expressed in the language of politics, law, morality, religion, metaphysics, etc. of a people. Men are the producers of their conceptions, ideas, etc. — real, active men . . . (*German Ideology*, p.37).

Because people lead different lives, are subject to different levels of control and respond to different needs, they develop differing images of reality. Their life chances are limited by the family, religion, ethnic group and social class into which they are born. The words they learn, the attitudes, values and social expectations to which they are exposed will not all be the same. The 'recipe knowledge' that guides everyday action and governs thought will vary from group to group. In other words, there is a multitude of *sub-cultures* in every complex society. But notice the implication of this term. A sub-culture is subordinate to a major culture. Conflicting definitions of reality can be maintained within a group but the sub-culture has less influence than the 'dominant' culture. The Aborigines have their culture but it was not the victor. Migrants have always brought with them their own ethnic cultures—dominant values in their home country but subordinate in the Australian context. A sub-culture is not just an individual style of life; it is an organized value and idea system which sustains meaning for an organized group.

In the chapters that follow, we shall be looking at the ways in which culture is transmitted: how real-life situations (in the family, at school, at work, in the wider community) structure meanings and life-orientations for various groups. Throughout, we shall be looking for the social structural conditions that serve to transmit, reinforce and reproduce the pattern of dominance relations in Australian society. This pattern of dominance is always under challenge, because not all people submit passively to a lack of control over their own cultural values or a denigration of them. But powerful forces are always at work to *legitimate* the status quo, to suggest to everyone that what *is* is what *must be*. For in the end it is not power based on force that matters; it is power that becomes 'authorized', legitimated and accepted by those whom it controls. As Horace Mann said in favour of public schooling in nineteenth-century Massachusetts, the citizen of tomorrow must 'think of duty rather than of the policeman' (quoted in Bowles, S. and H. Gintis, *Schooling in Capitalist America*, Basic Books, N.Y., 1976, p.170).

Both the threat and the hope are contained in many a child's schoolyard rhyme:

> I'll never go to school any more, more, more
> There's a big fat teacher at the door, door, door,
> She asked me a sum
> And she kicked me up the bum,
> So I'll never go to school any more, more, more.

(*Cinderella Dressed in Yella*, Ian Turner (ed.), Heinemann Educational, Melbourne, 1969, p.65)

Chapter 6

Structural Limits and Cultural Realities

6

Our culture offers us a set of guidelines for making sense of life. It comes packaged in words and signs and recipes for action—ready-made interpretations that help us understand what is going on. The trouble is that not all interpretations offer the same amount of control over life. Some cultural packages are outdated or distorted and they work against the premise that ideas are socially created and maintained. In other words they serve as 'blinkers' on our view of reality. They keep us on a narrow path so we never learn that the shadows are peopled with real things that can be altered by action. Ideas transmitted to us within the culture are then taken as absolutes. They are not questioned or examined to see if they really meet our needs, serve our interests, or give us control over our own lives.

Alienation

The term sociologists use to describe the separation of self from control over what we do is *alienation*.

The term alienation at first meant the transfer of ownership of a piece of property. It later came to mean a state of mental disorientation. Its sociological meaning derives from Marx's use of the term to describe the tension between the individual and the social structure of modern capitalist society. Marx argued that there was a close relationship between alienation and the system of mass production developing at the time. In the workplace, alienation describes the feelings of frustration and unhappiness—of powerlessness—felt by workers who have no control over how their labour is used.

When social inventions like ideas of *democracy* or *goodness* or *authority* or *laws* take on a thing-like quality, a reality of their own apart from man, we call the process *reification*.

For Marx, this is a form of alienation. Man is separated from the ideas he has created. The ideas have become *reified*. They then work back against man because their stubborn, thing-like quality takes on a power that is hard to see through. Notice the sense of shock many Australians felt at the first actions of the Whitlam Labor Government in December 1972. Whitlam recognized 'Communist' China, withdrew troops from Vietnam, and pardoned all 'draft dodgers'. Even people sympathetic with Labor's overall policy were heard to say 'But you can't pardon them; they've broken the law'. Their reality shock came when it was pointed out that the law had changed, that the law was not a 'thing' above men's actions, it was made, enforced and could be altered by the actions of people. In this case people with new values, an alternate view of reality, now held power, and they used that power to redefine reality for the whole of Australia.

Culture consists of the objects (both physical and mental) created by man's actions. Without symbols to 'objectify' meanings we could not communicate. Nor could we operate efficiently if we constantly challenged what society has already produced. When, however, we reify socially-produced objects such as 'the law', as though they exist of themselves and can never be changed, we are in trouble. For then we lose control over our cultural products and they may work against us. Rather, they will work against *some* of us. For cultural products (whether they be consumer items, religious values, racist attitudes, norms about the family or the 'Protestant work ethic') serve particular *interests*.

Marx saw alienation as a denial of a person's own free, conscious action. It was not until his *Economic and Philosophical Manuscripts* were translated into English in 1932, however, that the idea of alienation had much impact in sociology. It has now become a central linking concept between the individual and social structure, for alienation describes how the individual is set at a distance from society; how society becomes a 'thing' over which the individual has little or no power; how society may represent 'culture against man' (Jules Henry, 1963); and how the power of ideas may control action and reproduce the status quo.

Sociologists must therefore look at society and ask not just how things are, but also how they got to be that way and under what conditions (both structural and cultural) they might change.

The study of culture cannot be divorced from analysis of the social structure, the organized patterns that limit human action. For it is those structured limits that tie thought down. Nor will new ideas, or merely an awareness of how things work, be enough. For the structures of domination in society rest upon the social distribution of unequal resources, and knowledge is only one of those resources. But we must examine culture or we miss a key factor that explains how the social structure operates and is maintained. For as W. I. Thomas (1928, p.572) suggested, 'If men define situations as real they are real in their consequences'. That is, people act on the basis of their own assessments and understandings of what is needed. Whether or not they are 'objectively' wrong, their culture, their definitions of reality, will have important social consequences.

Situations and Cultural Relevance

Our subjective beliefs, our values and our motivations, are all limited by our pasts and our presents. Our life *situations* determine our needs, what is relevant, what is 'typical' and taken-for-granted as 'real' for us. In a complex life, we operate on various levels of alienation, with varying degrees of control. We operate in situations that present us with multiple (and at times contradictory) realities.

W. H. Auden's poem, *The Unknown Citizen*, illustrates a number of the points we have considered and raises others for further debate.

The Unknown Citizen

(To JS/07/M/378)

This Marble Monument

Is Erected by the State
He was found by the Bureau of Statistics to be
One against whom there was no official complaint,
And all the reports on his conduct agree
That, in the modern sense of an old-fashioned word, he was a saint,
For in everything he did he served the Greater Community.
Except for the War till the day he retired
He worked in a factory and never got fired,
But satisfied his employers, Fudge Motors Inc.
Yet he wasn't a scab or odd in his views,
For his Union reports that he paid his dues,
(Our report on his Union shows it was sound)
And our Social Psychology workers found
That he was popular with his mates and liked a drink.
The Press are convinced that he bought a paper every day
And that his reactions to advertisements were normal in every way.
Policies taken out in his name prove that he was fully insured,
And his Health-card shows he was once in hospital but left it cured.
Both Producers Research and High-Grade Living declare
He was fully sensible to the advantages of the Instalment Plan
And had everything necessary to the Modern Man.
A phonograph, a radio, a car and a frigidaire.
Our researchers into Public Opinion are content
That he held the proper opinions for the time of year;
When there was peace, he was for peace; when there was war, he went.
He was married and added five children to the population,
Which our Eugenist says was the right number for a parent of his generation,
And our teachers report that he never interfered with their education.
Was he free? Was he happy? The question is absurd:
Had anything been wrong, we should certainly have heard.

Notice how the *Citizen* is treated by different groups in society according to what they want him to be. But notice also that he plays out the roles expected of him without objection. Does that necessarily deny his human integrity? Was he *alienated* if indeed he was unaware that a better mode of life might have been available to him? To that question we would answer 'yes', because he has *reified* the ideologies of his society and has therefore lost control over his life.

It was the theorist Alfred Schutz who most clearly outlined how the 'life-world' is structured.

> The world of everyday life is the scene and also the object of our actions and interactions. We have to dominate it and we have to change it in order to realize the purposes which we pursue within it among our fellow men. Thus we work and operate not only within but upon the world (Schutz, in Wagner, 1970, p.73).

But that world is determined for us by our physical and social location, so our status and role and our moral and ideological position will affect our efforts to 'dominate the world of everyday life'. Schutz shows that our social location limits our share in the 'stock of knowledge' available. That stock of knowledge offers us a scheme of interpretation of past, present and future events. Human interests are structured by that scheme of interpretation and our interests in turn determine what is relevant to our immediate purposes-at-hand. The Aborigine, the factory worker and the wealthy business man may share certain common elements of the stock of knowledge, but their interests and purposes make sections of it more or less relevant to their daily lives.

Notice that this takes us towards social, not individual, concerns. Rather than stressing individual needs that give rise to interests, Schutz argues that interests (and thus needs) are defined for us by our situations and our share in the social stock of knowledge.

From those structured life interests arise more limited purposes-at-hand which define what in any situation is *relevant*, what is required to be selected for attention and action. For Schutz this means there is never any truth or certainty; culture is never fixed or final. Instead, all we normally seek is limited information on 'likelihood' and the 'chances or risks' involved if we take a certain line of action. Therefore what is relevant varies from situation to situation and knowledge (cultural values) is rarely, if ever, consistent.

> As a father, a citizen, an employee, and a member of his church he may have the most different and the least congruent opinions on moral, political or economic matters. This inconsistency does not necessarily originate in a logical fallacy. Men's thought is just spread over subject matters located within different and differently relevant areas, and they are not aware of the modifications they would have to make in passing from one level to another (Schutz, in Wagner, 1970, p.76).

What follows is that the more complex and varied the situations people face, the less likely we are to find a consistent set of cultural values. Instead, we will expect a separation between areas of life; between work and home, public and private life, religious, political, ethnic and occupational groups. One can be 'a mouse at home and a lion abroad'; a left-wing activist and a homeowner; a trade unionist and a member of the Liberal Party. Moreover, what we often hear described as 'apathy' or 'the great Australian stupor', may not be an abdication of responsibility or a feeling of powerlessness so much as a reflection of the segregated fields of relevance in people's lives.

Symbol Spheres and Recipes for Action

Schutz points out that what is relevant is limited by a group's interests and its share of the social stock of knowledge. It is the *folkways* (Sumner, 1906) of the group which serve as the standards by which the in-group 'defines its situation'. In other words, each group develops a culture that offers 'trustworthy recipes for interpreting the social world and for handling things and men in order to obtain the best results in every situation with a minimum of effort by avoiding undesirable consequences' (Schutz, in Wagner, 1970, p.81).

Such 'recipes' are taken for granted until such time as they fail to meet the tests of reality. Any new element will challenge the old ways. Interests alter and so new knowledge becomes relevant. But because most recipes for action carry the weight of group approval they will rarely be challenged; they tend to become reified as the only way to do things. Another way of putting this idea is to say (with Schutz) that when we *typify* situations and other people, we treat them at an *anonymous* level and assume nothing is problematic. It is only in intimate, face-to-face relations that we expand the *fullness of content* of our recipes for action. Symbols act as labels and those labels usually 'work' at an anonymous level quite efficiently. But if our view of the world is restricted and perceived largely in terms of such anonymous typifications, we are less likely to 'see through' the currently accepted, in-group norms, and we are thereby limited in our capacity to control our own lives.

Symbols may be manipulated by those who control the major means of communication. With mass media, more and more of our 'recipes' come pre-packaged. As we shall see in Chapter 10, this is one of the keys to the media's legitimization of the status quo. Many ideas, social rules and typifications may be experienced at an anonymous level and rarely in face-to-face situations, so the need to seek new knowledge that might redefine our situation may rarely arise. Schutz's critics have often held that he stresses the subjective and ignores the objective limits of social structure. A more careful reading suggests otherwise:

> ... institutional barriers allow only certain typical, socially determined persons to acquire determinate provinces of special knowledge ... knowledge can become more and more of a power factor in complex social distributions of knowledge. Groups of 'experts' form one of the institutional catalysts of power concentration. On the other hand, there is always the possibility of a conflict between different groups of 'experts' in a struggle for a 'power monopoly' ... The main characteristics of a complex social distribution of knowledge are 'inequality' in the distribution of general knowledge, progressive partitioning and specialization of special knowledge into various, more or less 'autonomous' provinces, and the corresponding institutional specialization of the transmission of special knowledge (Schutz and Luckmann, 1974, p.315).

In view of this, Schutz is closer to the views of 'radical' sociologist C. Wright Mills' views on culture than might have been suspected.

Gerth and Mills agree that language symbols, as the means by which we typify and handle the world, are locked into the power contexts of social institutions. High-brow pronunciation and group slang, family table-talk and the tête-á-tête of lovers, election speech and a sales-pitch all represent a form of symbol control. But some spheres carry more 'weight' and symbols become used to 'justify a social structure'. Gerth and Mills (1954, p.276) refer to them as symbols of *legitimation, master symbols,* or *symbols of justification.* For example, the notion of *motherhood* carries such emotional and moral weight that it is hard to argue in favour of any other forms of parenting and family structures. Anyone who questions the existing structure is immediately suspect.

In this way, interest groups avoid challenge by conjuring up moral symbols or shorthand terms. In the spheres of economics, the family, politics, the military order and status groups, sets of symbols serve to mark off those in command, of higher status, and to legitimate what is. Notions of good or bad taste, the use of foreign languages such as Latin, trade jargon, the unchallengeable symbols of 'private property', 'free enterprise', 'earning your own living', the sanctity of the home, the right to privacy, the labels 'dole bludger', 'fascist', 'sexist'; all represent emotional attachments to particular group interests and cultural values.

Gerth and Mills (1954) suggest that challenges to the symbols of legitimacy will arise when there is:

(a) a diversity of institutions, as when churches or political parties compete,
(b) a rapid turnover, as when a dictator seeks to debunk the previous institutional order,
(c) easy access to the channels of communication.

We should ask ourselves which of these conditions hold in Australia. But we should keep in mind that 'only if one set of symbols were successfully imposed upon virtually all of a population could we speak strictly of "common values" ' (Gerth and Mills, 1954, p.298). And we should remember in talking about culture, that action comes first.

> Propagation of symbols is effective only so long as they have some meaningful relevance to the roles, institutions and feelings that characterize a people. Symbols cannot create these roles (Gerth and Mills, 1954, p.298).

Following Schutz, the segregation of life situations in a modern society means that common values 'are *not* necessary in order to secure integration and unity' (Gerth and Mills, 1954, p.301), for the powerful can afford to tolerate diversity. Despite conflicting multi-cultural values, the prevailing social structure may continue to limit the life chances of some groups.

Apathy and Levels of Control

For such reasons we are highly sceptical of simple assertions about Australian 'apathy'. Apathy is a catch-all term that blames the individual for faults that are socially produced. In our examination of the family, the schools, work and the mass media, we shall be asking what is it that people take for granted, and why. We shall want to identify which groups do in fact take the existing structures of Australian society for granted and which groups challenge them or at least grumble under their weight.

All individuals seek some level of control over their environment. Without control we are less than human, dependent upon others and alienated from society and from ourselves. But people seek different *degrees* of control. If we cannot influence politicians, prices, or the laws, at least we can control our own family, the backyard, the new Holden or motorbike. At work we may not be boss, but there are always niches in which we can exercise control; there are people lower down the line who may be subject to our authority and influence.

It may be that work is less central a concern in some people's lives than we imagine, because they see it merely as a necessary evil, a means to other ends where money and leisure time are more vital. We shall have to examine how work of various kinds structures people's lives, their time, their routines, their expectations and value-orientations. It is likely that experience of control through authority at work will carry over into attitudes towards the rest of life, perhaps reproducing and perpetuating parental values in the values of their children. Certainly our work lives will affect what is relevant and what resources we will have available to achieve our day-to-day purposes and our longer-term life-goals.

There is a distinction to be made here that affects our sociological explanations. To some extent we behave as we do, and become what we are, *because* of circumstance; because our family background and the life chances over which we have little control press us in certain directions. Schutz (1972, pp.91–6) calls this the *because motive*, an explanation of action that can be found *objectively* in the person's life history and social circumstances. In contrast to this, however, he calls for the sociologist to consider *in-order-to motives* (Schutz 1972, pp.86–91; and in Wagner, 1970, pp.125–9). These are the subjective intentions, the future goals that motivate human action. The only way of finding out what a person intends is by asking the person himself. Straight answers are notoriously difficult to get but imputing motives to others can be most inaccurate. Yet if we ignore what motivates people to act in certain ways we lose much of the strength of explanation. That would force us back to explanations entirely in terms of 'because motives', as though people were just puppets pushed by situations and their past socialization to act in certain ways. That is, of course, why at law, 'motive' is always important in deciding guilt. It is assumed that a rational human being is conscious of why he acts, that is, 'before we carry it out, we have a picture in our mind of what we are going to do' (Schutz, in Wagner, 1970, p.129).

The problem is that those pictures of what is desirable, the goals we have in mind before we act, are not simply personal ones. They, too, are socially produced. Values are transmitted by society through its institutions, social norms and the social status accorded to certain groups and roles. We acquire values through our socialization in the family, the school, our work roles and via the other media of communication to which our society exposes us. So there will be *patterns* in our values, there will be a social distribution of in-order-to motives that will predispose us to act in certain ways.

We shall attempt to show how this structuring of cultural values takes place. In Australia, the family is still such an important institution that it forms the focus of most of our central values. Our self-image (our sense of who we are, of self-respect, of what we shall call *the competent self*) develops first in the family. If our experience in the family shows us to be members of a competent, respected, successful group with some status in society, then we are likely to approach life confident that our in-order-to motives can be achieved. On the other hand, if our parents are poor, of low status and exercise little control in the wider scheme of things, our horizons will be limited, our self-image will be less confident, our scope for initiative more constrained.

Such social messages come from our contacts with important social institutions. Where work status is low and the family income restricted; where the schools treat us with lack of respect and our own job future is unfulfilling; where our chance to exercise political control is confined to an occasional vote; and our lowly place in the social order is constantly reinforced by the media, we are unlikely to have many grandiose in-order-to motives. Our projected futures and our projected future selves will inhibit our options for acting *on* the world, as opposed to merely acting *in* it.

It is our contention that the worlds of home, school and work are closely intertwined. They reinforce and reproduce the dominant relations that exist in Australian social structure. Schooling seems to encourage an extremely limited range of abilities and to define competence as academic 'brightness'. Those who do not meet this 'norm' are 'cooled out' via competitive tests and are steered into a confined set of motives that aim at minimum levels of competence in literacy and numeracy (Martin and Meade, 1979, p.4). For only a few is brightness transformed into accreditation for the job market. Worse, however, the schools fail to help children understand the social structure and how Australian institutions operate. Group cooperation is discouraged and individuals are isolated and blamed for their own incompetence.

It follows that the occupations most people enter are likely to reinforce feelings of inferiority. As we shall see in Chapter 9, bureaucracy with its hierarchy of authority denies initiative, restricts control and channels competence in limited directions. That may be at the back of much industrial unrest. Management theories, personnel advisers, time and motion studies and so on cannot remove resistance to what may be an exploitative situation. This will explain the apparent contradiction between industrial unrest, go-slow or do-the-minimum techniques, and expressions of 'job satisfaction'.

Australia's wage levels are such that most workers are 'satisfied' and can 'use' their jobs for other, private, ends. This does not mean that all people enjoy their work. The strength of private, family-based, in-order-to motives for working, may direct attention away from that discontent and its structural causes. People continue to demand higher wages precisely because their private ends motivate their actions more than the jobs themselves, especially when economic forces or political policies threaten the viability of such extrinsic satisfactions.

If the education system fails to expose how such aspects of social relations are interconnected it may mean that people are prevented from articulating their felt unease.

This inability to articulate and thus act on what is wrong is not helped by the mass media. Representing the same commercial interests that structure much of the world of work, the media interpret Australian cultural values for the masses. Selective use of information, repetition of cliches, stereotypes and images that reflect a reality controlled by the few, inhibit the development of an informed and articulate Australian public. The media not only limit our capacity to understand, they limit what becomes a key part of the *social stock of knowledge*. The language and categories of the dominant interest groups pre-structure public debate on economic, political and social issues. Unions are often presented not as protectors of worker rights, but as striking radicals causing economic harm to all. Minority groups may be ignored or shown to be inferior. Unemployment may not be *explained* but discussed in emotive terms such as 'wage demands' and 'dole bludgers'. Political decisions may be made in the light of a media stress on economic issues which downplays other issues such as justice, equity, human rights and the monopoly of power. The question here is not whether there *are* dole bludgers, radicals and freaks but whether the media *explain* why, and whether they ever portray such groups in a less than negative light. The media, more than politicians, set the agenda for public understanding of public issues.

The argument put forward by David Kemp (1978) that Australians vote less and less along class lines because of increasing affluence and common values ignores the homogenization of values purveyed by our newspapers, radio and television outlets. It also selectively uses figures to make his conclusion a sort of self-fulfilling prophecy. Kemp's statement that manual workers' support for Labor had fallen from 74 per cent in 1946 to 58 per cent in 1975, could be equally well stated as the view that 'over half' the manual workers still support the Labor Party. His figures also show that support for Labor from the non-manual classes had risen from 32 to 38 per cent, and that *the knowledge elite* (Kemp, 1978, ch. 9) are more aware of underlying issues and more questioning of the status quo. They are less disposed to accept authority; more tolerant of 'permissive morality' and political challenges to the law; have less faith in existing institutions and feel big business has too much power in Australia. Kemp suggests that they, too, are disenchanted with the major political parties but are too small a group to challenge them. But he does acknowledge in referring to the educated elite that:

> as probably the most articulate and ideological section of the electorate, its discontents may become the discontents of a wider public, and in the traditional process of political change thereby come to influence the policies of the major parties (Kemp, 1978, p.344).

What needs to be spelt out further are the sociological *conditions* under which group interests can be changed; and how social action is altered by what groups see to be relevant to their purposes. The 'apathy' of the Australian public may not be the reason for lack of involvement. The structured absence of opportunities for the public to hear and explore alternate versions of reality may simply preclude more widespread activity. The very fact that large groups do protest and do espouse alternate views suggests that apathy, despite the effects of home, school, work and the media, is less enervating than some theorists of alienation or the 'end of ideology' have supposed. Culture reflects social conditions. As they change, the socially conditioned value-structures may no longer work. New meanings can be sought and new institutional arrangements may then emerge.

In the chapters that follow, we look more closely at the structural factors influencing cultural values in Australian society. We shall explore five broad issues involved in the construction, distribution and reproduction of competing cultural 'realities'.

The first is how individuals and groups *develop* a sense of reality, a view of the world, and a share of the social distribution of competence. This will involve studies of socialization, especially the important role of language in the creation of a social self, and comparisons across groups. (Chapter 7: The Family as Socializer)

The second is how socially structured opportunities, the life chances of various groups, affect *what* is available. Our focus here will be on resources, competencies and the relative sense of control groups have over their environment. (Chapter 8: Education as Cultural Reproducer, and Chapter 9: Work and Life Concerns)

The third is processes of *legitimation* via key communication mechanisms, in the home, the school, the media and at work. Problems of distorted communication; the limits set by myths, labels and stereotypes; and the manufacture of news and of reality itself. (Chapter 10: The Mass Media as Legitimators of Order)

The fourth is the effects of cultural life-concerns in *action*. How people behave. Their actual range for *praxis*, for breaking through an alienated failure to link thoughts and actions. Problems of conformity versus efficacy, and anxiety versus confidence need to be examined in the shifting contexts of the family, the school and the workplace, in order to see where one reinforces another or whether some compensate for what is missing elsewhere.

The fifth is how things *change*. Given the weight of socially-produced reality, the structures of inequality and the mechanisms of social reproduction, how do we explain the survival of counter-views, the presence of rebels, activists and individuals who never bow? Is there evidence of institutionalized resistance to change, of 'symbolic violence' in the form of meanings that are imposed 'as legitimate by concealing the power relations which are the basis of its force'? (Bourdieu and Passeron, 1977, p.4). (Chapter 12: Deviance and Social Restructuring)

Such questions are not easy to answer, especially given the limits of sociological research in Australia and elsewhere. Nor should they be taken without some scepticism about the levels of existential anxiety under which men and women suffer. The 'pursuit of loneliness' can become a social pastime, as institutionalized and integrating as anything else. Even change itself can come to be seen as normal, and people learn to cope.

Readings and References

AUDEN, W. H. (1964) *The College Anthology of British and American Verse*, A. Kent, Hieatt, William Park (eds), Allyn & Bacon, Boston.

BAUMAN, Z. (1973) *Culture as Praxis*, Routledge & Kegan Paul, London.

BOURDIEU, P. & J. L. PASSERON, (1977) *Reproduction in Education, Society and Culture*, Sage, London.

BRITTAN, A. (1973) *Meanings and Situations*, Routledge & Kegan Paul, London.

EDGAR, D. E. (1974) 'Reality Construction—Micro Processes and Macro Change', in D. Edgar (ed.), *Social Change in Australia*, Cheshire, Melbourne, pp.669-76.

FLETCHER, C. (1975) *The Person in the Sight of Sociology*, Routledge & Kegan Paul, London.

GERTH, H. & C. WRIGHT MILLS, (1954) *Character and Social Structure*, Routledge & Kegan Paul, London.

HENRY, J. (1963) *Culture Against Man*, Random House, N.Y.

HOLZNER, B. (1968) *Reality Construction in Society*, Schenkman.

ISRAEL, J. (1971) *Alienation: From Marx to Modern Sociology*, Allyn & Bacon, Boston.

KEMP, D. (1978) *Society and Electoral Behaviour in Australia: a Study of Three Decades*, University of Queensland Press, Brisbane.

LEFEBVRE, H. (1969) *The Sociology of Marx*, Vintage Books, N.Y.

McLELLAN, D. (1970) *Marx Before Marxism*, Penguin Books, U.K.

MARTIN, J. I. & P. MEADE, (1979) *The Educational Experience of Sydney High School Students*, Report No. 1, AGPS, Canberra.

OLLMAN, B. (1971) *Alienation: Marx's Conception of Man in Capitalist Society*, Cambridge University Press, Cambridge.

REX, J. (1974) 'Social Structure and Humanistic Sociology: The Legacy of the Classical European Tradition', in J. Rex, (ed.), *Approaches to Sociology*, Routledge & Kegan Paul, London, pp.187-204.

SCHUTZ, A. (1972) *The Phenomenology of the Social World*, Heinemann Educational, London.

SCHUTZ, A. & T. LUCKMANN, (1974) *The Structures of the Life World*, Heinemann Educational, London.

SUMNER, W. G. (1960 [1906]) *Folkways*, (3rd ed.) Ginn, Boston.

THOMAS, W. I. (1928) *The Child in America*, Knopf, N.Y.

WAGNER, H. R. (1970) *Alfred Schutz on Phenomenology, and Social Relations*, University of Chicago Press, Chicago.

Chapter 7

The Family as Socializer

7

As we saw in Chapters 4 and 5, the social structure of the family varies enormously from place to place and time to time, and sets limits to our life chances. Being born into a large extended family may expose us to a wider variety of social roles from which we can learn, but it may also restrict the resources of money, time and parental attention available for us to share. On the other hand, if we have only one or two siblings to rival our demand for parental care our relationships will be very different. Consequently, the ways in which we view the world will also be different.

So we cannot speak of *the family* as if it were a unitary thing. We must instead discover which factors are common to all families and which ones vary, and whether they produce different effects in behaviour. And we cannot accept that biological theories of child development explain social behaviour. Doubtless the human brain grows and cognitive powers develop in a biologically age-related way and we must take such developmental stages into account. But sociology aims to explain how *social* structures and processes relate to human behaviour, how social patterns are produced and reproduced, changed or violated, and how the individual relates socially to others. Thus we shall be interested in the *self* as a *social* entity rather than as a psychological one.

Socialization

We use the term *socialization* to describe how a new-born baby becomes a person, a unique self; how it becomes a social human being like others; how a society transmits its culture, its life concerns and the rules and practices of social groups. As individuals we like to think that we are unique, and so we are, but human beings would have no self, no sense of identity, without other people. It is through *interaction* with others that we learn to separate the self from other objects, to name other objects, to use language and other symbols that give meaning to life. Without others and their socially-developed symbol systems we would have no meanings by which to interpret action, no way of learning who we are or what we can be.

Human behaviour is not instinctive, it is learned. Identity, the social self, is learned, not inborn. You may be born female, but you learn to be 'a girl'. The genetic accident of skin colour is of slight significance compared with the social labels that become attached to it. But even derogatory terms such as 'Abbo', 'boong' or 'nigger' can be reinterpreted and changed. In the United States of America in the 1960s a new and proud self for 'black' people was asserted by the 'Black is beautiful' campaign.

This example also suggests that the self is always changing, that socialization is continuous through life, not just something that occurs in childhood. As our relationships change and we enter new social groups we learn new rules and behaviour. Schools and our relative success suggest whether we are 'academic' or 'good with our hands' or 'just plain dumb'. The jobs we enter likewise alter what we learn to do, with whom we interact, the rules that apply and how we regard others and ourselves. Even entering hospital requires us to learn new rules and new behaviour that attach to the 'sick role', or dying 'properly'. Thus socialization means learning to be a member of society and its varied social groups; acquiring a culture and its sub-cultures.

In Chapter 8 we shall look at the impact of formal education on socialization and in Chapter 9 we shall look at work as a crucial factor in adult (*secondary*) socialization. Here we are concerned with *primary* socialization as it occurs within the family. In many of our relations with others we learn new roles and values but the relationship is *secondary* because it is less intimate, less continuous and less important. In the family our relationships are *primary* because they are intimate, face to face, enduring and informal. We learn to be 'ourselves' in our primary groups. While play groups, peer groups, cliques and gangs are primary groups in this sense, the family is the most important of all.

Despite recurring fears that the family is dying, losing its functions and not socializing children properly, it is still the most basic institution for human socialization. Our first experience of social *others* takes place here; our first social *bonds* form here; our first experience of *roles* as patterns of expected behaviour is here; our early feelings of *power* and *authority* (in the shape of parental rights to control us) develop in the family. The structural location of our family in the wider society and the structure of relationships within the family will affect what we learn, how we learn and what sorts of persons we become. Because our class, status, religion and ethnic groups differ so much we should expect to see vast differences in the ways families socialize their young. Yet this should not blind us to the fact that such differences also reflect power differences of groups within the wider social structure. (See Chapters 3, 4 and 6.) It is in that sense that the family remains a chief mechanism for the 'reproduction' of existing power relations in society and the *social distribution of competence*.

Socialization processes tell us what is valued in a society or group, and what cultural norms, ideas and attitudes are seen as desirable. The culture is transmitted and reproduced through the lessons learned in the family, at school, at work and in everyday interaction with others.

Had you been born a boy in a Sioux Indian tribe no effort would have been spared to turn you into an aggressive, fearless, competitive, showy and independent man. But the Hopi Indians would see this as the opposite of all that a good man should be. Their arid, restricted land required a tightly-knit community. The boys were taught (as were girls) to fit in, cooperate, to be interdependent, non-assertive and non-individualistic. In the Israeli kibbutz, friendship comes first and competition second. The individual is taught to see himself to be less important than the social group. Our media-produced 'Ocker' image teaches boys to be rough, tough, pie-and-sauce eating, beer-swilling morons. Being nasty to girls is accepted; crying is not. But having a whinge seems good preparation for the adult male with 'a chip on both shoulders'. Just how 'real' this image is, of course, is a matter for research, but that the image exists and strikes a responsive chord tells us something about what to look for in Australian family socialization.

At birth, we have no culture and no words to express thought. All we experience are sense impressions: the frightening world of looming shapes, door bells, hard floors that come up to hurt our heads, and the nicer world of warm milk, soft blankets and gentle voices. Mother is not a person but a sort of benevolent monster who brings things to eat, pulls out nappy pins and comes on the run when we cry. This last suggests that children are not passive. Babies take a demanding, egocentric view of the world as something to be manipulated and controlled. So we should not think of socialization as a passive process. If we believe society to be structured around differences of power and inequalities arising from our exchanges of physical and intellectual resources with others, we can view the family as the first battleground of exchange. Socialization is an interactive process where others and the self negotiate over matters of control.

The family, in this light, is a central arena of conflict over power between the sexes, between young and old, and between siblings of roughly equal status. Parents have obvious resources such as age, education, money, physical size and greater know-how. Such resources give parents a clear advantage in negotiating control with their children. Parents differ, however, in how they *use* those resources, with the result that children grow up accepting parental values and parental control differently and with widely differing views of themselves and their own competence in coping with life.

The Competent Self

It is through communication that parental resources are translated into tools for individual action. The self emerges on the basis of what is communicated by *significant others*. Through symbols the human animal can socialize its young and transmit an entire cultural heritage. We can point or use signs (for example, by learning to associate two things like dark clouds and rain), but *symbols* must be *invented*. They do not exist in nature. They are learned through culture and our interactions with others. Language then (words, meanings and symbols) is at the heart of socialization. It is through *symbolic interaction* that we learn the meanings by which we can communicate and act socially and meaningfully with others.

Because symbols are invented, they differ from group to group and from culture to culture. As a stranger in a new land, we can only learn what the symbols in use mean by associating with others who know what the meanings are. A cross may symbolize Christianity, Nazism, a geometric form or medical help. Illness may be attributed to bacteria or to having offended the gods. Rubbing one's nose may mean an itch, an insult, or affection. Musical notes or mathematical symbols must be learned, as must every form of language. Meaning is necessarily social, based on agreement for purposes of common usage. Yet this too is power-based. Burning a flag may stimulate united passions of patriotism, but burning a bra will provoke more varied responses.

There is always a dominant or 'credentialled' version of the world. The extent to which our family of origin shares that version will affect our socialization into the dominant culture or some competing sub-cultural world-view. As Pollner (1975) suggests, while most of what we learn comes to be taken-for-granted, there is always a *choice* about which of several competing versions of experience will be credentialled as 'the correct' version of the world. William James long ago suggested that 'any object which remains uncontradicted is *ipso facto* believed and posited as absolute reality' (in Pollner, 1975). When we choose to act on one version or another (this is good/bad, right/ wrong, correct/incorrect, etc.) we engage in the 'politics of experience' and each set of competing symbols (the doctor's, the lawyer's, the psychoanalyst's, the priest's, the sociologist's, the mother's or father's versions of reality) tries to assert its superior competence in handling the world (Laing, 1974).

The family into which we are born affects our self-identification as one of the ignorant or knowledgeable, competent or incompetent, powerful or powerless people in the structure of things. That is, our family determines what share we shall have in the *social distribution of competence*.

It is in this sense that we can view the socialization of children in terms of competence and the extent to which different groups of children find their 'share' more or less limited. Competence in this usage refers not only to doing things well or as expected by others. For it involves the development of what Brewster-Smith (1968) calls *the competent self*, a view of oneself as being effective, able to control one's own life and make one's own way in it, as opposed to feeling ineffectual, powerless, controlled by others and having to conform to rules one has no chance of changing.

Two Views of Competence

Robert W. White (1959) spoke of 'Competence as a Basic Concept in the Growth of Personality' and Alex Inkeles (1966) presented 'A Note on Social Structure and the Socialization of Competence'. Their views take the two extremes in defining competence.

White stressed the active, spontaneous nature of the child's intrinsic motivation towards competence. Based on research by Harlow, Berlyne, Myers and others and arguing against the then orthodox theories of motivation, White held that every child, from infancy, experiences pleasure when it acts effectively on its environment. When the mother responds to a baby's crying, when the baby's hand gestures succeed in indicating what the baby wants or when a spoken word like 'No' alters a parent's behaviour, the child experiences *control*, i.e. a sense of efficacy which becomes the basis for an *intrinsic* motivation towards competence. Earlier theories had argued that motivations depended on external forces, either satisfying physiological drives such as hunger, or through socially approved ways of achieving a sense of competence. White did not want to rule out the importance of social approval and disapproval in setting the standards by which a child was judged and felt competent, but his work suggests that children feel the greatest sense of efficacy when they achieve goals set by themselves, perhaps especially when others have opposed or discounted them.

The implications of such a notion of competence motivation or 'effectance motivation' as White (1959) called it elsewhere are clear. Parents and teachers should encourage children to set and solve their own problems instead of providing ready-made solutions, so that *intrinsic* motivations deepen as the child experiences effective action. The aim is to develop self-directed behaviour rather than to rely on external incentives such as sweets, money, good grades and social prestige. Clearly such an approach informs much of the child development literature, ranging from Bruner (1956), Piaget (1952) and Kohlberg (1964) to the polemics about schooling of A. S. Neill (1962) or Ivan Illich (1971).

Against this view Inkeles (1969) argued that society, teachers and parents (the socializers) pre-define what forms of competence the child will develop. This differs across societies and across groups within societies, but there will be a common set of qualities that are necessary for survival in a particular society. But these qualities are not distributed evenly among social classes, ethnic groups or individuals because some families provide information, language skills, physical, financial and social resources denied to others. The problem for research then is to account for differences in the process, content and outcomes of socialization.

Inkeles, though, does not stress only the socially-defined forms of competence. While he argues that 'the objective of socialization is to produce competent people, as competence is defined in any given society' (Inkeles, 1969, p.265), he also builds in the child's capacity to actively choose new goals, new roles to aim for. He defines competence in general as:

> the ability to attain and perform in three sets of statuses; those which one's society will normally assign one, those in the repertoire of one's social system one may appropriately aspire to, and those which one may reasonably invent or elaborate for oneself (Inkeles, 1969, p.265).

He points out that people may have aptitudes or abilities but if these are not socially or legally valued they will not be seen as relevant competences. Skills are specially trained forms of aptitude, and some aptitudes are developed as skills at the expense of others. Obvious examples spring to mind, but the social consequences may be less obvious if we do not consider why some are valued and fostered more than others in the first place. Australian Aborigines were highly skilled, showed superb intelligence in surviving and adapting to a hostile environment, and had complex symbolic systems. But these competences were ignored by European settlers and are still not valued by most Australians. Minority groups (such as Black Americans or migrant Australians) have often been regarded and defined as incompetent to exercise citizenship rights and manage their own affairs. In our schools certain forms of competence are seen as desirable and others less so, resulting in a refusal to develop certain aptitudes and a verdict of failure on those who do not succeed academically.

These two broad aspects of competence are not, of course, unrelated. The sense of competence that arises from being effective on one's own initiative and the social judgements of others may be seen as two sides of the gradual emergence of self-confidence, self-esteem, and a shared self-concept. And they represent two sides of the reality-testing process everyone faces every day.

Different people have different notions of what is real, and a differing order of priorities about what is important in that reality. If I believe in God, that is real in its effects on my attitudes and actions (depending upon how important that belief is) in ordering my priorities. For a primitive tribe, evil spirits are real but disease-causing bacteria are not. For some, the moon is a magic symbol; for others it is a scientifically defined part of the physical universe. Santa Claus is real for children but 'dies' before adolescence. Democracy in the capitalist West means voting, choosing one's job, being free to read newspapers; in other societies it means working towards a common social goal under the guidance of 'the Party'. In Australia many of the affluent refuse to believe that people in other suburbs are starving or living in abject poverty. The 'reality' of statistics, surveys and poverty reports is denied within their system of relevance. Those in working-class suburbs may never see the reality of tree-lined streets and huge homes set in spacious grounds. So while we all know people are different, there are many 'realities' we do not share and do not even know exist.

The point is that our views of reality are constructed out of our past and present experiences. The objects we see from birth and the meanings that are attached to them, their relative importance to our lives and the lives of those around us build into a view of the world that in turn affects the way we interpret each new experience.

We know that in early life the baby is merely reactive, surrounded by non-meaningful sights, sounds and movements. As the stimuli change the baby reveals an *orienting response* of arousal and tension which then reduces (Hunt, 1965). As the stimuli are repeated and become familiar the child begins to recognize objects in its surroundings. This is the beginning of the child's active 'intentional' behaviour, for it tries constantly to match up new experiences and inputs with the mental images or inner standards acquired through previous experience. When things are matched, the child smiles. Every parent knows the smile of recognition, the joy when a child sees the things now known. Once familiar with the objects around, to the point where they do not arouse tension, the child seeks new stimuli. It is here that the importance of exploration and play can be seen and also the importance of the range and type of stimuli available to children in different socialization settings. In particular the role of language is vital in the way it allows children to identify, separate, objectify and symbolize one thing from another.

Piaget describes the stages through which this gradual process of the child's exploring its environment and learning to handle, manipulate, differentiate and understand passes (Edgar, 1973). From a sensori-motor stage in which the child constructs the basic patterns of objects and actions; through the pre-operational stage which marks the beginning of the use of language and symbolic capacities; to the stage of intuitive thought where the child is able to internalize actions into thoughts and group objects into classes—the child's capacity for understanding and mastering the environment gradually grows. If certain skills or understandings are not developed, we know that child will suffer disabilities in other areas of life.

It is here that the social distribution of competence becomes vital. Because each child is born into a different family, class, race or ethnic group, each with its own varied resources (shelter, food, clothing, money, parental education, know-how, value systems, etc), it is obvious that life chances will vary. The child whose parents have everything to offer (and who have the intellectual and emotional capacity to offer it constructively) is clearly going to develop differently from one whose parents are poor, or sick, or ignorant or vicious. The child who is allowed to play, to explore, to fantasize, without anxious parents over-protecting, restricting or worrying about such play being 'sissy' or 'mannish' or 'unreal and over-exciting' will learn more about himself or herself and about other people than the child who is coddled and constrained. Again, if the child meets, through parental contacts or discussion, a wide variety of people with differing personalities, capacities, roles, ideas and values, there will be a wider 'reality' against which that child can test himself or herself.

We can put this another way, and suggest that the child who is exposed to people who possess 'the right' skills in our society (good speech, pleasant manners, professional or managerial training, etc.), will learn more easily to present himself in a 'legitimate' way that meets the approval of the more powerful groups in society. As we shall see later, the school is a key legitimator of the social order and through its 'pedagogic work' (Bourdieu and Passeron, 1977) on children does 'symbolic violence' to those who have not developed in the socially defined 'correct' ways.

So in studying the socialization of children we must examine the social conditions that give rise to alternate world views. *Which* children grow up to conform and what conditions in the society make certain types of competence more useful in negotiating a successful place in society than others? For example, while we may praise imagination, high spirits, free-thinking, or gumption in young people, how many of that type actually rise to 'the top' in business or academia? If the reward system praises diligence; patient, plodding hard-work; accepting learning and regurgitating what is taught; being quietly pleasant rather than noisily aggressive and so on, the stolid hack is more likely to succeed than the budding genius. Organizations demand obedience, deference, decorum, punctuality and completion of tasks, so perhaps only those who conform to such demands will get promotion. Academic work requires students to be prepared to defer to 'experts'; to work long hours; to subject themselves to constant evaluation by superiors often expounding ideals of free speech and rational discourse but applying their own prejudices and jealousies in the same manner as other human beings. So perhaps only the intelligent 'good boys' can make it in the academic marketplace where there is room for only a few truly independent thinkers. The same could apply in other less pleasant settings. The delinquent sentenced to a youth prison may have to conform both to his peers and the officers. What skills, what forms of competence will serve best in that situation? Very likely, the capacity to get on with other people, interpersonal competence, will be more important than academic or practical skills, but we would need to look closely at how interpersonal skills were used in relation to the two different groups, peers and jailers. The 'front' that is presented may contrast strongly in the two situations, but the ability to present a front is needed in both.

Certain forms of competence will help one to conform, more or less successfully, to different types of social demand. What should be stressed is that each society is structured round the interests of competing groups which have differential access to the resources most relevant to serving their interests. If, as we have argued earlier in this chapter, the most basic motivation of all is to be in control of our own environment, then the skills and capacities, the resources needed to control that environment are the key to serving our interests. I may want to be a doctor or a shop owner, but if I have no access to the necessary resources (both physical and human) my interests will not be achieved. If the society dictates that to be successful I must command complex language skills, understand the mathematics of economic power and possess certain qualities of personality and character, then my chances are limited according to my access to the means of developing those forms of competence. That is why I feel it is more pertinent to speak of the *social distribution of competence* than the *social distribution of knowledge* (Berger and Luckmann, 1966). For knowledge is the universal set which may be regarded as both neutral and pluralistic, as though all knowledge were of equal worth and simply the possession of different groups in different life situations. Knowledge becomes power through its being put to use in the interests of a particular group, through their asserting its value to be greater than other forms of knowledge. Knowledge put to use is the action side of competence, *praxis*, the effecting of ideas in order to control. The main dilemma in life is to control or be controlled, with each of us controlling some areas and being controlled by others in other areas.

Notice that if we speak of competence only in terms of the individual, we miss much of the point. Or rather, we make a point about the nature of competence in capitalist societies. The rhetoric of capitalism stresses free, individual action rather than group action. Much of the vocabulary of educational psychology and sociology echoes the needs of the individual: *developmental tasks, individual differences, self-actualization, the autonomous self, discovery learning, equality of (individual) opportunity, free competition, reward for merit, mastery learning,* etc. What is concealed by such terminology is that the individual is *not* free to act alone in society and that regardless of individual talent or effort some can never succeed because society's rewards are unequally distributed. Moreover it conceals the group interests that lie behind much *apparently* individual action. The public school boy may be neither bright nor work hard, but the upper-class group to which he belongs will guarantee better job opportunities and social status for him than for the talented poor boy struggling along in the State school system.

The competent self emerges only through social interaction with others. Perhaps the most basic tools for development as a competent individual able to act with and upon others are those of language. Our symbolic capacity makes humanness possible. The physical environment is less important in socialization than the meaning environment. Symbols allow us to anticipate the future, deal with things not immediately present, to interpret, plan ahead, think, explain and understand ourselves within the limits of our social context.

The Looking-Glass Self

Charles Horton Cooley (1962 [1902]) used the term *the looking-glass self* to refer to the way others affect our learning of the culture and our place in it. The baby at first understands by associating one event or object with another. A bottle, breast or spoon indicates food, a 'No-No' suggests the likelihood of a smack. Repeated associations develop into symbols when a word can elicit a response even when the object or action referred to is not present. The emotional tone of parental talk gives some idea of the *value* placed on actions by others. The monster who feeds you reacts to your actions. It smiles and cuddles when you allow food into your mouth; it looks sour and yells when you throw the rattle out for the tenth time. At that stage the child's aim to please is not morality, just pragmatism. But the reactions of others show us how we appear to them and help us develop an image of *self* that is truly social because it is shared and based on *accepted* cultural values.

Cooley held there are three components to this process of the looking-glass self. First, we imagine how we appear to other people (as son, daughter, brother, mate, tired, upset, happy, etc.). Then we imagine their judgement of how we look (they like us, are pleased, annoyed, disappointed, indifferent, etc.). Then we react to that judgement (with feelings of pride, shame, confidence or self-doubt). In this way we learn not only to see ourselves as others see us, but also to *value* ourselves in relation to others. The child may begin to slap its own hand, to reprimand itself, to conjure up the words of others as a reminder of the social values and norms of behaviour that would typically apply in such a situation. It is the *typicality* that matters. One battle does not a victory make; repeated instances allow the general rule to emerge, the 'normal' to take shape, the categories to become clear.

The Self as Object

George Herbert Mead (1964 [1934]) describes this process of social development in terms of an increasingly general picture of self in relation to others. Mead saw the person as an acting and thinking agent, not merely as a responding or reacting organism. Self-control and empathy for others was the psychological basis of the social order, for without insight into the feelings of others the person could not participate successfully in social interaction and interpersonal relationships.

The key to the emergence of the self is the capacity of each of us to think of ourselves reflexively, to be an *object* to oneself. Just as we learn to attach meaningful symbols to physical objects (tree, dog, worm, Mum, Dad) so too we learn to think of our self as a separate, unique object. We can then think about our self, evaluate our self, communicate and interact with our self and, above all, *control* our self without recourse to others. Symbolic interaction is therefore not merely conscious, it is self-conscious. Our 'world' consists of the objects which we have built for ourselves from the symbols used by others to interpret the world to us. Those others are called *significant others*. Our parents and family obviously form the most significant of our early others.

Mead (1964 [1934]) showed that the self can only emerge through our ability to 'take the role of the other', to imagine the attitudes and responses of others to our acts. At about the age of two, children begin to use the words 'I', 'me', and 'you'; pronouns that take the place of self and others. In order to win the sorts of responses they want from others, children must be able to guess reactions by putting themselves in the other's position. Mead saw the 'I' as the spontaneous, experiencing, subjective part of self; and the 'me' as that part of the self that judges and reflects upon its actions, i.e., the self as *object*. 'I think she likes me', 'I hate myself', indicate this relationship.

The child's capacity to take the role of another and thus be self-aware, develops through three stages. The stages are not necessarily fixed to certain ages but develop more or less in order of age. They are the *play stage*, the *game stage* and the stage of *generalized other*.

The Play Stage

In the play stage, the child learns about others by playing alternately at various roles. A sort of 'conversation of gestures' goes on as the child plays both father and child, shopkeeper and shopper, dog and master. As yet the self is not an organized unity; it consists of 'the particular attitudes of specific others to himself and toward one another as they participate in specific social acts' (Mead, 1964 [1934]). The child can only see himself or herself as an object of social actions, of how others act towards him or her.

The Game Stage: Society as Drama

It is during this stage that a more organized personality develops and the child becomes aware of his or her power to influence the actions of others. It involves projecting the self into a variety of roles, learning the rules and learning how to play an assigned role in the game. Before you can play football, hockey, baseball or even hopscotch, you must know all the roles that others in the game play; what is expected of you and of them. The child learns then to 'take the role of all the others in the team as an organized unit . . . impersonal, standardized roles defined by norms that do not take individual personalities into account' (Blumer, 1969). This is truly role-taking and rests on the capacity to see the self both as subject and object; to step into a pattern of behaviour that exists quite apart from the subjective self. The essence of social exchange, the negotiation of identity and social control rests in this role-taking capacity. If you cannot observe analytically both yourself and your audience you are at a disadvantage in the construction of social action because you are acted upon rather than acting with the other.

Goffman (1959) sees all social behaviour in terms of 'actors' and 'audiences' who mutually construct a 'performance'. But his 'dramaturgic' perspective does not imply merely a stage drama where each actor learns and acts out the scripts exactly. This happens very rarely in real life because *roles* lay down only very broad expectations for the behaviour of persons holding certain status positions. Goffman sees social life as 'dramatic' in the sense that the self monitors its own performance, and dramatic action is always subject to re-interpretation of any role. We should add that the wider social structure is also 'dramatic' because action is constrained by the fluctuating power of others, by our own interpretation of roles and our ability to step outside roles and perform quite surprisingly counter to expectation.

The value of such a perspective lies in its insight into the individual's relative competence as an acting self. For Mead, role-taking was the key to influencing the actions of others. Goffman (1959) suggests that 'impression management' is a feature of all social interaction. When faced with other people in any situation, we try to get into the *back regions* of their minds (Cicourel, 1964). We apply a *norm of cynicism* to impute motives to others so we can react accordingly. If their performance is convincing we assume they are honest and sincere and we *trust* them (Nisbet, 1970). If it is not, we are on our guard. We may stereotype people, though we may not disclose our imputations about 'people like them' too openly. We 'present' our self by impression management techniques in order to minimize the dangers of self-disclosure and to 'maximize the efficacy and power of our performances' (Cicourel, 1964).

So this brings us to the second broad aspect of competence that must be examined, the *competent self*. For it is true that some people, despite the stereotypes, despite social limits, often even despite their own measured incompetence, do break through. Churchill and Einstein seem to be the favourite examples of people defined as incompetent (at school anyway) whose personal will and drive allowed them to develop new forms of competence that went beyond the normal definitions. Goldman's book *Breakthrough* (1968) describes several such people who became leaders in their fields against all predictive odds. What distinguishes them is a determination not to be put down by others and a capacity to grasp the few ledges on their perilous life space and pull themselves up. In other words they succeeded in exploring and mastering their environment better than most. They proved their own efficacy against extraordinary odds.

But they are merely the most dramatic end of the continuum. At the opposite extreme are the weak, the poor and the oppressed for whom life has never been kind. The life space in which they can be effective or exercise any sort of power or mastery is strictly limited. They are lions neither at home nor abroad. And we cannot accept an explanation of this in terms of personality alone. Personality is developed as we grow and is affected by life situations. Those life situations give people different access to resources, skills, ideas and chances to be effective, happy or sad. One's experience of being effective rather than ineffectual makes all the difference to one's personality and one's capacity to handle new problems in new situations.

This is why Brewster-Smith (1968) argued that the process of child socialization, of growing up, combines both the *equipment for competence* and *the competent self*. Skills, abilities and resources for coping with life are not evenly distributed. From birth there are differences in genetic makeup which give us unequal chances. Then society itself distributes food, clothing, shelter, money, schools, jobs, status and power unequally to different groups of people. Inevitably, then, some children will grow up seeing both their parents and themselves as being competent, as able to cope with most situations they face in life. If they succeed in mastering the side of a cot, they will be less afraid in tackling a ladder or a tree. If they learn to ride a tricycle, the bigger bicycle is less frightening. The more words they master the more control they have over what others do and say to them. If you master early reading skills and pass some simple tests, exams are there later as another potential victory. But experience the reverse, and failure after failure builds into a vicious circle of incompetence which colours the rest of life.

It follows that children who can draw on parents with resources that help master life's situations will develop a sense of self as competent. So we would expect some social class differences in self-esteem and feelings of efficacy or sense of power. But it will not be as simple as that because not all middle-class parents have the same resources and not all working-class children experience absolute powerlessness. Social definitions of competence may have common elements but different groups and classes will value other types of competence. Not being good at something will not necessarily mean a sense of lower self-worth. However, our starting point is to look at how children from different social groups see themselves and the forms of competence they have already developed or feel they lack, and then to examine the possible explanations for group differences.

The extent to which our early role-playing and role-taking experiences expose us to a wide variety of action skills and develop in us the ability to interpret the motives and intentions of others, will affect our competence in later life. The competent self that emerges will depend upon our symbolic capacity (which largely depends upon language) and the range of roles that are available to us. It will depend on our learning the skills of interpretation, presentation of self and impression-management, and the degree of cynicism with which we handle social situations. In short, our structural location in society (see Part 1, Introduction and Chapter 3) determines our chances of sharing the necessary *equipment for competence* that constructs our individual sense of *the competent self*.

Children are taught, through the family, then at school, the rules seen as most appropriate to the behaviour of each status group. If they fail to adhere to the basic ground rules they are in no position 'to negotiate successfully the hazards of living' (Cicourel, 1964). Implicit in this is the notion of power. 'Playing the game', 'It's not cricket', 'Going too far', 'Law and order' are all slogans that suggest the rules of a game in which some are winners and others losers. The child learns not only the rules appropriate to self and family, but also the rules that apply to the expected behaviour of superiors and inferiors. Thus Mead's *game stage* is more than just an innocent taking of roles. It is the stage at which we learn to establish and maintain our advantages at the expense of others.

The Generalized Other

Mead suggests the third stage of the development of a social self is that of *the generalized other*. During the game stage the roles and attitudes of others become more generalized and less dependent upon particular persons. Instead of '*Mother says* it's right', we now decide '*It* is right'. Sanctions, rewards and punishments for acting according to expectations, become more inclusive. Mead saw the generalized other as a stage of self-control, what is loosely called a person's 'character', acting on a set of principles, consistently applying social

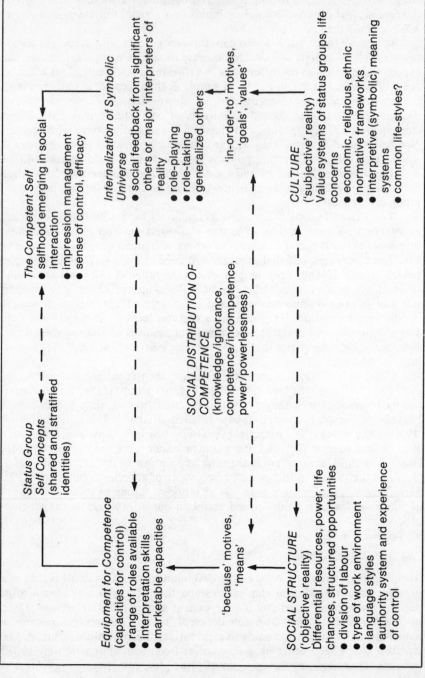

Figure 7–1   Socialization and the development of competence

The Competent Self
● selfhood emerging in social interaction
● impression management
● sense of control, efficacy

Internalization of Symbolic Universe
● social feedback from significant others or major 'interpreters' of reality
● role-playing
● role-taking
● generalized others

'in-order-to' motives, 'goals', 'values'

CULTURE
('subjective' reality)
Value systems of status groups, life concerns
● economic, religious, ethnic
● normative frameworks
● interpretive (symbolic) meaning systems
● common life-styles?

Status Group Self Concepts
(shared and stratified identities)

SOCIAL DISTRIBUTION OF COMPETENCE
(knowledge/ignorance, competence/incompetence, power/powerlessness)

Equipment for Competence
(capacities for control)
● range of roles available
● interpretation skills
● marketable capacities

'because' motives, 'means'

SOCIAL STRUCTURE
('objective' reality)
Differential resources, power, life chances, structured opportunities
● division of labour
● type of work environment
● language styles
● authority system and experience of control

standards of moral behaviour. It is through the generalized other that the community exerts control over the person without coercion; its standards have become internalized and accepted norms are applied whenever a situation prompts a 'typical' response where 'typical' or 'normal' or 'general' rules obviously apply.

Implicit in this rather vague notion is a more specific set of questions. Whose rules apply? In what situations? Which groups learn to internalize them? Who sees the rules to be generalized or typical? In whose interests do the norms operate? To whom and under what conditions are they *not* seen as general, normative, acceptable, legitimate? For the 'official' forms of role-taking, the appropriate general symbols of social recognition (proper dress, manners, deference patterns, etc.) are always set within a context of *competing* 'unofficial' definitions which are negotiated in interaction (Cicourel, 1964). General rules are only typical, not universal, and are always subject to challenge.

What emerges from our discussion of the self as a social object, then, is more than an individual, psychological concept. Since self-appraisal is largely derived from reflected appraisals, it is likely that self-images of the competent self will reflect *socially organized appraisals*. Self-views will be shared group views—identities embedded in life chances that are produced within the social structure and purveyed, maintained and reproduced by the valuations of culture. Kurt Lewin and others wrote about self-hatred among Jews. The 'Black is Beautiful' campaign reorganized the appraisal of racial identity. Where peer groups value social and sporting leadership over academic competence the most talented students drop their grade performances (Coleman, 1961). In Japan the chonin merchants were despised and the samurai soldiers praised but American and other capitalist societies value business acumen and success. In Chapter 9 we shall see how closely our work structures our sense of identity; our capacity to cope with the world. Now we will examine some of the evidence for the foundations of group identity and power in the socialization patterns of the family.

Social Class and Child-Rearing Differences

Researchers have long tried to explore family differences in child-rearing techniques. But their methodology has suffered from the theoretical assumption that 'social class' will explain differences between families, without considering the specific conditions or factors associated with social class which might alter family socialization of children.

For example, in 1948 Davis and Havighurst found a sample of Chicago middle-class parents were earlier in their weaning, spoon feeding and toilet training of children. They also found stricter father-child relationships, firmer discipline, higher educational and occupational expectations and greater demands for the child to assume responsibility. Race made no difference since middle-class whites and blacks were more alike than middle-class blacks and working-class blacks. They concluded that social class differences in child-rearing practices explained the greater achievement levels and success orientations of middle-class children. Working-class parents were more lax, so their children developed the 'wrong' attitudes for success in American society.

But the contention that there were such clear-cut 'class differences' in child-rearing was challenged. Critics pointed out that Davis and Havighurst's sample was based on only one city and that their method of interviewing parents gave data that did not reliably reflect actual parent behaviour. So in 1955 Havighurst and Davis revised their original data and agreed that they should not have tried to generalize to an entire social class. Middle-class parents in Boston were apparently later in their feeding and weaning practices than middle-class parents in Chicago. Moreover, they made the 'remarkable' discovery that the cultural differences they found between class groups (actually occupational groups) may have been due to religion, race and region. The broader culture had also changed because child-rearing practices were often based on manuals written for parents and 'desirable' practices had altered over time. (Even a Dr Spock can become outdated as wider cultural values change. Notice Spock's scramble in the 1970s to revamp his book so it contained no sexist references to what was 'good' for boys but not for girls.) In a society where children are given pride of place and education standards are rising, even the 'working class' might read and apply standards previously thought to be the preserve of the middle class. In sum, other factors needed to be looked at besides 'social class'.

In 1957 Sears, Maccoby and Levin conducted a very large-scale study of socialization processes in a representative sample of mothers of five-year-old children. The study reversed the Davis-Havighurst findings about social class differences. Working-class mothers were 'rejecting' rather than 'permissive', leaving the child alone or pushing it out of the way. They were also more severe with early toilet training, sexual behaviour, and in pressing for independent action and success. Middle-class mothers were found to permit more aggression, impose fewer restrictions and demands, and to use physical punishment and deprivation of privileges less in disciplining children than did the working-class mothers. What was to be made of this? It shattered the notion that working-class parents failed to socialize their children into 'acceptable' standards of behaviour: an explanation for their lower success rates and 'undesirable' traits in later life had to be found elsewhere.

The Sears *et al* study suffered from some methodological oversights. It failed to control for the mother's education level. Education is a factor strongly correlated with social class but it may have an independent effect on how mothers handle their children. The exhaustive interview data also ignored the role of the father and the impact of the family group considered as a whole. The sexist notion that only mothers are important in early childhood affected both the design of the study and the analysis of its findings. The study did, however, isolate several significant factors in the mother's reactions to the child. Permissiveness versus restrictiveness; aggressiveness versus punitiveness; warmth versus coldness—all seemed to relate to how children actually behaved.

In the same year (1957) Littman, Moore and Pierce-Jones replicated the Sears study, taking a sample in Oregon. They found no social class differences at all in feeding and weaning age, toilet training, aggressive treatment and so on. The only aspect that seemed the same across the three studies was that middle-class father-child relationships were better (though interaction was no more frequent) than for the working class. Littman *et al* concluded that while social class may be important for determining economic behaviour, it is not for parental socialization practices.

Amidst the mass of research on social class differences in family styles of child-rearing, the work of Melvin Kohn stands out for its theoretical and methodological superiority. Kohn studied the specific conditions that seemed to give rise to class variations in parental values. His 1959 study of 200 working-class and 200 middle-class mothers asked what values they would like to see embodied in their children's behaviour. He found they all wanted honesty, happiness, obedience, consideration and dependability, but the relative importance of each varied with the social status of the mother. For working-class mothers, happiness was less desirable for boys than being good students, ambitious and obedient. Girls should be neat, mannerly, clean and obedient. Middle-class mothers placed a higher value on consideration, self-control and curiosity. Beyond these differences, Kohn located considerable variations *within* social classes; the higher strata in both middle and working classes valuing curiosity, the lower strata valuing cleanliness, neatness and honesty.

Kohn's most significant finding was that middle-class parents, wanting to develop self-control in their children, based punishment on the child's intentions rather than on notions of respectability and obedience. Kohn and Carroll (1959) followed this up in a new study in which both parents and their children (400) were interviewed. The study repeated their previous finding about values and discipline. Middle-class parents punished on the basis of the child's intent, valuing the child's development of internalized standards. Working-class parents punished on the basis of the immediate consequences of the child's action, valuing qualities that ensure respectability. Further research in the United States and Italy consistently found a higher valuation of self-direction by middle-class parents and of conformity to externally imposed rules by the working class.

By 1969 Kohn and Schooler had managed to suggest several of the specific conditions associated with class that explain more closely its relation to socialization values. Their index of class was multi-dimensional, based on education and occupational levels. They defined values as 'standards of desirability, criteria of preference'. And they tested the hypothesis that it was the father's experience of 'occupational self-direction—that is, using initiative, thought and independent judgement in work' that explains class differences in values and orientation. Their findings are important because they show how close are the links between the institutions of family and work. They found present class position mattered more for values than did class origins, suggesting that one's present situation and one's current experiences of control can outweigh the effects of early childhood. This is crucial because it reminds us of the active, on-going and negotiable nature of all socialization processes. It saves us from Freudian fixations on childhood effects and from structural fixations on *social facts*.

What overrides 'social class' in Kohn's study is the father's experience of autonomy or self-direction at work. The higher his class position, the more he values personal and job characteristics indicative of self-direction. These include an interest in how and why things happen; good sense and sound judgement; responsibility; self-reliance; and ability to do well under pressure. Whereas working-class men value extrinsic job rewards (pay, fringe benefits, co-workers, hours of work and job-security), the middle-class value intrinsic rewards such as the job's interest level, amount of freedom and the chance to use personal abilities.

Perceptions of social reality and self-image are also related to social class. The working-class male is more authoritarian, conformist and opportunistic. He is also less open-minded, less responsible, less trustful of others and less receptive to innovation and change. But it appears that the cause is not simply social class (as measured by occupation and education levels). Rather it is specific job conditions which rub off on men and are communicated through socialization to their children.

When men are closely supervised at work, they value conformity for their children, stress extrinsic benefits, are distrustful, resist change, and lack self-confidence. Men doing complex work with people or data, value self-direction. Men working with things have conformist values and orientations. Where work allows a variety of approaches and work is more complex, men value self-direction for children, are tolerant of non-conformity and are more open-minded.

Thus Kohn and Schooler conclude that, while education may be the key to providing the intellectual flexibility and breadth of perspective that are essential for self-directed values, the social structure (in the form of occupational position and the nature of work) has pronounced and consistent effects on values.

> Self-direction is a central value for men of higher class position who see themselves as competent members of an essentially benign society. Conformity is a central value for men of lower social class position who see themselves as less competent members of an essentially indifferent or threatening society . . . these relationships . . . are substantially attributable to class-correlated variations in the degree to which jobs allow and require self-direction (Kohn and Schooler, 1969, p.675).

I have dwelt at some length on this research because we have some comparable Australian data.

In 1954 Oeser and Hammond conducted two studies, one in Melbourne, the other in a Mallee community in rural Victoria. At that time there seemed to be a high level of authoritarianism, especially in the handling of boys. In disciplining pre-school children, mothers used smacking (79 per cent), reasoning (52 per cent), scolding (17 per cent), isolating (14 per cent) and ignoring (10 per cent). Boys were taught 'functional adequacy', while girls were taught 'orderliness, attractiveness and cleanliness'. In Melbourne the study showed that there were differences according to occupational levels. Parents who were property owners or self-employed praised their children and were relatively unrestrictive, and there was a lower level of rebellion among their children. White-collar parents stressed being 'good' and 'well-mannered', with clear sex differences. Skilled workers' families were closely knit and valued 'conformity of character' more than of behaviour. The children of semi-skilled fathers were expected to cope with 'the day-to-day problems of the present', and not to worry about future success.

Katz's study in 1964 showed that middle-class Australian children defined success in status terms while working-class children reflected the extrinsic values of their parents who valued material rewards.

While Adler's 1965 study of authority patterns in the Australian family suggested a sort of 'matriduxy' where wives exercised dominant control and emotional authority over children, Fallding's 1954−5 (published in 1957) research revealed that in both tradesmen's and professionals' families the father exercised 'rightful patriarchy', controlling the family budget and all important decision-making. Only in a minority of families did 'partnership' exist where according to relative competence, husbands and wives left certain areas to one another. Bell's 1975 study of women's roles saw the husband to be of more help in looking after children and assisting with other family tasks where the wife was working, but Cass is correct in pointing out that this reflects the class nature of these women's opportunities (Davies, Encel and Berry, 1977).

Krupinski (1974) claims from his review of the literature (and Connell's 1975 study of Sydney youth supports him) that 'mothers are the focal point of the emotional relationships of family life'. They transmit conventional sex roles, standards of morality and work segregation because the father is so often absent. Yet that very absence reproduces the division of sexual and economic labour through demonstration. Just as feminists have argued it is the quality not the quantity of 'mothering' that counts, so too with the father as a socializing figure.

Edgar (1974 and 1977) conducted a longitudinal study of Victorian adolescents from 1971−76. In this he partially replicated the Kohn−Schooler research on class-related differences in socialization values, and highlighted the centrality of communication patterns within the family. One of the major findings was that girls at every social class level had a lower estimation of their own competence, even when their measured verbal intelligence was superior to boys'. This lower sense of power derived from parental resources and the lower status afforded the female sex. But where parental encouragement and resources permitted, girls could move outside the narrow circle of female incompetence and achieve more.

Beyond this sex difference, however, there were other important differences between occupational groups. Like the Kohn and Schooler study in the United States and Italy, this study also showed differences relating to the father's level of education and to his degree of occupational self-direction. Non-manual fathers liked their children to be interested in how and why things happen, considerate of others and self-controlled and responsible. The manual fathers ranked more highly good manners, being neat and clean, obeying parents and conforming to appropriate sex roles.

But are these values communicated to the children themselves? Are there the same consistent differences between children from different socio-economic groups as there are for fathers? Connell (1974) suggests there are not, but Edgar's data suggest otherwise. In a very broad categorization of socio-economic groups, ranging from 'professional' down to 'unskilled' there were found to be consistent differences in the values expressed by adolescents. The lower socio-economic groups are more conservative, perceive more external limitations on their life chances, blame themselves more, and have a lower sense of power. This does not prove social class differences of course, but it suggests substantial stratification and patterning of crucial value-orientations within this Australian sample.

Family Communication

The explanation for such value differences between social groups lies in the way parents communicate with their children. In all of the early childhood research two factors stand out as significant in how well children accept the values of their parents: the types of control techniques used and the degree of effect or emotional involvement.

		Control	
		High	Low
Affect	High	Strongest socialization effects	Uncertainty
	Low	Uncertainty	Lowest socialization effects

(from Edgar, 1974)

Where parents are strict but show little warmth, or where they are affectionate but exercise lax control, the effect on children is confusion. The best child-rearing technique (if one regards accepting and conforming to parental standards as good) results from parents setting clear limits and insisting on firm controls in a warm and caring way. The child then feels attached, wants to please, has a clear picture of what is permitted and can test the limits of selfhood against those standards. Without limits the tests of self become shadow-boxing and the looking-glass reflects a confused picture of how others see the self.

A study reported by Little and Holmström (in Davies, Encel and Berry, 1977) found the warmth of Australian parents towards their children was linked to children's responses favourable to authority. Whether the father or the family as a whole was demanding seemed to have no effect on attitudes to authority, but, where the mother was demanding, children responded unfavourably to authority.

Little and Holmström used the *semantic differential technique* (having people choose between contrasting word pairs such as trusting-distrustful, warm-cold, etc. to describe their feelings about things) to find responses to authority in a sample of 500 men and women 18 years of age and over in Melbourne. A substantial youth-age difference emerged, with younger people (especially younger women) chafing under authority demands more than the older groups. The study, however, did not consider differences between socio-economic or class groups.

Little and Holmstrom (1977) found women to be more dependent on the family and lower in their sense of potency (i.e. their ability to influence things), especially where the mother was 'boss' of the family. Their findings contradict the Herbst and Adler (1965) view of an Australian 'matriduxy'. Twice as many people in their sample reported that the father was 'the boss' even though the mother might have run things as the 'family executive'. Where a partnership existed the father was seen as warmer but the family was no less demanding than before. The impact of sex-role modelling is also shown in that men whose father had been boss of the family felt most potent under authority (i.e. less threatened, weak or worthless). Bossy mothers seem cold and this produces a sense of weakness in their sons.

Edgar's 1971—76 study of 1214 Victorian adolescents used different techniques, with rather different results. Adolescents were asked directly about their parents' current affection and control, and the fathers and mothers were asked parallel questions in a sub-sample of 100.

As with the previous research, mothers were found to be closer to their children than fathers and they played the leading role in disciplining their children. However these adolescents got on better with their mothers (61 per cent very well) than with their fathers (50 per cent very well), and adolescents (especially girls) expressed a sense of loss in not knowing their fathers more closely. While only 62 per cent saw fathers as being fair, 92 per cent accepted their mothers' treatment as fair, a clear indication of better communication. Note that this finding is in contrast to Little and Holmström's mother-as-'steward' hypothesis (mother acting only by grace of father and thus more likely to provoke hostility) and in contrast to Power's (1970) notion of the mother's function as 'wrist-slapping'.

Edgar's study also revealed occupational group contrasts. Children of professional men accepted their fathers' criticisms, while those of service workers and unskilled men saw them as much less fair. Service worker fathers got along less well than any other group with their teenage children. Daughters of managers got on better with their mothers than their fathers, but the sons of professional, skilled and unskilled workers did not relate as well to their fathers as one might expect. These fathers themselves reported a lack of closeness and more frequent clashes with their sons than with daughters. Businessmen, skilled and unskilled fathers praised less and criticized more than other groups, but it was the children of service workers who reported the greatest lack of communication and who said their parents did not understand 'the sort of person I am'.

In the middle-class groups there was more sharing of control between mothers and fathers, but again father's job and education altered the relationships. Professionals encouraged more open discussion at mealtimes but businessmen discouraged it and reported a lack of closeness with their children, often because they lacked the time but also because of conflicting attitudes. Middle-class mothers did not differ from working-class mothers in what they saw as the basic purpose of punishment. Half of both groups said they punished simply to get conformity, obedience and respect; the other half to teach children correct values, to 'do the right thing', to 'make the child stop and think'. Middle-class mothers, however, did stress firmness as a basis for learning self-discipline; the need to set standards and the use of 'love and understanding' more than 'smacking or punishing'. Working-class mothers wanted more obedience, and used physical punishment and deprivation of rewards to get it.

Overall, the findings suggest the same sort of 'conforming adolescent', that Connell's study of Sydney youth reported in 1975 and Little and Holmström's study confirms, that is, the adolescent is pretty firmly under the thumb of parents and not rejecting parental values. The Australian family appears to operate with that mixture of control and warmth that leads to acceptance rather than rejection of parental socialization; a deference to authority that perhaps carries over into later adult life. Where communication between parent and child is encouraged the socialization effects are often more marked in the child's acceptance of parental values.

Wider Family Networks

It is important to realize that it is not only mother and father who determine how early childhood will affect later values, attitudes and behaviour. The family as a whole and its place in a wider status group will also have an impact on socialization.

Few Australian studies have looked at the whole family and its 'group' impact on the child. Nor have many looked at the socialization effects of the family group on other members, such as father and mother. Yet obviously children affect parents, and family size, family interaction patterns, and family *networks* with relatives and friends will make a difference to the sorts of values learned.

Sex-role segregation for example, will reflect the wider group structures that affect the family. In 1955 Zelditch tested the hypothesis that the modern nuclear family would tend to produce more marked role segregation between husband and wife than existed in traditional extended families. The wife-mother would take on the role of *expressive-emotional* leader, while the husband-father would be the *instrumental-task* leader. This is partly because of innate sexual differences and partly because of economic needs and power, but it arises from the modern family's structure as a small group to cater for both the emotional and practical needs of its members. Cross-cultural data supported his hypothesis: 46 of his 56 cases did show this pattern of family role specialization. Critics have claimed Zelditch's view is a sexist one and Aronoff and Crano (1975), for example, show that women contribute significantly to the productive, instrumental tasks of the family in many societies. Of course this does not disprove Zelditch's view that a set of economic and child-rearing roles is regularly ascribed to husbands and wives across cultures, and that men hold major authority by virtue of their economic monopoly.

Within the family, however, husband-wife sharing may be influenced by other factors. Elizabeth Bott (1957) suggested that husband-wife roles were influenced by the nature of wider family networks. Where there was a close-knit network of friends and relatives, marital roles tended to be segregated. (A close-knit network exists where everyone knows and interacts with everyone else.) Where a wider social network existed it satisfied many expressive and instrumental needs and spouses were less dependent on one another. They continued to lead separate lives as before marriage. Where social networks are loose-knit and friends do not necessarily know one another or live near the family, the married pair are thrown together more for companionship, emotional support and help with instrumental tasks. They therefore develop a joint form of conjugal role organization. Bott's work has been supported (Nelson, 1966; Blood, 1969; Turner, 1967) but other studies (Udry and Hall, 1965; Aldous and Straus, 1966; Wimberley, 1973; Lee, 1977) suggest it is not the extent of network connectedness (close- or loose-knit) that causes the difference. Rather it is the extent to which each spouse is tied into a same-sex peer group. In other words, if a man continues his links with 'the boys' or his 'mates' after marriage, or if a wife retains her female friends, their dependence on each other within the marriage will be less. Their roles inside the family will be separate rather than shared.

In Lyn Richards' study of suburban Melbourne families (1978, ch. 10) there is evidence that isolated housewives lose their links with friends and have few chances of building new networks with neighbours. Moreover their sense of incompetence in coping with children (what every woman 'should know naturally') prevents them from venturing out to break the loneliness. The study showed there was no clear-cut middle-class/working-class difference in women's sex roles; rather a confusion as roles change, women continue to work, children arrive and alter conjugal role relationships.

Cultural differences between ethnic groups also make it dangerous to speak of 'the Australian family' or to think only in terms of social class variations. Bettina Cass correctly stresses the plurality of 'moral communities' in Australia's multi-cultural society (Cass, in Encel, Davies and Berry, 1975, p.167). In 1970 her own study of Sydney children's group affiliations found ethnic parents to be more likely to control the leisure time activities of their children than Australian born parents. Gillian Bottomley (1974) also found Greek parents encouraging participation in clubs and organizations which embed children in the ethnic community, thus limiting peer-group relationships. Jean Martin's (1967) classic study of kinship networks in Adelaide in 1965-6 found more evidence for the existence of extended family links than might have been expected. But here again there were class differences. In the old, working-class area, relatives often lived within walking distance of each other and went shopping, visiting and on outings together. But as suburban mobility increased this family solidarity was breaking down. Because they had access to 'resources' such as a car, telephone and money, middle-class suburbanites were able to maintain family contacts despite distance. Moreover the extended family was used to help find jobs and often provided direct financial help to the young in establishing their own 'independent' homes. Bryson and Thompson (1972) reported on a new working-class suburb in Melbourne in which, despite distance, the extended family network remained very important in providing child care, emotional support and weekend social visits.

Migrant families in particular reinforce the parents' efforts to socialize children into the values of their 'moral community'. The child's sense of identity may be split between the 'two worlds' of home and school, but the family influence remains very strong (Smolicz and Wiseman, 1971). Gillian Bottomley revealed the way Greek families' close-knit kin networks 'control behaviour by means of the positive sanctions of approval and prestige and the negative sanctions of gossip and ridicule'. Both men and women play a part in this though males hold the ultimate authority. Lyn Tisay (1979) in a study of Greek primary-school children and their families in Melbourne found children caught and confused between parental control values and the school teachers' insistence on greater independence on the part of children. Despite making their children attend ethnic schools after the school day finished, Greek parents ultimately conveyed (through their aspirations for children and their own deference to authority) that State-school values were important. Because State-school teachers themselves failed to understand or respect the children's home culture, however, these Greek primary-school children were suffering not only a hiatus in learning but also a loss of self-esteem and confidence.

Ethnic and class differences may isolate groups in other ways. Rena Huber's (1977) study of Italian farmers in Griffith, New South Wales, shows how separate farms prevent neither contact with nor the sense of obligation to help one's kin. But they do cut off ethnic families from the dominant Australian community. Similarly, Daphne Phillips' 1966—7 study of Italian tobacco-growers in the Ovens Valley of Victoria suggested a vast wall of misunderstanding and distrust. Despite similar work there was a lack of contact and an almost complete lack of 'resocialization' of migrants into the values and behaviour patterns of their Australian neighbours.

In 1978 the Centre for Urban Research and Action conducted another study of Italians in the King and Ovens Valleys, this time for the Country Education Project. In spite of 30 years of settlement there was still a strong Italian based community, 34 per cent of whom spoke little or no English and rarely interacted with the native Australian population. This (together with the fact that no teachers in the area spoke Italian) resulted in children in the schools performing at far lower levels than should be expected. In this case, however, there was a strong desire on the part of migrant parents to improve their relationships with the Australian community, and the action-research nature of the study has generated a new enthusiasm and interest on both sides.

For a brilliant description of cultural differences on a national scale on the socialization of children, see Urie Bronfenbrenner's (1970) book on the *Two Worlds of Childhood: U.S. and U.S.S.R.* Here at the macro-level can be seen two powerful 'moral communities' at work.

Language Codes

Language styles are the main guide to family and community interaction patterns. As Sue Harvey wrote when discussing national language usage among Dutch and Polish immigrant children:

> Society itself (and the essence of *their* social *being*) comes to children, and they to it, through language, spoken and written, more than through any other medium. Words are labels which help to focus, and to memorize, concepts; the labels are *socially given*; so are the definitions of when their use is appropriate. By learning *his* language the child joins *his* community—now he too can communicate ... Language is not only a *medium* of inter-communication, it is itself a *message* about the network of people that use it (Harvey, in Edgar, 1974, p.132).

Polish children reported using their native language frequently and especially with their families but Dutch children were much less active in their usage. As Smolicz and Wiseman (1971, pp.20−1) suggested, if the native language is devalued at school and retained for home use only, it is likely to become a kind of 'restricted code', limiting its users to a restricted social context.

This leads us to consider the language context within which family socialization takes place.

Work in England has gone further on this aspect than elsewhere. In 1968 Lawton reported significant social class differences in the speech and writing of twelve and fifteen-year-old boys. They were matched for verbal and non-verbal ability but the middle-class boys' essays were longer and more abstract. Working-class boys used fewer passive verbs, a less varied vocabulary and fewer subordinate clauses. Bernstein (1975) found middle-class children were more likely to use precise terms in offering general explanations whereas working-class children tended to list things concretely. He explained this in terms of differing socio-linguistic codes. Working-class people use a *restricted code* because their close-knit family, work and community experience makes detailed explanations of feeling and meaning unnecessary. Because everyone shares the same language context, they can predict more easily what is coming next and what is meant, so their speech is highly condensed. It is cliché-ridden, full of slang and almost unintelligible to the outsider. In contrast, middle-class people use a more *elaborated code* of speech which relies less on implicit (taken-for-granted) meanings and spells out in more complex ways what is intended. Not so tied to a narrow context, they can express individual intentions and motives more exactly and flexibly. This gives them control over a wider universe of meaning.

The explanation for such socio-linguistic codes lies in sub-cultural conditions of life and brings us back to status group differences in family socialization methods and their effects on children. Just as Kohn argued that the father's experience of self-direction at work affected his values for self and children, so Bernstein argues that the working-class family is more *position-oriented*. He argues that behaviour is controlled by role expectations, appeals to authority and rules that must be obeyed. In contrast, the middle-class family is more person-oriented and less reliant on accepted rules. Bernstein draws on Durkheim's contrast between *mechanical* solidarity and *organic* solidarity where more complex interdependence makes arbitrary rules and sanctions less appropriate. In the person-oriented family, everyone's wishes are considered, decisions are discussed, reasons are given and appeals to the child are personal.

Bernstein draws on Elizabeth Bott's work on the density of social networks and the segregation of father-mother roles to support his view that working-class families are *positional*, allowing less flexibility, offering more restricted roles for children to play and fewer opportunities for exploration of self.

Language may act as a form of social control, binding the child into a narrow context of meaning. Working-class families offer language resources that can be used in fewer contexts than the more elaborated code of the middle-class world. That code gives the child 'access to the sense that the world is permeable' (Bernstein, 1970, p.9).

As far back as 1955, Schatzman and Strauss (1955, pp.329–38) had argued that the middle class are more familiar with the task of transmitting information to strangers. Lower-class people, coming from a context in which people knew each other very well, assumed shared knowledge too readily. As a result they gave disjointed, concrete accounts.

When Australians say 'you know' as the conclusion to every other sentence they may be reflecting a working-class habit of appealing to what 'everyone knows'. Or it may be a call of despair in situations where their words fail to get through to those who do not 'know'. As Edwards suggests:

> where obedience is what matters, communication can be terse. Where the aim is self-control, the elaboration of feelings and reasons is essential. The difference is *not* one of relative punitiveness, but of making meanings individual and explicit. . . . (Kohn) can be criticized for concentrating too much on experience at work. Behind many other accounts of the group-centredness of working-class life are the additional factors of a common occupational status, a high density of housing, and a low level of geographical mobility. In such a community, relatives were also neighbours, and work-mates acquaintances of long-standing. Most interaction was between those familiar with each other's lives, and able to trade on a large store of common knowledge (Edwards, 1976, p.105).

Edwards and many others have been critical of Bernstein for implying too little richness and complexity in working-class and minority-group language (see Labov 1969, Rosen 1972, Byrne and Williamson 1972). But there can be little doubt that one's social class position limits opportunity to experience control and that those limited opportunities restrict access to elaborated codes of speech. And by nature those codes are 'expressions of questioning and challenge' (Edwards, 1975, p.106).

It is through the family that the child learns to see the world and conform to it as others do. In that sense Bernstein (1973, p.198) is right in claiming that the focus and filter of the family and its language codes are keys to the way class structure affects the social distribution of 'privileged meanings'.

As we shall see in the next chapter, the school goes on to reflect, reinforce and extend the 'cultural capital' the child has acquired in the family context. Advantages and disadvantages are magnified as the school takes over the more specialized aspects of the social distribution of competence.

Readings and References

a. Australian Society:

ADLER, D. H. (1965) 'Matriduxy in the Australian Family', in A. F. Davies & S. Encel (eds) *Australian Society: a Sociological Introduction*, Atherton, N.Y. pp.149-55.

BELL, D. (1973) *The Coming of the Post-Industrial Society*, Basic Books, N.Y.

BERGER, P. & T. LUCKMANN (1966) *The Social Construction of Reality*, Doubleday Anchor, N.Y.

BOTTOMLEY, G. (1974) 'Some Greek Sex Roles: Ideals, Expectations and Action in Australia and Greece', *ANZJS*, 10(1), pp.8-16.

BURNS, A. & J. GOODNOW (1979) *Children and Families in Australia*, Allen and Unwin, Sydney.

BRYSON, L. & F. THOMPSON (1972) *An Australian Newtown: Life and Leadership in a working class suburb*, Penguin, Melbourne.

CICOUREL, A. V. & J. I. KITSUSE (1963) 'The Educational Decision-Makers', Bobbs Merrill Inc. reprinted in Karabel, J. & A. H. Halsey (eds) (1977) *Power and Ideology in Education*, Oxford University Press, Oxford, pp.282-92.

CONNELL, W. F. (1974) 'The Causes of Educational Inequality: Further Observations', *ANZJS*, 10(3), October.

CONNELL, W. F. & R. E. STROOBANT, K. E. SINCLAIR, R. W. CONNELL and K. W. ROGERS (1975) *12 to 20, Studies of City Youth*, Hicks Smith, Sydney.

Country Education Project (Vic.) (1979) *Migrants and Education in a Rural Community: A Case Study of the Ovens and King Valleys*, Centre for Urban Research and Action, Melbourne.

CURA (1978) *But I Wouldn't Want My Wife to Work Here*, Centre for Urban Research and Action, Fitzroy, Vic.

DAVIES, A. F., S. ENCEL & M. J. BERRY (eds) (1977) *Australian Society, A Sociological Introduction* (3rd ed.), Longman-Cheshire, Melbourne.

DAWSON, M. (ed.) (1974) *Families: Australian Studies of Changing Relationships Within the Family and Between the Family and Society*, Searchlight, ANZAAS, John Wiley & Sons, Sydney.

EDGAR, D. E. (1974) 'Adolescent Competence and Sexual Disadvantage', *La Trobe Sociology Papers*, No. 10, La Trobe University, Melbourne.

EDGAR, D. E. (1977) 'Family Socialization Patterns and Adult-Adolescent Interaction': paper given to the ANZAAS Congress, Melbourne, August, 1977.

EDGAR, P. M. (1975) 'Sex Type Socialization and Family Comedy Programmes', in Edgar, D. E. (ed.), *Sociology of Australian Education*, pp. 232-47, McGraw Hill, Sydney.

EDGAR, P. M., D. EDGAR, M. POOLE, T. ROPER & M. HIGGS (1973) *Under 5 in Australia*, Wm. Heinemann, Melbourne.

FALLDING, H. J. (1957) 'Inside the Australian Family', in A. P. Elkin (ed.) *Marriage and the Family in Australia*, Angus and Robertson, Sydney.

HARPER, J. & L. RICHARDS (1979) *Mothers and Working Mothers*, Penguin, Melbourne.

HARVEY, S. (1974) 'National Language Usage among Dutch and Polish

Immigrant Children', in D. E. Edgar (ed.), *Social Change in Australia*, Cheshire, Melbourne, pp.131-43.

HICKMAN, D. C. (1971) 'Issues in the Interpretation of Adolescents in Society', *ANZJS*, Vol. 7, No. 2, pp.58-68.

HUBER, R. (1977) *From Pasta to Pavlova*, University of Queensland Press, Brisbane.

HUNT, F. J. (ed.) (1972) *Socialization in Australia*, Angus & Robertson, Sydney.

JAMES, K. (1979) 'The Home: A Private or a Public Place? Class, Status, and the Actions of Women', *ANZJS*, Vol. 15, No. 1, pp.36-42.

KATZ (1964) 'The Meaning of Success: Some Differences in Value Systems of Social Classes', *Journal of Social Psychology*, 62, pp.141-8.

KRUPINSKI, J. (1974) 'Family Relationships in Australia', in J. Krupinski and A. Stoller, *The Family in Australia*, Pergamon, Sydney, pp.31-6.

LEFROY, R. B. (1977) 'The Elderly Person and Family Life', *Aust. Journal of Social Issues*, Vol. 12, No. 1, pp.33-42.

LITTLE, G. & E. HOLMSTRÖM (1977) 'Family Authority' in A. F. Davies, S. Encel and M. J. Berry, *Australian Society, A Sociological Introduction*, (3rd ed.), Longman Cheshire, Melbourne, pp.176-88.

MARTIN, J. I. (1957) 'Marriage, the Family and Class', in A. P. Elkin (ed.), *Marriage and the Family in Australia*, Angus & Robertson, Sydney, pp.24-53.

MARTIN, J. I. (1967) 'Extended Kinship Ties: an Adelaide Study', *ANZJS*, 3, pp.44-63.

MERCER, J. (1977) *The Other Half, Women in Australian Society*, Penguin Books, Melbourne.

OESER, O. A. & F. EMERY (1954) *Social Structure and Personality in a Rural Community*, Routledge & Kegan Paul, London.

OESER, O. A. & S. B. HAMMOND (1954) *Social Structure and Personality in a City*, Routledge & Kegan Paul, London.

PHILLIPS, D. (1974) 'Italians and Australians in the Ovens Valley', in D. E. Edgar (ed.), *Social Change in Australia*, Cheshire, Melbourne, pp.121-30.

POWER, J. (1970) 'Family and Polity', in Mayer, H. (ed.), *Australian Politics*, Cheshire, Melbourne, pp.109-16.

RICHARDS, L. (1978) *Having Families: Marriage, Parenthood and Social Pressure in Australia*, Penguin, Melbourne.

RICHARDS, L. (1979) 'Good Mothers and Other Mothers: Family Style and Social Change', *La Trobe Sociology Papers*, No. 2 (new series), La Trobe University, Melbourne.

RUSSELL, G. (1979) 'Fathers! Incompetent or Reluctant Parents?', *ANZJS*, Vol. 15, No. 1, pp.57-65.

SAMPSON, S. (1975) 'The Australian Women's Weekly and the Aspirations of Girls', in Edgar, D. E. (ed.), *Sociology of Australian Education*, McGraw Hill, Sydney, pp. 248-60.

SMART, R. C. & M. S. SMART (1973) 'New Zealand preadolescents' parent-peer orientation and parent perceptions compared with English and American', *Journal of Marriage and the Family*, 35 (Feb.) 1973, pp.142-8.

SMOLICZ, J. J. & R. WISEMAN (1971) 'European Migrants and their Children',

Quarterly Review of Australian Education, Part 2, 4/3, September, pp.20-1.

TISAY, Lyn (1979) 'The Negotiation of an Identity: School-Child Community Relations in an Inner Suburban School in Melbourne'. Unpublished 4th year Honours thesis, Sociology, La Trobe University.

TURNER, I. (1969) *Cinderella Dressed in Yella*, Heinemann Educational, Melbourne.

WITTICH, E. (1974) 'Individual Constructions of Meanings and Communication Problems in Marriage', *ANZJS*, Vol. 10, No. 3, pp.164-9.

See also reference list at end of Chapter 5.

b. General:

ALDOUS, J. & M. A. STRAUS (1966) 'Social networks and conjugal roles: A test of Bott's hypothesis', *Social Forces*, 44 (June), pp.576-80.

ARONOFF, J. & W. D. CRANO (1975) 'A Re-examination of the cross-cultural principles of task, segregation and sex-role differentiation in the family', *American Sociological Review*, 40 (Feb.), pp.12-20.

ARIES, P. (1962) *Centuries of Childhood*, Knopf, N.Y.

BELL, N. W. & E. F. VOGEL (eds) (1968) *A Modern Introduction to the Family*, (2nd ed.), Free Press, N.Y.

BERGER, P. L. & H. KELLNER (1970) 'Marriage and the Construction of Reality', in H. P. Dreitzel (ed.), *Recent Sociology No. 2*, Macmillan, London, pp.49-72.

BERNSTEIN, B. (1961) 'Social Class and Linguistic Development: a Theory of Social Learning', in A. H. Halsey *et al* (eds) *Education, Economy and Society*, Free Press, N.Y.

BERNSTEIN, B. (1970) 'Education Cannot Compensate for Society', *New Society*, 387, pp.344-7.

BERNSTEIN, B. (ed.) (1973a) *Class, Codes and Control: Vol. 1 — Theoretical Studies Towards a Sociology of Language*, Routledge & Kegan Paul, London.

BERNSTEIN, B. (ed.) (1973b) *Class, Codes and Control: Vol. 2 — Applied Studies Towards a Sociology of Language*, Routledge & Kegan Paul, London.

BERNSTEIN, B. (1975) *Class, Codes and Control: Vol. 3 — Theoretical Studies Toward a Sociology of Language*, Schocken, N.Y.

BLOOD, R. O. Jr. (1969) 'Kinship interaction and marital solidarity', *Merrill-Palmer Quarterly*, 15 (April), pp.171-84.

BLUMER, H. (1969) *Symbolic Interactionism: Perspective and Method*, Prentice-Hall, New Jersey.

BOLI-BENNETT, J. & J. W. MEYER (1978) 'The Ideology of Childhood and the State: Rules Distinguishing Children in National Constitutions, 1870—1970', *American Sociological Review*, Vol. 43, No. 6, pp. 797-812.

BOTT, E. (1957) *Family and Social Network*, Tavistock, U.K.

BOURDIEU, P. & J. C. PASSERON (1977) *Reproduction in Education, Society and Culture*, Sage, N.Y.

BREWSTER-SMITH, M. (1968) 'Socialization and Competence', in Clausen, J. (ed.), *Socialization and Society*, Little Brown, Boston.

BREWSTER-SMITH, M. (1969) *Social Psychology and Human Values*, Aldine, Chicago.

BRIM, O. G. Jr. & S. WHEELER (1966) *Socialization After Childhood*, Wiley, N.Y.

BRITTON, J. H. & J. O. BRITTON (1971) 'Children's Perceptions of their Parents: A Comparison of Finnish and American Children', *Journal of Marriage and the Family*, 33 (Feb.), pp.214-8.

BRONFENBRENNER, U. & E. C. DEVEREUX, Jr. (1970) *Two Worlds of Childhood: U.S. and U.S.S.R.*, Russell Sage, N.Y.

BRUNER, J. S., J. J. GOODNOW & G. A. AUSTIN (1956) *A Study of Thinking*, Wiley, N.Y.

BYRNE, D. & B. WILLIAMSON (1972) *The Myth of the Restricted Code*, Durham University, Department of Sociology (Working Paper in Sociology, No. 1).

CARULLO, M., J. STACEY & W. BREINES (1977-8) 'Alice Rossi's Sociobiology and Anti-Feminist Backlash', *Berkeley Journal of Sociology*, Vol. 22, pp.167-78.

CICOUREL, A. V. (1972) 'Basic and Normative Rules in the Negotiation of Status and Role', in D. Sudnow (ed.), *Studies in Social Interaction*, Free Press, N.Y., pp.229-58.

CLAUSEN, J. A. (ed.) (1968) *Socialization and Society*, Little Brown & Co., Boston, (especially the articles by Maccoby, E.E., pp.227-69 and Brewster-Smith, M., pp.271-320).

COLEMAN, J. S. (1969) *The Adolescent Society*, Free Press of Glencoe, N.Y.

COOLEY, C. H. (1964 [1902]) *Human Nature and the Social Order*, Schocken, N.Y.

DANZIGER, K. (1971) *Socialization*, Penguin, U.K.

DAVIS, A. & R. HAVIGHURST (1948) 'Social Class and Color Differences in Child Rearing', *American Sociological Review*, 11, pp.698-710.

DEVEREUX, E. C., U. BRONFENBRENNER & R. R. ROGERS (1969) 'Child-Rearing in England and the U.S.: A Cross-National Comparison', *Journal of Marriage and the Family*, 31 (May), pp.257-70.

EDWARDS, A. D. (1976) *Language in Culture and Class*, Heinemann Educational, London.

ERIKSON, E. H. (1963) *Childhood and Society*, Norton, N.Y.

GOFFMAN, E. (1959) *The Presentation of Self in Everyday Life*, Doubleday Anchor, N.Y.

GOLDMAN, R. (ed.) (1968) *Breakthrough: Autobiographical Accounts of the Education of Some Socially Disadvantaged Children*, Routledge & Kegan Paul, London.

GOSLIN, D. A. (ed.) (1969) *Handbook of Socialization Theory and Research*, Rand McNally, Chicago.

HARLOW, H. F. (1959) 'Love in Infant Monkeys', *Scientific American*, 200, pp.68-74.

HAVIGHURST, R. & A. DAVIS (1955) 'A Comparison of the Chicago and Harvard Studies of Social Class Differences in Child Rearing', *American Sociological Review*, 20, pp.438-42.

HUNT, J. McV. (1965) 'Intrinsic Motivation and its Role in Psychological Development', in D. Levine (ed.), *Nebraska Symposium on Motivation*,

University of Nebraska Press, pp.189-282.

ILLICH, I. (1971) *Deschooling Society*, Harper and Row, N.Y.

INKELES, A. (1963) 'Social change and social character: The role of parental mediation', in N. J. Smelser & W. J. Smelser (eds), *Personality and Social Systems*, John Wiley & Sons, N.Y.

INKELES, A. (1966) 'Social Structure and the Socialization of Competence', *Harvard Educational Review*, 36, pp.265-83.

INKELES, A. (1969) 'Social Structure and Competence', in D. Goslin (ed.), *Handbook of Socialization Theory and Research*, Rand McNally, Chicago.

KAGAN, J. (1977) 'The Child in the Family', *Daedalus*, Spring, pp.33-56.

KANDEL, D. & G. S. LESSER (1969) 'Parent-adolescent relationships and adolescent independence in the United States and Denmark', *Journal of Marriage and the Family*, 34 (Feb), pp.348-58.

KOHLBERG, L. (1964) 'Development of Moral Character and Moral Ideology', in M. & L. W. Hoffman (eds), *Review of Child Development Research*, Russell Sage Foundation, Vol. 1, pp.383-431.

KOHN, M. L. (1959) 'Social class and the experience of parental authority', *American Sociological Review*, 24 (June), pp.352-66.

KOHN, M. L. (1959) 'Social class and parental values', *American Journal of Sociology*, 64 (Jan.), pp.337-51.

KOHN, M. L. (1963) 'Social class and parent-child relationships: An interpretation', *American Journal of Sociology*, 68 (Jan), pp.471-80.

KOHN, M. L. (1969) *Class and Conformity*, Dorsey Press, Ill.

KOHN, M. L. & J. CARROLL (1959) 'Social Class and Allocation in Parental Responsibilities', *American Journal of Sociology*, January.

KOHN, M. L. & C. SCHOOLER (1969) 'Class, Occupation and Orientation', *American Sociological Review*, Vol. 34, pp.659-78.

KOHN, M. L. & C. SCHOOLER (1973) 'Occupational Experience and Psychological Functioning: An Assessment of Reciprocal Effects', *American Sociological Review*, Vol. 38, No. 1, pp.97-118.

LABOV, W. (1969) 'The Logic of Non-Standard English', in J. Alatis (ed.), *Linguistics and the Teaching of Standard English to Speakers of other Languages or Dialects*, Georgetown University Press, Georgetown.

LAING, R. D. & A. ESTERSON (1964) *Sanity, Madness and the Family*, Tavistock, London.

LAWTON, D. (1968) *Social Class, Language and Education*, Routledge & Kegan Paul, London.

LEE, G. R. (1977) 'The effects of social networks on the family', in W. R. Burr *et al* (eds), *Contemporary Theories About the Family*, Free Press, N.Y.

LEWIN, Kurt (1941) 'Self-hatred among Jews', *Contemporary Jewish Record*, 4, pp.219-32.

LITTMAN, R. A., R. C. A. MOORE & J. PIERCE-JONES (1957) 'Social Class Differences in Child Rearing: a Third Community for Comparison with Chicago and Newtown', *American Sociological Review*, 22, pp.694-704.

MACCOBY, E. E. (ed.) (1966) *The Development of Sex Differences*, Stanford University Press, Calif.

MEAD, G. H. (1964 [1934]) *On Social Psychology*, A. Strauss (ed.), University of Chicago Press, Chicago.

NEILL, A. S. (1962) *Summerhill: a Radical Approach to Education*, Gollancz, London.

NELSON, J. I. (1966) 'Clique contacts and family orientations', *American Sociological Review*, 31 (Oct.), pp.663-72.

NISBET, R. A. (1970) *The Social Bond*, Alfred Knopf, N.Y.

PARSONS, T. & R. F. BALES (eds) (1955) *Family, Socialization and Interaction Process*, Free Press, Glencoe Ill.

PEARLIN, L. I. (1971) *Class Context and Family Relations: A Cross-National Study*, Little Brown & Co., Boston,

PEARLIN, L. I. & M. L. KOHN (1966) 'Social class, occupation, and parental values: A cross-national study', *American Sociological Review*, 31 (Aug.), pp.466-79.

PIAGET, J. (1952 [1932]) *The Moral Judgement of the Child*, Harcourt Brace, N.Y.

PIAGET, J. (1954) *The Construction of Reality in the Child*, Basic Books, N.Y.

POLLNER, M. (1975) 'The Very Coinage of Your Brain. The Anatomy of Reality Disjunctures', *Philosophy & Social Science*, 5, pp.411-30.

RAINWATER, L. (1966) 'Crucible of identity: The negro lower-class family', *Daedalus* 95 (Winter), pp.172-216.

RAPOPORT, R. & R. (eds) (1978) *Working Couples*, Routledge & Kegan Paul, London.

ROSEN, H. (1972) *Language and Class: a Critical look at the Theories of Basil Bernstein*, Falling Wall Press, U.S.A.

SAFILIOS-ROTHSCHILD, C. (1970) 'The Study of Family Power Structure: A Review 1960—1969', *Journal of Marriage and the Family*, 32 (Nov.), pp.539-51.

SCHATZMAN, L. & A. STRAUSS (1955) 'Social Class and Modes of Communication', *American Journal of Sociology*, 60, pp.329-38.

SCHLESINGER, B. (1978) *The One-Parent Family*, (4th ed.), University of Toronto Press, Toronto.

SEARS, R. R., E. E. MACCOBY & H. LEVIN (1957) *Patterns of Child Rearing*, Row, Peterson & Co., Ill.

SENNETT, R. & J. COBB (1973) *The Hidden Injuries of Class*, Vintage Books, N.Y.

SPIRO, M. E. (1958) *Children of the Kibbutz*, Harvard University Press, Cambridge, Mass.

STRYKER, S. (1972) 'Symbolic interaction theory: A review and some suggestions for comparative family research', *Journal of Comparative Family Studies*, 3 (Spring), pp.17-32.

THOMAS, D. L. & A. V. WEIGERT (1971) 'Socialization and adolescent conformity to significant others: A cross-national analysis', *American Sociological Review*, 36 (Oct.), pp.835-47.

TURNER, C. (1967) 'Conjugal role and social networks: A re-examination of an hypothesis', *Human Relations*, 20 (May), pp.121-30.

UDRY, J. R. & M. HALL (1965) 'Marital role segregation and social networks in middle-class middle-aged couples', *Journal of Marriage and the Family*, 27 (Aug.), pp.392-5.

WALTERS, J. & N. STINNETT (1971) 'Parent-child relationships: A decade review of research', *Journal of Marriage and the Family*, 33 (Feb.), pp.70-111.

WHITING, J. W. H. & I. L. CHILD (1953) *Child Training and Personality: A Cross-Cultural Study*, Yale University Press, New Haven, Conn.

WHITE, R. (1959) 'Motivation Reconsidered: The Concept of Competence', *Psychological Review*, 66, pp.297-333.

WHITE, R. W. (1960) 'Competence and the Psycho-sexual stages of development', in M. Jones (ed.), *Nebraska Symposium on Motivation*, University of Nebraska Press, Nebraska.

WILLMOTT, P. & M. YOUNG (1960) *Family and Class in a London Suburb*, Routledge & Kegan Paul, London.

WIMBERLEY, H. (1973) 'Conjugal-role organization and social networks in Japan and England', *Journal of Marriage and the Family*, 35 (Feb.), pp.125-31.

ZELDITCH, M. Jr. (1955) 'Role differentiation in the nuclear family: A comparative study', in T. Parsons and R. F. Bales, *Family Socialization and Interaction Process*, Free Press, N.Y., pp.307-52.

Chapter 8

Education as Cultural Reproducer

8

School has not always been necessary for nor available to everyone. Mass primary education emerged only in the mid-nineteenth century and mass secondary education not until after the turn of the century. Mass tertiary education now exists, more or less, only in advanced industrial countries such as the United States and the USSR.

Schooling and Society

In Australia the first Free School was established in 1809 and a school of arts was founded in Sydney in 1833. By 1848, separate National and Denominational School Boards had been set up by the New South Wales government.

The long sectarian battle over State aid to religious schools was settled by its total abolition in 1862 and the passage of Sir Henry Parkes' *Public Schools Act* in 1866. But it was not until 1880 that the *N.S.W. Public Instruction Act* consolidated free, compulsory and secular education. This meant that public schools became centrally controlled and Protestant, reflecting the dominant religion and the lack of local power. Attendance at many schools continued to be voluntary annd many required fees to be paid.

Until some high schools were built (and they served mainly as 'normal schools' for the training of teachers) the only schools at the secondary level were the elite private schools and a few Working Men's Colleges for the teaching of trade skills. The universities (established in the optimism of post-gold-rush affluence—Sydney University, 1850; Melbourne University, 1853) were modelled on elite British institutions and served a tiny minority of the urban elite. Just as in China and Egypt 2000 years B.C., schools trained priests and officials from and for 'the establishment', new forms of education have always developed to serve the interest of dominant groups or to provide for those groups whose interests are not served by the dominant system of education.

To explain the development of formal education requires more than a simplistic 'growth' model of society. To understand new structures of education we need to consider what changes there have been in the central institutions of society. These may be economic, political or religious. Unfortunately, part of the 'received wisdom' (what people see as 'common sense') is the argument that education grew simply to meet new job needs. Of course such a 'technical-function' theory is in large part true. When the home and family were the units of production, children were educated in specific skills in the home, not in schools. The family was both general socializer and specific educator. Schools were limited to teaching reading, transcribing and the scriptures. But when work was separated from the home and the factory system demanded workers who were literate and numerate, employers began to demand that public schools produce them. As technology develops and more specialized qualifications are required, educational institutions expand to teach special skills. These will include vocational and technical skills, and also 'service' skills such as accounting, management, psychological testing and so on.

But this theory of *technological functionalism* (New Jobs ⟶ Demand for New Forms of Education) does not explain very well *how* formal education developed. It does not tell us the whole story about *why* schools teach the sorts of things they do, handle people the way they do or are structured the way they are. These three elements (curriculum content; methods of teaching, learning and testing; and the formal organization of education into levels, types and grades) can, however, be explained in terms of *whose interests they serve* (Collins, 1971). Educational institutions, like any other institutions, did not simply happen. Nor did they simply grow the way they did because everyone agreed they should. Conflicting values and conflicting interests are resolved by the weight of competing resources. The more powerful win. But they win not merely by force. They win by convincing people that this is the way things *should be*. In the case of Australian education that schooling is 'naturally' individually-based, job-directed, competitive and selective.

For this reason we want to examine the evidence on education as a social institution in the light of what we have called the Social Distribution of Competence (see Figure 7—1). Note that it is an *active* process. A person's relative share of any social resource (wealth, property, language, knowledge, skills, moral values, political power, authority and so on) results not from 'natural' inequalities but from socially-produced ones. The 'self-made man' depending on his own wits and talents may have existed somewhere at some time. But when people today claim to be self-made, for the most part their claims are phoney. Their starting point was not equal to others and their location in the social structure gave them access to better life chances through no virtue of their own. As we have seen in Chapter 7, the family serves to transmit both worldly goods and a view of the world that makes one more or less effective in 'making one's own way' in life. The mere presence or absence of a kindergarten (or a good primary school or a technical rather than a high school) in one's neighbourhood will enhance or dampen those life chances. Neither their presence nor their absence depends upon chance or individual merit. It rests on political, economic and value decisions by those in power.

Competence in life varies in two broad ways. In each society there is a set of common tasks which all people must be able to perform in order to be regarded as *normal*. But there are also many other tasks, not common to all, which have become the rights or duties of certain people.

The tasks common to everyone include being able to walk, talk and handle things, find food, shelter, sexual partners and so on. The range of variations on that set of tasks alone is immense. Anthropology shows how every society varies in the way its members handle *universal* tasks.

But the province of sociology is that second set of tasks; those tasks not common to all the members of a society. Men and women may be assigned different roles, only some of which (like child-bearing and breastfeeding) might not be performed as well by the opposite sex. Children may not be expected to work, take responsibility or make decisions in the same way as adults. But while their physical and mental capacities prevent some things, many others are socially, not physically, proscribed. The more complex a society is, the wider will be the range of tasks to be assigned or chosen and the more differentiated will be the types of competence that might be achieved. When we specialize in an occupation we develop different skills from those of our friends and neighbours. Each role carries with it certain demands for skills, expertise, competence and know-how which must be learned if we are to perform that role competently. And this is where *stereotypes* start to interfere with social realities.

For example, parents may say of their children, 'He's no good at school work but he's good with his hands. His sister always loved reading, she's more the academic type'. Or of girls, frequently, 'Why should she stay on at school? She's happy with her friends; is a lovely warm girl and she'll probably marry and settle down in a year or so. That's what girls should do'. Parents may face the choice of technical or high school secondary education for their children with no more than a stereotyped notion that technical education is for boys who hate 'book-learning' and high schools are for boys and girls who have shown some academic interest. The fact that this typing (of both schools and children) is based on very thin information does not alter the fact that it involves a commonly accepted typology of competence.

That typology includes *is*, *ought* and *can* elements. A child *is* bright or dull, interested or bored, a bookworm or a sport, quiet or outward-going, practical or airy-fairy, academically talented or not too good at school. But the *oughts* often obscure what *is* and we may find that girls *ought* not wear trousers, do metalwork, lift heavy loads, study science or go into business; or that working-class kids *ought* to go to technical schools rather than high schools, become apprentices rather than go on to higher education, or leave school early if they show signs of failing. Moreover the typology tends to obscure or worsen the effects of the *can* element. Boys *can* go to technical schools in Victoria but often girls cannot. Teachers may tell less successful students they cannot do French or Maths/Science but must do the practical/commercial courses, or the 'alternate' fifth and sixth year. Not all successful pupils *can* get into the university or college course of their first choice even though the typology leads them to that expectation.

But because societal values of competence or the capacity to cope mix a limited view of what a child *is* able to do with a stereotyped view of what certain types of people *ought* to do, the limits on what one *can* do are often forgotten. Competence will be measured as an individual's capacity to measure up to arbitrary definitions of what *ought* to be done. If an individual fails to measure up, the individual will be blamed rather than the social definition or the social limits themselves which made it impossible for that individual to gain the required capacities.

Most people take for granted certain assumptions about schooling. Some are based on fact, others are not. We do vary individually in 'inherited' intelligence; we do find ourselves physically capable or clumsy; and we do compete and enjoy winning. One of the most remarkable things about

Australian society though, is how assumptions about such real, inborn differences have been used to obscure the equally demonstrable influence of social factors on them. The Jensen-Eysenck I.Q. controversy is less interesting for the 'evidence' it produces about 'nature versus nurture' than for the people it brings out of the woodwork on both sides of the controversy. The major proponents of the argument that intelligence is inherited, are those whose talents have already been developed and recognized by society and whose positions require a continuation of the status quo. Those who oppose the view that education should recognize innate (even racial) inequalities in intelligence are those whose talents have been developed by society but whose position has not been given equal recognition or status. Those whose talents have been neither developed nor recognized by society could not care less. They are the victims and their children will be processed by the education system in ways over which they have little control. They are the victims of the 'authorities' who impose their views on what education should be like. A sort of violence has been done to them which lays the blame for their lack of competence upon themselves.

Symbolic Violence

Bourdieu and Passeron (1977) call this state of affairs *symbolic violence*. Recall our discussion in Chapter 6 concerning C. Wright Mills' notion of *master symbols* where Mills argued that each status group produces its own view of the world and thus its own *vocabulary of motives*. But there are also more far-reaching symbols—social rules or moral imperatives—that come to be legitimated on a wider scale. 'Freedom', 'representative government', 'privacy', 'initiative', 'progress', are part of that vocabulary. Control over the means of communication confers power to spread such master symbols. The schools are a major means of communicating moral values, of indicating attitudes that either support or challenge the social structure as it is. So too are forms of mass media such as newspapers, radio and television. But because the media are controlled by people whose power depends upon continuation of the status quo, their 'messages' are not likely to challenge the master symbols or the dominant vocabulary of motives. Rather, they will reinforce them.

Durkheim recognized the central importance of education to the maintenance of society. According to Bourdieu and Passeron (1977, p.4) Durkheim saw education as 'the privileged locus of the illusion of consensus'. Marx's stress on the ruling ideas came close to seeing the power that cultural symbols achieve when those who are dominated come to accept that domination as legitimate. And, more than others, Weber stressed the power of legitimation to perpetuate existing structures of domination through rational bureaucratic forms of social organization. Bourdieu and Passeron (1977, p.5) claim that 'All pedagogic action is, objectively, symbolic violence insofar as it is the imposition of a cultural arbitrary by an arbitrary power'. This means that any attempt to teach (whether by a parent or a teacher) that is based on arbitrary power, does 'violence' to the child. That is, by imposing meanings as legitimate, it conceals the fact that those meanings could be challenged. For example, when a father says to a child 'you must behave because parents have a right to expect good behaviour', rather than 'if you don't behave I'll belt you', he is doing symbolic violence. The demand rests on power, but it is asserted as a legitimate right.

On a larger scale, when teachers present examinations, tracking, streaming, failing grades, arbitrary rules about dress, manners and school discipline as though they are unquestionably legitimate, they do symbolic violence. Their very right to impose arbitrary rules goes unchallenged because it is presented as legitimate. It denies the chance for people to consider whether they will confer legitimacy of their own free choice.

While the concept of 'authority' refers to power that has been legitimated (agreed to) by those below, authority may take unto itself powers not initially ceded by those subject to its control. It was Weber who first warned of the dangers inherent in bureaucratic authority. Though he regarded rational-legal authority as superior to the arbitrary forms of traditional authority, he saw organized bureaucracy as a threat—doing violence to man's freedom.

> Petrified spirit is also the living machine constituted by the bureaucratic organization, with its specialization of trained experts, its demarcation of competence, its rules and hierarchically ordered authority-relations. With the dead machine it works to produce the shell of a future serfdom, which may only and for all, like the fellaches in ancient Egyptian society, force man into impotent obedience. This will occur, given that the ultimate and only value is going to become a rational administration and distribution by functionaries, who determine the shaping of human affairs. Because this task is performed by a bureaucracy incomparably superior to any other authority structure (Weber, 1968, pp.111—12).

It was Weber, too, who recognized that teachers whose professional ideology asserts their right to communicate with students in a 'master-disciple' fashion, are behaving like 'little prophets in the pay of the State' and are, in fact, only the 'delegated holders of the right to exercise symbolic violence' (quoted in Bourdieu & Passeron, 1977, pp.20 and 24). Such a theory sounds very negative and highly critical of teachers and the State making any attempt to control our freedom. Yet Bourdieu is not calling for revolution or denying that people accept the naturalness of the way things are. For that is the point. Unproblematic social conditions *predispose* people to accept their social relations as natural.

In this sense then, it cannot be argued that the schools, or the mass media, *create* opinions or inequalities. Rather, they reinforce predispositions which are the result of social structures of domination and control. That is why we speak of education as *cultural reproducer*, rather than as *producer*. Education may have more power as an institution in modern society than it did previously, but it is always dependent upon other factors in society. Inequalities come first; educational provisions then serve to reproduce the structuring of resources in society. This is not to deny that education can serve as a pathway to success and social mobility. The questions are: *Under what social conditions is education allowed or even encouraged to open up new pathways*? and *In practice, when such pathways open up, who gets to take them*?

Technical Competence

We shall now consider the argument that the requirements of new jobs bring about changes in education. Davis & Moore (1945) argued that stratification develops from natural inequalities. As new jobs demanded new skills only those with native ability or special training would be able to attain higher status. That argument failed to examine how groups compete for status, a process that may better explain how education develops.

Collins (1971) found that only 15 per cent of the increase in education of the United States labour force in the twentieth century could be related to shifts in the number of jobs demanding higher skills. So the actual increase in educational levels is in excess of what jobs require. Something else must have been going on.

Other evidence on growth in Gross National Product (GNP) suggests the residual (what is left over when you discount the contribution to GNP of both increased capital and a growing labour force) cannot be attributed only to improved skills from better education. Studies of underdeveloped countries show that the take-off point for education to improve GNP occurs when the school enrolment level reaches 30–50 per cent of the 7–14 age-group. That is, mass literacy does seem to make a big difference to productivity (Katz, 1977). Beyond that, further advances in education seem to make little difference to economic growth. Again, there must be something else to explain the expansion of education.

The Williams Report (1979) is similarly cautious in its comments on the effect of education on residual GNP. While labour and capital are crucial inputs to economic growth, education and research help improve 'quality'.

> The quality of labour in production depends on attitudes engendered by the home and school environments and on the skills acquired in the process of education. Unless methods of production are static, some old labour skills cease to be needed and new labour skills come to be needed. The quality of the labour force therefore depends on the extent, relevance and adaptability of the education system, including education at the place of work (Williams Report, 1979, p.578, ¶13.09)

Ivar Berg (1970, pp.85–104 and 143–76) examines the data on the question whether better educated people are individually more productive as a result of their education. He concludes that they are not, and calls his book *Education and Jobs: The Great Training Robbery*. What the data do show is that most vocational skills are learned *on the job*, not in schools. In fact, graduates of specifically vocational schools are no more likely to get jobs than high school dropouts. In 1978 in Victoria, together with cries for a return to 'the basics', and more 'vocational training', the Employers' Federation also admitted that its members selected students from the 'better' high schools in preference to those from technical schools. Clearly they were looking for other qualities from education. Philip Foster (1965) describes the 'vocational school fallacy' as it was applied in Ghana, where academic schooling proved to be more 'vocational' (and popular) than agricultural schools because it led to higher status public service jobs.

In sum, the evidence supports neither the notion that schools develop only because skills are needed for new jobs nor the belief that schools are the places that actually teach job skills.

In Australia in 1976, the *Williams Inquiry on Education, Training and Employment* was initiated because schools were charged with failing to teach basic literacy and numeracy, resulting in the 'unemployability' of youth. Yet the evidence collected shows that unemployment is highest among those who leave school early, so despite its faults, more education means better 'employability'. Further, the Australian Council for Educational Research's (A.C.E.R.) national survey of literacy and numeracy showed that Australian children performed at the same levels as children in England, Scotland, the United States and New Zealand. Only 3 per cent of 10-year-olds and 0.8 per cent of 14-year-olds were unable to read simple sentences; and 4 per cent of 14-year-olds were unable to subtract and multiply because they did not know their number facts. The Williams Report assessed 25 per cent of 14-year-olds to need extra instruction in reading before they would have the capacity of independent reading and information-seeking and found that 'only 50 per cent of 14-year-olds could write a satisfactory letter of application for employment in terms of four basic criteria'. But the Williams Report agreed with the A.C.E.R.

Table 8 – 1   Full-time teenage students

Full-time students as a percentage of 15 – 19 age group

1. Japan	76.3
2. U.S.A.	72.0
3. Canada	66.4
4. Norway	63.4
5. Denmark	62.1
6. Belgium	61.3
7. Finland	60.8
8. Netherlands	57.5
9. Sweden	57.1
10. Switzerland	51.6
11. France	51.3
12. West Germany	51.3
13. Ireland	47.1
14. Australia	46.1
15. Greece	45.4
16. Britain	43.9
17. New Zealand	43.2
18. Italy	40.8
19. Austria	37.0
20. Spain	34.5
21. Luxembourg	33.5
22. Portugal	29.6
23. Turkey	12.7

(Source: O.E.C.D. Observer, 1978 — figures for 1975)

conclusion 'that there was no evidence to justify undue criticism of performance in Australian schools' (1979, p.93, ¶4.24). It also says that 'changes in the philosophy and administration of education should not therefore be blamed for the sharp increase in youth unemployment' (1979, p.85, ¶4.09). Other factors cause unemployment and most of them are beyond the control of the schools.

Other factors are also at work in the expansion of education. In the United States by 1840 nearly three-quarters of the population could read and write, although barely 20 per cent of jobs then required literacy (Katz, 1977; Tyack, 1974). Whereas in 1890 only 4 per cent of 17-year-olds graduated from high schools, by 1930 the figure was 47 per cent. By 1979, these *retention rates* had increased beyond anyone's expectations. They were so far beyond real job needs that a back-lash set in against 'over-education', the 'taxi-driver Ph.D.' and the senseless proliferation of credentials. Table 8−1 makes some international comparisons of retention rates in 1975 for the 15−19 year age group.

Table 8−2   School and tertiary education retention rates

	Year 10	Year 12	CAE's	Uni's
1957	—	—	3%	4.7%
1967	71%	23%	—	—
1977	88%	35%	9.6%	9.5%

(Source: Williams Report, 1979:7, ¶1.1)

Table 8−3   Retention rates[1] to final year of secondary schooling Australia: 1967 to 1977

Year	Males per cent	Females per cent	Persons per cent
1967	26.5	18.7	22.7
1970	33.0	25.5	29.3
1971	34.1	26.9	30.6
1972	35.7	28.9	32.4
1973	35.2	30.8	33.1
1974	34.1	31.6	32.8
1975	34.6	33.6	34.1
1976	34.6	35.3	34.9
1977	34.0	36.6	35.3

[1] Without adjustment for net immigration or grade repetition effects.

(Source: Commonwealth Department of Education, Williams Report, 1979, p. 11)

Notice in Table 8−3 the marked increase in retention rates for girls. The Williams Report also reveals that the rates show marked differences between the States (p.26, ¶1.39); that the number of Australian graduates by the year 2000 will be seven times the number at the time of the 1971 Census (p.29, ¶ 1.44); and that in the current economic climate, there has been a marked slowing down in the retention rate (p.42, ¶2.34). Whereas retention to year twelve rose 43 per cent between 1967—72, the increase over that was only 9 per cent between 1972—77.

People do not stay on at school only because jobs demand skills. The key fact is that employers demand *credentials*. If schools do not actually teach job skills, why are credentials demanded? The answer must be in terms of the existing structure of social relations.

Reverse the logic of the technical-function argument, that

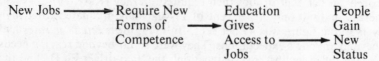

and you have an argument that

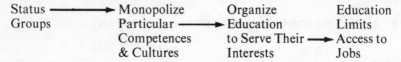

Randall Collins (1971) puts this as a plausible counter-theory to explain how education acts to reproduce the existing structure of status groups in society. People in status groups share a common level of equality and participate in a common culture. As we have shown in Chapter 6, such sub-cultures form the basis of our identity and transmit to us a particular set of moral values, a vocabulary of motives and our standards of evaluation. The sub-cultures may not be distinct groups as such but their 'moral evaluations' set apart the 'in-group' from 'outsiders'. Questions of taste, breeding and respectability are involved. The group's level of organization and cohesion will affect its ability to assert its definition of 'reality' against other, competing views. For that reason, *selection* into a status group will be important. It may be by marriage, employment or education. Important too will be the *manipulation* of those allowed to join (they have to be resocialized into 'acceptable' values) and of those excluded (they have to be taught to respect the superiority of those who 'belong').

In this regard, we may see 'retention rates' in an important new light. Schooling transmits a scholastic culture that is used as a basis for selecting 'suitable' candidates for particular jobs. The longer you stay on at school the closer you get to these models of suitability. Drop out early and your saturation in the scholastic culture is low. As Bourdieu & Passeron (1977, p.82) put it, '. . . at every stage in their school career individuals in the same class who survive in the system exhibit less and less the career characteristics which have eliminated other members of their category'.

Moral Competence and the Hidden Curriculum

Schools, then, are the distributing agents not only of technical or intellectual skills, but also of 'moral competence'. That is, distributors of the 'right' sets of values to the 'right' sorts of people. We will consider evidence that schools do provide training for the elite culture, or respect for it, and that employers do use education as a means of selecting people on the basis of their cultural attributes.

American research has gone further than Australian studies in providing evidence. Social historians like Michael Katz (1977) and David Tyack (1977) have documented the close links between technical and moral competence in public schooling. The demands of industry, the rural to urban population drift, massive immigration and the social chaos of growing American cities gave rise to demands for public education. Local, democratically run schools gave way to centralized and bureaucratically run schools because:
a) they suited rural needs but not large cities;
b) their 'democracy' gave school boards the right to impose local prejudices but a more standardized form of schooling was needed by business; and
c) there was a growing fear of:

> the cultural divisiveness inherent in the increasing religious and ethnic variety of American life. Cultural homogenization played counterpoint to administrative rationality. Bureaucracy was intended to standardize far more than the content of public business (Katz, 1977, p.387).

The solution was to make public education religiously and politically 'neutral', though the values imposed were strictly those of White Anglo-Saxon Protestant (WASP) elites. There was no pretence that public schools were to serve other than moral ends. Education was 'the balance wheel of the social machinery' (Bowles & Gintis, 1976, p.166). The poor would be taught 'to look upon the distinctions of society without envy . . . to understand that they are open to him as well as to others and to respect them for this reason' (Bowles & Gintis, 1976, p.167). Sewing would exert a 'moral influence' (Bowles & Gintis, 1976, p.168). The habits of 'prompt action in the performance of the duty required of the boy, (would become) in the man of business confirmed' (Bowles & Gintis, 1976, p.169). Many children 'have to receive their first lessons of subordination and obedience in the school room' (Bowles & Gintis, 1976, p.162). And the 'hidden curriculum of the school came increasingly to stress "heart culture over brain culture" ' (Bowles & Gintis, 1976, p.163).

As educators and business leaders in the late nineteenth century came to realize that mechanical drill in the 3 R's and strict discipline did not necessarily develop self-control and initiative, teaching methods changed. Legitimation of dominant cultural values became the goal. Schools became graded. Foreign languages, geography, history and even surveying were introduced (though they were taught in a moral rather than a practical or political way). Softer discipline, pleasure in learning and respect for the teacher were stressed 'so that the citizen of tomorrow will think of duty rather than of the policeman' (Bowles & Gintis, 1976, p.170). Female elementary school teachers were favoured, not only because they cost less to hire, but because the school increasingly took on the affective, moral role of the family. (See Parsons (1959) for a more recent analysis of the school's moral role. Parsons here draws heavily on Durkheim's views about education's moral functions for society.)

Bowles and Gintis (1976) also argue that the progressive education movement led by John Dewey (a close associate of George Herbert Mead at Chicago), was ideally suited to the new flexibility and specialization needed by corporate capitalism. Equalizing opportunity and full human development were central to Dewey's thinking but the needs of business carried more weight and set limits to schooling. Social unrest resulting from depressions and union strife in the 1890s raised fears about the cohesion of American life. The excesses of capitalist exploitation were exposed in the vivid, muckraking novels of Upton Sinclair, Sinclair Lewis, John Dos Passos, and Jacob Riis. See particularly Upton Sinclair's *The Jungle* on migrant workers in Chicago's meatworks and *The Goslings* on the 'Black Hand's' stranglehold on school buildings, supplies and textbooks. Dos Passos' massive *U.S.A.* still deserves to be read by everyone today. These novels resulted in governmental reforms and a renewed concern about the moral importance of education.

Stratification of Schooling: the Meritocracy

Out of these struggles emerged America's secondary schools. Pushed by business elites who wanted more specialized workers and supported by workers for whom education rather than private business or land now seemed the only path to advancement, security and social respectability, secondary schools grew apace. But as working class and immigrant children flooded in, moves were made to stratify the schools. No more was there the 'same-curriculum-for-all' argument that led to standardized primary schools. Liberal attacks on academic high schools preserved for the few found partnership with progressive education's call for education to be tailored to the 'needs of the child'. It played into the hands of an increasingly stratified system. Moves were made in the 1890s to establish 'vocational' schools for the working classes. Leading capitalists lent their support because they hoped an oversupply of skilled workers might destroy worker monopoly over apprenticeship and work conditions. Workers called these trade schools 'breeding schools for scabs' because they not only trained additional skilled-tradesmen but also the growing band of foremen whose loyalties were suspect. The Cooley Bill, introduced in 1913 to set up a dual system of vocational-secondary and academic-secondary education in Illinois, was defeated with Dewey and Chicago's teachers supporting the unions. And though the Smith-Hughes Act of 1917 gave federal funding for vocational education, it was restricted to those over 14 years of age.

So the American junior high school remained comprehensive rather than being split into two systems. The inevitable result, as Bowles & Gintis (1976, p.194) argue, was to produce a new form of stratification *within* the schools—'a tracking system which would separate and stratify young people loosely according to race, ethnic origins, and class backgrounds'. They outline the incredible growth of I.Q. testing and scholastic-aptitude testing and the growth of the vocational guidance profession through the early twentieth century. People now take for granted these forms of testing and they have only recently been challenged as *not* being 'culture-free'. The rigidity and arbitrariness of such tests as a form of 'symbolic violence' can be seen in Lewis Terman's view in the 1920s:

> that an I.Q. below 70 rarely permits anything better than unskilled labor; that the range from 70 to 80 is pre-eminently that of semi-skilled labor, from 80 to 100 that of the skilled or ordinary clerical labor, from 100 to 110 or 115 that of the semi-professional pursuits; and that above all these are the grades of intelligence which permit one to enter the professions or the larger fields of business ... This information will be a great value in planning the education of a particular child and also in planning the differentiated curriculum here recommended (quoted in Bowles & Gintis, 1976, p.197).

The effect of such testing was to reinforce and reproduce the existing social structure. Blacks, working class and ethnic groups were streamed and tracked according to measured 'ability'. Since I.Q. correlated closely with social status (largely because the tests used middle-class language and measured middle-class cultural attributes) the tests served to justify social inequalities and to promote an ideology of *meritocracy*. Michael Young in Britain describes this ironically as *I.Q. + Effort = Merit* that is, a belief that life chances are determined by one's own achievement rather than by one's social class. Numerous studies have shown this not to be so and that countries vary in the extent to which they encourage 'contest' versus 'sponsored' mobility (Turner, 1952). They have shown that schooling more often reinforces than alters the class structure.

Cicourel & Kitsuse (1963) studied the way testing and counselling operated in an American high school. They found that guidance officers 'read' test results differently according to what they knew of a student's background. Where a lower-class student scored low on Scholastic Aptitude but high on Grades, he was labelled an 'over-achiever'. Where a middle-class student had discrepant scores he was called an 'under-achiever' or the discrepancy was ignored and he was still regarded as a 'high achiever'. If a lower-class child showed high aptitude but got low grades, the potential was again ignored and he was called an 'opportunity' student and placed in a more vocational, less academic track. Their data suggests that counsellers interpret test scores in terms of known student status and future College plans and channel the less-articulate lower-class group into non-College tracks, regardless of their ability or actual achievement.

The famous study 'Pygmalion in the Classroom' by Rosenthal and Jacobsen (1968) found that teachers' expectations could influence I.Q. scores. A non-verbal I.Q. test was used to predict 'blooming intellect' in some children. Twenty per cent were picked arbitrarily by the experimenters and teachers were told that these children had scored highly on the test. The teachers were told the names of these 'high scorers'. Re-tests four months later and at the end of the year showed the children so labelled had gained in I.Q. score. Those not so labelled had not gained. More significant, though, were the attitudes of teachers. Pupils who had been expected to 'bloom' were seen as more interesting, curious, happy, affectionate and more likely to succeed. Pupils not in that group but who actually had very high intelligence were regarded by teachers as troublesome, less well-adjusted, less interesting and less affectionate. The major effects were seen at early grade levels where pupils' background performance was less well known but they went as far as the grade six level.

Elizabeth Cohen (1970) at Stanford University has extended this sort of research in a series of studies on 'assertion training' and 'diffuse status characteristics'. With groups of black and white students, ethnic minority and majority groups and male and female groups, she and her co-workers have shown how social status and the expectations that go with it alter task performance and affect the competent self-image. In small groups, simple tasks were tackled with more initiative by high status pupils. The minority status pupils held back, made fewer suggestions, deferred to the others and claimed incompetence. They were then given secret help before the group met, that is, they were fed 'resources' in the form of clues to solving the task and information related practice. They began to assert themselves in group interaction when they found their actual competence was superior to the higher status pupils.

This sort of *assertion training* proves how closely related are status, competence and power. In every case, the reversal of initiative proved a shock to those whose cultural status had led them previously to assume superiority and to take the lead. Their damaged *competent self* required boosting and they had to adjust their images of status to a more equal status situation.

Nothing akin to this research has yet been done in Australia, though there are related findings. Knight (1974) examines the 'school status' hypothesis to argue that by their very structure Australian schools 'cool out' the lower status students. He shows that teacher expectations are a crucial factor. Edgar's (1974) study of adolescents found that, despite higher verbal intelligence test scores, girls consistently express lower self-confidence and higher self-deprecation than boys. They have lower aspirations and blame their failings on themselves rather than external life limitations to a greater degree than boys do. Connell et al's (1975) study of Sydney city youth confirms this sex difference. It also shows self-esteem to be higher for pupils in selective private schools, reflecting their higher social status (Connell et al, 1975, pp.61−2), though the levels for sex difference seem high across every social class. Wright & Headlam (1976) report marked differences between the sense of competence expressed by youths who have stayed on at school and those who have been 'cooled out' by an alienating and irrelevant school system. And Campbell (1978, p.196) in a detailed study of West Heidelberg (Melbourne) schools, suggests that while working-class children can maintain a reasonable sense of self at primary school, their 'hopes and dreams have soured by mid-secondary school'. The personal collectivism of primary education gives way to:

> individualism, private ambition and egoism . . . Conformity to externals becomes increasingly irrelevant to mastery of subject material and teacher approval . . . the school rejects what you are and what you think you can do . . . Children seek status in the external symbols of adulthood, and in the derivative symbols of 'high-class' living. School and often family reject them as 'failures' so they turn elsewhere to rescue their integrity as persons (Campbell, 1978, p.197).

Campbell (1978, pp.199 and 200) sees the schools as providing such a child with 'a daily and official statement of his inadequacy and incompetence'; the system's barriers being 'less effective than the belief in the legitimacy of the system by most of the population'.

Such feelings of incompetence are reflected in the lack of influence lower-class parents have on school governance (Davies, 1978; Fitzgerald, Pettit & Musgrave, 1978) and the monopoly held by businessmen, middle-class 'organization' people and 'professional' teachers on school council membership (cf. Bowles & Gintis, 1976, pp.186−90).

The Williams Report of 1979 reveals how the interests of various status groups are reflected in what they want education to do (see pp.100−12 on 'Objectives'). Evidence given to the inquiry proved there is 'not a true consensus' in Australia and that definitions of desired competences (both intellectual and moral) vary enormously. The Tasmanian Education Department distinguishes, interestingly, between 'politically-based purposes' and 'educationally-based purposes'. The former include:

> the basic *skills*, the introduction to the *norms* of Australian culture, the provision of equal *opportunities*, the certification and ranking of students at the exit point to assist the *selection* process of society.

Politically-based purposes are 'outcomes and articulated by laymen rather than professionals'. Educationally-based purposes, on the other hand concern the *process* of schooling dealing with:

> pupils as individuals: the development of self-awareness, the transition from adolescence to maturity, the development of practical, intellectual, expressive and social competencies including the handling of information and linguistic competency, and the individual's understanding of work, personal relationships, values and political and ethical issues (pp.102−3, ¶4.46, 4.47).

Against such professional educational aims, the Central Industrial Secretariat argued that educationalists hold too much control, are not accountable to the community and that schools wrongly stress academic skills inappropriate for most students. The employers complained that 'schools were failing to assist the selection processes of society' and 'produced students who in the standard of their academic achievement and in their attitudes were not suitable for employment'. I.C.I. Australia criticized schools for encouraging 'excessive individualism', making it hard 'for students to adjust to employment' (Williams Report, 1979, p.104). Others called for more 'vocational training which commerce and industry should be involved in designing' (Williams Report, 1979, p.105). The A.C.T.U. complained that 'the job expectations of school leavers were often unrealistic and that they had little or no work orientation', and the National Youth Council deplored 'the schools' implicit devaluation of manual and technical skills' (Williams Report, 1979, p.108). While the Tasmanian Department of Education felt employers had a right to expect basic skills and responsible attitudes, they did point out that:

> the changing demands of modern work had caused employers, who sought not only 'obedience, submissiveness and a willingness to carry out mundane tasks cheerfully' but also initiative and adaptability, to raise their standards (Williams Report, 1979, p.109).

The Queensland Education Department commented that 'the education system could not cure problems which lay deep in the social and economic structure of the community' (Williams Report, 1979, p.109).

But the conclusions drawn by the Williams Committee are based on unsound logic. It argued that there is 'insufficient differentiation of programs' and quoted disapprovingly the TEND Committee's attack on testing:

> sorting on the basis of ability testing or school performance is nearly equivalent to sorting on the basis of class differences and that teaching based on ability grouping tends to increase the advantage that social class status brings with it (p.111).

Williams' comment is that:

> misjudged parental ambitions and fears that differentiation will reinforce class differences have helped to produce too homogeneous a pattern for secondary schools (p.111, ¶4.62).

The whole thrust of the 1979 Williams Report is to differentiate further the education system. It argues that CAE's and TAFE colleges should offer lower level, practical education for the less gifted; that universities should be highly selective and fees should perhaps be reintroduced. A fine compromise is effected in the Report between the interests of academics and business: university funding returns to triennial plans but while research is to be encouraged it is to be 'coordinated' and tied to practical needs. A slight obeisance to improving academic teaching skills is made; but lesser colleges will deal with the masses. A national system of testing literacy and numeracy should be established, so that 'weaknesses' in the school system can be identified. Yet, as we have seen, testing, tracking and curriculum streaming make education a more, not less, stratifying process.

The Outcomes of Schooling

What, in fact, are the effects of schooling? The A.C.E.R. Survey showed Australian literacy and numeracy rates to be equal to those of other advanced countries, though there was room for improvement. Those most in need of help were migrant children from homes where another language was spoken, Aboriginal students, and those with specific learning handicaps. The survey concluded that quality of teaching is most central to success and that efforts to improve mastery within these groups should increase. While it did not gather data on parental occupation levels, it did suggest that 'the social characteristics of the regions in which the homes were set were more likely to be factors on which compensatory programs might be based' (Bourke & Keeves, 1977, p.14).

It is ironic perhaps that the Williams Report should insist on testing all school children, with little acknowledgement of the effects of variations in their home backgrounds. The Schools Commission established by the Whitlam Labor Government in 1972 very firmly set its policy on the path of funding to meet needs and of overcoming the disadvantages produced by social class differences. The Williams Report (Ch.11, vol. 1) confines its comments on 'access' to figures on 'retention rates' and the problems of Aborigines and handicapped people. It does acknowledge the 'structural' problem that technical students have if they want to transfer courses. It also acknowledges that though 'the universities are not institutions for the exclusive possession of the very rich ... the socio-economic status of parents certainly influences the post-secondary participation rates of their children and the sector in which they participate'.

Table 8 – 4 Fathers' occupations of students in post-secondary education 1974

Fathers' Occupations	% Male Population (aged 45 – 54)	% Fathers of Students (F/T Students)		All Students
		Univ.	CAE	TAFE
Professional/Technical	7	24	17	7
Administrative/Executive	11	19	15	7
Clerical	7	5	5	6
Sales	5	5	5	7
Farming/Fishery	9	7	11	11
Mining/Quarrying	1	1	2	1
Communications	7	4	6	7
Tradesmen/Labourers	37	15	20	39
Services	4	3	3	4
Armed Forces	1	1	0	1
Other	11	16	16	9

(Source: Williams Report, 1978, p. 319, Table 7 – 6)

Table 8 – 5 Median income, by education level (full year, full-time workers only)

Qualifications	1968 – 69		1973	
	Males	Females	Males	Females
Degree, tertiary	$6620	$3210	$9210	$6790
Non-degree, tertiary	5110		7970	5210
Technician level	4610	2380	6940	4080
Trade level	3690		5680	3740
Other qualification	—	—	5290	3850
Left school, no subsequent qualifications				
— at Matric or age 18	3780	2370	5450	3750
— at 17	3300	2080	5190	3680
— at 16	3120	1950	4980	3400
— at 14 or 15	3090	1910	4850	3310
— at 13 or under	3010	1880	4700	3210

(Source: Fitzgerald, 1976, p. 30, Table 2.14)

But the Report (p.318) rather oddly regards TAFE courses as playing 'a part in overcoming the influence of the socio-economic status of parents on participation rates in post-secondary education'.

This is to ignore the qualitative differences within 'post-secondary education' and the close links between education levels and later job types and income earning levels.

Education and Jobs

If we look at earnings in relation to the levels of education gained, we get another picture of how limits in one resource carry over into another and reproduce inequalities in society.

One of the only areas in which qualifications do not significantly increase income is at the trade level and yet the qualifications being offered through the TAFE colleges are trade level qualifications. The only consolation to this increasing stratification of education levels is the fact that fees in Australia are either non-existent or very low. In the United States students have to pay fees of up to $7000 a year for a private university and between $1500 to $3000 for a State university. The fees are progressively lower for the State 4-year colleges, the 2-year junior colleges and the regional community colleges. Such fees make it impossible for lower-class people to enter anything beyond the lower status colleges and pursue lower status, vocationally-oriented curriculum programmes. The Australian system subsidizes all tertiary level education through government taxation and is therefore more open to anyone with talent. Fees, however, are only part of the 'opportunity costs' of education. Earnings foregone, living costs, books and other extras all make it harder for lower income parents to keep their children at school or beyond.

The Williams Report shows the intimate connections between qualifications and the type of job entered. The bottom line of Table 8—6 shows how few people in the Australian workforce actually have tertiary qualifications. Excluding trade level training, it is only 11.3 per cent. Within that group only 128 212 or 2.4 per cent have a degree and only 19 546 people or 0.4 per cent have a higher degree such as an M.A. or Ph.D. Most of the employed people with degrees are in 'community services' such as public administration and business. Manufacturing is the area most seriously in decline, yet that is the sector where most people with trade and other technical qualifications are employed. What then will happen to colleges of advanced education or TAFE colleges if job levels continue to drop?

When a measure of job prestige is used to see how education is distributed, a similar picture emerges. Fitzgerald in his report on *Poverty and Education in Australia, 1976*, shows that:

> Of those people who had never attended school, 77 per cent of males and 85.8 per cent of females were found to be in the two lowest prestige rankings which include shop assistants, process workers, domestic and service workers, and labourers. Among those who had attended only primary school, 59.8 per cent of males and 74.4 per cent of females were similarly at the bottom of the prestige scale. Of those

Table 8–6   Education and jobs: Industry by highest level of qualification obtained
(Employed Population 15 years of age and over, Australia, Census 30 June 1971)

Industry (Division)	No Qualification	Trade level	Technician level	Other tertiary	First Degree	Higher Degree	Total	%
Agriculture, Forestry, Fishing etc.	91.4%	3.2	3.1	.9	.5	.05	386 407	7.4
Mining	70.1	16.9	3.4	2.5	3.4	.8	76 023	1.4
Manufacturing	71.0	21.3	2.9	1.8	.9	.1	1 215 618	23.2
Electricity, Gas & Water	58.9	26.9	5.2	4.3	2.4	.2	91 252	1.7
Construction	57.0	37.5	2.3	1.3	.7	.06	412 229	7.8
Wholesale & Retail Trade	78.0	14.0	2.6	2.1	.7	.07	988 088	18.8
Transport & Storage	81.6	10.3	3.4	1.1	.4	.04	271 713	5.2
Communication	75.9	6.8	12.5	1.4	1.1	.06	103 485	1.9
Finance, Business Services, etc.	74.5	3.7	4.1	6.9	4.4	.4	363 418	6.9
Public Admin., Defence	68.9	10.1	6.7	5.3	5.1	.5	283 152	5.4
Community Services	46.6	4.7	12.0	19.8	11.2	2.2	564 649	10.8
Entertainment, Recreation etc.	80.1	12.4	2.7	1.5	.6	.07	267 511	5.1
Other & Not Stated	85.3	9.3	1.8	1.5	.8	.01	216 883	4.1
Total Employed	3 757 315	758 999	226 262	221 113	128 212	19 546	5 240 428	100%

who attended to level 10, nearly twice as many males and more than twice as many females are found in the highest prestige ranking (including upper and lower professional occupations, graziers, wheat and sheep farmers) compared with the two lowest rankings combined (Fitzgerald, 1976, pp.17—18).

At the top end, prestige depends less on education and more on property ownership and inherited wealth, but at the bottom end, lack of education acts as one of the barriers to prestige and enhanced life chances.

That in itself helps explain why education has been so highly regarded. It is valued as a pathway to social status, higher incomes and greater job satisfaction. The facts of life, however, speak louder than socially-approved values and not every child is able to stay on at school.

Retention rates reflect not simply a desire for more education or hopes for a better job. They reflect the value system of the school itself, a 'school climate' which conveys the importance of education and the school community's self-fulfilling expectation that pupils 'should' stay on or drop out early. In private schools, pupils stay on longer despite individual misgivings and dissatisfactions with schooling. Seventy-six per cent of students in government schools leave before the final year, compared with 48 per cent in non-government schools (Radford & Wilkes, 1975). Whereas in government schools only 24 per cent stay on to final year, the figure is 39 per cent for Catholic schools and 67 per cent for non-Catholic independent schools.

These figures mean that half Australia's young people leave school by age 16. Only about a third continue to final year and only about 70 per cent of them satisfy university entry requirements. Employers and the public service, however, increasingly require a pass in the final school certificate as an employability criterion.

Despite fears that modern societies produce too many 'over-qualified' people, the actual numbers of qualified people in Australia are not high. As Fitzgerald (1976, p.39) argues, there is an almost universal attitude in Australia that education gives access to good jobs and that good jobs, being scarce, can only be taken by those who have 'proved' themselves through long years of schooling. The undesirable effects of using education as a job ticket thus:

> entails a view of education that is seriously defective in that education is not valued for itself, as an activity worthwhile in its own terms . . . but rather as a means to an end . . . If less reliance were put on certificates, employers would have to be more careful in defining the actual requirements for jobs, and more inclined to inquire into the job-related capabilities of candidates. Third, this practice confirms the already strongly entrenched assumption that education should precede work, and that the time for education in the life cycle of individuals is in their childhood and adolescence, as a 'once only' process that is not relevant to adults (Fitzgerald, 1976, p.138).

Conclusion

The structure of society and its organization of institutions affects both the structure of education and its effects on the life chances of already unequal groups. If we can be permitted an aside on the Schools Commission and its work, we may pull together the major threads of this chapter on education as an institution of cultural reproduction.

Our theme has been that of competence: of how socially distributed resources are converted into the 'equipment for competence performance' and the social development of a 'competent self'. In this respect the Schools Commission, despite mammoth efforts to improve the quality and equality of Australian education has fallen victim of the dominant rhetoric. It has defined competence largely in individualistic forms. This conceals a central fact of modern life that is not ignored in practice: that no one person can carry through complex tasks alone, but has to rely upon the skills and cooperation of others. Successful coordination is, in fact, a group-based capacity to draw upon individual talents, to use those talents where they are most appropriate and not expect people to perform well in every facet of the task. This is a view I have expounded elsewhere in relation to 'the competent teacher' (Edgar, 1974), arguing that not every teacher is equally good at lecturing, explaining, group work, individual tutoring and administration. So teacher-training should be directed at developing particular talents to the full rather than at some idealized notion of the perfect all-round teacher. In business, no-one makes that sort of elementary mistake. It is recognized that each person's competence contributes in different ways to the overall goal. Where capitalism then distorts the cooperative contribution incentive, is in rewarding talents differently. A factory or office could not function properly without cleaners or maintenance people but they are paid less than the personnel manager or foreman or top executive.

The Schools Commission recognizes, however, that inequalities in Australian society are structured and that the disadvantages of poor home backgrounds are reflected in poor school facilities. Thus their thrust since 1972 has been to make the schools 'equal'. Per capita grants are based upon measures of each school's socioeconomic status. Wealthy private schools are given less per pupil than the poorer Catholic or State schools. In addition, supplementary grants are given to specially disadvantaged schools in each State.

While this has been a major step forward in rectifying inequalities of educational opportunity in Australia, several assumptions and consequences cause doubt. The worst assumption is that the schools can solve society's problems. That has never been possible. Of course the Schools Commission programme must be seen in the context of the massive programme of reforms proposed by the 1972 Whitlam Government in other areas of society: welfare, health, decentralization, city renewal and control of wages, prices and mineral resources. None of these reforms really struck at the basis of unequal property distribution, so opportunities remained within the competitive free enterprise system. But it was hoped that inequalities of starting points might in some way be affected.

The second major assumption of the Commission was that more money to the schools would improve the quality of education. While money may be a necessary condition for improvement, it is certainly not a sufficient condition. Structurally, the Schools Commission had no control over how the money would be spent by the States so no outcome could be guaranteed. Programmes to improve pre-school education and teacher education were also begun but were given neither the same priority nor funding. A case could be made, however, that these strike more directly at the heart of both educational quality and equality.

Thirdly, the Commission assumed that basic literacy and numeracy were the foundation stones of equal opportunity. Although we might agree, we need to consider the meanings of those terms and whether the schools, as presently organized, can provide them. We have seen that the culture of the home 'arrests' the language skills of many children. Restrictions on play, on exploratory activity, on asking questions and on expressing opinions, retard the growth of many children into fully competent adulthood. Can the school alone undo the damage? In that the Schools Commission encouraged parent-community participation in education it recognized the problem. But the barriers to successful participation were enormous. Not the least of them is the so-called 'professionalism' of teachers which asserts expertise and authority as a protective device.

The 'tyranny of subjects' works against the development of basic literacy and numeracy. Timetables, too rigid an interpretation of 'liberal' education and an academic orientation to subject divisions rather than an intellectual orientation to learning, all prevent a concerted attack on the basic competences. Many migrant children are condemned to illiteracy in the master language because teachers speak only English. Moreover, numeracy is interpreted as *mathematics*, one of the least generally useful and worst taught subjects in the school curriculum.

Literacy and numeracy are not the grammar or literature or mathematics we see outlined in a school syllabus. They are, instead, the modes of speech of the respectable classes. They are the ability to manipulate ideas and the capacity to see through the distortions and manipulations of others. They are the ability to 'read' the messages and rules of social life. When we emphasize exclusively the *mechanics* of literacy and numeracy, we neglect their basic political content as the equipment for competence and efficacy, for being in control of our environment.

It is this basic linguistic and communicative competence that lies at the core of political power and impotence. Bourdieu refers to it as *symbolic violence*—the subtle relationship between the mastery of language and the conservation of power.

The same point applies to the content of other school 'subjects'. Do our schools teach history as it is related to the social structures of capitalism? Is economics or consumer education taught as political economy? Do science teachers relate their subject matter to problems of growth, environment and mastery, other than in trendy and incidental style? Is the analysis of other cultures through their language styles put above mechanical linguistics? Unfortunately knowledge is divided and sub-divided and children get a smattering of everything but a deep analysis of nothing. The content of our typifications is very thin and is kept thin by both schools and the media. That is the essence of cultural reproduction.

The few who stay on at school manage to gain some insight into the system, some notion of how to use their resources in the pursuit of control. It is seldom a *critical* insight because most 'academic work' is directed against that, but it is an insight that preserves and maintains their initial advantage in the 'personality market'. That is why (Jencks (1972), Bowles and Gintis (1976), Bourdieu and Passeron (1977)) we find repeatedly that socioeconomic status is *still* the major determinant of what types of academic qualifications and career opportunities an individual will have access to.

Because it held individual competence to be the basis for equal opportunity, the consequences of the Schools Commission's findings have not been quite what was hoped for. There has been no major effort to alter the ways home background disadvantages or assists children at school. There has been no restructuring of the school curriculum to allow a concerted effort to improve literacy and numeracy in the terms outlined above. Money has often been spent on *things* rather than on improving *people resources* or *programmes*. Some of the more innovative programmes have involved parents and the wider community to redefine the nature of education, but the broader system runs on with separate schools, grade levels, subjects, certificates and 'professional' teacher domination. Funds have gone to individual schools and often to separate programmes within those schools, rather than to provide the means of sharing what exists a few blocks or a few kilometres away. There has been a rush for every school to have its own film projectors, video equipment, telescopes, camping gear, sets of remedial readers and so on, instead of an attempt at cooperative sharing of resources.

As a consequence divide and rule individualism remains with little recognition of the need to develop *group* capacities to act. The rhetoric about school-community interaction, about competence and removing inequality of opportunity, falls into the trap of stressing individual competences rather than group capacities to cope (Sennett and Cobb, 1973). It says little about competence in 'political' terms; of shared efficacy; of groups sharing in the decision-making process; of the curriculum being taught not as arbitrary subjects but as means to ends of effectiveness.

But a new initiative in Victoria through the Schools Commission Country Education Project stresses 'cooperative competence' and a broader communal involvement in education. The Project recognizes that continued emphasis on the development of individual competence neglects the role society plays in limiting the access children may have to the resources necessary to develop social competence.

It is political know-how that counts. We may well be able to produce more competent, efficacious, self-confident people by building on and sharing community competences than through individualized efforts. Above all, that means breaking down traditional educational 'sorting' processes.

Readings and References

a. Australian Society:

A.C.E. (1978) *Quality in Australian Education*, Australian College of Education, Melbourne.

ANDERSON, D. S. & J. S. WESTERN (1972) 'Denominational Schooling and Religious Behavior', *ANZJS*, Vol. 8, pp.19-31.

BATES, R. J. (1975) 'Trends in the Sociology of the School', *ANZJS*, Vol. 11, 1975, No. 3, pp.10-14.

BESSANT, B. & A. SPAULL (1976) *Politics of Schooling*, Pitman Books, Sydney.

BOURKE, S. F. & J. P. KEEVES (1977) *Australian Studies in School Performance*, Vol. III, The Mastery of Literacy and Numeracy: Final Report, E.R.D.C., A.G.P.S., Canberra.

CAMPBELL, F. (1978) *The School in Heidelberg*, unpublished ms, prepared for the Heidelberg schools.

CONNELL, R. W. (1970) 'Class Consciousness in Childhood', *ANZJS*, Vol. 6, pp.87-99.

CONNELL, W. F. (1970) 'Myths and Traditions in Australian Education', *The Aust. J. of Education*, Vol. 14, No. 3, pp.252-64.

CONNELL, W. F., R. E. STROOBANT, K. E. SINCLAIR, R. W. CONNELL & K. W ROGERS (1975) *12 to 20, Studies of City Youth*, Hicks Smith & Sons, Sydney.

DAVIES, J. (1978) *An Evaluation of School Councils*, unpublished MA thesis, La Trobe University.

EDGAR, D. E. (1974) 'Adolescent Competence and Sexual Disadvantage', *La Trobe Sociology Papers*, No. 10, La Trobe University, Melbourne.

EDGAR, D. E. (ed.) (1974) *The Competent Teacher*, Angus & Robertson, Sydney.

EDGAR, D. E. (1975a) 'Preparing Teachers for Change', *La Trobe Sociology Papers*, No. 32, La Trobe University, Melbourne.

EDGAR, D. E. (ed.) (1975b) *The Sociology of Australian Education*, McGraw Hill, Sydney.

EDGAR D. E. (1975c) 'Adolescent Competence and Educational Ambition', in Edgar, D. E. (ed.), *The Sociology of Australian Education*, McGraw Hill, Sydney, pp.3-13.

EDUCATION AND THE ARTS (1977) AGPS, Canberra.

FENSHAM, P. J. (1975) 'School and Family Factors among Commonwealth Secondary Scholarship Winners in Victoria, 1964-1971', in D. E. Edgar (ed.) *Sociology of Australian Education*, McGraw-Hill, Sydney.

FITZGERALD, R. T. (1976) *Poverty and Education in Australia*, Fifth Main Report of the Australian Govt. Commission of Inquiry into Poverty, AGPS., Canberra.

FITZGERALD, R. T., D. PETTIT and P. W. MUSGRAVE, (1978) *The New School Councils*, Burwood State College, Melbourne.

FOSTER, L. (1976) 'Phenomenology in the "New" Sociology of Education',

ANZJS, Vol. 12, No. 1, pp.2-8.

GIRLS, SCHOOL AND SOCIETY (1975), Schools Commission, Canberra.

HICKMAN, D. C. (1975) 'The Sociological Dimensions of Educational Ideologies', *La Trobe Sociology Papers*, No. 15, La Trobe University, Melbourne.

KNIGHT, T. (1974) 'Powerlessness and the Student Role: Structural Determinants of School Status', *ANZJS*, Vol. 10, No. 2, pp.36-9.

LEVER, C. (1975) 'Social Theory, Child Failure and the "Missionary" School', in Edgar, D. E. (ed.), *The Sociology of Australian Education*, McGraw-Hill, Sydney, pp.146-56.

MARTIN, J. I. & P. MEADE (1979) *The Educational Experiences of Sydney High School Students*, AGPS, Canberra.

(MARTIN REPORT) (1965) *Tertiary Education in Australia*, AGPS, Canberra.

MERCURIO, J. E. (1974) 'Caning: Educational Ritual', *ANZJS*, Vol. 10, No. 1, pp.49-53.

MILLER, A. (1977) 'Social-Cultural Theories of Education and the Sociology of Education', in Edgar, D. E. (ed.), *The Sociology of Australian Education*, McGraw Hill, Sydney, pp.423-44.

MOL, J. J. (1968) 'The Effects of Denominational Schools in Australia', *ANZJS*, Vol. 4, pp.18-35.

MURRAY, K. A. H. (chairman) (1957) *Report of the Committee on Australian Universities*, AGPS, Canberra.

MUSGRAVE, P. W. (1979) *Society and the Curriculum in Australia*, Allen & Unwin, Sydney.

RADFORD, W. C. & R. E. WILKES (1975) *School Leavers in Australia, 1971-72*, A.C.E.R., Melbourne.

RIST, R. C. (1974) 'Why Public Schools Don't Change: An Assessment of Current Attempts at Educational Reform in the U.S.', *ANZJS*, Vol. 10, No. 1, pp.26-30.

SPAULL, A. (1979) 'Education', in B. Head & A. Patience, *From Whitlam to Fraser*, Oxford University Press, Melbourne, pp.125-39.

TAFT, R. (1975) 'Secondary Scholarship Holders and Their Background', in Edgar, D. E. (ed.), *The Sociology of Australian Education*, McGraw Hill, Sydney, pp.14-25.

TOOMEY, D. (1974) 'What Causes Educational Disadvantage?', *ANZJS*, Vol. 10, No. 1, pp.31-7.

TOOMEY, D. (1976) 'Educational Disadvantage and Meritocratic Schooling', *ANZJS*, Vol. 12, No. 3, pp.228-35.

WALKER, B. M. (1976) 'Ideological Underpinnings of Education—China and the West', *ANZJS*, Vol. 12, No. 2, pp.101-5.

(WILLIAMS REPORT) (1979) *Education, Training and Employment: Report of the Committee of Inquiry into Education and Training*, 3 vols., AGPS, Canberra.

WRIGHT, A. F. & F. HEADLAM (1976) *Youth Needs and Public Policy*, A.C.E.R. and Victorian Department of Youth Sport and Recreation, Melbourne.

WRIGHT, A., F. HEADLAM, U. OZOLINS, R. T. FITZGERALD, & R. E.

STROOBANT, (1978) *Outcomes of Schooling: Aspects of Success and Failure*, Commission of Inquiry into Poverty, AGPS, Canberra.

b. General:

BEN-DAVID, J. & A. ZLOCZOWER (1962) 'Universities and Academic Systems in Modern Societies', *European Journal of Sociology*, 31, pp.45-85.
BERG, I. (1970) *Education and Jobs: The Great Training Robbery*, Praeger, N.Y.
BERNSTEIN, B. (1972) 'Sociology and the Sociology of Education', in *18 Plus: The Final Selection*, Units 15-17, School and Society, Open University Press, U.K.
BERNSTEIN, B. (1977) *Class, Codes and Control, Vol. 3, Towards a Theory of Educational Transmissions*, (2nd ed.), Routledge & Kegan Paul, London.
BOURDIEU, P. & J. C. PASSERON (1977) *Reproduction in Education, Society and Culture*, Sage, N.Y.
BOWLES, S. & H. GINTIS (1976) *Schooling in Capitalist America*, Basic Books, N.Y.
CICOUREL, A. V. & J. I. KITSUSE (1963) *The Educational Decision-Makers*, Bobbs Merrill Inc., reprinted in Karabel, J. & A. H. Halsey (eds), *Power and Ideology in Education* (1977) Oxford University Press, Oxford, pp.282-92.
CLARK, B. R. (1962) *Educating the Expert Society*, Chandler, N.Y.
COHEN, E. G. (1968/1970) 'Interracial Interaction Disability' and 'Expectation Training 1: Altering the Effects of a Racial Status Characteristic', *Technical Reports* Nos. 1 and 2, Stanford Center for Research & Development in Education, Stanford University, California.
COHEN, E. G. (1970) *A New Approach to Applied Research: Race and Education*, Merrill, Columbus.
COLLINS, R. (1971) 'Functional and Conflict Theories of Educational Stratification', *American Sociological Review*, 36, pp.1002-19.
COSIN, B. R., I. R. DALE, G. M. ESLAND & D. R. SWIFT (1971) *School and Society: A Sociological Reader*, MIT Press, Cambridge, Mass.
DAVIS, K. & W. MOORE (1945) 'Some Principles of Stratification', *American Sociological Review*, 10, pp.242-9.
DURKHEIM, E. (1977 [1969]) 'On Education and Society', in J. Karabel & A. H. Halsey (eds), *Power and Ideology in Education*, Oxford University Press, Oxford, pp.92-104.
EGGLESTON, J. (1977) *The Sociology of the School Curriculum*, Routledge & Kegan Paul, London.
FOSTER, P. (1965) 'The Vocational School Fallacy in Development Planning', reprinted in Karabel, J. and A. H. Halsey (eds), *Power and Ideology in Education*, Oxford University Press, Oxford, pp.356-65.
FREIRE, P. (1972) *Pedagogy of the Oppressed*, Penguin, U.K.
GARTNER, A. & F. RIESSMAN (1977) 'The Assessment Controversy', *Social Policy*, Vol. 8, No. 2, pp.2-3.
HABERMAS, J. (1970) 'Toward a Theory of Communicative Competence', in H. P. Dreitzel (ed.), *Recent Sociology No. 2*, Macmillan, London, pp.115-48.

HALSEY, A. H. (1977) 'Towards Meritocracy? The Case of Britain', in J. Karabel & A. H. Halsey (eds), *Power and Ideology in Education*, Oxford University Press, Oxford, pp.173-85.

HOLT, J. (1969) *How Children Fail*, Penguin, U.K.

ILLICH, I. (1971) *Deschooling Society*, Harper & Row, N.Y.

JENCKS, C. (1972) *Inequality: A Reassessment of the Effect of Family and Schooling in America*, Basic Books, N.Y.

KATZ, M. B. (1977) 'From voluntarism to bureaucracy in American Education', reprinted in J. Karabel & A. H. Hasley (eds), *Power and Ideology in Education*, Oxford University Press, Oxford.

KOHN, M. L. (1969) *Class and Conformity: A Study in Values*, Dorsey Press, U.S.A.

OPIE, I. & P. (1977) *The Lore and Language of Schoolchildren*, Paladin, U.K.

PARSONS, T. (1959) 'The School Class as a Social System: Some of its Functions in American Society', *Harvard Educational Review*, 29, pp.297-318; reprinted in A. H. Halsey, J. Floud & A. C. Anderson (eds) *Education, Economy and Society* (1961) Free Press, N.Y., pp.434-55.

PRICE, R. F. (1977) *Marx and Education in Russia and China*, Croom Helm, U.K.

ROSENTHAL, R. & L. JACOBSEN (1968) *Pygmalion in the Classroom*, Holt, Rinehart & Winston, N.Y.

SCHATZMAN, L. & A. STRAUSS (1955) 'Social Class and Modes of Communication', *American Journal of Sociology*, Vol. 60, pp.329-38.

SCHULTZ, T. W. (1977 [1961]) 'Investment in Human Capital', in J. Karabel & A. H. Halsey (eds), *Power and Ideology in Education*, Oxford University Press, Oxford, pp.313-24.

SENNETT, R. & COBB, J. (1973) *The Hidden Injuries of Class*, Random House Vintage Books, N.Y.

SEWELL, W. H. & V. P. SHAH (1977 [1967]) 'Socioeconomic Status, Intelligence and the Attainment of Higher Education', in J. Karabel & A. H. Halsey (eds), *Power and Ideology in Education*, Oxford University Press, Oxford, pp.197-214.

SILBERMAN, C. E. (1970) *Crisis in the Classroom: The Remaking of American Education*, Random House (Vintage), N.Y.

TURNER, R. (1952) 'Sponsored and Contest Mobility and the School System', *American Sociological Review*, 25, pp.855-67.

TYACK, D. B. (1974) *The One Best System: A History of American Urban Education*, Harvard University Press, Cambridge, Mass.

TYLER, W. (1977) *The Sociology of Educational Inequality*, Methuen, U.K.

WEBER, M. (1968) *Economy and Society*, Bedminster Press, N.Y.

YOUNG, M. F. D. (ed.) (1971) *Knowledge and Control, New Directions in the Sociology of Education*, Collier Macmillan, U.K.

YOUNG, M. F. D. (1958) *The Rise of the Meritocracy 1870-2033*, Thames & Hudson, London.

Chapter 9

Work and Life Concerns

9

Studs Terkel begins his book about '*Working*' with the words:

> This book, being about work, is, by its very nature, about violence — to the spirit as well as to the body. It is about ulcers as well as accidents, about shouting matches as well as fistfights, about nervous breakdowns as well as kicking the dog around. It is, above all (or beneath all), about daily humiliations. To survive the day is triumph enough for the walking wounded among the great many of us ... It is about a search, too, for daily meaning as well as daily bread, for recognition as well as cash, for astonishment rather than torpor; in short, for a sort of life rather than a Monday through Friday sort of dying. Perhaps immortality, too, is part of the quest. To be remembered was the wish, spoken and unspoken, of the heroes and heroines of this book (Terkel, 1974, p.1).

If that quotation strikes a few surprising notes and shakes a few taken-for-granted assumptions about work, then it is worth re-reading. For Terkel vividly sums up several of the key sociological issues that make work of such central concern.

Work is, first of all, a means of survival. Without it we would not satisfy our most basic needs.

Secondly, work is an integral part of social life. Whether or not we choose to think of work and leisure, or work and home as separate, the time we must spend working affects our family relationships, our friendships and our capacity for private social activity.

Thirdly, work extends our range of social relations. It structures us into new sets of roles, expectations, statuses and forms of authority and control. The nature of those new networks may alter the impact of earlier childhood socialization in the family and the school. Whatever competences, skills, interests, motives or values we have acquired will be important for selection into a job but will very likely be modified by those we contact in a new work situation. Especially if we anticipate a career and stay in that line of work, our personalities and life-styles take on a new colour.

That suggests the fourth element: our sense of identity. Our sense of self-respect and of social status will depend in part upon the sort of work we do. We become an *organization man*, an *ordinary working man*, a *born nurse*, a *career girl* or *just a housewife* according to how we and others evaluate our work roles.

Fifthly, because work is so closely tied to public evaluations, it can do violence to the self. It can alienate us from our nature, the products of our labour and from being effectively in control of our own lives. Such cultural effects clearly relate to the socially structured relations of work, relations that limit life chances and affect our sociological futures.

The Centrality of Work

We may not baldly assert that work is a central life concern. We need to consider for whom and under what conditions. Work itself must be defined not only in terms of producing food, houses and clothing. For work can be 'non-production' work, contributing indirectly to producing material goods but having no tangible output to measure. Teachers are often accused of being non-productive and of bludging on fat government salaries. They are charged with being on the job only for its long holidays, security of tenure and future superannuation. Public servants, bureaucrats, administrators, personnel experts and academic researchers may also be seen to be wasteful, non-productive and expendable. Sociologically, however, the roles of teachers and other 'service' workers have developed because there was a need. Although their links with productivity may be distant or tenuous, we must see them within the broader structure of organized work.

Work can also be 'over-productive'. The advanced societies manufacture and waste more energy, food and 'unnecessary' consumer items than the rest of the world put together. Surplus in one nation does not necessarily go to the needy in another. Families enjoy, but do not 'need', two cars or two television sets, a holiday house, a swimming pool or a yacht. But they work to get them. Work goes well beyond satisfying basic survival needs. It responds to cultural values and serves status goals. Our motives and particular interests will affect how central work is to us as a life concern.

One of the most basic shifts that accompanied modern industrialization was the separation of work from the home. Farming retains some of the characteristics that formerly integrated work with the rest of life. A rural family may still work together to produce food and sell the surplus, the rhythm of their life fluctuating with seasonal demands. But it may have milk and bread delivered; keep children at a school away from the farm; employ others to do the dirty work and separate private lives from public places.

Work for most people has become identified with the 'public' side of their existence — the train, office, city street, factory cafeteria, union meeting. Formal relationships based on a hierarchy of impersonal authority force them into public associations. Home, leisure or 'non-work' time, the back garden, become private refuges from the stresses of work. Sociologically, then, we might expect to find a variety of *work cultures* that affect people at work but do not necessarily carry over into their private life concerns.

When we consider how consistent work behaviour is with private behaviour, we may hypothesize about it and test for it—but we may not assume it. People may be 'working class' but not vote for the Labor Party; they may be ruthless businessmen but also devout Christians who do much volunteer community work; they may be liberated career women and devoted mothers and wives. Such contrasts bother us because we like consistency; we prefer our 'labels' to work for us across situations so that we can 'typify' whole groups of people and 'control' them, at least within our own cultural world view. Because of the complex division of labour, people in some work situations never see how others work. If social contacts are few at work or outside it, labels may become stereotypes based on ignorance and mass media images.

In contrast to the divided lives of the modern industrial state, consider the lives of the Maring, a remote group of tribesmen living in the Bismark Mountains of New Guinea. Harris (1977) tries to explain why these people 'love' pigs, and does so in terms of the close links between work, war and cultural belief systems. The Maring treat pigs like children. They love them and almost worship them. Every twelve years or so, however, there is a massive pig slaughter and gorging feast. Known as the *kaiko*, it sometimes spreads out over a whole year. The slaughter is to thank the ancestors for giving them good pigs. It is accompanied by uprooting the small rumbin trees planted twelve years earlier, so signalling armed combat with enemy clans.

Rappaport (1967) and Harris (1977) explain this strange cycle in terms of workload. It is the Maring women who must tend the forest vegetable gardens and the beloved pigs. As baby pigs mature they cost each woman as much effort to feed as an adult human. The women plant more yams, taro and sweet potatoes, but have to walk further to and from the villages to do so. Eventually adult pigs break the fences, tired women get irritable and social pressure builds up to hold another kaiko. The exact time varies but is signalled by having enough mature pigs to trade off to other clans in military alliances. Tribes are invited to competing kaiko slaughter-feasts and the group with most pig-meat to give away gains most allies. It therefore wins more battles and is better able to take over new territory. New land is vital because forest burning to clear and fertilize the soil depletes areas for vegetable production. Defeated villages are not taken over but abandoned and left fallow for ten to twelve years.

For the Maring, warfare is a sort of population pressure valve, not in terms of killing off surplus males, but as a ritual means of moving people round a limited ecological area. So the answer to the cultural question 'When do the Marings have enough pigs to thank the ancestors?' is a structural one: 'They have enough pigs when the forest has grown back over the routed group's former garden area' (Harris, 1977, p.57). The cycle of work for women and men is integrally tied to their cultural valuation of pigs and the need to honour their ancestors.

In modern society work is similarly bound to cultural values but the structure of relationships may not be so closely linked to it. Time is more segmented and wage labour is based on limited 'contracts' for sections of our time. Work is not an ongoing part of everyday life. E. P. Thompson (1967, p.61) contrasts 'task orientation' in earlier societies with 'clock time' of the present day. Where time was once seen to accord with the regularity of milking, harvesting, planting or the length of time it took to complete a whole task, 'clock time' now separates work from the rest of life. It regulates and organizes people in complex structures called 'formal organizations', and time is 'not passed but spent'. Moreover, the 'work ethic' may have changed its cultural meaning rather than 'disappeared' or 'declined' as some disgruntled employers claim.

Structure of the Workforce

Before we can understand the importance of work institutions in the cultural life concerns of a society, we need to consider how work is structured. In Chapter 3 we considered some of the structured inequalities in Australian society. We may now add to the picture by focusing on the Australian workforce.

Figure 9–1 Australian workforce (1976–1977)

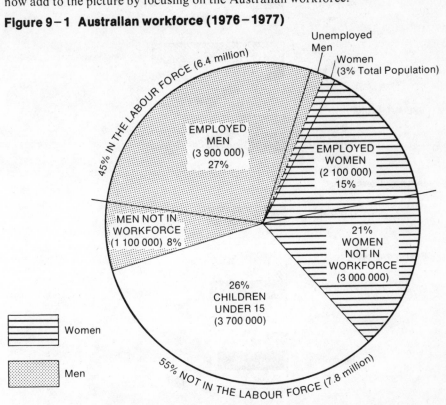

(Source: Based on the 1976 Census, reported in Social Indicators No. 2, 1978, Australian Bureau of Statistics, Canberra)

Note: These are the latest figures available. Figures vary greatly from month to month, so a yearly average gives a more reliable figure.

It is worth noting from Figure 9–1 that paid work is a part of the lives of less than half the Australian population and that it is a male dominated activity. Growing numbers of women are entering the workforce, however, and married women dominate the female workforce.

For whom do people work and what is the nature of the major tasks that occupy them? Some cross-cultural comparisons may illustrate how economic growth and technological advances alter the working lives of large sectors of the population.

Table 9−1 Percentage of the economically active population in various sectors of the economy, 1965−6−7

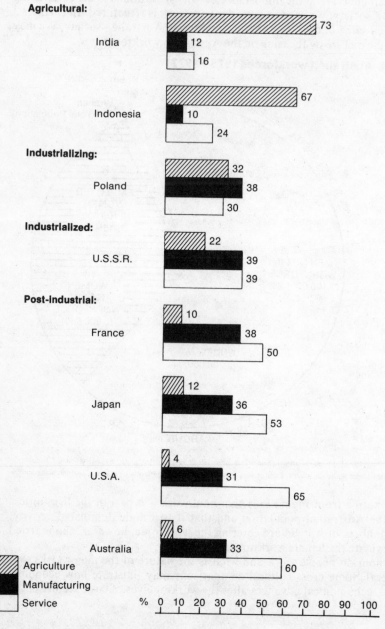

Agricultural:

India: 73, 12, 16

Indonesia: 67, 10, 24

Industrializing:

Poland: 32, 38, 30

Industrialized:

U.S.S.R.: 22, 39, 39

Post-industrial:

France: 10, 38, 50

Japan: 12, 36, 53

U.S.A.: 4, 31, 65

Australia: 6, 33, 60

Agriculture
Manufacturing
Service

% 0 10 20 30 40 50 60 70 80 90 100

(Source: ILO Year Book of Labour Statistics, 1978)

Table 9−2 shows shifts in technology and the social division of labour that occurred in Australia in the relatively few years between 1947 and 1976.

Table 9−2 Shifts in technology and the social division of labour

Growth Sectors			Stable Sectors			Declining Sectors		
1947	1976		1947	1976		1947	1976	
5.6%	13.4%	Community Services	6.3%	6.4%	Agriculture	12.6%	6.9%	Transport & Storage, Communication
18.4%	25.2%	Wholesale and retail trade, Finance, real estate & bus. services	7.4% 6.0%	7.4% 4.9%	Construction Entertainment recreation, restaurants, hotels & personal services	31.0% 2.0%	19.7% 1.3%	Manufacturing (rose from 22%, 1933) Mining

(Source: Yearbook 1947; Census, 1976)

Table 9−3 shows the distribution of the Australian workforce at the time of the 1976 Census.

Table 9−3 Employed Population x Industry Sector: 1976

	%	Persons 1000	Women as % of total
Manufacturing	20	1139	26
Wholesale and retail trade	18	1044	40
Community services (incl. teaching, health, welfare)	13	780	62
Construction	7	430	9
Agriculture	7	405	32
Finance, real estate, business	7	418	45
Public admin., defence	6	324	27
Transport & storage	5	289	14
Entertainment, recreation etc.	5	282	56
Communications	2	111	25
Electricity, gas, water	2	103	8
Mining	1	73	7
	91	5397	
Other	7	391	
(not 100% due to rounding)	98%	5788	36

(Source: Census, 1976)

The greatest decline has been in the proportion of the population engaged in manufacturing, an area currently suffering major unemployment problems because of the small home market, high costs of labour and competition from cheaper imports. But the decline of manufacturing jobs has not meant declining affluence overall. There has been major growth in wholesale and retail trade and in business and community services such as health, education and welfare.

Certain status groups within the community suffer or gain unequally as the distribution of valued resources alters. Sociological analysis focuses on the groups differentially affected by such shifts, for they are structural changes producing structural unemployment. Moving into new job areas requires much more, socially, than simply shifting to 'where the jobs are'. Massive retraining efforts may be required, buffered by welfare relief for those displaced. But first there must be a cultural recognition that old values, old stereotypes and old solutions are inadequate to meet the new conditions.

Class Structure?

We may now consider the classic *owner* v. *non-owner* split in the context of the Australian workforce. Table 9−4 shows how small are the numbers of owners or self-employed people.

Table 9−4 Employment categories

Employed:	1976%
employer, self-employed	13.2
wage and salary earners	80.9
unpaid helpers	1.4
Total Employed	95.6
Unemployed	4.4
Total Labour Force	100.0
Employers and self-employed as % of total employed population	13.9%

(*N* = 802 000 (20.2% of employed) of which 240 000 (i.e. 30% are women); cf. 1947, *N* = 640 000 of which 71 000 (i.e. 11%) were women)

Strangely, although fewer people in total were their own bosses in 1976 than in 1947, more women appeared to be their own mistresses! That, however, may be due to the income-dividing practice of registering wives as co-employers in small business enterprises to minimize taxation.

Most people then are not owners of the means of production; they sell their labour for wages. In Chapter 3 we saw that we could not discuss notions of '*social class*', '*class consciousness*' or a class '*for-itself*', without evidence of a subjective kind. We would need to know, for example, whether members of the 'working class' thought of themselves in that way, felt a unity of interests, recognized their common needs and problems and joined together to act to achieve joint ends. But we do not need such evidence to show (with Weber and Marx) the structural existence of economic classes (class *in* itself) in any capitalist society. Owners of the means of production buy labour from those who have only their labour to sell.

Capitalist production rests on the accumulation of capital from profits and workers demand their 'fair share' of those profits in wages. Wage demands threaten profits and thus capital, so they will be the focus of conflict under capitalism. Trade unions lead reform movements to prevent exploitation in the form of profit from going too far. Some radicals see this trade union 'economism' to be one of the factors delaying the development of a truly radical working-class consciousness. They see the focus on better wages and working conditions to distract attention from the 'real' issues of political power and control over the means of production. But given the long and bitter struggles of trade unions to improve working conditions, such a critique seems unhelpful.

Sociologically it is more important to analyze the conditions under which the wages-profits struggle has radical or conservative results. Under conditions of affluence reforms may keep workers 'happy' and divert attention from the structural causes of poverty, racism and inequality. Shorter working hours, higher basic wages and better conditions may be won but unemployment may still persist; pockets of poverty may continue and capital continue to be directed to military or monopoly interest group purposes rather than to broader social ends. But wage demands are not the only pressures on capital. World oil prices, changes in the balance of world trade, political decisions to end wars and foreign investment may have far more drastic effects than a strike for better overtime rates.

The Role of the State

In any modern society the State plays a significant role in determining the structure of work.

In 1947 only 26 per cent of all wage and salary earners worked for the government but by 1976 the figure had grown to 31 per cent. Table 9—5 shows the proportional changes since 1933.

Table 9—5 Government versus private employers

% of wage and salary earners (excluding rural, defence, and private female domestic workers) working for:

	govt. %	private %	TOTAL (000s)
1933	23.2	76.8	1333
1939	23.4	76.6	
1947	25.6	74.4	2430
1966	25.3	74.7	3804
1971	27.2	72.8	4422
1976	30.2	69.8	4709
1977	31.0	69.0	4726

In Australia the State also interferes in market processes in significant ways. Protective tariffs on farm produce and manufactured goods support owners and protect jobs. Economists may argue over the relative long-term merits of tariffs and open trade competition but the social consequences of the

215

removal of tariffs are immediately apparent. 'Buy Australian' campaigns are ineffective against the lure of lower prices.

The State determines how large the national deficit will be, regulating the balance of trade between import and export flow. This in turn affects the money supply available for investment and borrowing through the Reserve bank, other trading banks and lending societies. It is the State which determines interest rates in the light of this money flow.

Attempts to regulate or 'index' wage rises and price rises through institutions such as the Conciliation and Arbitration Commission and the Prices Justification Tribunal also represent the guiding hand of the State. In June, 1979, the president of the Arbitration Commission, Sir John Moore, called for a conference on the future of wage indexation, because neither Government nor unions seemed willing to help the system work.

The political and cultural values of the government in power will determine the monetary policies affecting jobs and 'business confidence'. Because world economic trends continue regardless of most Australian government decisions, however, 'the State' may here mean not the particular party in power, but that permanent group of public servants which advises every government on financial policy—the Treasury. Peter Sheehan (1979) argued in 1977 that Australian society's power structure comprised five major groups: entre-preneurs, managers, bureaucrats, workers, and a growing new proletariat of the disadvantaged. Despite their lack of direct ownership, Sheehan argues that the bureaucrats, especially those in the Treasury, hold the greatest power.

We may not, however, baldly assert the State to be the 'instrument of capitalism', simply a part of the ideological apparatus that maintains the legitimacy of capitalism as a system of control. Sociology insists on evidence for any such assertion. We need data on *how* the State acts, in whose *interests* it acts, and the *effects* of State intervention on diverse groups in society. Judgements vary, but at times the State does act against the interests (at least in the short-term) of the economically dominant class. It does this every time it legislates for a system of compulsory negotiation over industrial disputes, for health laws or factory acts, for minority group rights, equal pay for women, or accepts a wage case decision by the Arbitration Commission. While every such action by the State may be interpreted as 'in the long run' maintaining the capitalist system, the State as an institution has achieved some autonomy from the rest of the system.

While we might cynically see State reforms in health, education and welfare as maintaining the status quo, as the State's attempts to maintain its own legitimacy, the reforms are a sociological reality and can have effects contrary to the interests of capital. We see the response in the 'investment strike of capitalists' when reforms appear to be going too far. The toppling of the French Popular Front government of the 1930s, the Allende government in Chile in 1974 and the Whitlam government in Australia in 1975 are some examples.

Nor does the fact that 'capital sets the outer limits to reform' (Dreier, 1979, p.7) mean it has total control over either the State or society. The right to vote and to organize politically; progressive reforms against racism and sexism; and

Table 9−6 Inflow of foreign investment in enterprises in Australia, by country

($ million)

Year	United Kingdom	U.S.A.	Canada	Japan	E.E.C. (a)	Other countries	Total
1971−72	391	562	40		463		1455
1972−73	106	92	8	51	58	161	476
1973−74	87	188	18	75	85	11	464
1974−75	114	346	15	71	156	181	882
1975−76	264	380	22	80	−30	29	744

(a) includes Belgium, Denmark, France, Federal Republic of Germany, Ireland, Italy, Luxembourg and Netherlands from 1972−73 onwards.
Minus sign (−) denotes outflow.

(Source: Year Book, Australia No. 62 1977−78, p.663)

better health, education and working conditions, have come through the politically legitimated struggles of organized workers against the interests of capital. That the structural conflict still exists is not evidence that victories have not been won. Even though some political parties when they control 'the State' may use it to further the interests of capital against labour, change is still possible.

Bureaucracy

Working for the State is to work for a large bureaucratic organization. But this is the lot of many people in modern society. For, as Weber put it, bureaucratic administration is:

> superior to any other form of precision, in stability, in the stringency of its discipline, and in its reliability. It thus makes possible a particularly high degree of calculability of results . . . and is formally capable of application to all kinds of administrative tasks (Weber, 1964, p.337).

This is in theory. Today practical experience and research on how formal organizations operate suggest that bureaucratic administration might not be so superior. Bureaucracy has become one of the 'master symbols' of modern capitalist and socialist societies, serving the interests of dominant groups but not necessarily those of the wider community. Certainly people complain of 'red tape'; of bureaucrats who treat them as mere 'files' or 'numbers'; and there are charges that the bureaucracy is lazy, complacent and inefficient. But 'the bureaucracy' of such attacks has become synonymous in people's minds with government and public service departments, and the critique often stops there. Sociologically, bureaucracy is much more pervasive than that. If we are to understand how work structures social relations and affects people's lives and values, we will need to study bureaucracy more closely. Its claims to rationality and efficiency may be myths.

Weber saw bureaucracy as part of a most significant change in modern social institutions—their reconstruction in terms of 'rational-legal' authority rather than traditional adherence to loyalty to a person. Durkheim (1964 [1933]) also saw the old forms of legal sanctions to be changing to a new form. The old legal sanctions were based on a consensus about moral values which made social cohesion relatively 'mechanical'. Punishments were therefore 'repressive' because they bore the whole weight of social disapproval. But as the division of labour became more complex, the 'collective conscience' became less unified. People had their own beliefs and interests and their own moral values based on their segmented life experience. For Durkheim, this meant society no longer held together because of common agreements about right and wrong, but because the divided parts had to depend upon one another. Despite different functions and interests, different groups were inter-dependent. Modern society had an 'organic solidarity' rather than a 'mechanical' form of cohesion. Laws, therefore, could not be excessively repressive because that would set key 'parts' against the organic whole of productive society. Instead, laws would reflect interdependence by stressing 'restitution', the rehabilitation of offenders and the maintenance of the sick.

This more 'rational' form of social organization causes change between institutions. Economic, political and educational forms may become more interdependent and their functions may be linked in complex ways. But it may also produce new and separate institutions. Typically, law becomes more complex and highly organized. Medicine becomes organized and special institutions develop to handle particular problems. Education becomes separated from home and work activities and society becomes 'schooled'. Production itself sprouts new structures, such as market research, advertising, personnel management, industrial relations, and so on.

Bureaucratic organization pervades social life; it is not limited to the structure of government departments. What we now call bureaucratic administration grows precisely because a complex of highly specialized and interdependent parts requires coordination. Raw materials have to be delivered on time in the processing plant; component parts have to be in place on the assembly line; orders must be met; inquiries have to be answered and payments made at specified times.

The great ability of bureaucracy to cope with the complexity of such supply and delivery systems was what Weber admired, though he could see the social costs involved in placing efficiency demands and an authorized hierarchy of power ahead of human needs. As an *ideal type* though he saw bureaucratic formal organization as having the following characteristics:

An explicit purpose or *goal*, often defined by charter or statute, towards which all activities in the organization are directed.

Specialization of spheres of competence, of work roles and authority roles, to ensure the most efficient way of achieving the organization's goals.

Rules that specify clearly who will do what, how, in what order, and who is responsible to whom.

A *hierarchy* of responsibility and authority based on the legality of power positions within the organization.

Clear channels of communication to ensure coordination between specialized roles.

Routinized and systematic decision-making defined by the rules and the hierarchy of authority.

Rational career lines resting on *merit*, not favouritism or nepotism.

Staffing by full-time 'professionals' committed to the organization and loyal to its goals.

(See Weber, 1964, pp.328−41, and Gerth and Mills, 1958 [1946], ch.8.)

Weber's model specifies what *should* characterize an organization based on criteria of rational efficiency. We can thus use the *ideal type* as a model with which to compare actual organizations as they operate.

Notice first though, a contradiction within the ideal model. Specialization requires that the specialist be left alone to do what he or she is best at. Rules and the demands of coordination, however, may interfere with the specialist's autonomy and disallow what may be the most efficient method. Authority based on position (often seniority) may then conflict with authority based on skill.

That contradiction has caused major problems in actual formal organizations. We will now see how other elements of the *ideal type* are observed in practice and what their outcomes might be.

Formal organizations may have clear goals, but they are the goals of those in power. A goal may be 'maximum efficiency at lowest cost' but if either of those elements harms the personal or group interests of workers lower down the hierarchy, those workers may work against the organization's interests. *Rationality* may also become a master symbol, being presented as an absolute 'good' rather than as 'good for . . .' particular interest groups. Further, an organization's goals may conflict with those of 'outsiders'. That happens in competitive business. It happens when the goals of private industry are not in the public interest. It is cause for conflict between freeway authorities and local community groups. Multiple goals within an organization may similarly cause confusion and lack of 'efficiency'. The modern university may pretend to pursue 'truth' yet bend the knee of scholarship to the offer of funds for 'applied' research (Chomsky, 1969). Academics may profess the importance of teaching but when promotion is being considered numbers of pages published in refereed journals outweigh service to students. An organization's formal goals may not always be the best guide to its operations in the real world.

Specialization is essential to the advance of business and industry. Some tasks are so complex that it takes years to master the specialist theory and techniques involved. Professions develop where there are new bodies of theory and skills which are teachable and therefore monopolizable. But there is increasing concern about the minute 'specialization' of individually meaningless tasks such as those on an assembly line. The separation of workers into parts of a whole job is one cause of the alienation felt in modern society.

Scott and Dornbusch (1967) see it to be the root of many authority problems in industry. Bureaucracy assumes that tasks can be converted into routines. The early factory lines designed by Taylor (1911) were deliberately set up to separate worker from fellow worker. An assembly line rests upon an extreme subdivision of jobs. Each process requires little skill. Work methods are predetermined and there is no room for initiative or variation. There is a set speed for the conveyor belt. (Charlie Chaplin's *Modern Times* shows a man's plight in a nightmare world of machine-paced repetition where workers have no control over their environment.) Kornhauser (1965) shows that job satisfaction and mental health vary according to skill level of the job, being lowest with men on assembly lines.

Scott and Dornbusch (1967) claim that many tasks cannot be converted to routines because they are *active*. Digging a ditch or placing lids on boxes can be routinized because task resistance is *inert*. But teaching a student at school or serving a customer across the counter, may present *active* resistance. While inert tasks can be routinized and *directives* given on how the task is to be performed, 'active' tasks require *delegation*, leaving room for variation and initiative.

The criteria for evaluating inert, routine tasks are easier to devise because the outcomes are more predictable. If a bricklayer fails to follow the rules, the wall will be crooked or unstable or messy, and he can be easily judged. But since people are active and variable, how can we evaluate the outcomes of tasks such as teaching or counselling or advising on complex social issues? When tasks are delegated and rules not laid down, attempts to evaluate may be seen as illegitimate. They may be rejected as unfair if the criteria of judgement differ from those used by the one who carried out the task. Hence the refusal of professionals, such as lawyers and doctors, to allow anyone other than the professional colleague group the power to judge their work. Unfortunately, many other areas of work which involve relatively 'active' tasks are evaluated in routine and arbitrary ways. Workers in these jobs may rebel against the illegitimacy and inappropriateness of such controls but their managers fail to see the problem in the same way.

The rules insisted on by bureaucracy may have outcomes beyond the ones desired. Impersonal rules may ensure uniformity of treatment but not fairness. Rigidity in following rules may also reflect uncertainty concerning social relationships in the organization. The further workers are away from the central decision-makers, the less they will know about the overall aims of the organization and the more likely they will be to adhere rigidly to the stated rules. The boss can always 'bend the rules' but the junior cannot. That is why people say 'it pays to go straight to the top' if they want an answer to go their way.

Communication and coordination depend upon the social networks within an organization. Many studies have shown how *informal organizations* of workers cut across the formal organization and its hierarchy of rules and authority (Burns, 1955; Gouldner, 1955; Kapferer, 1969; Dalton, 1950; Katz and Kahn, 1966; J. D. Thompson, 1967).

The key to understanding how and why some workers cope with conditions an outsider might find unbearable lies in the informal structure of work organizations. Values and norms that set basic attitudes to work and serve as controls on both management and fellows develop within groups of fellow workers. The groups may become cliques, interest groups or friendship groups that restructure the status and power relations of the formal organization. Informal privileges accrue to group members and bosses may be wise to turn a blind eye. In a recent study of Melbourne abattoir meat workers, Sheila Wynn (1977) found evidence of widespread stealing. Buckets of 'lights'—livers, brains, and other offal—were taken and sold to local butchers. Only certain men were allowed to do this and if they took 'too much' both informal and formal control measures were taken. The role of the foreman may be particularly tricky because he falls between the formal and informal lines of command and communication. Elizabeth Cohen (1966) found men in such positions were likely to press their sons to do well at school and aim at a college level education so they could go beyond their father's twilight area of control.

Finally actual bureaucracy is often less than rational in its staffing procedures. Selection is not always based on merit. If courses and access to qualifications are open only to selected status groups, social position will outweigh actual competence. Credentialling itself may restrict *from* access the people best suited for the job. For example, to be a good doctor may require relatively high intelligence and very high interpersonal competence. But because competition for the high status and material rewards available to doctors is so fierce entry may be limited to the highest exam scorers regardless of their personal qualities. As a consequence social medicine may suffer. As we saw in Chapter 8, Berg and others suggest it is often not 'what you know' but 'who you know' that gets you into jobs and pushes you up the promotion ladder. Preference for people with certain qualities (a public school accent; good manners; neat dress; a particular religion or political allegiance) often works against promotion on merit in terms of task skills. Our earlier distinction between technical or intellectual competence and moral competence carries over into the workforce and may explain apparently 'irrational' decisions. Both published and hidden criteria exist. Where contenders for a position have the same sets of credentials and talents, it is likely that hidden criteria will be used in choosing between them.

The Professions and Social Prestige

Because the professions have the most highly developed skill levels, professional workers tend to dominate the authority structure of modern organizations. Management and administration has itself become 'professionalized.' Evidence the proliferation of new degrees and courses in every aspect of business. Business is controlled more by economists, accountants and lawyers than it is by the actual owners of majority shares. Lawyers, business and other professional men are predominant in both the government and the public service. For that reason, new debate has arisen about who comprises 'the ruling class': the owners of the means of production or the technocratic professionals who run business and government for them? (Sheehan, 1979).

In terms of prestige ratings, the professions consistently rank high. The best known occupational rank ordering is that carried out by North and Hatt in America in 1947 and replicated by Hodge, Siegel and Rossi in 1963. Using random samples of American adults they asked people to rate 90 occupations as excellent, good, average, below average, and poor. Each job was given a score depending on the number of times it was rated in each category. Table 9–7 lists the top 90 occupations in order of their prestige in American society, an order that had remained fairly consistent from 1947 to 1963. Controversy of course raged round methodological issues. Did people rank jobs on the same criteria? Which was uppermost in their minds: salary received, power held, education level needed, community importance, respectability or their own personal feelings towards each job? Moreover, the picture is not inclusive of all aspects of prestige in American society. A small town grocer's prestige may jump if he is elected mayor; military honour, notable service to the community or the sudden

Table 9–7 Occupational prestige ranks in the United States, 1963*

Rank	Occupation	Rank	Occupation
1.0	U.S. Supreme Court Justice	49.5	Radio announcer
2.0	Physician	49.5	Bookkeeper
3.5	Nuclear physicist	51.5	Insurance agent
5.5	State governor	53.0	Carpenter
8.0	U.S. representative in Congress	54.5	Manager of a small store in
8.0	College professor		a city
11.0	Chemist	57.0	Mail carrier
11.0	Lawyer	57.0	Railroad conductor
14.0	Dentist	57.0	Travelling salesman for a
14.0	Architect		wholesale concern
17.5	Psychologist	59.0	Plumber
17.5	Minister	60.0	Automobile repairman
17.5	Member of the board of	62.5	Barber
	directors of a large	62.5	Machine operator in a factory
	corporation	62.5	Owner-operator of a lunch-
17.5	Mayor of a large city		stand
21.5	Priest	65.5	Garage mechanic
21.5	Airplane pilot	67.0	Truck driver
24.5	Banker	70.0	Clerk in store
29.5	Accountant for a large	70.0	Streetcar motorman
	business	72.5	Restaurant cook
29.5	Public school teacher	74.0	Singer in nightclub
31.5	Owner of a factory that	75.0	Filling station attendant
	employs about 100 people	77.5	Coal miner
31.5	Building contractor	80.5	Restaurant waiter
34.5	Musician in a symphony	80.5	Taxi driver
	orchestra	83.0	Janitor
34.5	Author of novels	83.0	Bartender
39.0	Electrician	86.0	Soda fountain clerk
44.0	Farm owner and operator	87.0	Sharecropper — one who
44.0	Undertaker		owns no livestock or equipment
44.0	Welfare worker for a city		and does not manage farm
	government	88.0	Garbage collector
46.0	Newspaper columnist	89.0	Street sweeper
47.0	Policeman	90.0	Shoeshiner
48.0	Reporter on a daily newspaper		

* Based on Robert W. Hodge, Paul M. Siegel, and Peter H. Rossi, 'Occupational Prestige in the United States', 1925–1963. *American Journal of Sociology*, 70, No. 3 (November 1964), pp. 286–302, table 1. Reprinted from Theodore Caplow, *Elementary Sociology*, 1971, Prentice-Hall, Englewood Cliffs, New Jersey.

inheritance of wealth can affect prestige rankings. The election of a Catholic President or one from the Southern states can alter the social prestige of an entire status group, certainly in their own eyes.

Weber held that social stratification and inequalities of power could be based on *class* or *status* or *party*. While *class* rested on the distinction between propertied and propertyless, *status* groups rested on their prestige and honour within a society's value system. Weber felt that when rapid economic change was taking place class stratification would be more noticeable. During stable periods, however, differences of life-style based on consumption levels (and thus status) would prevail. Status groups are therefore always more aware of their common life-styles and visible differences from other groups; they are subjectively aware 'communities'. For Weber, 'party' meant any voluntarily formed group whose aim was control of an organization's policy (whether a sporting club or a political party). Parties may arise from, but cut across, classes and status groups. (See also Wild, 1978, ch.6.)

Professional groups are, in this light, status groups but may be regarded as 'parties' where they have succeeded in seizing control over their organization's policy. The Australian Medical Association (A.M.A.) and the Bar Association qualify as parties in Weber's sense. More importantly, since income, spending, conspicuous consumption and life-styles form the most common basis for recognizing stratification in Australian society, prestige rankings are often confused with class structure. Professionals may consequently be seen to be part of 'the ruling class' and subjected to some abuse. Whether they deserve it is not the point here; 'professional' is a *status* group distinction rather than a *class* one.

Giddens (1976) argues that class is not a particular form of stratification but is the basic division that explains the more complex and more easily described structures of social relationships through which life chances are distributed.

The professions have cornered a monopoly on certain 'marketable skills' (Weber). They maintain their prestige by controlling access to the profession (ensuring scarcity and thus good bargaining power for rewards), and by asserting internal group rights of self-evaluation. Professionalization is, then, a process of gaining a monopoly and then legitimating it. Codes of ethics, public assertions of the difficulty of learning a profession's theoretical body of knowledge and the structured reality of limiting access to the few, serve that legitimation purpose. Some of the tables in Chapter 8 show the degree to which access to the professions is limited.

Contrary to the image of the specialized individual possessed of great wisdom working alone as an autonomous expert making his own decisions, most professionals now work in large organizations (Blau & Scott (1963), Vollmer & Mills (1966)). Sociologically, this is not at all surprising. Advanced capitalism is a corporate affair, linking experts across nations in complex ways. Being specialized, the expert is by definition dependent upon other people. He needs a coordinated structure to supply him with both the materials and the time to 'do his own thing'. Being expert, he automatically enjoys some autonomy, because if he suffered constant interference to his work the organization would not benefit from his expertise. But it is a constricted and coordinated form of autonomy that he enjoys. We should therefore look more sceptically at the claims to independence, free enterprise and professional autonomy made on behalf of the professions.

Figure 9–2   Sources of class structuring

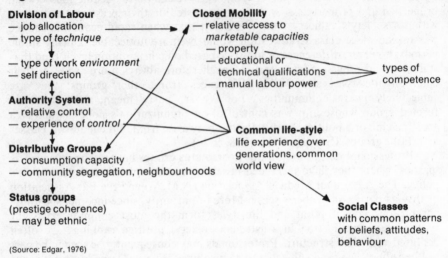

(Source: Edgar, 1976)

The medical profession, for example, is one greatly aided by State support (Medibank, hospital funds, etc.) and solidly embedded in large bureaucratic structures. Attempts by nurses to assert a new professionalism have been thwarted as much by doctors' attitudes as by the 'trained incompetence' of nursing courses and the poor career orientation of nursing recruits (Rollins, 1977).

Mobility Chances

Joseph Schumpeter (1950) and Joseph Ben-David (1963–64) both instanced the key role of the professions in the class structure of modern societies. As technology and research developed whole new fields of study—in physics, medicine, biology, manufacturing, psychology, electronics, and so on—the possibility for *mobility* greatly expanded. Social mobility (upward), in this sense means the opportunity to climb the 'stratification ladder' by achieving a higher status or moving into a higher class than that of one's parents. Strictly, to change classes would involve something as major as moving out of a wage-labour family to acquire property or ownership of the means of production. Gaining ownership of one's own home, becoming self-employed or starting a small business, might qualify one for membership of the 'middle classes'; but to achieve the degree of mobility required to gain the ownership of any major means of production would be a rags-to-riches story indeed. Ben-David found that the chance for new forms of competence to develop, for new areas of learning to open up, depended in part on how closed or open was the existing class structure of society. For example, while psychology was founded by Wundt in Leipzig and by Freud in Vienna, it was resisted in Europe as a new discipline because of the conservative traditions of European universities. Instead, it grew apace in the more open tertiary education scene in the United States. In America competing colleges were quick to seize upon new areas of specialization and so education as a form of 'marketable skill' or 'cultural capital', had greater impact on mobility chances there than elsewhere (see also David Apter (1965) on Africa). Joseph Kahl finds that since the start of the nineteenth century middle- and upper-class families in America have tended to restrict their family size, while farm labourers and working-class people have not. If the professional classes do not reproduce sufficiently to replace their own numbers, upward mobility for some of the lower classes will be possible. The possibility will vary according to the nature of power and the rate of economic change in the society.

The typical model used to explain social mobility is one which tests the relative strength of various 'paths'. For example Sewell and Shah (1967) measured the relative importance of the father's education and occupation, the level of education achieved by the son, and the son's first job in determining the son's eventual place in the occupational structure. They found that education had become more important in affecting life chances but that social class background was still influential *through* the sorts of educational opportunities that parents made available to their children. Halsey (1977) has demonstrated that even the British 1944 Act which introduced free, comprehensive secondary schooling, has not much improved the mobility chances of the lower classes. New jobs have demanded higher education, and the levels of education for all social groups has risen significantly but those from poorer backgrounds have still been left at the bottom of the pecking order.

It is often claimed that social mobility in Australia is high. In 1954, Oeser and Hammond found high rates of upward mobility (from manual to non-manual, 24 per cent) and downward mobility (from non-manual to manual, 37 per cent). By 1969 Broom and Lancaster-Jones had completed a national sample study for Australia which they compared with figures from Italy and America. They found that *structural mobility*, resulting from rapid economic changes to the occupational structure, was highest in America, but Australia had more *circulation mobility*, that is, movement between jobs. They also found for Australia that *inter-generational mobility* (the difference between job levels of father and son) might have been as high as 71 per cent and *career mobility* (the change in job level within an individual's life-cycle) as high as 59 per cent. Nevertheless they state that career 'mobility across the boundaries of non-manual, manual and farm strata is the exception rather than the rule', and it is much harder to rise from unskilled and semi-skilled jobs than it is from higher levels.

In a replication study in 1973, the Australian National University team found upward mobility to be still as high as 44 per cent (Broom, Jones & Zubrzycki, 1976). Encel's survey of access to the upper-class agricultural and business elites and his findings concerning the public school backgrounds of political leaders, however, suggest that *class mobility* is not high (Encel, 1970; West, 1965; Baldock, 1978, pp.98−100). Shifts within the same occupational status level may reflect the unsatisfying nature of the jobs involved or the search for better pay and better conditions. But because this is *individual mobility* it will have little effect on the underlying class structure.

The classic study of Luton manufacturing workers by Goldthorpe, Lockwood, Bechhofer and Platt (1969, p.56) revealed that 'only a little over a fifth had been entirely confined in their working lives to semi-skilled and unskilled manual work'. But they put up with worse conditions in their present jobs because the pay was better, suggesting that much so-called *social mobility* is *money mobility* rather than a shift either in job status or class position.

Recent Australian figures (*Social Indicators*, 2, 1978, Table 4.10, p.87 and Table 4.9, p.86), show white-collar workers are more likely to have left previous jobs to take 'better positions' (31−33 per cent of job movers in this category), while blue-collar workers are more likely to have left because they were 'laid off'. One in three tradesmen, production process workers and labourers have been 'mobile' because they were 'laid off'. Rural workers, fishermen and timbergetters (29 per cent) left mainly because it was seasonal or holiday work. Only 21 per cent of blue-collar workers left jobs to get a 'better position'; 14 per cent left because of unsatisfactory working conditions; 13 per cent left for health and medical reasons. For women the picture is much the same: blue-collar workers being 'laid off', or leaving because of working conditions or health reasons; white-collar women to get a better position or because they were transferred. So figures on personal 'career mobility' may conceal a number of complex issues.

The figures also deal with the lengths of time people in different occupational groups had held their current jobs. If it can be assumed that holding a job is important for career, income gain and security, then a surprisingly high number of Australian men (22 per cent) had been in their current (August 1976) job less than one year. Figures are highest for farmers, fishermen, timbergetters (32 per cent), sales workers (32 per cent), service, sport and recreation workers (28 per cent) and tradesmen, factory workers and labourers (24 per cent). They are lowest for white-collar administrators (10 per cent), professionals and technicians (15 per cent) and clerical workers (15 per cent). The relative 'stayers' are shown in Table 9−8.

Recent critiques of social mobility studies have suggested that path models rely too heavily on the dubious assumption that status can be attained readily through individual effort. As Horan (1978) points out, a status attainment model seen:

> in terms of individual resources or liabilities which contribute to the individual attainment process . . . by way of the differential distribution of rewards across the positions . . . serves to reinforce the individualist and voluntarist tendencies noted above by invoking a neo-classical, free market conception of occupational placement . . . (it) assumes an open, fully competitive market process . . . ignoring structural market characteristics in the analysis of individual attainment (Horan 1978, p.537).

Both Coser (1975) and Burawoy (1977) have criticized the model for its

Table 9—8   Relative permanence In employment

	Been in job 10 years or more	
	% Males	% Females
Professional	31	10
Administrative	42	31
Clerical	30	9
Transport	34	13
Tradesmen, factory workers	24	Blue-collar manual —
Farmers, fishermen, etc.	17	11
Miners, etc.	24	
Service, sport, recreation	20	8
Sales	18	

Note: The A.B.S. figures for women are very sparse and may be unreliable because sampling frames are based on males, and because categories often fail to accommodate the different circumstances of being in the workforce. Non-registration of women who do not 'have' to work makes unemployment figures similarly suspect.

failure to accommodate the assumption of a homogeneous market rather than a segmented one or to allow for the fact that:

> differential class power and social advantage operate in predictable and routine ways, through specifiable social interactions between classes or interest groups, to give shape to determine social structures and to create differential life chances (Coser, 1975, p.694).

Horan suggests that it is not the method of path analysis that is at fault; rather it is the theory-laden nature of current status-attainment studies. *'The assumption of fully open and competitive allocation of individuals to jobs (i.e. of market homogeneity) provides a source of justification for restricting attention to the individual characteristics of job-holders'* (Horan, 1978, p.538). In contrast, the work of Bonacich (1975), Beck et al (1978) and Wright and Perrone (1977), has begun to document the segmentation of the market structure by which people from different social positions face different opportunity and reward structures.

It is the structuring of life chances for different groups that should be emphasized rather than the idea that every man is the master of his own destiny. But two problems arise. In the first place, individuals do make voluntary choices, however limited their options may be. Hence our focus in Chapter 7 on the competent self, the sense of power or efficacy which enables people to cope against life's limits and to control their own environment. Note, however, the *socially constructed* nature of such a sense of efficacy. To say that individual *A* has a 'competent self' while individual *B* has not is merely to describe an end result. Just as housing, income, educational and job opportunities are socially distributed in different amounts to different social groups, so too are the chances to develop a competent self. Our model must accommodate structured factors in the development of self-views, world-views and life chances related to family, education and work.

This suggests a second problem. Because the notions of a 'competent self' and of 'equipment for competence' are historically individualistic, research procedure almost inevitably takes the form of measuring individual characteristics rather than the structural properties of groups. Wright and Perrone (1977, p.35) suggest most survey classifications of jobs are inadequate for identifying class positions. Instead, they use data on ownership of the means of production and the purchase, control and sale of labour to distinguish four class categories: employers, managers, workers and petty bourgeoisie. Their findings support the contention that education operates differently in producing income for different classes. In similar vein, Averitt (1968), Bluestone et al (1973), Bibb & Form (1977) and Beck et al (1978) use the *dual economy* literature to define economic sectors which may override individual abilities in the attainment of status. The size of the firms people work for, their levels of skill and their places of residence may do more to explain differences in income than their individual abilities. The difficulty, of course, is that such structural properties are rarely measured in 'normal' survey research.

In Australia we lack comparative data on social mobility rates and class awareness at times when occupational mobility chances are relatively open or relatively blocked. Edgar (1976) (in line with Weber, Ben-David and Giddens), argues that the degree to which mobility chances are open or closed may explain the role of education in producing marketable capacities and the development of status group and/or class consciousness.

The current 'over-supply' of teachers is a case in point. Teachers will be unlikely to claim 'professionalism' if they are out of work and will be unlikely to accept the argument that they 'ought to behave professionally'. Their more militant group action may signify a new sort of group consciousness now that their chances for upward mobility are less open. Lerner (1979) has described teachers (and social workers and government administrators) as 'increasingly proletarianized professionals'.

Work Roles and Life Orientations

Status groups are aware of themselves as communities with distinctive life-styles. Religious groups, racial and ethnic groups and small rural town communities obviously have distinct life-styles and their members may identify with them.

Occupational groups, however, may not have all the characteristics of a distinct status group. One's sense of identity obviously rests in part on one's job. We may say about ourselves: 'I'm a truck driver', or 'I'm a teacher', or 'I'm a student', or 'I'm unemployed', and in that way allow the role we play to become part of our self-image. The work role, however, is only part of our life and its importance for us may vary according to the kind of job we have. Moreover, since work is separated from home life and other non-work activities, we may more often identify ourselves in terms other than work roles. Our multiple roles are constrained by their breadth or specificity. For example, for a woman, the role of 'female' may pervade many areas of conduct, while her specific work role of accountant or machine process worker may not 'carry over' to the same extent into the rest of her life.

As the life-cycle progresses, work roles may also become more, or less, important. At school, formal 'work' is not usually expected, yet occupational ambitions may have important 'anticipatory socialization' effects (Brim & Wheeler, 1966). We may project ourselves into the future, model ourselves on those already working at what we want to be and acquire the forms of competence (technical, intellectual and moral) that will increase our chances of being selected into the chosen field. A single person may have a different perspective on work from that of a married person; commitments outside the job may encourage people to stick at a job they dislike. So too, will external economic conditions; in times of high unemployment, any job may be better than none. Such a social context may also constrain protest; students today may still resent 'the system' as much as those in the 1960s did, but student 'apathy' may be the result of fear or self-interest rather than unconcern.

So hypotheses about work roles and life orientations must be cautious, taking into account the relative importance of concurrent roles; the networks that bring workmates together or segregate areas of their lives; the stages of the life-cycle and the choices that are faced in the wider economic and political context. Nevertheless, there are several interesting studies that examine such matters and place the institutions of work within the wider socio-cultural context.

In Chapter 7 we referred to Kohn's study concerning the effects of paternal occupation on children's attitudes and values. Kohn argued that the experience of *control* over one's work situation, the degree of self-direction as opposed to close supervision, and the extent to which a job demands flexible decision-making (particularly with people), would reinforce class-related attitudes towards authority, idea-conformity, trustfulness, self-confidence and optimism.

Edgar's partial replication of Kohn's study with an Australian sample suggested similar influences. The actual nature of a man's job was found to relate consistently to differences in his children's value-orientations, findings which may contradict Connell's (1977, ch.8) assertion of no 'class' differences. They indicate technique, type of work experience and experience of control to be important sources of potential social class structuring—or at least of differences in values for status groups based on occupational criteria. Men who experienced little self-direction or flexibility were significantly more conservative, authoritarian, anxious, self-deprecating and less self-confident.

Individual items on the attitude scale can of course be challenged as vague, arbitrary or hard to interpret. Consider, for example, the following items:

On the whole I think I am a happy person
I wish I could have more respect for myself
There are very few things about which I'm absolutely certain

One needs to maintain a healthy scepticism about the conclusions which might be drawn from forced responses to them. But when the items scale reliably (indicating consistent responses to different statements designed to reveal similar attitudes) and when different groups of people respond in ways consistent within the group but markedly different from other groups—some confidence may be placed in the findings.

Table 9−9 highlights the most dramatic differences by comparing some of the attitudinal responses of adolescent boys and girls with those of their fathers.

Table 9−9   Value orientations of fathers and their adolescent children

Questionnaire Item	% Strongly Agree or Agree		
	Boys %	Girls %	Fathers %
Authoritarianism Conservatism			
1. The most important thing to teach children is absolute obedience to their parents	36	36	57
2. Young people should not be allowed to read books that are likely to confuse them	33	22	46
3. People who question the old and accepted ways of doing things usually end up causing trouble	33	22	70
4. In this complicated world, the only way to know what to do is to rely on leaders and experts	23	13	68
5. Any good leader should be strict with people under him in order to gain their respect	40	37	31
6. It's wrong to do things differently from the way our forefathers did	10	5	87
7. Once I've made up my mind, I seldom change it	41	40	38
8. It generally works out best to keep on doing things the way they have been done before	32	22	61
Trustfulness			
9. Do you think that most people can be trusted?	39	35	26
10. If you don't watch out, people will take advantage of you	70	58	32
Self-Confidence			
11. I take a positive attitude towards myself	56	41	7
12. I feel I'm a person of worth, at least on on an equal plane with others	75	65	2 (90.2% disagree)
13. I am able to do most things as well as other people can	78	75	11.8 (77.7% disagree)
14. I generally have confidence that when I make plans I will be able to carry them out	70	66	4 (86.1% disagree)
15. On the whole, I think I am quite a happy person	81	78	4.7 (84.9% disagree)
Self-Deprecation			
16. I wish I could have more respect for myself	38	30	62.8
17. At times I think I am no good at all	43	64	69.5
18. I feel useless at times	44	66	50
19. I wish I could be as happy as others seem to be	41	37	67
20. There are very few things about which I am absolutely certain	35	41	53
N =	660	554	792

(Source: Edgar, 1976)

We may notice a number of important differences between the values and attitudes held by boys and the values and attitudes held by girls, but the picture of their fathers that emerges is one of sheer despair. Occupational and educational differences within the father group might have been expected but not the huge gap between child and adult on what might be called broadly the *pessimism-optimism* dimension. Only 7 per cent of these fathers see themselves positively; 90 per cent disagree that they are persons of worth equal to others; 78 per cent say they are not able to do most things well; 86 per cent say they have no confidence they can carry out the plans they make; 63 per cent wish they had more self-respect; and 85 per cent disagree that they are a happy person even with the qualification 'on the whole'. What a sorry picture of Australian manhood that is! Ironically, they appear to think that their fellows are happier than they are, are more worthy and more capable than themselves.

In contrast, their adolescent children reflect the expected optimism of youth. They feel worthy, capable and confident their plans will succeed. They are happy, have self-respect and take a positive attitude towards life. There are, of course, structured social differences between them on most of these issues, but the broad picture is one of facing life confidently and cheerfully. What an affront they must be to fathers whose past or present looks so bleak. It is significant, too, that the fathers tend to see less need for change in society than their offspring do. One might hope that if they believed life had passed them by they would want social change to provide better prospects for their sons and daughters.

The findings suggest that later life experience, especially in one's occupation, alters one's view of the world. The objective limits become translated into subjective attitudes, values, concerns and self-views. The degree of control one can exercise at work is likely to be of crucial importance in sustaining a view of oneself as 'effective', as worthwhile, as having some significance in the world.

Randall Collins puts the issue thus:

> The situations in which authority is acted out are the key experiences of occupational life. Since one cannot avoid having an occupation or being cared for by someone who does, it influences everyone. On this basis, three main classes (sic) can be distinguished: those who take orders from few or none, but give orders to many; those who must defer to some people, but can command others; and those who are order-takers only (Collins, 1975, p.63).

But the implications may not be, as Collins implies, rigid 'class' structures. If, as we have seen, bureaucratic controls limit one's power at work to a narrow role within the hierarchy, several reactions are possible. It may be that everybody in the modern organization is happy because the organization provides some area for everyone in which to experience control. The evidence, however, seems to show otherwise. Most people at work are controlled by others. Their own areas of decision-making are limited. Rules are laid down and routines must be followed. Bureaucracy distributes control unequally.

Another result may be that workers denied any degree of control or self-direction at work will seek it elsewhere. Private life may offer substitute means of controlling some small corner of life. A 'functional' argument might suggest that anti-social behaviours like gambling, drinking, reckless driving, male chauvinism and violent sport have been publicly legitimated in Australia because they serve the 'purpose' of directing attention away from the lack of control people suffer at work and in the political and economic spheres. But demands for more money, more worker control over decision-making and a more participatory form of democracy (all of which attack more pertinently the structures of inequality) are not so readily tolerated.

And this may be the key to the way hegemonic control operates. In a segmented, differentiated society, all people have their own areas of control. There is room for the competent self in all walks of life. If effective control is reinforcing in itself and of itself people may have no desire to extend their areas of control. That being so, we need to consider the ways society structures its socialization and opportunity channels to ensure that most people will not want broader areas of control.

Legitimation will be one of the factors (Gramsci, (1957); Habermas (1976); Bourdieu and Passeron (1977)). Obviously formal agencies of social control need to be seen to be legitimate if people are to obey them willingly. But legitimated authority or control through the exercise of naked power may not be necessary if most people are willing to accept the degree of control they have over their own lives (their exercise of 'the competent self'). If people are kept separate from activities or ideas which may cause them to rethink, control of the overall structuring processes may remain in the hands of a few (Edgar, 1974, pp.670—6).

But people operate in society in and through groups. Identity or 'self' is segmented according to the groups to which an individual belongs. It may therefore be more fruitful to highlight the structured opportunities for a group self to be competent than to discuss the individual characteristics that might constitute a 'competent self'.

We need to begin by explaining how groups differ from each other in the opportunity structures available to them and in their conceptions of the desirable, the possible, the acceptable and the 'inevitable'. A group's location in a particular segment of the broader occupational structure, or of the educational system, or of other possible relevance structures (Holzner, 1968) will be crucial in explaining the extent to which its members conform, and to what they conform. Some of the studies relevant to the discussion indicate how people cope with the structured demands of work.

Varieties of Coping—Health, Hours, Satisfaction   *executive*

Different occupations involve different strains and pressures. Hetzel (1976, p.88) suggests executive level work leaves little time for wife and family, and 'increased tension is associated with heavier food and alcohol intake, cigarette smoking and less exercise, a life style . . .(linked to) coronary heart disease and lung disease, which are the major causes of death in men'. However, other research has found that managers had gained confidence in decision-making and were more likely to see obstacles as challenges rather than threats, and consequently maintained a more optimistic outlook. And as far as alcohol intake is concerned, the data show that of 22 000 drivers positively breathalyzed in 1972, a third were under 25 and about 70 per cent were blue-collar workers (Hetzel, 1976, p.121). The problems of coping may be greater for working-class people.

McClelland in America suggests that alcohol is associated with increased thoughts about power, especially in working-class men and he sees gambling and drinking 'as a major outlet for the frustrations of the working man' (Hetzel, 1976, p.135). Other studies suggest that heart disease is lower for executives and those with a tertiary education than for foremen and the less well-educated (Hetzel, 1976 p.162). Absence rates are similarly higher for manual workers (4.8 per cent for unskilled) than for non-manual workers (1.8 per cent for males, 2.9 per cent for females) (Harkness & Krupinski, 1977).

Though little statistical work of any substance has been done in Australia, there are clear indicators of stress and health problems varying by type of occupation.

Working hours reflect and affect relations in the social structure. Long hours at work mean absence from home and family, fatigue and limited leisure activities. The standard working week restricts shopping and leisure opportunities, creates the sociological institutions of 'weekend', 'rush hour', 'pay day and the pub' and 'Saturday football'. Changes to working hours would bring about major changes to social relationships.

The most comprehensive Australian study of the capacity to cope as it relates to people's occupations was made by Rosemarie Otto (1976). Hypothesizing (in line with Kohn and Edgar) that lower status groups and women would have fewer resources for coping and a lower sense of 'the competent self', she tested samples of teachers, clerks, managers and skilled and semi-skilled factory workers for variations in their reactions to stress and the frequency with which they sought medical help. She considered sources of strength for coping; 'oral comforts' and other forms of tension release; the use of interpersonal relationships; and levels of 'fatalism' versus 'self-reliance'. Otto is cautious about generalizing from the study and calls for closer case study methods to clarify the social processes but she presents several occupational 'profiles' of coping responses:

> *Managers* are assertive and confident, use more work rather than less to cope with stress and see the family as their main source of support. Forty per cent smoke or drink to relieve tension.
> *Semi-skilled factory workers*, express fatalism about life, and are more passive in their responses to trouble. Over 60 per cent smoke under stress and the intakes of alcohol for men and analgesics for women are higher than for any other group. Despite having good 'mates' at work and the pub, these men prefer to be self-reliant (40 per cent) and to keep their troubles to themselves (60 per cent). Religion, as for all groups in the study, is rarely a source of comfort.
> *Skilled workers* drink less, smoke less and are less fatalistic. They are more assertive and are more inclined to seek help from 'experts'.

Teachers seek escape in divergent leisure activities and the family. They discuss problems with others more than any other group. They smoke and drink less and take analgesics less often, but women teachers may use eating as a source of consolation.

Clerical workers lie between teachers and the semi-skilled in the degree to which they use smoking, eating and divergent activities to help them cope. Female clerks rank second to the semi-skilled in fatalism but find friendships a major source of support.

The study indicates that cultural patterns, in particular those relating to stress and coping with problems, 'are distributed in such a way as to favour those who are already advantaged', while reinforcing the powerlessness of those whose lives are already most constrained' (Otto, 1979, p.26). Occupations may be seen to reflect and reinforce the unequal distribution of life chances and to sustain the particular cultural value systems that dominate people's lives.

Levels of job satisfaction may be related to the different degrees of control that different occupational groups experience. Money, short hours, clean work, enjoyment and interest value, however, may all lead to a level of job satisfaction. But it may be (following Herzberg, 1959) that these are not so much indicators of a person's *being satisfied* as they are of his *not being dissatisfied*—at least, not sufficiently to quit.

In Edgar's study of adolescents and their parents, the fathers' responses to the question concerning job satisfaction clearly reflect *work situation* differences. People at different occupational levels experience different levels of self-direction and different levels of control over their work. Even unskilled and service workers experience some level of control over their daily work lives and levels of satisfaction are sometimes quite high—even when others give directives and supervision is frequent. In other words, though the trend is fairly consistent (as Kohn found) for men who experience self-direction at work to be more satisfied, other men do not need (or perhaps want) autonomy in order to be satisfied with their jobs. (See Tables 9—10 and 9—11.)

Another indicator of relative job satisfaction ought to be rates of turnover. Bad jobs are likely to have higher turnover because they are not only less well paid but also less intrinsically satisfying or worthwhile. A 1972 South Australian report found the following groups had the highest turnover rates:

Women (usually young) working as binders in the printing industry (300 per cent).

Food processing (repetitive) workers (200 per cent).

Semi-skilled operators in rubber manufacturing (200 per cent). (One company had a daily absence rate of 7 per cent).

Unskilled brickyard labourers (100 per cent).

Other manufacturing industries such as agricultural implements, electrical cables, aluminium door and window frames, steel tubing products, etc.—unskilled (170 per cent) semi-skilled (85 per cent), and skilled workers (60 per cent). Many men stayed for a month or so, then abandoned working altogether for a while.

(*Report of the Survey of Training Needs in Industry, Commerce and Government in South Australia, 1972*, quoted in Fitzgerald, 1976, pp.153—4).

Table 9 – 10   Occupation levels and experience of control at work

% Experiencing

	Professl.	Entreprl.	Rural	Service	Skilled	Unskilled
A lot of job variety	46.6	54.3	27.8	42.4	42.9	23.9
Not much, routine	8.0	12.1	14.8	20.0	14.8	35.8
Work with — People	74.1	74.1	5.9	58.3	30.3	15.1
(mostly) — Things	16.5	17.2	90.2	17.5	61.7	77.4
Autonomy —						
Decide Myself	61.4	82.8	92.5	38.7	46.8	17.6
Others Direct	3.4	3.4	7.5	6.5	13.8	28.7
Supervision —						
None	75.0	81.7	88.5	63.7	61.7	44.0
Occasional	25.0	16.5	9.6	30.6	34.6	45.0
Frequent	—	1.7	1.9	5.6	3.7	11.0
(Total *N* = 681) *N*=	88	116	54	125	189	109

Table 9 – 11   High job satisfaction and experience of control at work

% High Satisfaction

	Professl.	Entreprl.	Rural	Service	Skilled	Unskilled
A lot of job variety	57.1	59.4	33.3	43.8	57.5	22.2
Not very much, routine	14.2	17.3	40.7	35.4	15.1	25.0
Work with — People	55.6	64.0	0	38.6	56.1	25.0
— Things	71.4	50.0	54.3	47.6	35.3	32.9
Autonomy —						
Decide Myself	59.3	61.5	55.1	52.1	52.3	42.1
Directives	33.3	50.0	0	0	23.1	32.3
Supervision —						
Work Alone	62.1	59.6	54.3	43.0	45.7	39.6
Frequent	36.4	0	0	28.6	0	16.7
(Total *N* = 681) *N*=	88	116	54	125	189	109

The view that wages are what matter and 'some people don't care whether a job is satisfying or not' is given the lie by such figures. Not shown by mere figures are working conditions, levels of stress and physical effort that would appal many people who work in white-collar jobs.

In some kinds of white-collar work, however, levels of job satisfaction have changed. When office work was an indicator of higher status, monotonous clerical or administrative work was tolerated. As more people have entered this type of work, however, status has decreased, wages have levelled out and white-collar workers have begun to unionize to avoid being treated as just another group of wage labourers (Martin, 1975).

Embourgeoisement?

There can be no doubt that the changing division of labour continues to affect social relations and institutional and cultural patterns. The old Marxist predictions, however, that increased exploitation would lead to working-class awareness, solidarity and eventual revolution have not been fulfilled. As we have tried to suggest, the structure of control is central to any attempt to explain social behaviour. We might ask, then, why men do not rebel if modern work denies them control. It may be that their ways of life and the possibilities for control outside their jobs alters the central position of work in their lives. It may be that increasing affluence allows everyone to identify with 'the system' that produces it.

One of the turning points in the continuing sociological debate about class, occupational status groups and life-style differences was use of the concept of *embourgeoisement*. It meant the tendency for working-class people in advanced capitalist societies to adopt middle-class (bourgeois) values. In a sense it was a red herring that drew attention away from underlying structural differences towards more superficial, cultural life-style similarities. But it did help clarify some of the complex links between social structure and culture. It arose from a central problem of sociological theory: why the working class, instead of becoming more radical as a result of class exploitation, in fact voted Conservative (as they did in the U.K. of the 1950s) and seemed to be adopting middle-class values and life-styles.

Engels, in the 1870s, had wondered why the English working class had not used their new (1867) voting rights more vigorously to prevent their own exploitation in the workforce. Three possible explanations were offered for the phenomenon: that capitalism brought greater affluence rather than worker poverty and allowed the 'middle' strata to expand; that the State had come to play a more vital role in guaranteeing political, civil and social rights; that status differences (based on education, income and occupation) had superseded class conflict. Economic change, it was claimed, had 'homogenized' incomes and living standards; technological advances had broken down the manual/non-manual labour distinctions and made work more rewarding and less alienating; urban growth had broken up traditional working class communities with their close kinship and neighbouring networks into new, segregated suburbs. Research focused on 'New Towns', network patterns and the new concern with status. In other words, the premise was that the working class was becoming more 'bourgeois'.

But, as Goldthorpe, et al (1969, p.14*ff*), point out it was not at all clear what this thesis was actually saying. Marcuse (1964), for one, argued that the worker's integration into a middle-class style of life might represent an increase in, not an end to, alienation; the worker becomes so indoctrinated, so involved in satisfying 'false' needs that he becomes 'one-dimensional'. Attention was thus directed towards the cultural legitimation processes of modern capitalism. The notion of 'hegemony' suggested by Gramsci (1971) holds that the dominant class can exercise its power by authority rather than force; and by controlling the means of creating consciousness as well as the means of production and the means of violence. Notice that the explanation of embourgeoisement at that point shifts from changes in the *material* conditions of life to changes in the subjective, cultural, *meaning* bases of social life.

Other critics pointed out that affluence could just as readily produce a sense of relative deprivation. Better education levels and greater understanding of the causes of oppression might develop aspirations for an even better way of life. Goldthorpe et al (1969, pp.24−6) cited five concerns with the embourgeoisement thesis:

1. *The problem of definition*. Embourgeoisement might be defined in any one of three different ways. Or else all three conditions might be held to be necessary for the process to have occurred. The separate indicators include: higher wages; the development of new social norms; equality in the nature of social relationships between working-class and middle-class groups.

2. *The problem of relativity*. Middle-class conditions and life chances are still superior despite apparent similarities in consumption styles between working-class and middle-class groups. The process may not have gone very far.

3. *The problem of adaptation*. The development of new forms of home and family-centredness might be the result of adaptations of old ways to new conditions rather than indicators of changes in values.

4. *The problem of social relationships*. There must be evidence of changes in social relationships between manual and non-manual occupational groups for the thesis to have any great social significance.

5. *The problem of 'normative' change*. Economic aspirations are not the same as status aspirations. The working class may not change its identity or accept middle-class values simply because it aspires to the same material consumption patterns as the middle-class.

As a result, they set out to test the lesser hypothesis of the *convergence* of the two classes at the level of values and aspirations, rather than the more dramatic one of *assimilation* of the working class into middle-class structural relationships. *Convergence* in this sense occurs when the working class takes to itself some middle-class values and the middle class takes to itself some working-class values. For example, it is arguable that the working class has shifted away from the values it once placed on kinship and the extended family towards the middle class values of individualism and family centredness. It may be likewise arguable that middle-class 'instrumental collectivism' is no more than a euphemism for the white collar equivalent to the working-class trade union. The problem, of course, is as we have stated earlier: the shifts may be no more than changes to *behaviour* in response to changing conditions. There may be no accompanying change to the underlying social class *values*. The middle class may use white-collar trade unions for practical ends while remaining disenchanted with the concept of unionism itself.

The results of the Goldthorpe et al (1969, pp.158−65) study, however, showed that the embourgeoisement thesis, while it might have been theoretically convincing, was faulty at several points.

a) Claims that working conditions were 'more equal' had been exaggerated: Workers still suffered worse conditions and more strain. Their leisure was restricted by shifts and overtime. Work for them still meant selling labour for wages with minimal opportunities for control.

b) Higher consumption levels for the working class had been exaggerated. They were not reflected in the development of middle-class patterns of sociability or in the establishment of new social relationships with white-collar workers.

c) The Luton workers wanted more money, but did not aspire to, or expect to become, 'middle class' in status.

d) Workers who were most 'bourgeois-like' had many prior white-collar connections through family and work. 'No more than one or two of the 70 couples in question here could be realistically represented as being even "on the road" to a middle-class pattern of social life' (Goldthorpe et al, 1969, p.160).

e) Since the sample had been specially selected as a 'critical' test of the thesis (that is, a sample most likely to reveal trends *to* embourgeoisement), the findings challenge the whole notion that western industrial societies are becoming more middle class. But even if the results had shown shifts in value orientations, no necessary shift in class structure or social stratification would have been proved because those are 'ultimately a matter of sanctioned social relationships' (Goldthorpe et al, 1969, p.162).

Goldthorpe et al maintained that their alternative thesis of *normative convergence* was closer to the mark. The manual workers in their study were leading more family-centred and privatized styles of life and economic advancement for their families was their main concern. Work was valued for its instrumental rather than intrinsic benefits and there were few ties of solidarity with fellow workers outside working hours. Neither class consciousness nor status consciousness were apparent, these workers expressing 'money models' of social structure instead. Nor was trade unionism 'on the wane'. Though they did not actively participate in union affairs and agreed that unions had too much power and that the leaders were out of touch, their trade union membership was increasing and they found union collective action advantageous to their own interests. Moreover, most of these 'affluent workers' were Labour Party (U.K.) supporters and personal exposure through social networks to white-collar life-styles, rather than affluence, explained Conservative voting tendencies.

The study supported the view that alienated workers might see work only as a means to satisfy other needs. Many workers actually gave up more satisfying jobs to earn more money. Family commitments here seemed to affect job values rather than job values to influence family life. So Goldthorpe et al (1969, pp.183—7) called for 'a new empirical sociology of consumption' rather than the emphasis they saw being placed on the central significance of 'work activity and relationships to any understanding of working-class social being and consciousness'. But here their conclusions seem to overstep the limits of their data. As we have seen, the Kohn/Schooler studies reveal the quite significant effects working conditions may have on value-orientations and on the wider social experience of control.

Australian research has shown there to be similar convergences of the classes where income levels and family-centredness are concerned. But the same theoretical problems obtain. *Normative convergence* is neither the same as acceptance into middle-class relationships nor an indicator of structural change, and Australian community studies examining social relationships between classes and status groups have demonstrated very little withering away of the divisions between the working and the middle classes (Broom & Zubrzycki, 1968; Parsler, 1970, 1971; Kriegler, 1976).

Moreover, we may have overstated the case for a convergence of incomes in Australia. Table 9−12 shows there to be significant differences between the professional and managerial occupational groups in relation to all other groups.

Table 9−12   Mean weekly earnings, by occupation, August, 1977

	Men $	Women $
Professional, technical	254	189
Admin., executive, managerial	264	183
Clerical	188	143
Sales	183	121
Farm workers, etc.	139	98
Transport & communication	189	142
Tradesmen, factory process workers, labourers	172	126
Service, sport and recreation	180	130
Average:	192	147

(Source: Labour Statistics, 1977, p. 54)

Unfortunately, the figures combine tradesmen, factory workers and labourers, but on average, they earn 46 per cent less than the professional-technical 'middle class'. Clerical workers get 33 per cent less. The average for women is only 77 per cent of the average male wage; rural workers get 75 per cent. Earnings for clerical and other white-collar jobs are not much higher than for blue-collar workers.

The Future of Work

Hopes for and doubts about the future rest upon different assumptions concerning work. To say that work is clearly divided from leisure and most jobs are segregated from home life is to say the obvious. But not so obvious may be the effects of unemployment, non-work, flexitime and job-sharing on life-styles and work as a life concern.

There is, of course, no necessary connection between decreased work and increased leisure. Unemployment means empty time, but it is not necessarily 'leisure'. Not only that, but 'growth' as an ideology in modern societies may have its limits. Fred Hirsch argues (1977) that growth may be limited more by social conditions than physical resources. The good things in life cannot be constantly increased without some decline in quality. As societies become richer, the demand for a share of consumer goods goes up—'a demand that can be satisfied for some only by frustrating demand by others'. The result is an increase in welfare needs and increasing governmental action and collective regulation—of course running counter to the value we place on individual freedom of action (see Williams Report, 1979, ch. 12, p.544*ff*).

Others claim that Hirsch's argument is merely justification for maintaining the unequal status quo and that technology, in fact, promises an affluent future for all. At this point, the future of work involves both empirically based projections and the speculations of 'futurologists'.

In Canada in 1972 the Commission on Educational Planning posed two possible alternative futures. In a 'second phase industrial society' economic values might continue to put individual needs below the requirements of industry and technology. If that happened, a professional and intellectual elite would dominate; work and leisure would continue to be separate with more leisure for all but the top technical and managerial positions. Work would continue to be alienating and education would remain a separate social institution focused on training and credentialling. Social unrest would grow and increased conflict over law and order would lead to repression and resistance. Alternatively, society could become 'person-centred', putting technology at the service of human needs. In that event, needs rather than the market system would determine distribution, people would participate more in decision-making, and the distinctions between work, leisure and education would break down. As a result, education would become more central to society and lifelong learning would reduce alienation and the rigidities of grading and credentialling. The choice between the alternatives clearly rests on values and depends upon the power of vested interests. The Canadian Commission was not optimistic that the second 'choice of futures' would be made.

Herman Kahn's team report for the American Academy's Commission on the Year 2000 predicted the same contrast, where:

> Work-oriented, achievement-oriented, advancement-oriented values and 'national interest' values erode, and sensate, secular, humanistic, perhaps self-indulgent, criteria become central, as do intellectual institutions (quoted in Williams Report, 1979, p.554, ¶12.38).

The Williams Report, however, suggests that a decline in the work ethic is not compatible with a situation of increasing scholarship and research.

Current indications are that work participation rates are increasing rather than declining and especially for married women. As the 'Jackson Report' (1975) suggested, a decline in the work ethic may not mean that the demand for work is less. Rather, the meaning of the 'work ethic' may have changed resulting in a demand for different kinds of jobs.

> The human resource is unique, in that it is the only resource that cares how it is used. Affluent better-educated workers are asking for work to have meaning in itself, and to have purpose to which they can subscribe. But there is no clearcut evidence that people do not want work at all. Rising educational standards and the demands discussed above are simply incompatible with a large pool of people willing to do dirty, unpleasant, monotonous work (quoted in Williams Report, 1979, p.556, ¶12.42).

As we have seen earlier, 'dirty work' has always been allocated to lower status workers, whether nurses, cleaners or ditch diggers. If technology concentrated on removing 'dirty work' and provided opportunities for more satisfying, meaningful work to replace it, the social consequences might be highly desirable.

We need a renewed interest in the sociology of work; concern less with fine theoretical discussions about whether 'classes' exist and more for the way actual worklife structures social relations, reinforces or alters cultural values and limits or extends the competence or powerlessness of people. The first step might be to map the various 'communities' of work as they reflect the social distribution of competence and the structured limits to *praxis*.

Subjective and objective realities may reinforce one another or they may produce tests of reality to challenge the status quo. Through the study of occupational structures and cultures (especially those undergoing change), we may better understand the processes involved.

Readings and References

a. Australian Society:

A.C.T.U. (1976) *Social Policy and Problems of the Work Force*, Vol. 1, Melbourne.

A.I.P.S. (1972) *Parliament, Bureaucracy, Citizens: Who Runs Australia?* Angus & Robertson, Sydney.

ANCICH, M., R. W. CONNELL, J. A. FISHER & M. KOLFF (1969) 'A Descriptive Bibliography of Published Research and Writing on Social Stratification in Australia,' 1946-1967, *ANZJS*, Vol. 5, pp.48-76 and pp.128-52.

BALDOCK, C. V. (1971) *Vocational Choice and Opportunity*, University of Canterbury Publications, Christchurch.

BALDOCK, C. V. (1978) *Australia and Social Change Theory*, Novak, Sydney.

BLAIKIE, N. W. (1974) 'Altruism in the Professions: The Case of the Clergy', *ANZJS*, Vol. 10, No. 2, pp.84-9.

BORDOW, A. (ed.) (1977) *The Worker in Australia: Contributions from Research*, University of Queensland Press, Brisbane.

BOREHAM, P. et al (eds) (1976) *The Professions in Australia*, University of Queensland Press, Brisbane.

BROOM, L. & F. LANCASTER-JONES (1969) 'Career Mobility in Three Societies: Australia, Italy and the United States', *American Sociological Review*, 34, pp. 650-8.

BROOM, L., F. LANCASTER-JONES and J. ZUBRZYCKI, (1976) *Opportunity and Attainment in Australia*, A.N.U. Press, Canberra.

BROOM, L. & J. ZUBRZYCKI (1968) 'Social Stratification in Australia', in J. A. Jackson (ed.), *Social Stratification*, Cambridge University Press, Cambridge.

BRYSON, L. & F. THOMPSON (1972) *Australian Newtown*, Penguin, Melbourne.

CONNELL, R. W. (1977) *Ruling Class, Ruling Culture*, Cambridge University Press, Cambridge.

CRAWFORD REPORT (1979) *Study Group on Structural Adjustment*, AGPS, Canberra.

CURA (1978) *'But I Wouldn't Want My Wife to Work Here'*, Centre for Urban Research and Action, Victoria.

CURTHOYS, A., S. EADE & P. SPEARRITT (eds) (1975) *Women at Work*, Australian Society for the Study of Labour History, Canberra.

DEPARTMENT OF PRODUCTIVITY (1978) *Worker Participation in Australia*, A Selected Bibliography 1970-76, A.G.P.S., Canberra.

EDGAR, D. E. (1974) 'Reality Con-Struction: Micro Processes and Macro Change', in Edgar, D. E. (ed.) *Social Change in Australia*, Cheshire, Melbourne, pp.670-6.

EDGAR, D. E. (1975) 'Preparing Teachers for Change', *La Trobe Sociology Papers*, No. 32, La Trobe University, Melbourne.

EDGAR, D. E. (1976) 'Social Class Differences and the Structure of Education', *La Trobe Sociology Papers*, No. 34, La Trobe University, Melbourne.

EDGAR, D. E. (1979) *School-Work Transition in Rural Areas*, Commonwealth Department of Employment and Youth Affairs.

EMERY, F., M. EMERY, G. CALDWELL & A. CROMBIE, (1974) *Futures We're In*, Centre for Continuing Education, A.N.U., Canberra.

EMERY, F. E. & C. PHILLIPS, (1976) *Living at Work*, A.G.P.S., Canberra.

EMY, H. V. (1974) *The Politics of Australian Democracy*, Macmillan, Melbourne.

ENCEL, S. (1970) *Equality and Authority: A Study of Class, Status and Power in Australia*, Cheshire, Melbourne.

FITZGERALD, R. T. (1976) *Poverty and Education in Australia*, A.G.P.S., Canberra.

FOX, L. (1974) *Australia Taken Over?*, Quality Press, Sydney.

GIBBONS, A. R. (1977) 'Extending Flexitime to Shiftworkers', *Work and People*, 3 (1), pp.10-12.

GILMOUR, P. & R. LANSBURY (1978) *Ticket to Nowhere: Training and Work in Australia*, Penguin, Melbourne.

HALL, B. (1974) 'Competence and its Assessment in a Professional Training Situation', *ANZJS*, Vol. 10, No. 3, pp.221-2.

HARKNESS, R. & B. KRUPINSKI (1977) 'A Survey of Absence Rates', *Work and People*, 3 (2), pp.3-9.

HARVEY, L. V. (1978) 'Work and Family—Interacting Environments', *Work and People*, 4 (1/2), pp.33-6.

HAZLEHURST, C. & J. R. NETHERCOTE (eds) (1977) *Reforming Australian Government: The Coombs Report and Beyond*, RIPA, with A.N.U. Press, Canberra.

HELLER, F. A. (1979) 'The Future of Worker Participation', in Edgar, D. E. (ed.) *Australia's Changing Future*, Sociology Department Monograph, La Trobe University.

HETZEL, B. S. (1976) *Health and Australian Society*, Penguin, Melbourne.

HILL, S. C. (1973) 'Professions: Mechanical Solidarity and Process', *ANZJS*, Vol. 9, No. 3, pp.30-7.

HILLER, P. (1973) 'The Subjective Dimension of Social Stratification: The Case of the Self Identification Question', *ANZJS*, Vol. 9, No. 2, pp.14-21.

HILLER, P. (1974) 'Social Reality and Social Stratification', in Edgar, D. E. (ed.) *Social Change in Australia*, Cheshire, Melbourne, pp.71-88.

ISAAC, J. E. & G. W. FORD (eds) (1975) *Australian Labour Relations*, Sun Books, Melbourne.

JACKSON REPORT (1975) *Policies for Development of Manufacturing Industry*, A.G.P.S., Canberra.

JONES, F. E. & F. L. JONES (1972) 'Occupational Prestige in Australia and Canada: A Comparison and Validation of Some Occupational Scales', *ANZJS*, Vol. 8, No. 2, pp.75-82.

JORDAN, A. (1974a) 'Living Death in the Social Policy Section', in Edgar, D. E. (ed.) *Social Change in Australia*, Cheshire, Melbourne, pp.409-25.

KRIEGLER, T. (1976) 'An Empirical Test of the Embourgeoisement Thesis: The Australian Case', unpublished M.A. thesis, A.N.U., Canberra.

LANSBURY, R. (1975) 'Unionization of New Professionals', *ANZJS*, Vol. 11,

No. 2, pp.60-2.

LANSBURY, R. (1977) 'White Collar and Professional Employees', in A. Bordow (ed.), *The Worker in Australia*, University of Queensland Press, Brisbane.

LANSBURY, R. (1978) 'Unemployment and Social Class: The End of Embourgeoisement?', *ANZJS*, Vol. 14, No. 3 (Part 1), pp.259-65.

MCQUEEN, H. (1978) *Social Sketches of Australia, 1888-1975*, Penguin, Melbourne.

MARSHALL, I. (1974) 'Pressure and the Pressman: Journalists at Work', in Edgar, D. E. (ed.), *Social Change in Australia*, Cheshire, Melbourne, pp.365-78.

MARTIN, R. M. (1975) *Trade Unions in Australia*, Penguin, Melbourne.

MERCER, D. (ed.) (1977) *Leisure and Recreation in Australia*, Sorrett, Melbourne.

MILTON, P. (1975) 'Work and Leisure—What is the Link?', *Work and People*, 1 (3), pp.27-31.

MURPHY, D. J. (1975) *Labor in Politics: The State Labor Parties in Australia, 1880-1920*, University of Queensland Press, Brisbane.

OESER, O. A. & S. B. HAMMOND (1954) *Social Structure and Personality in a City*, Routledge and Kegan Paul, London.

OTTO, R. (1976) 'Patterns of Stress, Symptom Awareness and Medical Help-seeking Among Men and Women in Selected Occupations', Unpublished Ph.D. thesis, La Trobe University.

OTTO, R. (1979) 'Varieties of Coping and Defence', *La Trobe Sociology Papers*, No. 6, La Trobe University, Melbourne.

OXLEY, H. G. (1974) *Mateship in Local Organization*, University of Queensland Press, Brisbane.

PARSLER, R. (1970) 'Some Economic Aspects of Embourgeoisement in Australia', *Sociology*, 4, pp.165-79.

PARSLER, R. (1971) 'Some Social Aspects of Embourgeoisement in Australia', *Sociology*, 5, pp.95-112.

PERETTI, P. O. (1976) 'Effects of Community, Family and Home Variables on Job Satisfaction', *Australian Journal of Social Issues*, Vol. 11, No. 3, pp.222-9.

PETER, H. W. & R. N. DICK (1977) 'Changing Attitudes in a Mail Exchange', *Work and People*, 3 (3/4), pp.37-53.

PHILLIPS, C. R. (1977) 'The Disadvantaged Worker', in A. Bordow (ed.), *The Worker in Australia*, University of Queensland Press, Brisbane.

PLAYFORD, J. & D. KIRSNER (1972) *Australian Capitalism, Towards a Socialist Critique*, Penguin, Melbourne.

RICHMOND K. (1974) 'The Workforce Participation of Married Women in Australia', in Edgar, D. E. (ed.), *Social Change in Australia*, Cheshire, Melbourne, pp.267-307.

ROGERS, P. H. (1976) 'Shiftwork: How Acceptable is it?', *Work and People* 2 (1), pp.20-6.

ROLLINS, B. (1977) 'Socialization Into a Professional Occupation: A Study of Student Nurses', unpublished M.A. thesis, La Trobe University, Melbourne.

SHARP, G. (1974) 'Interpretations of Poverty', *ANZJS*, Vol. 10, No. 3, pp.194-9.

SHEEHAN, P. (1979) 'Social Forces in the Australian Economy', in Edgar, D. E. (ed.), *Australia's Changing Future*, Sociology Department Monograph, La Trobe University.

STOLZ, P. (1975) 'A Multi-million Dollar Problem in Industry—Alcohol and Drug Dependence', *Work and People*, 1 (1), pp.19-25.

SYMONS, A. (1978) 'Varied Working Hours—Here to Stay?', *Work and People*, 4 (1/2), pp.5-12.

TERNOWETSKY, G. (1976) 'Occupational Primacy and Socio-Economic Status: A Comparative Discussion of American, Brazilian, Mexican and Australian Findings', *ANZJS*, Vol. 12, No. 1, pp.64-8.

TRAHAIR, R. C. S. (1977) 'The Men on the Mine', in A. Bordow (ed.) *The Worker in Australia*, University of Queensland Press, Brisbane, pp.25-66.

WELLER, P. & J. CUTT (1976) *Treasury Control in Australia*, Novak, Sydney.

WESSON, G. (ed.) (1976) *Brian's Wife Jenny's Mum*, Dove Publications, Melbourne.

WEST, K. (1965) *Power in the Liberal Party*, Cheshire, Melbourne.

WHEELWRIGHT, E. L. & K. BUCKLEY (eds) (1975) *Essays in the Political Economy of Australian Capitalism*, Vol. 1, Australia and New Zealand Book Co.

WILD, R. A. (1978) *Social Stratification in Australia*, Allen & Unwin, Sydney.

WILLIAMS, A. J. (1977) 'The Independent Entrepreneur', in A. Bordow (ed.), *The Worker in Australia*, University of Queensland Press, Brisbane.

WILLIAMS REPORT (1979) *Education, Training and Employment*, Report of the Committee of Inquiry Into Education and Training,' 3 Vols. A.G.P.S., Canberra.

WINDSCHUTTLE, K. (1979) *Unemployment: A Social and Political Analysis of the Economic Crisis in Australia*, Penguin, Melbourne.

WYNN, S. (1977) 'The Social Structure of an Australian Abattoir', unpublished Ph.D. thesis, La Trobe University, Melbourne.

b. General:

ANDERSON, P. & R. BLACKBURN (eds) (1965) *Towards Socialism*, Fontana, London.

APTER, D. E. (1965) *The Politics of Modernization*, University of Chicago Press, Chicago.

AVERITT, R. T. (1968) *The Dual Economy: The Dynamics of American Industry Structure*, Horton, N.Y.

BECK, E. M., P. M. HORAN & C. M. TOLBERT 11, (1978) 'Stratification in a Dual Economy: A Sectoral Model of Earning Determination', *American Sociological Review*, in press. Referred to in P. M. Horan, 'Is Status Attainment Research Atheoretical?' *American Sociological Review* Vol. 43, August 1978, pp.534-41.

BEN-DAVID, J. (1960a) 'Roles and Innovations in Medicine', *American Journal of Sociology*, 65, pp.557-68.

BEN-DAVID, J. (1960b) 'Scientific Productivity and Academic Organization in Nineteenth Century Medicine', *American Sociological Review*, 25, pp.828-43.

BEN-DAVID J. (1963-4) 'Professions in the Class System of Present-Day Societies', *Current Sociology*, 12, pp.247-330.

BEN-DAVID, J. and R. COLLINS (1966) 'Social Factors in the Origins of a New Science: the case of Psychology', *American Sociological Review*, 31, pp.451-65.

BENDIX, R. (1956) *Work and Authority in Industry*, Wiley, N.Y.

BERGER, P. (ed.) (1964) *The Human Shape of Work*, Macmillan, London.

BIBB, R. & W. FORM (1977) 'The Effects of Industrial, Occupational and Sex Stratification on Wages in Blue Collar Markets', *Social Forces*, 55, pp.974-96.

BLAU, P. M. (1963) *The Dynamics of Bureaucracy*, (2nd ed.) University of Chicago Press, Chicago.

BLAU, P. M. & W. R. SCOTT (1963) *Formal Organizations: A Comparative Approach*, Routledge & Kegan Paul, London.

BLAUNER, R. (1964) *Alienation and Freedom: The Factory Worker and His Industry*, University of Chicago Press, Chicago.

BLUESTONE, B., W. M. MURPHY and M. STEVENSON (1973) *Low Wages and the Working Poor*, Institute of Labor and Industrial Relations, University of Michigan, Ann Arbor.

BONACICH, E. (1975) 'Advanced Capitalism and Black/White Relations in the U.S.: a Split Labor Market Interpretation', *American Sociological Review*, 41, pp.34-51.

BOURDIEU, P. & J. C. PASSERON (1977) *Reproduction in Education, Society and Culture*, Sage, N.Y.

BRIM, O. G. & S. WHEELER (1966) *Socialization After Childhood: Two Essays*, Wiley, N.Y.

BURAWOY, M. (1977) 'Social Structure, Homogenization and the Process of Status Attainment in the United States and Great Britain', *American Journal of Sociology*, 82, pp.1001-42.

BURNS, T. (1955) 'The Reference of Conduct in Small Groups, Cliques and Cabals in Occupational Milieux', *Human Relations*, 8, pp.467-86.

BURNS, T. (ed.) (1969) *Industrial Man*, Penguin, U.K.

CAREY, A. (1967) 'The Hawthorne Studies: A Radical Criticism', *American Sociological Review*, 32, pp.403-17.

CHOMSKY, N. (1969) *American Power and the New Mandarins*, Penguin, U.K.

COHEN, E. G. (1965) 'Parental Factors in Educational Mobility', *Sociology of Education*, Vol. 38, pp.405-25.

COLLINS, R. (1975) *Conflict Sociology, Toward an Explanatory Science*, Academic Press, N.Y.

COSER, L. A. (1975) 'Presidential Address: Two Methods in Search of a Substance', *American Sociological Review*, 40 pp.691-700.

CROZIER, M. (1964) *The Bureaucratic Phenomenon*, University of Chicago Press, Chicago.

DALTON, M. (1950) 'Conflicts Between Staff and Line Managerial Officers', *American Sociological Review*, June, pp.342-51.

DREIER, P. (1979) 'The Case for Transitional Reform', *Social Policy*, Vol. 9 No. 4, pp.5-17.

DUBIN, R. (1956) 'Industrial Workers' Worlds: A Study of the Central Life

Interests of Industrial Workers', *Social Problems*, Vol. 3, No. 3, Jan., pp.131-42.

DUBIN, R. and D. R. GOLDMAN (1972) 'Central Life Interests of American Middle Managers and Specialists', *Journal of Vocational Behaviour*, Vol. 2, No. 2, April, pp.133-41.

DUMAZEDIER, J. (1974) *Sociology of Leisure*, Elsevier, N.Y.

DUNKERLEY, D. (1975) *Occupations and Society*, Routledge & Kegan Paul, London.

DURKHEIM, E. (1964 [1933]) *The Division of Labour in Society*, Free Press, N.Y.

GERTH, H. H. & C. WRIGHT MILLS (1958 [1946]) *From Max Weber: Essays in Sociology*, Galaxy ed. Oxford University Press, Oxford.

GIDDENS, A. (1976) *The Class Structure of the Advanced Societies*, Hutchinson, London.

GOLDTHORPE, J. H., D. LOCKWOOD, F. BECHHOFER & J. PLATT (1969) *The Affluent Worker in the Class Structure*, Cambridge University Press, Cambridge.

GOODE, W. J. (1967) 'The Protection of the Inept', *American Sociological Review*, 32, pp.5-19.

GOULDNER, A. W. (1955) *Patterns of Industrial Bureaucracy*, Routledge & Kegan Paul, London.

GRAMSCI, A. (1957) *The Modern Prince and Other Writings*, International Publishers, N.Y.

GRAMSCI, A. (1971) *Selections from the Prison Notebooks*, Lawrence and Wishart, London.

HABERMAS, J. (1976) *Legitimation Crisis*, Heinemann Educational, London.

HALSEY, A. H. (1977) 'Towards Meritocracy? The Case of Britain', in Karabel, J. & A. H. Halsey (eds) *Power and Ideology in Education*, Oxford University Press, Oxford, pp.173-85.

HARRIS, M. (1977) *Cows, Pigs, Wars and Witches: The Riddle of Culture*, Fontana, London.

HERZBERG, F., B. MAUSNER, and D. B. SNYDERMAN, (1959) *The Motivation to Work*, Wiley, N.Y.

HIRSCH, F. (1976) *Social Limits in Growth*, Harvard University Press, Cambridge Mass.

HODGE, R. W., P. M. SEIGEL & P. H. ROSSI (1964) 'Occupational Prestige in the United States, 1925-1963', *American Journal of Sociology*, 70, 3, pp.286-302.

HOLZNER, B. (1968) *Reality Construction in Society*, Schenkman, London.

HORAN, P. M. (1978) 'Is Status Attainment Research Atheoretical?', *American Sociological Review*, 43, pp.534-41.

HUGHES, E. C. (1958) *Men and Their Work*, Free Press, N.Y.

JACKSON, J. A. (ed.) (1968) *Social Stratification*, Cambridge University Press, Cambridge.

KAHL, J. A. (1953) 'Educational and Occupational Aspirations of "Common Man" Boys', *Harvard Educational Review*, 23 (3), pp.186-203.

KAHL, J. A. (1957) *The American Class Structure*, Holt, Rinehart & Winston, N.Y.

KAPFERER, B. (1969) 'Norms and the Manipulation of Relationships in a Work Context', in J. C. Mitchell (ed.), *Social Networks in Urban Situations*, Manchester University Press, Manchester, pp.187-244.

KATZ, D. & R. L. KAHN (eds) (1966) *The Social Psychology of Organizations*, Wiley, N.Y.

KORNHAUSER, A. (1965) *Mental Health and the Industrial Worker*, Wiley, N.Y.

LERNER, M. P. (1979) 'Surplus Powerlessness', *Social Policy*, Jan/Feb, pp.19-27.

LIPSET, S. M. & R. BENDIX (1959) *Social Mobility in Industrial Societies*, University of California Press, Berkeley.

MCCLELLAND, D. C. (1970) *Alcohol and Human Motivation*, Free Press, Glencoe.

MARCUSE, H. (1964) *One-Dimensional Man*, Beacon Press, London.

MARSH, J. G. & H. A. SIMON (1958) *Organizations*, Wiley, N.Y.

NORTH, J. and P. R. HATT (1947) 'Jobs and Occupations: A Popular Evaluation', *Opinions News*, Vol. 9, Sept pp.3-13. See also Hatt (1950) and Hodge, Seigel and Rossi (1964).

PARKER, S. (1972) *The Future of Work and Leisure*, Paladin, London.

RAPPAPORT, R. A. (1967) *Pigs for Ancestors: Ritual in the Ecology of a New Guinea People*, Yale University Press, New Haven.

ROY, D. (1952) 'Quota Restriction and Goldbricking in a Machine Shop', *American Journal of Sociology*, 57, pp.427-42.

SCHUMPETER, J. A. (1950) *Capitalism, Socialism and Democracy*, Harper & Row, N.Y.

SCOTT, W. R., S. M. DORNBUSCH, B. C. BUSCHING & J. D. LAING (1967) 'Organizational Evaluation and Authority', *Administrative Science Quarterly*, 12.

SEWELL, W. H., and V. P. SHAH (1967) 'Socioeconomic Status, Intelligence and the Attainment of Higher Education', *Sociology of Education*, 40, pp.1-23; reprinted in Karabel, J. & A. H. Halsey (eds), *Power and Ideology in Education*, Oxford University Press, Oxford, pp.197-215.

SHOSTAK, A. B. (1969) *Blue Collar Life*, Random House, N.Y.

TAYLOR, F. E. (1911) *The Principles of Scientific Management*, Harper, N.Y.

TERKEL, S. (1974) *Working*, Penguin, U.K.

THOMPSON, E. P. (1967) 'Time, Work-Discipline, and Industrial Capitalism', *Past and Present*, Vol. 38, pp.56-97, referred to in P. Worsley, *Introducing Sociology*, (1970) Penguin, U.K. p.211.

THOMPSON, J. D. (1967) *Organizations in Action*, McGraw-Hill, N.Y.

TOURAINE, A. (1971) *The Post-Industrial Society*, Random House, N.Y.

VEBLEN, T. (1970 [1899]) *The Theory of the Leisure Class*, Unwin Books, London.

VOLLMER, H. M. & D. L. MILLS (1966) *Professionalization*, Prentice-Hall, New Jersey.

WEBER, M. (1964 [1922/1947]) *The Theory of Social and Economic Organization*, Free Press, N.Y.
WHYTE, W. H. (1956) *The Organization Man*, Simon & Schuster, N.Y.
WRIGHT, E. O. & L. PERRONE (1977) 'Marxist Class Categories and Income Inequality', *American Sociological Review*, 42, pp.32-55.

Chapter 10

Mass Media as Legitimaters of Order

Media Control

Media Images of Society

The News

The Portrayal of Social Roles

Distorted Communication

10

The mass media are just one of the institutionalized ways knowledge is transferred and information about the world and our place in it is communicated. Whether the mass media are more important in this regard than family or education or our social relations at work, is a matter for testing. And the tests are not easy.

So far, our emphasis has been on the social distribution of knowledge and ignorance, of competence and incompetence, of power and powerlessness in society. We have seen how the family limits that distribution through the roles it teaches us to play, the levels of control our parents experience and permit us to develop and the flexibility of language skills it allows us to acquire. We have also seen how education serves to reinforce those initial inequalities by defining competence in special ways, by giving selective access to different forms of competence and by certifying people both as intellectually and morally competent members of society. Work also confirms or denies our sense of competence and the legitimacy of what we know. It distributes material and status rewards and sets limits to the range of control we may exercise in life.

In all these ways, we acquire a share in the social stock of knowledge. Those elements of knowledge that are relevant for everyone are the building blocks of social communication. Unless we shared some form of common knowledge, we would all be 'strangers', able only to interact hesitantly and with distrust. As we saw earlier, we learn to categorize the world, to typify things in symbolic ways so that most of our everyday activities can be taken for granted. We desire our world to be unproblematic and predictable.

These ways of typifying the world of everyday life, however, vary in their degree of *content*. Close, face-to-face interaction with the members of our family teaches us in detail how they think and how they are likely to behave. But a great deal of what we 'know' is unlike that. For example, we do not know in detail how the mail is processed and delivered; we simply assume it will arrive. We do not personally know the President of the United States or how trade union leaders make decisions or how people in India or Morocco live. We 'type' them nonetheless and we often react to *stereotypes*, the contents of which may be very 'thin'.

Since our personal social world is inevitably limited to our own particular life situations it is likely that much of our knowledge of the 'public world' will be of this kind—thin in content, vague and at an 'anonymous' level. That is not to say, however, that it will be any less 'real' or important in its consequences for our social behaviour. But it does mean that the media through which we learn to typify the public world will be particularly influential. How we 'see' the world may be structured for us by the media of communication.

The term 'mass media' implies a lack of intimacy: the opposite of personal face-to-face communication. It also implies an audience on a large scale, undifferentiated according to class, race, religion, status, or personal or individual criteria. The media are communicating information and ideas to a relatively passive audience that cannot answer back.

The degree of passivity, however, may vary. For example, while we may not talk back to the television set, we can turn it off. We can stop buying a particular paper or write a letter to the editor. However, less interaction is possible than at, say, a public meeting where the audience can affect what is being said.

The kinds of media outlets and the dispersal of their ownership and control will also determine how 'mass' the media are. If every group had the opportunity to run its own newspaper, radio or television station, its views could be heard and the 'mass' audience could choose the messages it preferred to hear. We shall see that in Australia and other modern societies, this is less and less likely to occur.

Media Control

Few people would argue that ownership of Australia's media is not concentrated in the hands of a few. The Annan Report (1977) on the future of broadcasting in Great Britain, commented that Australia had one of the most monopolistic press systems in the world.

In 1923 there were 26 capital city newspapers owned by 21 different proprietors. By 1976, however, the number had shrunk to 18 and these were owned by as few as three proprietors: the Herald and Weekly Times; John Fairfax & Sons; and News Limited (Rupert Murdoch). The same groups hold controlling interests in the major radio and television outlets, further restricting the opportunity for Australians to be exposed to a diversity of media news and opinion.

Alan Brown (1976) has made a comprehensive listing of Australian media ownership. Table 10—1 shows how many different forms of the media are located in the hands of the single owners. (See Edgar (1979b) for a full list.)

Australian law states that no one company may hold a controlling interest in more than two television channels, or more than one radio station, in each capital city. But there is no limit to joint ownership of television, radio and newspaper outlets.

Mr Paul Keating, MLA, introduced a *Broadcasting and Television Amendment Bill* (No. 2) in November, 1976, with the words:

> The incestuous nature of the interlocking companies and directorships provides this small clique of proprietors with perhaps the most effective grip on the instruments of a national media that could be witnessed in any part of the western world . . . But no positive moves have been made by any government to break up the multi-media combinations . . . What also makes the situation frightening is that most of the proprietors who operate these groups share a common social background and in political terms share a common point of view (Quoted in Edgar, 1979b, ch.1).

The government's refusal to allow AM radio operators to expand into FM radio

Table 10 – 1 Media interests of the five major media groups

Media Outlets	ABC	Herald & Weekly Times	News Ltd. (Murdoch)	Fairfax & Sons	Consolidated Press Holdings Ltd. (Packer)
Metropolitan daily newspapers	—	9	4	5	—
Metropolitan weekly newspapers	—	5	6	3	—
Regional daily newspapers	—	11	3	4	4
Regional non-daily newspapers	—	4	12	2	11
Suburban & free newspapers	—	23	37	20	7
Magazines	3	6	4	11	30
Metropolitan radio stations	20	5	—	6	2
Regional radio stations	71	6	—	1	3
Metropolitan TV stations	7	4	1	3	2
Regional TV stations	77	—	1	1	—

(Source: Brown, A., *Australian Media Ownership*, Occasional Media Monograph, No. 1, Department of Economics, University of Queensland, 1976, p. 2)

will prevent the Herald and Weekly Times and Fairfax & Sons from doing so, but Packer's Consolidated Press and Murdoch's News Limited will be able to expand their media power into FM because they have not owned sufficient AM radio stations to disqualify them (*National Times*, 16 June 1979, p.26). The introduction of FM radio may also allow new groups to join the ranks of media owners. On the other hand, the closure of 3ZZ in 1977 and the low-frequency range of community radio stations such as 3RRR and 2VV limits the variety of views that may be put to counter the commercial world view.

So we have little control over the ideas presented by our mass media. We may choose not to watch and not to listen but whenever we do switch on a television set or a radio we will be exposed to typifications of the world decided for us by those who control the stations.

Kippax and Murray (1979) present statistical data describing the size and nature of the Australian television viewing audience.

a) 96 per cent of households (4.1 million) have a television set;

b) 62 per cent of households own a colour television set;

c) there are 87 national (ABC) television stations;

d) there are 50 commercial stations (clustered mainly in urban areas);

e) on average, Australian children spend more time watching television (an average of 21 hours a week) than in school;

f) of regular ABC viewers, 16.3 per cent watch television for more than three hours a day;

g) of regular commercial television viewers, 38.8 per cent watch for more than three hours a day.

Because it has access to such a large captive audience, commercial television commands a large share of the consumer advertising dollar. From a start in 1956—57 of just over $6 million gross income, the commercial channels grossed $303.7 million in 1977 (Kippax and Murray, 1979). Viewers may think that television entertainment is 'free' after the purchase price for the set has been paid but as economists say, 'there is no such thing as a free lunch'. Advertising costs reappear in the price structure of consumer goods.

But the media do more than transmit information and entertainment; they are integral to production and consumption in capitalist society. As McQueen (1977, p.10) puts it, the media are not merely financed by advertising: 'the commercial mass media are advertisements which carry news, features and entertainment in order to capture audiences for advertisers'. Kippax and Murray (1979, pp.21—31) detail the complex nature of investment, advertising costs and media profits.

Media Images of Society

What images of society are transmitted by the mass media of television, radio and newspapers? Do they simply put a mirror up to life and show society as it is? Or are particular group interests, tastes and moral values selected for special emphasis, giving a distorted picture of people's lives?

Several limits to media objectivity are immediately obvious. First, the majority of media outlets are commercially owned. As such, they aim to make a profit and depend upon advertising for revenue. If there is a commercial side to much of what is shown that should not surprise us. Programmes will be geared to the most 'popular' level, to as big a 'mass' audience as possible, rather than to minority tastes. Programmes attracting the largest audience, of course, attract the greatest advertising revenue. The same applies to newspapers, though it is possible for newspapers to run at a loss and to be stridently commercial, if that loss can be buffered by profits in another sphere such as television or radio. Newspapers, in fact, may serve as advertising media for television channels owned by the same company, a situation that causes doubt about the 'objectivity' of some programme reviewers and critics.

Also, the number of media outlets will affect the variety of world views presented in any society. In China and Russia, for example, centralized State control narrows political, social and economic messages to the one currently accepted 'line'; no counter-views are permitted. Free enterprise systems offer conditions for more variety through competition, but since commercial groups share a common interest in maintaining the current economic system, one 'line' may still dominate. Governments recognize this and fund independent media outlets such as the ABC and the BBC. Their brief is not merely to cater for minority tastes and interests (though commerical operators would like this to be the case), but to offer news, entertainment and culture untainted by commercial values or economic constraints. So-called left-wing political bias in ABC current affairs programmes may be no more than the presentation of counter views.

In Britain, BBC 1 caters for the 'mass' audience and competes successfully against commercial television. Its BBC 2 channel offers specialized programmes for minority audiences. In Australia, the 1979 inquiry into the ABC will have to decide whether to allow it to continue to compete against commercial television or to restrict it to programming for minority tastes. Since many rural areas are only catered for by the ABC, problems are bound to arise. And attempts by commercial interests to develop and control a national satellite system will compound the problems. Just as all televised cricket has fallen into the hands of one commercial operator so may other areas of the 'national culture' come under similar control.

Historically, newspapers used to be directed at small, specialized audiences. For example, in 1725 in Leipzig there was even a special newspaper for women. Mergers and monopolies, however, have reduced that kind of variety.

It is to say the obvious that the smaller the number of newspapers available to us, the more limited will be the choice we may exercise over whose views we will read. And of course, our chances of being heard, of having our own views printed, will be similarly limited.

The worldwide wire services of AAP and Reuter control most of the world's news (Tunstall, 1977). Their very structures, however, limit what may constitute 'news' for them and consequently what we read as news. In many of the developing countries, they do not employ journalists: so vast areas of the world may never appear in the 'reality' of news broadcasts or reports.

We hear the predictable: famine, floods, disease or political upheaval. Disaster colours our picture of the developing world and 'fits' comfortably into our superior self-view. Third-world countries increasingly protest the distortion and lack of access to the world's communication channels, which, they claim, damage their political and economic well-being (Tiffen, 1974 and 1976).

There is a further constraint on how the mass media communicate a version of reality. Like all other institutions the media operate through formal organizations with their own peculiar rules, routines and processes. Information coming in will emerge transformed by internal organizational processes. Deviant views will be pressed into an acceptable mould. Some recent studies have examined how organization structures and policy-making procedures of media companies in Australia affect their presentations of the news. Edgar (1979b) and Vigo (1980) relate some vivid examples of 'in-house' pressures as seen by Australian newspaper journalists.

Given these constraints (the commercial domination of the media, the limited number of media outlets and the internal rules of media organizations), we may not be surprised to find a significant degree of uniformity in Australian media images of society. There is, however, another constraint. Australia's economy is closely linked with overseas economies. In particular, the United States dominates consumer production and the popular entertainment field—especially film and television production. Despite attempts by the Australian Broadcasting Tribunal to impose Australian content quotas, the fact remains that most music, films and television programmes come from the United States. And it seems we pay heavily for the privilege. Because Australia has three competing commercial television networks, the prices paid are higher than in other countries which also purchase the products of the American media

(*Australian Financial Review*, 14 June 1979; see also Tunstall, 1977). So the world view portrayed by much of the Australian media may not even be determined by Australian tastes. In the next sections we shall look at the nature of the world views displayed through the Australian media.

The News

Perhaps because it offers the greatest opportunities for deliberate manipulation and distortion, the news and its presentation has been the focus of considerable sociological interest.

The communications revolution of the nineteenth century created a vast increase in available information. As a result, the problem of *the meaning of meaning* became more acute. People began to realize that there was no necessary connection between *facts* and *history* or *truth*. Information is *processed* and every report reflects the interests and ideologies of those who give meaning to the facts. Gouldner (1976, p.91*ff*) argues that the search for meaning from this mass of new information also created a 'news-reading public'.

A *public* emerges when close, face-to-face interaction declines. In a *group*, meanings emerge from mutual interaction and shared interests, but a *public* may have things in common and share information and cultural values without social interaction. The *mass* media makes this possible by conveying meanings and common world views through means other than direct interpersonal communication. As Gouldner points out, sharing information without close contact makes the job of *evaluating* information more difficult. We may not question or interrupt to ask for clarification.

At first, the news-reading public really comprised several specialized publics, each buying and reading newspapers which reflected the kind of news and political comment relevant to it. Time, however, has seen the amalgamation of these kinds of specialist papers into the comprehensive newspapers we have today. Modern newspapers continue to appeal (after a fashion) to different publics through special sections and supplements. We have only to notice how different people turn first to the sports pages or the business section or the literary supplement to see that different reading publics still exist.

Gouldner (1976, p.96) argues that a 'news reading public' emerged as people began to talk about the diversity of views reported in order to evaluate the true meanings. Newspapers, then, had the potential to increase public rationality by allowing alternate views to be presented, discussed and evaluated. But such 'talk' required room, some private time and space, for questioning, discussion and criticism. Lewis Coser (1965) describes the gradual shift in the nature of this 'safe space' where talk about news and its meaning could occur. The earlier aristocratic salons were often private homes and open only by invitation. The bourgeois public of the later nineteenth century, however, made access easier through their use of the public cafes as centres for intellectual discussion. But since sitting talking during the day required leisure-time and money, and night-time sessions were restricted to males, Gouldner (1976, pp.101–3) is probably correct in claiming that this early mass media public was 'open only to the economically and sexually privileged' and was 'premised on the patriarchal family system'.

Paradoxically, then, the growth of the *public* and the growth of the *private* went hand in hand in the eighteenth and nineteenth centuries. Public matters are those we may discuss whether or not we have personal experience of them. They go beyond the family and workplace; but the continued existence of public figures requires that there be a private world of the family to which they might retreat to rest. In the family there are bonds of affection, loyalty and authority to limit challenges to what may be said; but the public is not so restricted and may demand full explanations of what is done and why. Gouldner argues that public scrutiny reinforced the need for a family retreat, a private world of refuge, but at the same time encouraged concealment, secrecy and censorship in the public world.

Because of its necessary orientation to newness, the news rarely depicts the routines of everyday life. This, Gouldner says, has the effect of tacitly dividing the world into 'the seen but unnoticed regularities of everyday life' and 'the news which *is* seen, the departures from regularity'. Thus at the same time that:

> news *focuses* notice, it also *de*-focalizes notice, censors and occludes aspects of life . . . its silences generate an 'underprivileged social reality', said to be unworthy of attention (Gouldner, 1976, p.107).

But Gouldner does not encompass the point that the news places these departures from routine *within a recognized framework*. The news has its own set of conventions which make the unusual seem normal, and if we are continually exposed to these kinds of conventions we may learn to expect life always to be like that. Schutz and Luckmann (1974, pp.282–3) describe this process of selective construction in terms of 'motivated over-statements and motivated deceptions'. The more remote and anonymous the information being transmitted, the more prone it is to become 'the social dissemination of "false" knowledge'.

In other words the news may be *constructed* by a few people who decide what is, and what will not be, news. The roles of owners, editors and journalists are all of major importance in defining the 'reality' of news (Baker, 1980).

One further implication of the processing of news bears on the legitimation of an ordered, standardized world view. Gouldner (1976, pp.107–8) argues that the selection of departures from normality for treatment as news, implies its converse: what *is* normal, to be taken-for-granted, not to be upset in the social order. 'Dog Bites Man' is not news, but 'Man Bites Dog', might be. Reporters and editors 'print all the news that is fit to print', but *they* decide what that will be. One does not need to suggest they deliberately censor the news for the argument to hold. Every social being has an in-built censor. We view the world through our interests as well as our eyes and we try to arrange it so that our perceptions will not conflict with our values. We may not be surprised to find that newspaper proprietors and editors (as well as the journalists working for them) do likewise, reporting positively on items consistent with their own 'images of the desirable' (Gouldner, 1976, p.108), and discrediting those that seem to threaten the status quo. The problem is not that they do it; every society, group and individual does it. Rather, the problem is that people may believe that the news is the objective truth, the whole truth and nothing but the truth. Sociologically, news is no more than a construction of meaning refracted through the lens of particular interests.

Journalists may deny that they share common interests with their editors or proprietors, but they work within organizations that have their own rules and traditions necessarily limiting absolute freedom of reportage.

News journalists develop sets of standardized news stories and ways of treating them. They rarely lead the reader to see reality in new ways: rather the reader is led to come to terms with new realities in old ways. On the whole, news stories convert unconventional views to a set of 'normal' typifications that reinforce the status quo. For example, the Jensen-Eysenck IQ-heredity debate of late 1977, and Bennett's challenge early in 1978 to the accuracy of accepted figures on the Nazi holocaust, may illustrate how rarely contrary views are presented simply by the degree of controversy that follows when they are.

Normal handling of news stories leads people to accommodate the news (and any challenges to the status quo which it might contain) within the framework of the existing legitimations of the existing social structures. Langer (1980) argues that the 'management' of news items to ensure they fit the kinds of expectations the audience has, is similar to the way genre operates in film. A western movie, for example, always has 'goodies' and 'baddies' and themes and motifs which the audience expects to see unfold as part of the cowboy genre. So too, news stories have their generic qualities. Human interest stories, for example, fall into five recurring themes: animal stories, lost child stories, change of fortune stories, romantic adventure stories, and 'life's little ironies' stories.

Visual images in particular may strengthen beliefs that the news we see is objective truth. In television news especially, film conveys the message that what has been said in words really did happen. The picture is proof. Events as shown, however, may not be as they actually happened. Film footage may be cut to fit the commentary, the journalistic *interpretation* of events. Thus, Langer (1980) comments:

> The dominance of 'journalistic logic' in the structuring of news film means selecting and isolating visual symbols which will activate sources of meaning and instantaneous recognitions and will help control the viewer's 'reading' of a particular news story without the assistance of a completed narrative.

Ian Baker (1980) extends this point with an analysis of the sorts of people appearing most frequently on the news. He analyzed all stories filed in his ABC news office late in 1977, and scored them according to the mention of 'known regular news figures' and 'unknowns'. Over 80 per cent of news items mentioned known 'primary' figures and on only one day did the number of 'unknowns' rise above 20 per cent. Moreover, the style of 'mention' varied. Unknowns did not have their opinions reported; they were 'written about because they represented the end result of violence or the atypical'. They had been bashed, robbed, drowned or killed on the roads. Women and migrants appeared in no other category. In contrast, 'primary' figures (like Bob Hawke, Premier Hamer and

John Halfpenny) were reported for what they had said, for their opinions rather than for having done something (or having had it done to them). In addition to the really famous ones, there was an established and recurring group of 'spokesmen' used to comment on specific areas such as the police, football, the law, business, education and so on. As Baker (1980) puts it:

> We can establish a firm probability that rather than being open to all members of the community, the media is in fact closed to all but a miniscule power elite as a medium for communicating ideas, thoughts and the bases for public debate . . . All primary news figures represent authority in differing degrees.

The primary news figures gain their access to the media as a result of institutionalized patterns of news gathering. In Baker's study, over 89 per cent of stories filed originated from the *rounds* structure, the set rounds journalists are assigned to cover: political, industrial, police, finance, sporting and courts. There is no conspiracy deliberately to deceive the public but what is *normal* or *expected* or *legitimate about our institutional structures tends to define the sorts of reality* that will be presented as news. Even when nothing of note happens on a particular day, journalists and editors must still fill their papers with news. Because their rounds are set and their contacts are limited it is likely they may ask some notable to make a statement. Authority is always in the best position to win the opportunity to put its point of view.

At times, of course, the news must include items that run counter to media interests: counter views, social upsets that disturb order and challenges to legitimate social institutions. The vocabulary used to report them is likely to be negative, but the very fact that such items are reported may give them a level of legitimacy.

John Sinclair's (1974) study of the Melbourne *Herald's* reporting of the 1960s 'counter-culture' is a case in point. In the early stages the media presented 'hippies' and 'flower people' as figures of fun but that changed to real hostility as the counter-culture revealed itself to favour drugs, unlegitimated sex and alternative political forms.

Despite the disapproval, however, the *Herald* became a vehicle for transmitting the messages of the counter-culture to a wider public. Sinclair argues that much of the counter-culture was 'co-opted', that is, taken over as a legitimate part of the dominant bourgeois culture. Long hair, blue jeans, pop posters and heavy rock music could be turned to commercial advantage, and were. Over time, even the reporting of all drugs as dangerous changed to a more tolerant line differentiating between 'soft' and 'hard' drugs. But the elements of the counter-culture most threatening to the legitimate social order continued to be excluded: communal living, group marriage, environmental protection and radical political action. The media presented the individualistic, self-searching, free expression side of the counter-culture, and ignored, or disapproved of, the sharing, group-based, political aspects. In so doing, the media made the counter-culture no longer 'counter' because individualism, self against others and the hedonistic pursuit of pleasure are themselves *master symbols* within modern capitalist societies. In the end, rather than trying to change the inequalities and oppression they saw in legitimate society, most members of the counter-culture simply turned inward to explore new forms of individual self-expression. Perhaps their socialization made this inevitable but in the short run, the media helped divert attention from their less legitimate group activities directed at the power bases of existing social institutions.

At times, however, the media may be more deliberately goal seeking in its treatment of news. The press, like every other form of mass media, has its own internal and external political agenda. In a new study of the way the Australian press treats elections and the role of the Canberra 'press gallery', Patricia Edgar shows how a press purporting to be 'balanced' and 'unbiased' can distort reality for its public.

An important aspect of media influence resides in its power to set the agenda for debate, to define the issues and confine discussion within the limits it wishes to set. Using detailed interview data with newspaper proprietors, editors and journalists, together with a content analysis of the press treatment of the major political parties in the 1972 and 1975 elections, Edgar (1979b) found that no newspaper lived up to its claims of 'balanced' reporting. Only *The Age* gave equal space (column centimetres) to both major political parties, but its bias was shown in other, more subtle ways. By determining the space and prominence given to competing electoral issues, *The Age* clearly conveyed its own political preferences. Constitutional issues involved in the dismissal of the Whitlam government faded as newspapers highlighted Labor's prior economic 'mis-management', the 'improprieties' of its Ministers, growing inflation, the 'loans scandal' and Whitlam's 'style' as a leader.

Many journalists will disclaim overt bias in their reportage but the interviews in this study reveal a number of factors which may give rise to a form of self censorship to set limits to public understanding of electoral debate. The factors include:

a) traditional news values (or what was considered to be newsworthy);
b) knowledge of proprietorial or editorial preferences;
c) journalists' own preferences;
d) the selective nature of in-house editorial style.

At this time, however, there were overt attempts to censor reports that ran contrary to newspaper policy. For the first time in Australia's history, journalists went on strike because of what they saw to be unwarranted interference. On 8 December 1975, journalists working for Murdoch's *Australian* held a one-day strike in protest against direct editorial interference with the news stories they filed. Yet, as Edgar (1979b, ch.7), concludes:

> At critical points of history, given enough pressure, the press will respond with all its resources to see that the view they support prevails. But there is rarely the need for that kind of overkill, for the other factor that operates continually, is that the acceptance of particular news values and a standard approach to appointing journalists and news gathering ensures that the conservative viewpoint is perpetuated. A serious newspaper is a broker within the system and above all it is a source of ideological legitimation of the system itself. It can determine the outcome of a contest, but it also plays the continuing strategic role of maintaining the credibility of the system, a system which gives the Press its role as a key broker.

In such ways the media legitimates the dominant culture and the institutions that make up Australia's social structure. Consumption-oriented production values set the agenda for much of the news and systematically bias the portrayal of key social roles.

The Portrayal of Social Roles

Recent Australian research has begun to throw light on the way the media portray the broader roles in society. The way they present the family, the roles of women, the place of work and minority groups tends to reflect the master symbols of the dominant Anglo-Saxon middle-class way of life.

The picture of the 'typical' family in family television comedy shows seems consistently to comprise a professional and dominant father, an attractive, stupid-but-understanding, ever-present-in-the-kitchen mother, and children who enjoy luxury living and the constant attention of their parents. Patricia Edgar's 1973 study of such family shows revealed strong sex role stereotyping of women's roles. The message was that girls had no future other than through marriage and they had to be both manipulative and attractive to have any hope of ensnaring the 'right' man. (See also Edgar, 1974, pp.232−47.)

Obviously those kinds of role models are misleading for children of impressionable age, but 'typical' parent behaviour is also distorted and implies criticism of real parents who might be less perfect or 'provide less well' for their children. By omission, these shows redefine family life and men's and women's roles, so that differences in class, ethnicity and occupational and social level do not exist in the media view.

A study by Shirley Sampson (1975) revealed similar sex-role stereotyping in the *Women's Weekly* magazine. With a weekly circulation of 820 000 copies per week (in 1971), this magazine reached over 50 per cent of Australia's women and one home in every four. Again the picture conveyed was of a life based on housework, children, the need to please men, and the maintenance of youthful beauty. There was scant recognition of women's work roles, the importance of education or the realities of poverty, ethnicity and old age. Sampson suggests that while this may be a true reflection of social values, it reinforces rather than alters them, ignores conflict and social change and locks females into old 'realities' no longer appropriate to today's world.

Though new women's magazines such as *Cleo* and *Cosmopolitan*, and new television programmes such as *Policewoman* and *Charlie's Angels* show women in more active, 'liberated' roles, content analysis of the values expressed reveals them to be exploitative and sexist. They continue to idealize, exaggerate and distort by overlooking the real worlds of Australian family life or the lives led by ordinary women. Some programmes like *Family* or *Eight is Enough* tackle more controversial issues but they do so in the same context of patriarchal, middle class, consumer-oriented values.

A report on women in the media released by the Women's Bureau of the Federal Department of Employment and Youth in May, 1979, suggested that sex stereotypes have not decreased in current television shows. On Channels 9, 7 and 0, 80 to 88 per cent of lead characters or presenters were male, over 90 per cent of characters shown in paid work were in sex-stereotyped occupations, and close to 80 per cent of performers in advertisements were males. The report argues that trivializing women's concerns has a negative impact on society's attitudes to women and lowers the dignity of women at home and at work. Many daytime viewers suffered low self-esteem and agreed that television programmes reinforced that feeling.

The sociological question here concerns the effects of the media on people. It may be argued that people do not take the shows seriously; that they are just 'entertainment' and that if ratings are high they must be 'what people want'. But that argument ignores the limits on choice. When people come home from work and have little access to other forms of entertainment outside the home, and if their education has not taught them to enjoy music or reading and intellectual games, radio and television become invasive, attractive, ready-made forms of easy entertainment. Switching channels is little real choice when channels schedule programmes of the same type, at the same time, to compete with one another. And choosing to watch at all is no indication that people would not prefer something else if it were available.

In the controversy over classification of children's television programmes, the 'popularity' argument has been used to hide the facts. Commissions and Advisory Committees in 1956, 1968, 1971, 1973, 1976, 1977 and 1978 all expressed disappointment at the failure of commercial television companies to plan and pay for quality children's programmes. Each of them called for controls, quotas and more thought and money to be invested. Yet in 1979, when a new Children's Programme Committee drew up guidelines for quality C-classified programmes, the commercial television world reacted with shock, anger and obstruction. They had hidden from the public that the proportion of television time devoted to children's programmes had in fact declined from 8.9 per cent in 1960 to a mere 3.9 per cent in 1978 (Edgar & Callus, 1979, p.71).

In 1978 the Federation of Australian Commercial Television Stations claimed that advertising on children's television was desirable because children 'must learn to be consumers'. Cynically, needs, desires and choices could be deliberately created to produce effects necessary to the continued welfare of those who control the media.

Research on media effects is particularly difficult because so many other factors operate at the same time (Comstock, et al, 1978). For the most part, communication research has consisted of controlled experiments which isolate one media 'cause', and attribute any effects to it. But this is to ignore the social contexts within which children are exposed to the mass media. We know that people are influenced more by interpersonal, face-to-face discussion than by remote factors (see Edgar & Edgar, 1971–2, pp.608–12). We know, too, that shy, retiring people are more likely to watch television because it helps them avoid other people (Himmelweit, 1966, p.427; Hazard, 1967, pp.461–9; Edgar, 1977).

So our discussion concerning media effects will be more complex than such simple hypotheses as 'television violence leads to real life aggressive behaviour', or 'media sex role stereotypes cause women's lower status or lower self-esteem'. Writers such as Riley and Riley (1951), Maccoby (1954), Hazard (1967),

Himmelweit (1972) and Katz, Gurevitch and Gans (1973) argue in terms of a 'uses and gratifications approach'. They argue that people adapt the media to their needs rather than being influenced directly by the media. Edgar (1975) however, argues that such an approach is misleading. It assumes people are aware of their needs and ignores the way needs may be 'manufactured' within the social structure. The uses and gratifications view plays into the hands of mass media organizations by agreeing that the audience is getting something it wants. Television and radio may 'function' as an escape for housewives or as a substitute for excitement, but this tells us little about either causes or effects. Nor does the simple assertion that media content and people's needs are related to an 'interactive' way (McQuail, Blumer & Brown, 1972). Instead, Edgar suggests a *reality constructionist* approach which stresses the way typifications are shared and taken-for-granted, and can be 'constructed' by media organizations. She insists on the active, interpretive role of individuals but also on the parallel, socially circumscribed limits within which those interpretations of media content are made. Her model of media effects shows the need to examine not only audiences and content, but also media organizations, policies and ideologies and the way *production* of media content pre-structures the perceptions and interpretations that are possible (Edgar, 1975, pp.21–6).

In her own research on *Children and Screen Violence*, (1977a) Edgar found that both sex and self-esteem determined the way children responded to violence. Contrary to the conclusions of much of the earlier research she found that children were not upset by scenes of violent death because they had learned to perceive this as a stylized form of 'morality play' in which none of the actors really got hurt. Violence did disturb them when it came close to their own life experience. A mother dying, a child having her hair cut off as a punishment or an animal being hurt, were more upsetting than shootings and stabbings. The news was considered to be the most violent show of all, and a simulated documentary of a nuclear attack on Britain (*The War Game*) was upsetting to every group because of its realism and its news-type format. Boys with high self-esteem were best able to cope with realistic screen violence. Low-esteem children and particularly girls, preferred to escape into fantasy programmes and were likely to be upset by the content of their viewing.

This suggests that the study of media effects should be made from a *reality constructionist* stance. Children, like adults, have already formed some views of 'reality'. It is not simply that they use the media to gratify certain needs. Rather, they react differently to the content of media programmes on the basis of their previous socialization. They have already constructed an image of reality so the reality shown by the media will be interpreted in the light of that pre-existing world view. Sweeping condemnations of media violence divert attention from the central issue which ought to be to teach those most vulnerable to media influence how to 'read' its content more effectively.

Edgar's 1977 research has been confirmed in a 1979 study of children's responses to innovative children's programmes (Edgar & Callus, 1979). Again children with low esteem were found to be the highest viewers, to be most likely to be upset by what was shown and to be envious of the more competent, more fortunate people they saw. The research demonstrated that:

Children's viewing patterns are extremely complex and do not always indicate that the programs viewed are genuinely interesting to the viewer. They are simply 'less boring' than doing nothing. The diversity and uniqueness of children's tastes are not being catered for or developed (Edgar and Callus, 1979).

Thus the damaging effects of the media are on those who can least well cope. Because it is implied that they have failed to meet certain standards and because they are not recognized in the world of the mass media, they are made to feel even more inferior.

In this sense the media are legitimaters, rather than creators, of the current social order. They give pride of place to people with high status: they give low status people no place at all, or else cast them as victims or outcasts. If that is the way the world is, the media hold out little prospect that anything might change.

It is the same in the world of work. Connell (1977, pp.198—9) shows how much easier it is for some people to be presented in the news than others. Over 80 per cent of people mentioned in Sydney newspapers were from white-collar occupations. While 59 per cent of Australia's population work in blue-collar jobs, they represent less than 20 per cent of newspaper mentions. When they are, it is for their roles as sportsmen, victims or villains. The work of the working class is not news but the daily work of politicians and businessmen is. Ian Baker's (1980) study of primary news figures and the reporting of 'unknowns' as victims confirms this view of how the media structure a public image of worthy and unworthy occupations.

John Goldlust (1980) examines the portrayal of trade union strikes in the media and finds a pattern of typifications that again supports the dominant structure of Australian life. His study suggests that:

> the significance of the media's hostility to strikes lies beyond the opinions expressed in newspaper editorials and, more importantly, permeates the structure and presentation of general reporting of 'industrial unrest' both in the press and on television newscasts (Goldlust, 1980).

Just as the Glasgow University Media Group found little reportage concerning the *cause* of a strike or the background that led to a dispute, Goldlust found for Australia that each time a strike occurred, the media resurrected a standard set of typifications to portray it as illegitimate. The media's 'common sense' approach interprets strikes as irrational and out-dated, to cause severe economic disruption, and to reveal 'excessive' trade union power within society (Goldlust, 1980, referring to Hyman, 1962, p.140, and Westergaard, 1977, p.109; see also Moreley, 1976). For the most part, the media concentrate on the *effects* of strikes and fail to explain the *reasons*. While bosses may be interviewed in person, workers tend to be interviewed in noisy groups. Strikes are 'bad news', while their termination is 'good news'. Goldlust argues that journalists, over time, build up 'a standardized vocabulary of social typifications' through which they portray the world. Thus they do not deliberately distort what is reported or deliberately attempt to deceive the public. Rather they simply reflect, in the symbols they choose and the language they use, a particular world view that legitimates some groups and de-legitimates others. In examining the strike by air-traffic controllers in May, 1977, Goldlust finds that the media reported virtually nothing about the background to the strike (dating from 1971). Rather, it concentrated on the salary claims (seen to be undermining the government's current call for a voluntary wages and prices pause), alternative transport available to the public (it was school-holiday time), detailed reports of the chaos and personal upset to travellers, and the economic costs of the strike to airlines, other employees and passengers. Selectivity thus diverted attention from the issues, and portrayed air-traffic controllers in terms of the standardized symbols through which all strikes are portrayed. When the media focus on effects, the implication is that strikes simply 'happen' without social structural causes and that all strikers (even professional air-traffic controllers) are irrational militants influenced by a radical few.

Another case in point occurred following the arrest on 13 June 1979 of trade union officials in Western Australia for holding an 'unauthorized' public meeting. A clause in the Western Australian Police Act gave the Police Commissioner power to authorize any public assembly. At the time, the Western Australian government said it would not apply to union meetings but the police applied it. Because the law might have been seen to strike at the heart of the democratic freedom to assemble the dispute presented the media with a dilemma. Their standard typification for radical trade union leaders had to be set against the slogans of democracy—an uneasy balance. Some awkward decisions had to be made: it would rest uneasily with the media to extend public sympathy to 'communists' who had broken the law, but the law itself was in violation of the International Labour Organization (U.N.) convention on freedom of association and the right to organize. The problem would be to condemn the law while also condemning as illegitimate the strikes with which unions were protesting the action throughout the rest of Australia.

The media found that legitimations could be tricky things when a case did not readily fit their typifications. We sometimes see where the media suggest that strikes against a single employer are in fact strikes against the whole of society, but this was quite a different situation. This was an act by police, authorized by a democratically elected government, against basic democratic rights.

Crises like these afford us the opportunity to see power structures and the pressures of legitimation at work. The Western Australian newspaper *Daily News*, printed its first-ever editorial in defence of its right to print the facts of the Pilbara arrest, despite Premier Court's 'railing at the media' for their pro-union bias (15 June 1979). By 16 July 1979, Sydney radio personality John Laws, supported by media magnate Kerry Packer, was calling for a million signatures to support the federal government in its anti-union stance.

Distorted Communication

We have been describing examples of distorted communication. Filtered through the lens of commercially controlled media interests, women look stupid and inferior and families appear normal, well-adjusted, happy and affluent; violence is acceptable and seems to emanate from individual deviants rather than the nature of the social system; and strikers are irresponsible wreckers of legitimate social order.

Distortion can take several forms and, as we have seen, may not always be part of a deliberate conspiracy to deceive. When it is, however, we can call it *repressive communication*. This is Mueller's (1973) term for any situation where specific interest groups predefine issues and offer public explanations of events in terms of their own interests, in order to prevent other groups 'locating' themselves in society and properly expressing their own interests. Mueller has in mind an 'ideal' model of open communication that serves to point out contrasts. In the ideal model, everyone has equal linguistic skills, is able to analyze issues equally well to reach conclusions, and shares (or at least understands) the values and expectations of everyone else. In addition, there are no boundaries between private and public language so everyone's wishes can be articulated publicly. Flexible rules allow new views open access to all channels of communication (Mueller, 1973, p.20).

Clearly no real-life situation permits such open communication. The most extreme contradiction of such ideals, though, occurs where communication is 'directed'. Government control, blatant censorship and re-definition of the meanings of words aim to prevent subversion of the dominant group by denying the growth of counter symbols. Mueller cites examples of President Nixon's 'double think' where lies made previous facts 'inoperative'; of Hitler's systematic distortion of words and invention of new words to stereotype Jews and develop a new political vocabulary (Mueller, 1973, pp.24–42).

Less obvious, but no less influential, is what Mueller calls *constrained* communication. This is similar to the notion of *master symbols* or the *vocabulary of motives* used to describe a world taken-for-granted. Such *agenda-setting* is a subtle form of control. It takes the form of jargon and cliches and messages couched in language that conceals other intentions and other assumptions. The mere withdrawal or withholding of information by selective reporting constrains public communication to the *agenda* set by those in control (Gerbner & Gross, 1976; McCombs & Shaw, 1972; Tipton, Haney & Baseheart, 1975). Where fragmented pieces of official information are offered but the contexts and relationships left out, people lose track of how and why decisions are actually made. They are thus constrained to act within an officially defined information framework; their ignorance excludes them from effective political communication. People may then be forced into distorted (because incomplete) communication with others or a distorted monologue with themselves (Hannah Arendt's *privatization of meaning*).

Other institutions also play parts in constraining communication. If the education system developed efficient language skills in all and showed how decisions are made, distorted forms of communication could be more easily challenged. (See *Journal of Communication*, Spring, 1979, for a series of articles on the 'Politics of Language'.) A third form of distortion, Mueller calls *arrested* communication. It is the limited capacity to interpret, to de-code language, that handicaps certain social groups (Mueller, 1973, p.43–85).

Bernstein's (1971) *restricted language code* is a case in point, where localized jargon and linguistic styles limit a group's ability to understand and communicate with 'outsiders'. But language may go further than to create a barrier to communication with others: it may limit self-reflection and the capacity to 'think through' situations so they can be brought under our control.

It is here that the mass media are most open to criticism. The continued use of standard images and clichés, serves to trigger standard public responses and deny the need for careful thought. 'Dole bludgers', 'welfare', 'ivory tower academics', 'striking unionists', 'crisis', 'economic harm', 'wage rises', 'inflation', 'abortion', 'crime', 'long school holidays', 'serious consideration', and 'the community', are some of the shorthand terms that serve to conjure up standardized thought associations. Those associations develop through repetition, juxtaposition (of photographs and words for example), and the omission of alternate terms that might alter the picture. Public dialogue may thus become an exchange of media cliches which set the linguistic limits to thought and discussion.

Just as power can be located in non-decision-making as well as actual decisions made (Lukes, 1974, pp.18—20), so too can the agenda for public discussion be set by inclusion and exclusion of selected issues. This process is at work in media campaigns (such as *The Age* 'Insight' team reports on freeways, police corruption, housing deals, etc.) which reassure the public that something is being done about abuses of political or economic power. The campaigns are usually dropped as soon as public interest is exhausted (and the stories no longer sell papers) or if the stories run counter to the interests of their favoured party when an election looms.

By adopting the norm of separating 'information' news reports from explicitly labelled 'opinion' pieces, the media have answered the charge that their presentation of the news deliberately (or unwittingly) sets the agenda for public debate. They have also found strength in their claim to the 'ethic' of objective reporting and the concept of 'balance'. Yet as Patricia Edgar puts it,

> The concept advanced to produce so-called objective reporting is 'balance'. The force for good comments on the force for evil. The result is, of course, consensus, not genuine critical conflict. The ABC presents the most cautious news coverage we have and as the polls show, the public say they trust the ABC news more than any other news service. But what the ABC serves up as news is designed to cloud issues and prevent viewers from thinking . . . the idea that presenting two opposing views clarifies an issue is nonsense. There may be fifty different views, but the nature of the media means that the number of views that can be put is limited (Edgar, 1977b, p.48).

Politicians are past masters at this sort of impression-management via the mass media. The topics that dominate political communication are those most central to sustaining economic growth. The standard of living, costs and wages, education, medical care, welfare, social security and affluence, are all used as issues for public debate. But, in fact, they are only secondary to underlying economic structures; they divert public attention from structural problems while creating an illusion of participation.

The mass media have diverted attention further from the real issues by focusing on the personal lives of political leaders. Their intentions and motives have assumed greater importance than their policies or actions and have obscured their work in office.

The cult of the personality in politics may be a reflection of the *personalization* of life in the wider social context. Richard Sennett (1974, ch. 11) argues that social dislocation caused by industrialization and the decline of politics forced people to search for meaning in themselves and in their families. He argues that fear of public life gave rise to the concerns for privacy, close personal relationships and an emphasis on individual personality. In turn, these weakened further the will to become involved in public life. Thus he sees people wanting to be left alone and not wanting to become involved in attempts to change the complex world they fear. He further believes that people have lost the ability to play on the public stage because they have forgotten how to wear the mask of public civility. Such is people's concern with their private images of themselves (the desire to be seen as *sincere* rather than *manipulative*; *genuine* rather than *phoney*) that they have ceded political power to others and have lost the belief that they might be able to mould the world to suit their own needs better. And consequently they will be more inclined to accept those images of reality which the media present.

As Sennett (1974, p.282) points out, the electronic forms of the mass media take this process of *privatization* to an extreme. They destroy the *public* nature of experience. By *public* experience he means both experience of diversity in life and experience outside one's intimate groups. Radio and television break both those definitions of *publicness*. Although the media increase the common stock of knowledge enormously, they do so inside the family and restrict public contact to a minimum. We watch silently and cannot interrupt if we want to hear; the message itself becomes more 'mass' because it cannot be qualified to serve the needs of diverse groups. Thus the content becomes more abstract, treating everyone in the audience as if they were identical, as though they shared a common culture and equal life chances. Because of the absence of feedback, the emotional content of face-to-face talk is absent (Schutz & Luckmann, 1974, p.282) and intentions of media performers become separated from the real-life effects of their actions.

The role of the mass media then is revealed to be much more crucial than many people may recognize or wish to admit. Reaching every home in a way few other institutions can, the media portray political and social realities through a filtered lens. The main media outlets are controlled by the financial power brokers of Australian society. There is therefore a set of common criteria for selecting the aspects of legitimate and illegitimate behaviour to be presented and it is likely that they will aim to preserve the social structure as it stands. As we have seen, this goes beyond any simple-minded notion of conspiratorial manipulation. The dominant cultural values permeate every aspect of the media's portrayal of 'normal' family life, sex roles, work, politics and social order. Strikes, radical action or alternate life-styles may be the subjects of 'news', but they are usually reported in a negative way or else co-opted into the structure of a set of standard typifications that reinforce the *world taken-for-*

granted. Like disasters, they punctuate normal routines and strengthen the desirability of the legitimate order.

The public is thus shown a parade of leaders, radicals, unknowns and entertainers. The realities of underlying power structures are obscured, the links between issues and events rarely explained. Media content is therefore 'thin', seldom fleshed out with complex explanations and rarely raises the curtain of cliche which veils public debate. The very processing of news is constrained by journalistic categories that make media treatment of events predictable and seldom comprehensive or 'deep'.

In a society whose system of education is geared to credentialling people for narrow work roles rather than giving them political know-how or a comprehensive understanding of the social structure, our media keep an uninformed public in ignorance. Trivial issues presented in stereotyped ways form the basis of public discussion. Roles are reinforced to keep people in their socially constructed places. The master symbols of individualism, self-blame, competitive achievement and conspicuous consumption dominate both news and media entertainment. The result is to drive an already privatized 'public' further into its private world. The values we learn in our homes lead us to reproduce the culture into which we were born and afford us just sufficient control over our own lives for dissatisfaction to remain latent rather than overt. Controlling the switch or turning the page are poor substitutes for having some say in the way Australian society runs. Australian apathy may therefore be less a reflection of 'couldn't-care-less' attitudes than the result of the activities of education and the media to restrict the individual's understanding of how society could be any different from 'the way she is'.

Readings and References

a. Australian Society:

BAKER, I. (1980) 'Looking inside the media as an institution', in *The Journalism of Exception*, P. M. Edgar (ed.), Sun Books, Melbourne, forthcoming.

BARR, T. (1977) *Reflections of Reality: the Media in Australia*, Rigby, Sydney.

BRENNAN, P. (1973) 'Pressure Groups for Change Within the Australian Mass Media 1971–73', *ANZJS*, Vol. 9, No. 3, pp.58-63.

BROWN, A. (1976) *Australian Media Ownership*, Dept. of Economics, University of Queensland (Occasional Media Monograph, no. 1).

BUTTON, J. (1979) 'Media Controls in Australian Society', in Edgar, D. E. (ed.), *Australia's Changing Future*, Monograph, La Trobe University, Department of Sociology.

CONNELL, R. W. (1977) *Ruling Class, Ruling Culture*, Cambridge University Press, Melbourne.

COUNIHAN, M. (1975) 'Notes on the Problem of Media Content', *ANZJS*, Vol. 11, No. 2, pp.31-6.

DAY, P. A. (1977) 'Child and Adult TV Fiction in New Zealand', *Delta Eleven*, Nov. pp.13-25, reprinted in O. F. Dent, P. Kringas & S. K. Mugford, *Readings in Social Research and the Life Cycle*, ANZ, pp.219-31.

EDGAR, D. E. (ed.) (1979) *Australia's Changing Future*, Monograph, La Trobe University Department of Sociology.

EDGAR, P. M. (1973) *Sex Type Socialization and Television Family Comedy Programmes*, Technical Report no. 2, Media Centre, La Trobe University, Melbourne; also in D. E. Edgar (ed.), *Sociology of Australian Education* (1974) McGraw-Hill, Sydney, pp.232-47.

EDGAR, P. M. (1974) 'Self-Perceptions and Mass Media Violence', in D. E. Edgar (ed.), *Social Change in Australia*, Cheshire, Melbourne, pp.496-513.

EDGAR, P. M. (1975) 'Directions in Mass Communications Research', *ANZJS*, Vol. 11, No. 2, pp.21-7.

EDGAR, P. M. (1977a) *Children and Screen Violence*, University of Queensland Press, Brisbane.

EDGAR, P. M. (1977b) 'The Media as a Rival Seat of Learning', Meredith Memorial Lectures, 1977, La Trobe University.

EDGAR, P. M. (1979a) *The Politics of the Press*, Sun Books, Melbourne.

EDGAR, P. M. (1979b) 'Radio and Television', in A. Patience and B. Head, *From Whitlam to Fraser*, Oxford University Press, Melbourne, pp.214-32.

EDGAR, P. M. (ed.) (1980) *The Journalism of Exception*, Sun Books, Melbourne, forthcoming.

EDGAR, P. M. & U. CALLUS (1979) *The Unknown Audience*, Centre for the Study of Educational Communication and Media, La Trobe University, Melbourne.

EDGAR, P. M. & R. CROOKE (1976) *Families Without Television*, Media Centre Papers No. 3, Centre for the Study of Educational Communication and Media, La Trobe University, Melbourne.

EDGAR, P. M. and D. E. EDGAR (1971-2) 'Television Violence and Socialization Theory', *Public Opinion Quarterly*, 35 (4), pp.608-12.

GOLDLUST (1980) 'The Mass Media and The Social Typification of Industrial Conflict: The Case of the Air Traffic Controllers' Strike', in *The Journalism of Exception*, P.M. Edgar (ed.), Sun Books, Melbourne, forthcoming.

HARDING, R. (1979) *Outside Interference, The Politics of Australian Broadcasting*, Sun Books, Melbourne.

HEWAT, T. (1975) *Advertising in Australia*, Ure Smith, Sydney.

HORNE, D. (1976) *Money Made Us*, Penguin, Melbourne.

KIPPAX, S. & J. P. MURRAY (1979) *Small Screen, Big Business*, Angus & Robertson, Sydney.

LANGER, J. (1980) 'The Structure and Ideology of the "Other News" on Television', in *The Journalism of Exception*, P. M. Edgar (ed.), Sun Books, Melbourne, forthcoming.

McQUEEN, H. (1977) *Australia's Media Monopolies*, Widescope, Melbourne.

MAJOR, G. (ed.) (1976) *Mass Media in Australia*, Hodder & Stoughton, Sydney.

MAYER, H. (1964) *The Press in Australia*, Lansdowne, Sydney.

MURDOCK, G. (1975) 'The Sociology of Mass Communications and Sociological Theory', *ANZJS*, Vol. 11, No. 2, pp.27-30.

MUSGRAVE, P. W. (1969) 'How Children Use Television', *New Society*, 20 Feb.

RICHARDS, L. (1978) 'Displaced Politics: Refugee Migrants in the Australian Political Context', *La Trobe Sociology Papers*, No. 45, La Trobe University, Melbourne.

ROSENBLOOM, H. (1976) *Politics and the Media*, Scribe, Melbourne.

SAMPSON, S. (1975) 'The Australian Women's Weekly and the Aspirations of Girls', in D. E. Edgar (ed.), *Sociology of Australian Education*, McGraw-Hill, Sydney.

SINCLAIR, J. (1974) 'Mass Media and Society: Critical Theory and Critical Research', in Edgar, D. E. (ed.), *Social Change in Australia*, Cheshire, Melbourne, pp.618-29.

SINCLAIR, J. (1975) 'Mass Media and the Dialectics of Change: The Melbourne *Herald* and the Counter-Culture in the Late 60's', *ANZJS*, Vol. 11, No. 2, pp.46-9.

THOMSON, R. J. (1959) *Television Crime-Drama: Its Impact on Children and Adolescents*, Cheshire, Melbourne.

TIFFEN, R. (1974) *Communications and Politics*, ACFOA, Melbourne.

TIFFEN, R. (1976) 'Australian Press Coverage of the Third World', *ANZJS*, Vol. 12, No. 1, pp.9-13.

VIGO, K. (1980) 'The Education and Training of Journalists', unpublished paper, Media Centre, La Trobe University.

WESTERN, J. & C. A. HUGHES (1971) *The Mass Media in Australia*, University of Queensland Press, Brisbane.

WHITE, B. (1975) *White on the Media*, Cassell, Sydney.

b. General:

ANNAN REPORT (1977) *Report of the Committee on the Future of Broadcasting*, HMSO, London.

BACHRACH, P. & M. S. BARATZ (1970) *Power and Poverty: Theory and Practice*, Oxford University Press, N.Y.

BELSON, W. A. (1967) *The Impact of Television*, Crosby Lockwood & Son, London.

BENSMAN, J. & B. ROSENBERG (1963) 'Mass Media and Mass Culture', in P. Olsen (ed.), *America as a Mass Society*, Free Press, N.Y.

BERELSON, B. & M. JANOWITZ (eds) (1966) *Reader in Public Opinion and Communication*, (2nd ed.), Free Press, N.Y.

BERNSTEIN, B. (1971) *Class, Codes and Control*, Vol. 1, Routledge & Kegan Paul, London.

BLUMLER, J. & D. McQUAIL (1968) *Television in Politics: Its Uses and Influence*, Faber & Faber, London.

COHEN, S. & J. YOUNG (eds) (1973) *The Manufacture of News. Deviance, Social Problems & the Mass Media*, Constable, London.

COMSTOCK, G. et al (1978) *Television and Human Behaviour*, Cambridge University Press, N.Y.

COSER, L. A. (1965) *Men of Ideas, a Sociologist's View*, Free Press, N.Y.

DORFMAN, A. & A. MATTELART (1975) *How to Read Donald Duck*, International General, N.Y.

FESTINGER, L. (1957) *A Theory of Cognitive Dissonance*, Row, Peterson, Ill.

GANS, H. J. (1972) 'The Famine in American Mass Communications Research: Comments on Hirsch, Tuchman and Gecas', *American Journal of Sociology*, 77(4), pp.697-705.

GERBNER, G. & L. GROSS (1976) 'Living with Television: the Violence Profile', *Journal of Communication*, 26(2), pp.173-99.

GOULDNER, A. W. (1976) *The Dialectic of Ideology and Technology*, Macmillan, London.

HALLORAN, J. D., P. ELLIOTT & G. MURDOCK (1970) *Demonstrations and Communication: A Case Study*, Penguin, U.K.

HAZARD, W. R. (1967) 'Anxiety and Preference for Television Fantasy', *Journalism Quarterly*, 44(3), pp.461-9.

HIMMELWEIT, H. T. (1966) 'Television and the Child', in B. Berelson & M. Janowitz, (eds), *Reader in Public Opinion and Communication*, Free Press, N.Y., pp.418-45.

HYMAN, R. (1962) *Strikes*, Fontana, London.

KATZ, E., M. GUREVITCH & H. GANS (1973) 'On the Use of the Mass Media for Important Things', *American Sociological Review*, 23, pp.164-81.

KNIGHTLEY, P. (1975) *The First Casualty*, Andre Deutsch, London.

LUKES, S. (1974) *Power: a Radical View*, Macmillan, London.

MACCOBY, E. E. (1954) 'Why do Children Watch Television?' *Public Opinion Quarterly*, 18(3), pp.239-44.

McCOMBS, M. E. & D. L. SHAW (1972) 'The Agenda-Setting Function of the Mass Media', *Public Opinion Quarterly*, Vol. 36, pp.176-87.

McQUAIL, D. (ed.) (1969) *Towards a Sociology of Mass Communications*, Collier-Macmillan, London.

McQUAIL, D., J. BLUMLER & J. BROWN (1972) 'The Television Audience: A Revised Perspective', in D. McQuail (ed.), *Sociology of Mass Communication*, Penguin, U.K., pp.135-65.

MORELEY, D. (1976) 'Industrial Conflict and the Media', *The Sociological Review*, May, 1976, pp.245-68.

MUELLER, C. (1970) 'Notes on the Repression of Communicative Behaviour' in H. P. Dreitzel (ed.), *Recent Sociology No. 2*, Macmillan, London, pp.101-13.

MUELLER, C. (1973) *The Politics of Communication*, Oxford University Press, Oxford.

PACKARD, V. (1957) *The Hidden Persuaders*, McKay, N.Y., (Penguin ed. 1960).

RILEY, M. W. & J. W. RILEY Jr. (1951) 'A Sociological Approach to Communications Research', *Public Opinion Quarterly*, 15, pp.445-60.

ROSZAK, T. (1971) *The Making of a Counter Culture*, Faber, London.

SCHILLER, H. I. (1976) *Communication and Cultural Domination*, M. E. Sharpe Inc., Pantheon Books, N.Y.

SCHUTZ, A. & T. LUCKMANN (1974) *Structures of the Life World*, Heinemann Educational, London.

SENNETT, R. (1974) *The Fall of Public Man*, Cambridge University Press, Cambridge.

SCHULMAN, M. (1973) *The Ravenous Eye*, Cassell, London.

SUSSMAN, L. R. (1977) *Mass News Media and the Third World Challenge*, Sage Policy Paper, No. 46.

'Third World News and Views' (1979) *Journal of Communication*, 29(2), pp.134-98.

THOMAS, W. I. (1928) *The Child in America*, Knopf, N.Y.

TIPTON, L., R. D. HANEY & J. R. BASEHEART (1975) 'Media Agenda-Setting in City and State Campaigns, *Journalism Quarterly*, 52, pp.15-22.

TUNSTALL, J. (ed.) (1970) *Media Sociology*, Methuen, London.

TUNSTALL, J. (1977) *The Media are American*, Columbia University Press, N.Y.

UNITED STATES (1972) *Report to the Surgeon General*, U.S. Public Health Service, 5 volumes on 'Television and Social Behavior', Govt. Printing Office, Washington D.C.

WESTERGAARD, J. (1977) 'Power, Class and The Media', J. Curran, M. Gurevitch and J. Woollacott, (eds), *Mass Communication and Society*, Free Press, N.Y.

WILLIAMS, R. (1968) *Communications*, Penguin, U.K.

Chapter 11

The Treatment of Ethnicity

11

The title of this chapter is deliberately ambiguous. The adjective *ethnic* may be defined as *relating to a nation, race or people discriminated on the basis of physical and mental traits, common customs and characters* (Webster's), so the term mixes aspects of biologically determined *race* and socially structured group *culture*. Ethnic groups are a key to understanding both social structure and culture. They offer a critical test not only of how life chances are limited by the status groups into which one is born, but also of how group cultures reflect particular life concerns and values. Hence the way ethnicity is 'treated' (i.e. studied) by sociologists is of theoretical interest. So too is the way ethnic groups are 'treated' (i.e. behaved towards) by the dominant culture.

The Dominant Culture

We have already discussed the meaning of culture and the ways in which competing values become *institutionalized* in social relationships. The groups with the greatest control of the *resources* most relevant to the particular time, place and circumstance impose their values, their expectations, their needs and their interests upon the society as a whole. In simple societies there will always be competing individual interests. People's needs and resources in simple societies, however, are so similar that no *groups* as such emerge. There may be a sexual division of labour and thus a sexual stratification; there may be age-related status group distinctions too; but the entire set of social relationships is seen as serving (and serves fairly effectively) the interests of all. Here we may speak of *the* culture of a society, but not of a *dominant* culture.

As soon as the division of labour becomes more complex, however, class and status group divisions become more important. Separate functions and unequal resources create more rigid barriers between sections or groups within the community. And each group may be relied upon to pursue its own interests according to its own values. For example, if a priestly class develops, its members may demand rewards, respect and obedience for the services it performs or for the sanctions which it might invoke. And the presence of a dominant warrior class may mean that men who plough rather than fight will be treated as an inferior group. Lowest in the pecking order of any society, however, is the slave. The use of captives as slaves brings an entire group of strangers into a community. The culture of these strangers is likely to be despised because it is both different and defeated. Of course, slaves have no rights at all and they may be dominated by everyone who belongs to the dominant culture.

Strangers, however, may join a society in times of peace as well as war.

Migrants come in search of food; to escape overcrowding or enemy attack; to promote trade or a religious gospel. When they arrive, the migrants have to establish relationships with the natives. The first impact is likely to cause culture shock as both migrants and natives suddenly become aware of a group of people who behave differently, who have different values and expectations, and who do not fit neatly into the social structure to which they are accustomed.

It is then that the issue of *dominant* versus *minority* cultures raises its head. If a society claims to be democratic its members will likely claim that it is necessarily *pluralist* and that no single group does or can dominate.

Ethnicity and Pluralism

The idea of pluralism is essentially a *balance of power* thesis about social structure. Society is pictured as a complex of many competing interest groups; power is seen as being widely distributed throughout the society. Since each group has veto powers which can counter threats to its own interests, most societal decisions are held to be compromises arising from the overall balance of power (Reisman, 1951, pp.242—55). Some theorists, then, see ethnic groups as elements in a pluralist society, not necessarily maintaining their cultural differences (*cultural pluralism*) but forming cohesive groups representing their own interests (*structural pluralism*). In some cases, however, such ethnic groups are fragmented, are not strong enough to exercise any real power in their own interest, compete with one another (often at the lower end of the social scale), but are unable to touch or be heard by the major structures of power. In other cases, an ethnic minority group can become so powerful that it dominates the major social structure. The British in colonial India and the Chinese in Malayan Singapore provide two historical cases in point.

Pluralism is a desirable goal for those who see competition as a way to prevent monopolies of power. Leadership roles are likely to be more widely distributed in a community where many people belong simultaneously to a variety of organizations. In such a community, too, there is likely to be a greater distribution of the skills and experience of leadership and decision-making (Cox, 1976; Ronan, 1974). In the words of de Tocqueville: 'If men are to remain civilized, or to become so, the art of associating together must grow and improve in the same ratio in which the equality of conditions is increased' (quoted in Broom and Selznick, 1977, p.575). Notice that the emphasis here is on association, on cross-cutting memberships, shared decision-making and shared power. Even in a representative democracy, however, such ideal conditions rarely exist. If people do not belong to large and powerful organizations they are not protected and have little power. Power is not equally distributed because resources are distributed unequally; the power to decide what colour to paint the school hall is not the same as the power to refuse to build it. Democracies, furthermore, elect leaders who may promise all sorts of things before the elections but who may forget their promises when the elections are over.

Moreover, where pluralist groups are strong, their veto power can block all

277

action. This happens in the United Nations Organization. It happens less formally, but more often, when a government deliberately declines to act because it sees that any course of action will offend at least one major bloc of voters.

It is thus rather naive to suggest that a country with many ethnic groups is therefore *pluralist*. Ethnicity may be one of the very factors that decreases group power. Both their low status and their inferior resources make it less likely that ethnic groups will be part of the pluralist balance of power. The more common assumption is that ethnic groups will 'melt' into the more dominant economic and social organizations, thereby gaining their share of social power. But if they do, it follows that they are no longer illustrative of either cultural or structural pluralism.

American interest in ethnicity as a field for study peaked in the 1920s (Thomas and Znaniecki, 1927; Wirth, 1928); thereafter it declined because most social scientists assumed that the American 'melting pot' had worked so well that there was little to be studied. (There is a concise review in the first chapter of Martin, Jean I., *Community and Identity, Refugee Groups in Adelaide* (1972), A.N.U. Press, Canberra, pp.1–8). Glazer and Moynihan's *Beyond the Melting Pot* (1963) shattered some of those complacencies, however, and the huge minority group disturbances since the 1960s have guaranteed renewed attention for ethnic groups. Debate has focused round the notion of *pluralism*. While some,

> have been loath to admit that ethnic loyalties could exert any influence on the making of American public policy . . . we have conceived of political interest based upon ethnicity as 'un-American' and have often sought to stamp out such influences (quoted in Martin, 1972a, p.3, from Bailey, H. A. & E. Katz, *Ethnic Group Politics*, Merrill, 1969, p.vii),

others have argued that pluralism, the existence of groups strongly representing different values and interests, is the very essence of democratic freedom (Veidemanis, J. quoted in Martin, 1972b, p.3).

Gordon (1964) claimed that such groups survive either to protect ethnic identity against host society hostility, or else because that society erects structural barriers to ethnic assimilation. A different view is taken by others who, like Sklare (1965), believe that ethnic groups persist for the more positive reasons of preserving 'a long and profound tradition'. Structural pluralism might also develop as minority groups pursue their interests, or because these groups are sustained by larger structures, such as a political party or a church.

To decide what form structural pluralism takes and the extent to which it exists at all one would need evidence of the links between ethnic groups and other structures of power; of the degree of ethnic group solidarity; of the relative influence of such groups; and of the extent to which the interests underlying group membership are served by ethnic community life.

The terms *dominant culture* and *minority culture* may deceptively imply both superior numbers and superior power for the dominant culture. In South Africa, however, the whites are a numerical minority, yet they dominate and enforce their views on the black majority whose culture is considered to be inferior. *Apartheid* as a policy claims to view Bantu and other black cultures as equal but different. However the way the policy is implemented, which involves keeping entire racial groups separate and on unequal terms, does not support the claim. The term *minority group*, then, often refers to a social *condition*, a set of dominance relations, rather than to the numerical size of a social group.

In a similar way, *race* and *ethnicity* may also be confused. Strictly speaking, *race* refers to inherited, genetic differences such as skin colour, hair type and eye shape. *Ethnicity* as such is only partly inherited. It is also acquired, learned and transmitted through socialization processes. One's ethnic identity is revealed through language, nationality, dress, cultural mannerisms and so on, all of which are learned within the ethno-groups we grow up in. Despite this distinction, people often speak of ethnic groups as if they were totally distinct races. Hitler managed to transform non-Aryan racial origins into a stigma for all Jews (a religion, not a race), regardless of their country of birth or racial make-up. Even the French-Canadians and Anglo-Canadians at times refer to one another as different races. In Australia, as in America, waves of new migrant ethnic groups are often seen as 'foreign races'.

Thus it is important to identify clearly the tests and categories that are socially used when people are defining different racial or ethnic or minority groups. Later in this chapter (Table 11–5) we will see that many Australians are happy to speak of Jews (a religious group), Greeks (an ethnic group) and Chinese (a race) as if they were equivalent categories.

The Roots of Prejudice

Prejudice means, literally, pre-judging. In everyday life we pre-judge most things as a kind of shorthand for experience. The labels, and classifications that we use to 'type' people, events and ideas, help us sort out new experiences and to *typify* them in a way that makes them meaningful to us. We 'fit them in' to our view of the world. Because our experience is necessarily limited, many of our labels come to us second-hand. For example, if I have never been to Egypt I must rely on pictures, stories and other people for my interpretation of life there, an interpretation made up of pictures of pyramids, women in veils, and 'Arabs'. Such a label, 'Arabs' then is not full of 'content' for me, it is an anonymous type that I use as a shorthand categorization of millions of different people. Stereotypes are thus heightened types: a few characteristics are taken to represent multiple realities. The Scot is 'canny'; the Jew is 'shrewd'; the Australian is a 'spendthrift' in a 'lucky country'. Such labels can be favourable or unfavourable.

We are forced to abandon these labels only by *contact*, which forces us to adopt a more detailed category system and to abandon unreal stereotypes. Our contact with members of another group may be pleasant or unpleasant. It may be with people who are fairly representative of the group or with people who are quite unrepresentative. The sort of contact we have will inevitably colour the new evaluations that we form.

There is, therefore, a clear process which produces racial and ethnic stereotypes. Just as in early childhood socialization the 'looking-glass self' (Cooley's concept for our seeing how we appear to, and are evaluated by, others), serves to develop our personal identity, so too in every new encounter, we expect to see our identity mirrored in our 'we-relations' with others. As Schutz puts it:

> ... to every concrete situation in which I meet an Other, I bring with me my stock of knowledge, i.e., the sedimentation of past experiences. This stock of knowledge naturally includes as well a network of typifications of men in general, their typically human motivations, patterns of action, hierarchies of plans ... my knowledge of objective sign systems, especially of a language ... the natural attitude is characterized by the assumption that the life-world accepted by me as given is also accepted by my fellow-man as given ... a breaking off, or even just a radical restriction, of the continual confirmation of this character of the world has grave consequences for the normal development of its intersubjectivity ... self-evidences (are) the underpinning for the life-world to which we are accustomed ... (Schutz & Luckmann, 1974, pp.67−8).

In other words, the 'stranger' who brings a new cultural life both heightens our sense of identity and threatens it. 'We' are felt anew as being different from 'them'. If they happen to be in a minority or primitive or non-aggressive or disunited, they can be destroyed, 'treated' calmly or ignored. Our perceptions of strangers and our tactics for dealing with them will always reflect our interests and reality-views. Jean Martin suggests that the migrant as 'stranger' may show a 'new way', may be an innovator in the receiving country. Unfortunately, most studies treat migration through *stunting* theories rather than through *liberating* ones (Martin and Meade, 1979).

Because we develop (through socialization), a constantly reinforced stock of taken-for-granted knowledge, we can control the world accordingly. Our theories about *reality*, about what constitutes truth, normality, wisdom and morality, meet constant *reality tests* which either confirm or modify them. In everyday life most of our assumptions, typifications, beliefs and theories are confirmed by the others around us. The self is safely *lodged* in the security that others share our views (Denzin, 1969), know that we share theirs, are therefore fairly predictable in their actions and reactions, and can be trusted. In such cases we enjoy a 'safe' social existence. But if the confirmations of others are removed, if what is accepted as typical or normal is challenged, then our individual and group identities are immediately threatened.

Like the deviant, the stranger or minority group member conforms to different social norms. The stranger's own ethnic group's norms, its stock of taken-for-granted knowledge, *is* reality, and gives him *his* sense of identity in the context of a valued past sedimented in tradition. The migrant is not a stranger in his own land, only in another. The expression 'like a fish out of water' applies to any cultural outsiders who feel embarrassed in unfamiliar settings. The academic in a working-class pub, the bashful adolescent on his first date and the untrained person tackling a highly skilled task are all unaware of how they should behave. However the migrant is the ideal type of the sociological *stranger*.

Stages of Ethnicity

This suggests that there are likely to be stages in the treatment of ethnicity. At first the new arrival will be 'strange', both to himself and to the people of the host country and the extent to which the social networks of the host country are open or closed will alter the conditions of the stranger's acceptance or rejection. The uses to which minority cultures are put (they may be slaves, unskilled labourers, religious scapegoats or expert elites) will also condition their relevance and importance to the interests of other groups. The migrant may be seen as threatening, as insignificant or as a valuable contributor.

But immigrants are not passive. They, too, have their interests and purposes. The decision to seek a new life may represent despair and disgust with the old; it may reflect new hope and determination; it may reflect either a long-term 'settlement' goal or the short-term goal of 'striking it rich' and then returning home.

Similarly the host community is not monolithic. Different structures —churches, political parties, school, sporting and social organizations—will receive and be acted upon by ethnic groups in a variety of ways. As a result, terms such as *assimilation*, *integration* and *settling in*, must be treated with the same caution as the term *socialization*.

How long does it take to absorb an ethnic group into a host society? Before we may answer such a question we must clarify what we mean by *absorption*. If our concern is with *assimilation* we may want evidence that 'they' have become more like 'us', or 'we' like 'them', or both. If, on the other hand, we are looking not for assimilation but merely for *integration*, we will be less concerned with subjective change on the migrant's part; instead we might merely hope that the migrant group will be accepted into the wider community. (Note that we have said nothing about the levels of the social system into which the group will fit.)

A concern for integration may well reflect an acceptance that ethnic groups are not necessarily a threat to national identity even if they succeed in preserving their own cultures. In Australia the new policy encourages a *multi-cultural* society, with the recognition of the worth of other languages and other life-styles and of the rights of other groups to preserve their own identities through group cultures, ethnic schools and organizations. That acceptance, of course, could change if ethnic groups started to pursue divisive political goals (as with the recent crackdown on the Ustashi and the concern over competing Vietnamese political groups in Australia (*National Times*, 26 May, 1979, p.14)). It could change, too, if such groups were to challenge the structure of Australian institutions.

We must remember, too, that statements of government policy are not always matched by action nor always accepted throughout the dominant culture.

In Australia in the 1940s and 1950s assimilation was generally seen as the logical and desirable consequence of the nation's immigration policy. The term *New Australian* symbolized the expectation that migrants would learn and adopt our culture in the way that babies do. It was expected, further, that migrants would abandon their own cultures. There was no expectation that native Australians would adopt any part of any ethnic culture that migrants might bring with them.

It was only in the late 1960s that most Australians came to expect integration rather than assimilation. This shift followed the gradual realization by Australians that most migrants really did not wish to be assimilated.

It was only after 1972 that governments began to spend significant amounts of money (for example on ethnic radio) in order to help ethnic groups preserve their identities. The emphasis until then had been on helping the cause of assimilation by providing English Language courses for migrants. More recently, the 1978 Galbally Report (in Victoria) has firmly supported the new approach of multi-culturalism. The Report welcomed the cultural differences that migrants bring with them and accepted their rights to separate organizations, educational curricula, media outlets and cultural expressions. Yet there is still little indication that the Australian-born population is any less prejudiced, or less intolerant of migrants who seem unwilling or unable to abandon their native languages and cultures.

The 'Uses' of Migration

It is rare for a country's immigration policy to be motivated either by altruism or by a desire to diversify the national culture. Economic factors usually hold sway. The most common economic motivation is that of increasing the workforce. After World War 2, because of the fear Japan had struck into a nation of chiefly empty spaces, the Labor government saw the need for Australia to extend its manufacturing industries. Large development works like the Snowy River Scheme were started and an active immigration policy was renewed. Though Labor Party leader Calwell hoped 'that for every foreign migrant there will be ten people from the United Kingdom', successive governments have shaped a country where 4 million people are first or second generation immigrants, over half of whom are of non-British origin. 'Outside Israel and the OPEC Arab region, Australia has the most diverse workforce of any present western industrialized country' (Storer, 1979, p.62).

As Jean Martin suggests, an 'analytically distinct situation arises when the population of an established society becomes rapidly more differentiated in a short span of time' (Martin, 1978, p.15). Those whose interests define existing institutions must then, even if reluctantly, take notice of 'the migrant presence' and adjust the webs of meaning that their culture maintains and enforces (Martin, 1978, pp.20−6).

Australia is, of course, not alone in facing institutional problems caused by migration. West Germany for example has even greater problems. During post-war reconstruction millions of people moved their homes in Europe. But even in the last ten years, 15 million people have migrated from southern to northern Europe, and West Germany now has four million 'guestworkers'. The term reflects the early expectation that these guests were welcome but would eventually return home. With the 1973 recession not only was their welcome worn out: their chances of returning to their home countries and finding jobs were actually reduced. In the Bavarian south, the government assumes that guestworkers will go home. Therefore it refuses to socialize dependent children into the German way of life but instead imports foreign teachers to teach a foreign-language curriculum. In the north, authorities are facing up to the likely permanence of guestworkers and have designed an 18 month transition curriculum for pupils moving from foreign language to German language classes.

According to Rist (1979) the dominant West German view is that one cannot maintain what he calls a *hyphenated-identity*. One either stays a Turk in Germany or one becomes a German, but to be a German-Turk or a Turkish-German is not possible (Rist, 1978; Rist, 1979). The Australian view differs, perhaps because so many of our population have always held hyphenated-identities, or perhaps because a peculiarly Australian national identity is less rigidly defined or less emotively asserted. From 1831 to 1850, close to 223 000 immigrants were assisted to come from Europe to Australia. The goldrushes of the 1850s and further assisted passages swelled the population to 350 000 in New South Wales and to 540 000 in Victoria by 1860. Thus Australia has had a polyglot population for a long time. It has been dominated by people of Anglo-Saxon and Celtic origin, but 'foreigners' in Australia are hardly a recent phenomenon.

What happens to these newcomers now? How are they treated by the host country? What does their treatment tell us about the Australian culture and about how its institutionalized values are translated in social structures and the distribution of life chances?

Table 11−1 shows the areas in which people from different ethnic groups are currently employed. Clearly, non-English-speaking (NES) migrants cluster in the semi-skilled and unskilled labour areas.

In the early post-war years there was an urgent need for unskilled labour. Migrants were placed in factory work, car production, road building and sewerage and water works. The policy, however, allowed few skilled migrants to enter and excluded professional people. As both Bourke (1971) and Martin (1972a) have shown, these overseas-born were generally better educated than the Australian-born. Refugees, often intellectuals and professionals, were forced to do physical labour for two years under contract in jobs to which they were assigned. This policy caused not only a waste of talent, but also a psychological and status shock to people who had formerly belonged to a privileged class (Johnston, 1977, p.68). Up to 1952, when the Displaced Persons Scheme ceased, such migrants were placed in unskilled jobs, often remote from the capital cities. Australia's skilled needs were met by the United Kingdom Assisted Passage Scheme, a scheme aimed at attracting skilled tradesmen for post-war reconstruction and at competing with Canada and the United States for the migrant 'brain gain'. New agreements in 1952−3 with the Netherlands, West Germany and Italy for assisted passage still gave the Australian government the right to place immigrants in jobs for a compulsory two years, but there was an avowed intent to place skilled people in appropriate jobs (Salter, 1978, pp.42−3).

Because of the fears of trade unions and professional associations,

Table 11–1 Occupation of major birthplace groups: per cent distribution and total numbers of employed persons aged 15 years and over. Census 1971

Persons	Australia	UK/Eire	Italy	Greece	Germany	Yugo-slavia	Other	Total Overseas born	Total
	%	%	%	%	%	%	%	%	%
Professional, technical and related workers	10.6	11.2	1.8	1.0	10.5	2.2	12.2	9.2	10.2
Administrative, executive, managerial workers	6.9	6.7	4.2	5.0	6.1	1.8	7.0	6.0	6.7
Clerical workers	17.5	15.7	4.6	2.4	13.7	2.6	12.2	11.5	15.8
Sales workers	8.5	8.1	5.5	9.1	6.3	2.1	6.2	6.8	8.1
Farmers, fishermen, hunters, timber getters etc.	9.2	2.9	8.2	2.2	2.4	3.4	3.0	3.5	7.7
Miners, quarrymen, related workers	0.7	0.7	0.4	0.2	0.8	0.9	0.6	0.6	0.7
Workers in transportation and communication	6.1	5.0	3.5	3.1	3.6	2.3	4.0	4.1	5.5
Tradesmen, production-process workers, labourers, etc.	27.6	36.5	57.2	59.5	42.9	68.1	41.2	44.2	32.1
Service, sport and recreation workers	7.0	8.6	7.2	8.6	8.7	7.8	8.4	8.4	7.4
Members of Armed Forces	1.4	1.4	0.2	0.1	1.4	0.1	0.6	0.9	1.2
Occupation inadequately described, not stated	4.5	3.2	7.2	8.8	3.6	8.7	4.6	4.8	4.6
Total %	100.0	100.0	100.0	100.0	100.0	100.0	100.0	100.0	100.0
Nos. (thousands)	3836.6	540.9	170.2	98.5	70.0	79.1	445.1	1403.8	5240.4

(Source: *First Report, National Population Inquiry*, 1976, A.G.P.S., p. 129)

however, many of those with specific skills were unable to find proper places. In 1951, for example, 70 per cent of European skilled tradesmen asking for employment in the metal and electrical trades were being rejected (Salter, 1978, p.43). And Kunz (1969) estimates that while 10 per cent of all immigrant males were professionally qualified or had partial university certification, only 20 per cent of them were to be found in professional or executive positions twenty years after their arrival in Australia (Salter, 1978, p.86).

A 1973 survey (Table 11–2) found that 23 per cent of migrant family heads were holding jobs inferior in status to those they had held overseas. Only 59 per cent of them claimed to be satisfied with their type of job and position. Many migrants, then, did not realize their hopes of a new life in a new country with new opportunities for upward mobility.

Table 11–2 Heads of migrant families with regressive employment histories

Occupation overseas and at time of survey (1973)

Usual occupation before migrating to Australia	Regressive employment histories — % of total
Professional, technical workers	31
Managers, workers on own account etc.	64
Clerical workers	7
Skilled workers	29
Semi-skilled workers	12
Unskilled workers	—
Total	23

(Source: *A Decade of Migrant Settlement* Australian Population and Immigration Council, 1976, A.G.P.S., Chapter 3. As reported in *Migrant Services and Programs*, May 1978, A.G.P.S., p. 148)

Mobility chances vary by ethnic group. On average, Northern Europeans are better educated than Southern Europeans. Whereas 34 per cent of Australians in 1966 held white-collar jobs, the relative figures for Germans and Dutch were 25 per cent, 17 per cent for Poles and only 8 to 10 per cent for Greeks, Italians and Yugoslavs. Johnston (1977) suggests that many migrant families have experienced mobility but often only to a limited degree. For example, a labourer father may have a craftsman son; a mother who worked as a domestic cleaner may see her daughter become a clerk or a shop assistant.

Migrant families, of course, try to make good in their new country. Their aim may be to buy a new home and settle or to make enough money to return to their country of origin and 'buy into' a higher status there than they could previously afford. (See Harvey, 1979 on Dutch returnees.) Workforce participation levels for migrants at every age level are higher for both men and women (*The Labour Force*, A.B.S., Feb. 1978).

But their occupations remain largely at the lower status levels. The 1971 Census showed, for example (Storer, 1979, p.62):

More Yugoslav, Italian and Greek born males work in manufacturing industry than those born in Australia, Britain or Germany; Italians and

Yugoslavs work more in construction industries; people born in Australia, the United Kingdom and the United States comprise a far larger proportion of the public service than they do of the adult population.

Constance Lever's (1975) detailed study of the 1961—1971 statistics confirmed her conclusion that:

> The proportion of migrants in certain, mainly low-status, manual occupations, is rising faster than is their proportion in the population. Australian and British-born are leaving these jobs while non-British migrants are either entering them, staying in them, or leaving them more slowly than are Australian or British workers.

The extent of non-English speaking (NES) migrant poverty is, as a consequence, higher (12.5 per cent of income units) than the Australian average (6.7 per cent). And studies of income reveal that migrant workers from Mediterranean countries earn $20—$40 less per week than Australian-born or English-speaking migrants. Storer holds that there are thus two essential types of migrants, in terms of their structural location in Australian society:

> The professionals or skilled migrants from English speaking or Northern European countries;
> Unskilled labourers from non-English speaking countries.

Table 11—3   Mean average weekly earnings by birthplace (August 1976)

	Aust.	Main English Speaking	F.R. Germ.	Greece	Italy	Yugo-slavia	Other	Total Average
	$	$	$	$	$	$	$	$
Males	173	188	191	152	152	155	174	174
Females	131	140	141	114	111	122	136	131

(Source: *The Labour Force*, March, 1978)

Not only are migrant incomes lower, but rents and mortgage repayments for migrants appear to be higher. Indeed the more recently arrived the migrant, the higher his household expenditure is likely to be.

When we consider that migrant workers are more likely to suffer the impact of structural shifts in unemployment, the claim that some ethnic groups form a sort of 'underclass' in Australian society does not seem exaggerated. The stereotype of migrant workers holding down multiple jobs, getting rich and moving out to showy suburban houses must also be modified. The example of a few, or their clustering in a particular suburb, does not accurately represent the structural life chances of every ethnic group in Australian society. The symbolic few may legitimate indifference or complacency; but they will not help explain sociologically the perceptions of ethnic groups themselves or the existence of resentment, hostility and cultural conflict.

Unemployment rates are clearly higher for females and especially those from Southern Europe. They are higher still for new migrant arrivals, and higher for migrant youth than for anyone else. Between 1971—1977 there was a loss of 156 000 jobs in manufacturing, of 50 000 jobs in building and construction, and of over 25 000 jobs in agriculture. These are the areas in which most

Table 11 – 4   Unemployment rates

	Males	Females	All Persons
	%	%	%
All Australian born	5.0	8.5	6.3
All Overseas born	6.2	9.5	7.3
Greece	8.3	10.9	9.0
Yugoslavia	7.8	9.6	8.4
U.K.	6.2	9.2	7.2
Arrived 1971–76	7.9	11.0	9.1
Arrived since Jan. '77	—	27.7	16.7
Aged 15–19 Austn. born	14.7	19.7	17.1
Aged 15–19 Overseas born	20.3	22.1	21.2

(Source: *The Labour Force*, March 1978)

migrants, especially the non-English speakers, have had to find their jobs. The fact that a further 485 000 jobs have been provided by the tertiary (largely service) sector has not helped the desperate plight of NES migrants. Women, especially have had to move into part-time work. The CURA study of Melbourne clothing factories is aptly titled *But I wouldn't want my wife to work here*. However, part-time work at home (like making clothes, packing plastic bags for supermarkets, and so on), is even less visible, more open to the exploitation of migrant women, and has more drastic effects on family life (see also Hurwitz, 1977, pp.222–67).

Attitudes to Migrants

How has adjustment to the migrant presence in Australia been effected? Have old prejudices paled with familiarity, contact and media coverage? Is lower occupational status really a result of active discrimination?

Structurally, some answers may already be apparent. If ethnic groups have entered different kinds of jobs, Australian attitudes to them will have been coloured by the status of those jobs. Following Elizabeth Cohen's school experiments with groups of black and white students we may hypothesize that unequal status and unequal resources will affect patterns of social interaction. Merely being exposed to lots of people with ethnic backgrounds in Australia will not alter stereotypes; it may reinforce them. For example, having migrant neighbours may create a better understanding of their cultural patterns, but contact will be limited if language and status barriers exist. We are forced to re-think our *self-other* evaluations only as a result of contact with people equal in status to ourselves. All the figures, however, suggest that most migrants, apart from those from Britain and Northern Europe, have entered low status occupations.

Johnston (1977, pp.70–71) argues that language, rather than discrimination, is the problem (although her own more detailed interview studies reveal a substantial amount of other sorts of prejudice). Many employers refuse to employ any migrants, but their reasons vary. British and Dutch building workers seem to arouse more animosity than most, perhaps because they are better educated or are believed to be arrogant or because they are prominent in trade union action. Some firms refuse to employ NES migrants: their personnel offices administer English reading tests over the job-application counter. Such firms claim that workers must be able to read warning signs and that it would be 'impractical' to have signs in several languages or to run their own courses in safety and sign-recognition.

Early studies by Taft and Robbins (1955), Borrie (1954), Oeser and Hammond (1954) showed that Australians were either indifferent or hostile towards migrants, but preferred those most likely to assimilate. Most hostility was directed at the better educated migrants and at those from rural areas. By the 1960s opinion polls showed a more favourable attitude (Richardson & Taft, 1968; Taft, 1965; Johnston, 1977, p.74). It seemed that women and especially school children were more likely to be accepting, and willing to adopt the ethnic cultural styles of their friends. Yet Buchanan (1976) shows teenage girls to be most negative, especially when they are out of school and working, and Martin and Meade (1979) found quite startling hostility to migrants in their sample of teenage school children in Sydney.

Maris Buchanan in 1976 tried to replicate the 1954 Oeser and Hammond study to see whether any changes had taken place in Australians' knowledge of and attitudes towards migrants. Her sample was of 2652 married women aged 15−60 in metropolitan Melbourne. It was a stratified random sample representing the occupational distribution. Oeser and Hammond had found a hierarchy of 'preferred' migrant groups, ranging from Northern European to Southern European, to 'coloured'. Buchanan found that these preferences had hardly changed since 1954. Perhaps because of the impact of a tenfold increase in Asian immigration to Australia since the 1950s, the Chinese had lost favour. Jews were now more popular. Arabs and Turks (groups hardly represented in 1954) were very low on the 1976 list. As Buchanan comments:

> It is thus interesting to note that despite Grassby's assertions that Australian society is becoming more unified and more tolerant in its attitudes towards immigrants, many of the prejudices of the 1950's remain (Buchanan, 1976, pp.17−18).

Table 11−5　Hierarchy of preferred immigrant groups

	Hammond Study 1954	Age Poll ASRB, 1971	Melbourne (Buchanan) study
Most preferred group	English	English	British
	German	German	German
	Chinese	Italian	Jew
	Greek	Greek ⎫ equal	Italian
	Italian	Jew ⎭	Greek
Least preferred group	Jew	Negro	Chinese
	Negro	Chinese	Negro

(Source: Buchanan, 1976, p.18.)

According to Buchanan, people see the greatest benefit of Australia's migrant population to be *diversity of culture* (47 per cent) yet they also see *clashes of culture* to be the biggest problem (39 per cent). Twenty-nine per cent say migrants help the country's economic growth and development, but contrary to Oeser and Hammond's (1954) suggestion, educated people are not more favourably disposed. Rather they seem more aware of the social and economic cost of large-scale immigration. Nine per cent of the sample saw no advantages at all, though all people surveyed could list some disadvantages. Apart from culture clashes, other disadvantages seen were the effect of immigration on housing shortages (12 per cent), education (10 per cent), crowding and pollution (8 per cent), crime and violence (6 per cent), effect on incomes (3 per cent) and too many southern Europeans or some other specific group (4 per cent).

The language gap again appeared to be the most central aspect of the *culture clash*. The antagonism of this sample of women was particularly motivated by their feeling that language problems lead to lower standards of education in the schools. Given the reduction of the northern European inflow (Martin, 1972a; Johnston, 1977), this problem is likely to worsen as the average level of education of migrant parents declines. Certainly, schools in Victoria and New South Wales—the States with the highest migrant concentrations—are now accepting their responsibilities for teaching English as a second language, and for developing a more positively multi-cultural curriculum. The new wave of immigrants from Latin America and South-East Asia may alter this picture in schools, for, on the whole, they are a better educated group.

Buchanan's study also allows a limited test of the *status-contact* hypothesis: does familiarity breed contempt or does it reduce ethnic prejudice? In suburbs with high migrant populations (particularly NES, and thus low status, ethnic groups) attitudes are more negative. In these suburbs, people want less immigration and are worried about the quality of schooling. Buchanan found the most liberal attitudes to be in the eastern and outer suburbs of Melbourne where the population tends to be better educated and to contain a high concentration of professional people, but where migrant concentrations are low. Unfortunately, the study cannot tell us whether education or income level is more important as a determinant of attitudes. Education seems to be more important but in any event, since the sample is restricted to women, Buchanan thinks their chances of contacting immigrants would be lower than for men who make wider contacts at work. The study is also limited in that the tendency to give the socially desirable response is apparent in some findings. People may be prejudiced but try not to show it, and the methodology used to collect data will affect the findings. Ninety-three per cent of these women agreed that 'Once you get to know people it doesn't matter what their race is'. Perhaps a better indication, however, may be the reactions they gave to a series of hypothetical situations (Table 11–6).

Notice that although the Chinese were ranked as among the least desirable of immigrant groups, they score better than Italians as possible neighbours but worse as possible sons-in-law. Obviously differing stereotypes and criteria of judgement are being applied in each situation.

Table 11−6   % Australlans 'Displeased' or 'Very Displeased' with possibilities, for ethnic groups

Hypothetical Event	British %	Dutch %	Italians %	Chinese %
Migrated to Australia in quite large numbers	15	17	40	43
Bought houses in your suburb in large numbers	13	16	41	40
Moved into the house next door	8	12	34	29
Attended your child's school in large numbers	4	9	21	18
Married your daughter	9	19	40	54

(Source: Buchanan, 1976)

The controversy in June 1979 over a Victorian Government sponsored survey of attitudes to migrants rested as much upon the wording of questionnaire items as it did upon its reported findings of wide-spread hostility towards migrants. Methodologically such studies leave much to be desired. In the search for a properly stratified random sample and for 'hard facts' to convince government policy-makers, researchers too often neglect the human, meaningful side of the lives they are studying. It is one thing to ask people how many migrants they know, whether they approve of them and how they would respond in certain circumstances: it is quite another matter to capture the actual social relations that pattern their lives.

In Australian sociology, as elsewhere, there has been too much emphasis on *distributive* studies and not enough on *relational* studies (Wild, 1971). As Wild pointed out:

> For Beteille, the distributive aspect is only a pointer towards delineating the more relational aspects, that is, the way in which individuals interact with each other in socially significant ways ... Weber was aware that the objective factors of the situation could not be considered apart from the qualitative ideas and values of the individual or status group because both affect social behaviour and the social consciousness (Wild, in Edgar, 1974, p.234).

Wild's own study, *Bradstow*, was an attempt to examine in-depth social relations in a small community. But there have been few such attempts in the study of migration and ethnicity. Fiona Mackie's second thoughts about her study of Greek diversity may point the way:

> I am now much more interested in approaches which do not accept the assumptions in the label 'migrant' as straightforward, but are concerned more with the actual perceptions of those so labelled. I am even more suspicious of a structural approach that starts by accepting organizations as if they were real, and more concerned to start with the individual's perceptions of what is significant in defining his experience, plotting his relationships in terms of 'networks' which may indicate the existence of group and organizational ties, but do not presume them at the outset (Mackie, in Edgar, 1974, p.152).

Perhaps the most systematic of the more recent studies to have avoided the traps hinted at above are those of Jean Martin. From her early studies that led to the book, *Refugee Settlers* (1965), her anthropological interests have led her to look at the networks—the webs of affiliation which help migrants sustain their ethnic identity and negotiate the institutional structures that face them in the new land. In 1965 she felt the 'Displaced Person's' adaptation to life in Australia 'could best be understood in terms of individual rather than group processes' (Martin, 1965, p.10). Later, her focus moved more towards group processes of support within the ethnic communities as they sustained their cultures in the Australian context. In her 1972 study of refugee groups in Adelaide, she examined their relative social cohesion as separate groups, their residential concentration, their rate of naturalization and the levels of their workforce participation, for insights into patterns of community development. One of her aims was to examine why *structural pluralism* (the existence of groups based on ethnic origin) persists, while *cultural pluralism* (their life-style distinctiveness) seems to fade. She also wanted to challenge the simple dichotomy of host society versus minority group.

> ... in reality many different minorities and many different structures within and outside the host society contribute towards the development of the definition of the situation which is salient for the outcome of any particular occasion of interaction, and the interaction itself may involve several minority and host structures just as readily as the duality of a monolithic host vis-a-vis a monolithic minority (Martin, 1972a, p.117).

The model Martin constructs (1972a, p.115) shows a cycle of more complex interactions which produce definitions of the migrant situation by multiple hosts and minorities, which in turn lead to more complex re-definitions on both sides of the 'migrant' situation and then to re-negotiated interaction patterns. Her conclusions rest upon close study of the networks (mainly in community life and schools) that link these Adelaide refugee groups to one another and to multiple structures in the 'host' society. Minority groups with a strong religious orientation seem more 'introverted' (turned in on their own group structures) and are thus not so well assimilated. Ethnic minorities that are cohesive, strong and secular, seem to take more notice of (and thus reap more rewards from) Australian society. At other times minority fragmentation (rather than cohesion) seems to push minority members towards the Australian community. Martin (1972a, p.132) concludes that:

> Australia is not a plural society in the sense that our polity is based on ethnic segments, but in the more limited sense that ethnicity is a source of formal and informal groupings and of some cultural differentiation.

Contrary to Milton Gordon's view that ethnic groups continue as a defense against the 'prejudices of the majority', Martin (1972a, pp.132−3) holds that ethnic community life is a positive move to maintain cultural, and thus personal, identity and continuity.

Rena Huber, in a study begun in 1968, and continued over several years, describes richly the lives of Italian settlers in urban Sydney and rural Griffith (Huber, 1977). Italians are the largest, single, non-English speaking group to migrate to Australia (Price, 1977, p.18). Instead of providing broad statistics however, Huber concentrates on small groups of families and is thus able to show them going through stages of treatment, response and action as new citizens of Australian society. The stages of settling in (Huber, 1977, pp.139−41); the return visits to Italy (which seemed to make them more satisfied with living in Australia (pp.97−8)); snobbery and inequality in country towns (pp.116−19); their status goals in life (p.149); the social support for their own clubs and societies (pp.98−100, 157): all give a more vivid picture of life than statistical samples can convey. She concludes (see Summary Chart p.208) that it has been easier for Italians to adapt and reconstruct traditional social institutions in the country than in Sydney, where work and family were more separated. Though Italians in Griffith did not choose to live with their extended families they retained close links with them. The earlier authoritarian relationship between father and son was replaced by something more like a partnership. In rural areas their lack of education was less important. Religion helped hold the community together. They were familiar with farming and had come to settle. On the other hand, their city confreres found adjustment to urban life more difficult because they lacked solid ethnic institutions and networks of support.

Prejudice at Work

If work is a central arena for the exercise of authority and of other less legitimate forms of control, attitudes and behaviour on the factory floor may also be a more reliable indicator of prejudice than the expressed preferences of women. Economic sanctions make it possible to express prejudice more openly: people who object may get the sack. Ignorance of ethnic values may lead employers to establish work routines which suit the dominant cultural patterns, but which may offend the migrant's moral code and make difficult the observance of religious practices and social taboos. Jean Martin's comment is apt here:

> The most fundamentally powerful 'effect' is the effect of ruling out certain objects as objects of public knowledge. P. Bachrach and M. S. Baratz call this *nondecision-making* . . . 'a decision that results in suppression or thwarting of a latent or manifest challenge to the values or interests of the decision-maker' (Martin, 1978, p.23).

Even to focus on attitudes, as we have done in the previous section, is to assume that all that is

> needed for ethnics to be successfully incorporated into the society is fundamentally a change of heart: understanding, sympathy and tolerance on the part of the host community, adaptability and optimism on the part of the ethnics can effect what no social rearrangements could do, and so render structural change redundant (Martin, 1978, p.216).

If we agree that there is a close relationship between the structures that maintain and reproduce cultural institutions and the relationships of dominance inherent within them, we may agree with Jean Martin that purely 'subjective' changes will not solve ethnic problems. Even these subjective changes are unlikely to arise unless there are changes in the structured relations of Australian society.

Until recently Australia has managed to avoid the most difficult challenges from other cultures. The so-called *White Australia Policy* preserved the domination of Western, and largely Anglo-Saxon, peoples. The languages of most migrants may have seemed strange, as did some of their communal habits, but their traditions in Graeco-Roman and European culture were the same. While their food, drink or dress may have seemed exotic, their religions were usually Christian and their experience of religious, political and economic institutions was at least comparable. However, an increased flow of southern European and Islamic populations, and the removal of racial barriers against 'coloured' people, are now exacerbating both the sense of cultural difference and the need for institutional change.

Consider, for example, the plight of Moslems within our Turkish and Arabic ethnic communities. Australia has approximately 150 000 Moslems from 21 countries, of whom 70 000 live in Victoria—85 per cent of them in Melbourne. Their religion is the second largest in the world, with 800 million adherents. The new upsurge of Islam in Iran and the Middle East seems likely to herald a change in the future balance of power. Yet Australian institutions remain unchanged, and Australians generally are neither aware of their problems nor motivated to solve them.

In schools, the language problem is not the only one for Moslem children. In their homes they are taught to lower their heads and to speak softly in the presence of their seniors. Australian teachers, however, are likely to interpret such deference as shyness or lack of confidence. Moslem boys may help with housework at home, but feel disgraced if asked to do it publicly. Because Moslems stress modesty in female dress and behaviour, compulsory school uniforms, sports dresses, school camps, excursions and school dances may cause embarrassment. During the Holy Month of Ramadan, when Moslems fast, Moslem children fear to swim in case they swallow water. Their holy days fall on a Thursday and Friday, and two of the five times when men and boys must pray on Friday fall during school (and working) hours. Yet in our supposedly free, compulsory and secular school system, a Christian-based religious instruction is often foisted upon them. And if not that, then generally a system which through inflexibility or ignorance does not allow for cultural differences.

For adults, similarly, rigid working hours make religious observances difficult. Turkish men are used to male-only coffee shops but must eat in mixed cafeterias. Turkish women suffer even more as a result of the failure of Australians to understand or cater for their needs for modesty. Many women used to living in discrete domesticity are forced out into unfamiliar work situations. Many are reluctant to mention pregnancy and other health problems. Few commercial firms bother to provide translator services to cater for their needs (Hooks, 1979, p.14).

Being a migrant woman at work is to be at the very bottom of the totem pole. In a society where sex, occupation and ethnicity all contribute to social status, working migrant women are seen to be inferior on every count. In her study of migrant women in the Leyland factory at Waterloo, Sydney, Helen Hurwitz (1977) found that sexual politics affected ethnic discrimination. Foremen favoured pretty and docile women, were often overly familiar and were generally feared by all the women. They did not value women who put their work first and who refused to play 'flirt' games. While the women could not understand these indignities, factory men (even migrant men) excused such harassment by arguing that it was a logical consequence of the desire of women to be treated as workers in their own right on the job: in effect the argument of sexual liberation was inverted.

Many taken-for-granted conventions of the Australian work place may also contribute to the discomfort migrant women workers must endure. Working closely with males, being photographed with them or even being the recipient of a peck on the cheek from the factory foreman at Christmas time—may all be disconcerting experiences. Johnston (1977, pp.243—5) found that many of these women were often afraid to ask for the simplest of things to which they were entitled (like permission to go to the toilet, or a lighter kind of job when they were pregnant). They often took pills for 'nerves' without any idea of what the real effects of the pills might have been.

Many of the women needed the money, but claimed that they would work anyway because social isolation at home would be unbearable. Having lived until recently within a full and satisfying domestic subculture, they found inner-city and suburban living in Australia 'very frightening' (Hurwitz, 1977, p.232). Unlike the old context of flat living, shared child-minding, chatting and talking a lot with other women, domestic life for them in Australia was monotonous, lonely and hectic.

Authoritarian, masculine traditions bear heavily on the working wife in many ethnic groups. The husband wants her financial contribution but continues to expect her to carry the full traditional burdens of wife and mother. It is culturally unacceptable for males to help with housework at all. Thus women feel rushed; they worry about their children; they often seek a solution in separate shift work, causing further tensions between husband and wife (Johnston, 1977, p.250).

Business organizations, however, rarely consider the possible structural alternatives. Flexitime, permanent part-time work, job-sharing, in-plant health and gynaecological clinics, child care, using workers as paid translators, education programmes for line supervisors and other managers are all possible. Such alternatives are costly, however, and are likely to be considered unnecessary by any employer who sees the migrant as the one who has to make the adjustment.

Johnston reports (1977, p.75) a 1972 study which showed that a quarter of Australian males actually felt migrants should *not* have equal opportunities to work, and that Australians should have preference in their own country. While they admired migrant workers for their 'diligence' they disliked their use of foreign languages and their clannishness. While Australian teenagers at school may get on well with migrants, those at work tend to be intolerant. Both Zubrzycki (1964) and Johnston (1972) found that Polish mine workers were given the dirtiest and hardest jobs. Johnston describes parallel experiences for professionals, hospital workers, migrants in a soap factory in Perth, and in the building and transport industries (Johnston, 1972, pp.93–102).

Fewer migrants than Australians find their work interesting. Like Australians they want fair supervision and friendly workmates as well as good pay. Migrants, however, are more ambivalent than Australians about the trade unions. It is not just that their experiences of unions in the home country affect their attitudes here—there is also evidence of prejudice and discrimination on the part of the unions. Jean Martin argues that there have been four phases in union responses to migrants over the past thirty years. At first, right-wing migrant support was sought against communist union leaders (Richards 1974). Next, union leaders sought merely to recruit migrants; non-decision-making was the mode. By the third phase, a greater concern was being shown for migrant welfare, communication and their position as 'exploited victims of capitalism'. And, more recently, in a fourth phase, union leaders have recognized their own ignorance, their responsibility for, and indeed their active connivance in, the low status of migrant workers. Unions have now made links with ethnic organizations and community groups and are finding that some migrant groups now demand changes in union structures and accountability (Martin, 1978, ch.7; Martin, R. M., 1975, p.136; Johnston, 1977, p.102–12; Hearn in Birrell and Hay, 1978, pp.116–32).

Migrant Education and Identity

Education affects identity and self-esteem through the access it allows to the development of competence. For migrant children, living in 'two worlds', and having to decide which is most relevant to their own particular needs and interests, the problem of competing realities and the domination of favoured knowledge is acute. Their native languages are not accepted as a proper medium of communication; their customs are seen as odd or funny; and time is not given in class to teaching others about their cultures. The whole institutional weight is against their stock of knowledge. A new stock of knowledge, both general and specific, must be acquired, or social respect, honour, prestige and trust will be denied. Once these children realize that those others most significant to them, their parents and family members, have no social standing in the wider community, their identities are really threatened. The structures of Australian institutions and their lack of response to migrant needs, may be in themselves the elements of an education in self-deprecation for ethnic communities.

Refugees generally have no place to return to: they have arrived without possessions, have no relatives left at home and have no hope or even desire to revisit a past of misery. On the other hand, the migrant retains some links. Certainly to emigrate is a severe break, but if the intention is either to save enough to return or to bring out the entire extended family, then the attack on migrant identity by the host country will be experienced in a different way.

As far back as 1962 Charles Price had located a substantial *departure* rate, which demonstrated that the immigrant was not necessarily a permanent settler.

Australian concerns about 'settler loss' became highest in the 1960s. Price found in 1971 that over a fifth of all German migrants had returned, as had 18 per cent of the Dutch and British, and 13 per cent of the Italians (see Martin, 1978, pp.30–3). From what we have seen of migrant employment patterns, it is not surprising that so many wished to return. Economic conditions in Europe had also improved, so there was now less reason to stay in Australia. Sue Harvey (1979) argues that the Dutch, particularly, were enticed to return home once economic conditions improved. It should be noted, however, that some migrants, particularly Italians, came with little intention of staying in Australia; not all 'returnees', then, reflected Australia's failure to prove attractive.

By the late 1960s there was a new recognition that better housing, welfare and employment opportunities would have to be offered to attract prospective immigrants. Jean Martin suggests (1978, p.33) that it was not until the 1966 Henderson Poverty Inquiry found substantial pockets of economic disadvantage among ethnic groups, that governments began to question seriously their earlier assumptions about the benefits of immigration for the immigrant. Labor Party campaigns in 1969 and 1972 made much of the exploited situation of migrants and of community neglect. The new professionals, Jupp's (1966) 'so-called social experts' were at times resented for treating migrants as 'problem children', but they at least provoked some institutional response (see Martin, 1978, pp.36–49).

Part of that response is likely to have been an increased awareness among migrant groups of their own spoiled identities. Grassby's 1973 call for 'A Multi-cultural Society for the Future' went so far as to suggest that Australia might have to allow social and political pluralism as well as cultural pluralism (Martin, 1978, p.55). But the severe recession of the early 1970s led the Labor government to cut the migrant intake severely, in line with the recommendations of Borrie's 1974 National Population Inquiry. The new Liberal-NCP government in 1975 had already realized the importance of the migrant vote and embodied this realization in its Department of Immigration and Ethnic Affairs, so-named to show their concern for immigrant cultures. They have supported the ethnic press, radio and television (albeit in controversial ways), maintained Al Grassby's Commission on Community Relations, and tackled the Asian refugee problem more vigorously than their predecessors (see Price, 1979). Perhaps the height of the new awareness of ethnic affairs and immigration policy was marked by the 1978 La Trobe University Meredith Memorial Lectures. A new publication by Birrell and Hay (1978), had deplored the government's decision to again increase the migrant intake. The lectures offered a forum for attack and counter-attack on what that book had argued. Spokesmen for several immigrant groups actually expressed support for a policy of lower intake, given the increasingly competitive job market.

In an editorial putting the economic point of view, the *Financial Review* (21 June 1979) revealed that the old attitude to migration still exists. While denying such 'baser motives', as the use of 'cheap captive labour for decentralization', the editorial called for Australia to accept a massive influx of Vietnamese refugees. They would help productivity and would not take jobs from Australians. It was argued that our housing, medicine and education services were so over-supplied that:

if there was ever a time at which we could afford to open our doors to take in large numbers of migrants, it is now . . . To put it harshly, the industrial cannon fodder which was provided by the post-1945 immigration, and upon which much of our current high living standard is based, is now once again available to us. Not at a wage level below the award wages which are paid to Australian workers, nor in conditions which would be totally unacceptable to Australian workers, but in the form of a willingness to perform jobs which Australian workers are reluctant to take (*Australian Financial Review*, 21 June 1979, p.2).

Ethnic groups in Australia, however, no longer accept their *treatment* passively. New self-assertions by ethnic organizations, new media outlets, greater realization that existing institutional structures must change or be changed, all make it likely that the 30 per cent of our population which consists of post-war immigrants and their children will be heard and will have a more profound impact on Australian society than they have hitherto been allowed to have.

Aborigines as 'The Recurring Forgotten'

It would be optimistic to predict that the Aboriginal ethnic group will have a similar impact on Australian society. Comprising only 0.9 per cent of Australia's total population, the Aborigines are often forgotten in discussions of minority ethnic groups. They are, of course, a distinct race and comprise a wide variety of tribal cultures, many of which have their own languages. Estimates put the number of Aborigines at 300 000 before Australia's colonization, but since censuses ignored them until the 1930s, no accurate account can be given of the rate of their decline. Many were shot, poisoned and driven off traditional hunting grounds; others starved and died of European diseases. The entire Tasmanian Aboriginal race was exterminated. On the mainland the Aboriginal population was reduced by the 1930s to about one-fifth its original size; since then numbers have stabilized and started to grow. Today Aborigines number 106 290 (1976 Census), with about 44 per cent of them living in urban areas. Queensland has 23 per cent of the total Aboriginal population, but only in the Northern Territory do Aborigines comprise a significant proportion of total population (just over 20 per cent). Thus, as an ethnic group, the Aborigines have been truly a 'minority' in numbers and have come to public attention only intermittently.

It was only when the Aboriginal population had been nearly destroyed that Aboriginal Protectorates were established. As McQueen documents, Aborigines were never as passive as white history suggests in accepting the treatment meted out to them by the dominant white society. In retaliation they killed sheep, drove out Church of England missionaries from the Forrest River area in 1898 and attacked pastoralist expansion in Western Australia in the early 1900s.

In 1928 Aborigines in Western Australia even formed a union which demanded full equality. Nevertheless they were driven off their own farms, out of schools and into restricted reserves closer to settlers in need of cheap labour (McQueen, 1978, pp.30–1). In these degrading reserves into which they were herded, very few were able to preserve their traditional ways of life. The Aborigines suffered a similar fate to the American Indian. Their power to resist was limited. They had to contend not only with the superior force of the colonists, but with the colonists' belief, as a central part of their culture, in white supremacy. This belief justified colonization itself; it made it easy for governments to overlook the occasional massacre of Aborigines by settlers or the police; it was at the root, even, of the public outcry against Katherine Susannah Pritchard's novel *Coonardoo*, which told of a white man's love for an Aboriginal girl (McQueen, 1978, pp.114—5).

Yet the Aborigines have not been totally forgotten; their pride in race and their political and social presence makes them 'the recurring forgotten'. The Aborigines refuse to go away.

The 1967 referendum gave the Commonwealth government power to make laws affecting Aborigines who had previously been the responsibility of the States. A Council for Aboriginal Affairs was set up and an Office for Aboriginal Affairs was established to formulate policy. Land rights became an issue when the government's refusal to recognize the claims of the Gurindji and Yirrkala led to the famous 'Aboriginal Embassy' on the lawns of Canberra's Parliament House. This demonstration emphasized to an almost unprecedented extent, the political nature of ethnic discrimination. It made it more urgent for the Labor Party to enact those policies in its 1971 platform which promised equal rights and positive discrimination in the provision of health and education services.

Though much was done in the Labor years, 1972—75, Lippman (1979, ch.10) claims that both residual paternalism and deliberate bureaucratic sabotage, from within the new Department of Aboriginal Affairs, has led to chaos, unfulfilled expectations and disenchantment. Land Rights Councils were set up in the Northern Territory: the National Aboriginal Consultative Council gave Aborigines an official voice for the first time (though advisory only) and $163.6 million was allocated to Aboriginal programmes. But Queensland refused to cooperate, and media backlash helped to discredit what was achieved. Since then the *Aboriginal Land Rights (N.T.)* Act has been passed (1976) and the Ranger Uranium mining agreement has been signed (3 Nov. 1978). However the Queensland government has successfully resisted attempts to give self-determination to Aborigines on the Mornington Island and Aurukun reserves, and the Fraser government has changed its policy to one of 'self-management', reducing spending on Aboriginal programmes by 22 per cent.

The status of Aborigines as an ethnic minority can be seen in a few facts. In 1974—5, '11 000 Aboriginal families were without adequate shelter and were being joined by 1200 additional homeless families each year' (Lippman, 1979, pp.182—3). By June 1978 the housing loan list had been frozen. Infant mortality in 1977 was 75 per 1000 live births for Aborigines in the Northern Territory. (The white mortality rate is 16 per 1000.) Unemployment among Aborigines is six times the national average. Even the provision of more and better schooling seems unlikely to enable the current generation of Aboriginal children to break out of the pattern. As Lippman comments:

Despite some transfer of resources and responsibilities to Aboriginal communities, there was no real autonomy; despite the enthusiasm, goodwill and considerable increase in expenditure, moneys were controlled by white bureaucrats acting on behalf of a white society to make certain that white norms and values were being upheld. In traditional areas, it was white society that decreed that conventional schooling should take priority over adult education and that economic enterprises must show quick profit, rather than be viewed, temporarily, as learning experiences. In urban centres, complex accounting procedures and endless delays in project approvals brought home to Aboriginal self-help groups their total dependence on the major society (Lippman, 1979, p.187).

If we desire to understand the *treatment* of ethnic minority groups within any society we shall need to find adequate answers to questions like these:

How equal is the power of each group in a so-called *pluralist* society?

What motives, interests and purposes lie behind the treatment of ethnic groups?

How do minority groups themselves *define the situation*?

How do institutional structures, organizations and community associations, help or hinder minority group life-chances?

What networks operate either to 'absorb' ethnic groups or lead them to maintain a cohesive identity?

What forms can ethnic identity take?

What are the roots of prejudice?

What value is placed on the cultural worth of ethnic groups and how does this value affect their self-respect and their wider status?

Do attitudes and structures (of work, school, community) reflect a dominant culture doing symbolic violence to minority people?

What forces for change seem to be operating?

Readings and References

a. Australian Society:

BAILEY, J. P. (1978) 'Immigration and Ethnic Relations—the British in Argentina', *La Trobe Sociology Papers*, No. 44, La Trobe University, Melbourne.
BESWICK, D. G. & M. D. HILLS (1969) 'An Australian Ethnocentrism Scale', *Australian Journal of Psychology*, Vol. 24, pp.211-25.
BIRRELL, R. & C. HAY (eds) (1978) *The Immigration Issue in Australia*, Dept. of Sociology, La Trobe University, Melbourne.
BORRIE, W. D. (1954) *Italians and Germans in Australia*, Cheshire, Melbourne.
BOTTOMLEY, G. (1974) 'Some Greek Sex Roles: Ideals, Expectations and Action in Australia and Greece', *ANZJS*, Vol. 10, No. 1, pp.8-16.
BOTTOMLEY, G. (1976) 'Ethnicity and Identity Among Greek Australians', *ANZJS*, Vol. 12, 1976, No. 2, pp.118-25.
BOURKE, J. E. (1971) 'Educational Attainment and Migration' *Australian Journal of Education*, Vol. 15, pp.1-15.
BROOM, L. & P. SELZNICK, (1977) *Sociology* (6th ed.), Harper, N.Y.
BUCHANAN, M. E. (1976) *Attitudes Towards Immigrants in Australia*, Research Report No. 3 to the National Population Inquiry, A.G.P.S., Canberra.
BULLIVANT, B. M. (1976) 'Social Control and Migrant Education', *ANZJS*, Vol. 12, No. 3, pp.174-83.
BURNLEY, I. H. (1975) 'Ethnic Factors in Social Segregation and Residential Stratification in Australia's Large Cities', *ANZJS*, Vol. 11, No. 1, pp.12-20.
BURNLEY, I. (1975) 'Immigrant Absorption in the Australian City, 1947-71', *International Migration Review*, 9, pp.319-53.
CASS, B. (1976) 'Women at University: Pt. 1, Family and Class Background', *Refractory Girl*, 10, pp.6-11, 13-19 March.
CLAYDON, L., T. KNIGHT & M. RADO (1977) *Curriculum and Culture: Schooling in a Pluralist Society*, Allen & Unwin, Sydney.
COUNTRY EDUCATION PROJECT (Vic.) (1979) *Migrants and Education in a Rural Community. A Case Study of the Ovens and King Valleys*, CURA, Melbourne.
COX, D. P. (1976) 'Pluralism in Australia', *ANZJS*, Vol. 12, No. 2, pp.112-17.
CURA, (1978) *But I Wouldn't Want My Wife to Work Here*, Centre for Urban Research and Action, Victoria.
FEATHER, N. T. & G. WASYLUK, (1973) 'Subjective Assimilation Among Ukrainian Migrants: Value Similarity and Parent-Child Differences', *ANZJS*, Vol. 9, No. 1, pp.16-31.
GALBALLY REPORT (1978) *Review of Post-Arrival Programs and Services for Migrants*, AGPS, Canberra.
GEORGIOU, P. (1973) 'Migrants, Unionism and Society', *ANZJS*, Vol. 9, No. 1, pp.32-51.
GRASSBY, A. J. (1976) 'Towards a Multicultural Society', *Social Policy and Problems of the Work Force*, Vol. 1, A.C.T.U., Melbourne.

HARRIS, R. McL. & J. J. SMOLICZ, (1976) 'Anglo-Australian Views of Ethnics', *ANZJS*, Vol. 12, No. 2, pp.148-51.

HARVEY, S. (1974) 'National Language Usage Among Dutch and Polish Immigrant Children', in Edgar, D. E. (ed.), *Social Change in Australia*, Cheshire, Melbourne, pp.131-43.

HARVEY, S. (1979) 'Dutch Return Emigration: North Brabant Farmers' Sons: A Case Study of Settler Loss', *La Trobe Sociology Papers*, No. 4 (new series), La Trobe University, Melbourne.

HEARN, J. (1976) 'Migrants in the Work Force', *Social Policy and Problems of the Work Force*, Vol. 1, A.C.T.U., Melbourne.

HOOKS, B. (1979) 'A Clash of Cultures', *The Age*, 22 May 1979, p.14.

HUBER, R. (1977) *From Pasta to Pavlova*, University of Queensland Press, Brisbane.

HURWITZ, H. (1977) 'Factory Women' in A. Bordow (ed.), *The Worker in Australia*, University of Queensland Press, Brisbane, pp.222-67.

INGLIS, C. (1974) 'Chinese in Australia', in Edgar, D. E. (ed.), *Social Change in Australia*, Cheshire, Melbourne, pp.154-70.

JOHNSTON, R. (1972) 'The Concept of the "Marginal Man" ', *ANZJS*, Vol. 12, No. 2, pp.145-7.

JOHNSTON, R. (1977) 'The Immigrant Worker', in A. Bordow (ed.), *The Worker in Australia*, University of Queensland Press, Brisbane, pp.68-112.

KOVACS, M. L. & A. J. CROPLEY (1975) *Immigrants and Society*, McGraw-Hill, Sydney.

KUNZ, E. F., (1969) 'Engineering Profession and the Displaced Person Migrant in Australia', *International Migration*, Vol. 7, pp.22-3.

LEVER, C. (1975) 'Migrants in the Australian Workforce', *La Trobe Sociology Papers*, No. 14, La Trobe University, Melbourne.

LEWINS, F. (1976) 'Ethnic Diversity Within Australian Capitalism', *ANZJS*, Vol. 12, No. 2, pp.126-35.

LEWINS, F. (1977) 'The Australian Catholic Church and the Migrant', *La Trobe Sociology Papers*, No. 22, La Trobe University, Melbourne.

LEWINS, F. (1978) *The Myth of the Universal Church: Catholic Migrants in Australia*, A.N.U. Press, Canberra.

LIPPMAN, L. (1975) 'Aboriginal Education', *ANZJS*, Vol. 11, No. 2, pp.13-19.

LIPPMAN, L. (1979) 'The Aborigines', in A. Patience & B. Head (eds), *From Whitlam to Fraser*, Oxford University Press, Melbourne.

LOWENSTEIN, W. & M. LOH (1977) *The Immigrants*, Hyland House, Melbourne.

MCQUEEN, H. (1978) *Social Sketches of Australia, 1888-1975*, Penguin Books, Melbourne.

MACKIE, F. (1974) 'Some Suggestions on Greek Diversity', in Edgar, D. E. (ed.), *Social Change in Australia*, Cheshire, Melbourne, pp.144-53.

MADDOCK, K. (1972) *The Australian Aborigines: A Portrait of Their Society*, Penguin, Melbourne.

MARTIN, J. I. (1965) *Refugee Settlers*, A.N.U. Press, Canberra.

MARTIN, J. I. (1967) 'Extended Kinship Ties: An Adelaide Study', *ANZJS*, Vol. 3, pp.44-63.

MARTIN, J. I. (1972a) *Community and Identity*, A.N.U. Press, Canberra.

MARTIN, J. I. (1972b) *Migrants: Equality and Ideology*, Meredith Memorial Lectures, La Trobe University Press, Melbourne.

MARTIN, J. I. (1976) 'Ethnic Pluralism and Identity', in S. Murray-Smith (ed.), *Melbourne Studies in Education*, Melbourne University Press, Melbourne.

MARTIN, J. I. (1978) *The Migrant Presence*, Allen & Urwin, Sydney.

MARTIN, J. & P. MEADE, (1979) *The Educational Experience of Sydney High School Students*, Report No. 1, A.G.P.S., Canberra.

MARTIN, R. M. (1975) *Trade Unions in Australia*, Penguin, Melbourne.

MATTHEWS, P. W. (1977) 'Multicultural Education in Australia: An Historical Overview, 1970-76', *Child Migrant Education Newsletter*, (NSW Dept. of Education), Vol. 6 (Sept.) pp.3-7.

MEDDING, P. Y. (ed.) (1973) *Jews in Australian Society*, Macmillan & Monash University, Melbourne.

Migrant Services and Programs (1978) A.G.P.S. Canberra.

NICOLL, P. (1977) *Directions for Research in Migrant Education*, Dept. of Education, Canberra.

OESER, O. A. & S. B. HAMMOND (1954) *Social Structure and Personality in a City*, Routledge & Kegan Paul, London.

OXLEY, H. G. (1974) *Mateship in Local Organization*, University of Queensland Press, Brisbane.

PEARSON, D. G. (1976) 'Directions in Ethnic Relations Research: Britain and New Zealand in Comparative Perspective', *ANZJS*, Vol. 12, No. 2, pp.107-11.

PHILLIPS, D. (1974) 'Italians and Australians in the Ovens Valley', in Edgar, D.E. (ed.), *Social Change in Australia*, Cheshire, Melbourne, pp.121-30.

PITTOCK, A. B. & L. LIPPMAN (1974) 'Aborigines', in Forward, R. (ed.), *Public Policy in Australia*, Cheshire, Melbourne, pp.55-92.

POOLE, M. (1975) 'Learning More About Migrants: Some Adolescent Views', *ANZJS*, Vol. 11, No. 3, pp.66-9.

PRICE, C. A. (1962) 'Overseas Migration to and from Australia, 1947-1961', *Australian Outlook*, Vol. 16, pp.160-74.

PRICE, C. A. (1963) *Southern Europeans in Australia*, Oxford University Press and Australian National University.

PRICE, C. A. (1979) 'Immigration and Ethnic Affairs', in A. Patience & B. Head (eds), *From Whitlam to Fraser*, Oxford University Press, Melbourne.

PRICE, C. A. (1977) 'The Immigrants', A. F. Davies, S. Encel and M. J. Berry (eds) *Australian Society*, Cheshire, Melbourne.

PUTNINS, A. L. (1976) 'Immigrant Adjustment: A Note on Kovacs and Cropley's Model', *Aust. J. of Social Issues*, Vol. 11, No. 3, pp.209-12.

RICHARDS, M. (1974) 'The Immigrant's Experience', in Edgar, D. E. (ed.) *Social Change in Australia*, Cheshire, Melbourne, pp.109-20.

RICHARDS, L. (1978) 'Displaced Politics: Refugee Migrants in the Australian Political Context', *La Trobe Sociology Papers*, No. 45, La Trobe University, Melbourne.

RICHARDSON, A. & R. TAFT (1968) 'Australian Attitudes Towards Immigrants: a Review of Social Survey Findings', *International Migration Review*, 2, pp.46-55.

RIVETT, K. (ed.) (1962) *Immigration: Control or Colour Bar?*, Melbourne University Press, Melbourne.

ROBINSON, C. (1979) 'Vietnamese Bring Their Politics to Australia', *The National Times*, 26 May 1979, p.14.

RONAN, M. J. (1974) 'Two Approaches to Power in a Pluralistic Australia', *ANZJS*, Vol. 10, No. 2, pp.117-19.

RONAN, M. J. (1975) 'Speaking in Two Tongues', *Polycom*, Vol. 8, pp.17-20.

ROWLEY, C. D. (1975) *The Destruction of Aboriginal Society*, Penguin, Melbourne.

SALTER, M. J. (1978) *Studies in the Immigration of the Highly Skilled*, A.N.U. Press, Canberra.

SGRO, D. (1976) 'The Italian Espresso Bar: a Case Study', *La Trobe Sociology Papers*, No. 24, La Trobe University, Melbourne.

SHAVER, S. (1977) 'The Care-taken Network', in McCaughey, J. et al, *Who Cares?*, Macmillan, Melbourne.

SMOLICZ, J. J. & R. WISEMAN (1971) 'European Migrants and Their Children', *Quarterly Review of Australian Education*, Part 2, 4/3.

SOMMERLAD, E. A. (1977) 'Aboriginal Children Belong in the Aboriginal Community: Changing Practices in Adoption', *Aust. J. of Social Issues*, Vol. 12, No. 3, pp.167-77.

STEVENS, F. S. (ed.) (1972) *Racism: The Australian Experience*, Vols. 1 & 2, Australia & New Zealand Book Co., Sydney.

STORER, D. (ed.) (1975) *Ethnic Rights, Power and Participation: Toward a Multi-Cultural Australia*, Monograph No. 2, CURA, Melbourne.

STORER, D. (1979) 'How Recession Hits Migrants Hardest', in *The National Times*, 26 May 1979, p.62.

SUMMERS, J. (1975) 'Aboriginal Policy', in Gibb, D. M. & A. W. Hannan (eds), *Debate and Decision, Political Issues in 20th Century Australia*, Heinemann Educational, Melbourne, pp.110-39.

TAFT, R. (1965) *From Stranger to Citizen*, University of Western Australia Press, Perth.

TAFT, R. & D. CAHILL (1978) *Initial Adjustment to Schooling of Immigrant Families*, A.G.P.S., Canberra.

TAFT, R. & J. GOLDLUST (1970) 'The Current Status of Former Jewish Refugees in Melbourne', *ANZJS*, Vol. 6, pp.28-48.

TAFT, R. & R. ROBBINS (1955) *International Migration*, Ronald Press, N.Y.

TISAY, L. (1978) 'The Negotiation of an Identity: School—Child Community Relations in an Inner Suburban School in Melbourne' unpublished 4th Year Honours Thesis, Sociology, La Trobe University, Melbourne.

Two Worlds: School and the Migrant Family, (1971) Brotherhood of St Laurence, Melbourne.

UNIKOWSKI, R. (1978) *Communal Endeavours: Migrant Organizations in Melbourne*, A.N.U. Press, Canberra.

WEBBER, D. L. (1978) 'Interpersonal Behavior in Relation to Aboriginal Programs', *Aust. J. of Social Issues*, Vol. 13, No. 1, pp.61-71.

WHITE, I. (1974) 'Aboriginal Women's Status: A Paradox Revisited', in Edgar, D. E. (ed.), *Social Change in Australia*, Cheshire, Melbourne, pp.210-21.

WILD, R. (1971) 'Social Stratification or Statistical Exercises?', *Politics*, Vol. 6, No. 2, pp.169-77; reprinted in Edgar, D. E. (ed.), *Social Change in Australia*, Cheshire, Melbourne, pp.227-35.

ZUBRZYCKI, J. (1964) *Settlers in the La Trobe Valley*, A.N.U. Press, Canberra.

b. General:

DENZIN, N. K. (1969) 'Symbolic Interactionism and Ethnomethodology: a Proposed Synthesis', *American Sociological Review*, 34, pp.922-34.

GEERTZ, C. (1973) *The Interpretation of Culture: Selected Essays*, Basic Books, N.Y.

GLAZER, N. & D. P. MOYNIHAN (1963) *Beyond the Melting Pot: The Negroes, Puerto Ricans, Jews, Italians and Irish of New York City*, M.I.T., Cambridge, Mass.

GORDON, M. M. (1964) *Assimilation in American Life*, Oxford University Press, N.Y.

HOLZNER, B. (1968) *Reality Construction in Society*, Schenkman, Cambridge, Mass.

REISMAN, D. (1951) *The Lonely Crowd*, Yale University Press, New Haven, Conn.

RIST, R. C. (1978) *Guestworkers in Germany: The Prospects for Pluralism*, Praeger, N.Y.

RIST, R. C. (1979) 'Migration and Marginality: Guestworkers in Germany and France', *Daedalus*, Spring, in press, pp.95-108.

RYAN, W. (1971) *Blaming the Victim*, Orbach & Chambers, London.

SCHUTZ, A. (1944) 'The Stranger', *American Journal of Sociology*, Vol. 49, pp.499-507.

SCHUTZ, A. & T. LUCKMANN (1974) *The Structures of the Life World*, Heinemann Educational, London.

SIMPSON, G. E. & J. M. YINGER (1972) *Racial and Cultural Minorities: An Analysis of Prejudice and Discrimination* (4th ed.) Harper & Row, N.Y.

SKLARE, M. (1965) 'Assimilation and the Sociologists', *Commentary*, Vol. 39, No. 5, pp.63-7.

THOMAS, W. I. & F. ZNANIECKI (1927) *The Polish Peasant in Europe and America*, Knopf, N.Y.

VAN DER BERGHE, P. L. (ed.) (1972) *Intergroup Relations: Sociological Perspectives*, Basic Books, N.Y.

WAGNER, H. R. (1970) *Alfred Schutz on Phenomenology and Social Relations*, University of Chicago Press, Chicago.

WIRTH, L. (1928) *The Ghetto*, University of Chicago Press, Chicago.

Chapter 12

Deviance and Social Restructuring

12

Throughout this book we have emphasized the way in which resources and access to them are distributed unequally in society. Conflicting interests do not make for a pluralist society which 'balances out' people's lives in polite, ordered exchanges. The outcomes are always stratified. Degrees of control build into structures of domination that have clear effects on the world views and life concerns of different groups. Yet society presents an image of order that seems to deny conflict as a theoretical explanation. In Australian society, at least, 'life mooches on' with an apparent calm, an apparent agreement about what 'counts' and how things ought to be.

In this chapter we will examine the problem of social order and control. Our image of the social order may be an accurate one. On the other hand it may be that we experience chaos and domination but seek refuge in convenient but inaccurate images as part of our 'flight from reality' (Kirsner, 1972).

Perhaps life has never been 'authentic' in the sense that Kirsner (1972) and R. D. Laing (in *The Divided Self*, 1965) use the word. Perhaps everyday life has always been a 'tyranny' and other people have always been a threat.

Such pessimism seems unwarranted in the light of the sociological and historical evidence. Social orders certainly reflect inequalities of exchange, but social orders change and will always change. If reality is socially constructed, and if their symbolic capacity allows people to see through the social realities that are imposed by dominant groups, it should follow that there is cause for hope rather than despair. Sociology has been presented here as a 'debunking' discipline, as one which insists on 'seeing through' the master symbols and the vocabulary of motives, to challenge the agenda-setting that places blame upon the individual victim and directs attention away from the structural effects on social life. The social construction of reality depends upon negotiation, and every person is, every day, negotiating a niche in life with every 'other'. Certainly subjective awareness is not enough to change the inequalities of things, but all changes require some quantum of awareness in the first instance. We are not speaking here of population change or of environmental effects which may go on unnoticed while drastically changing life chances. We are concerned with people as social beings and with the levels of awareness and control that may develop among them. There is no limit to power in that sense; the human capacity is infinite given suitable social conditions. History and anthropology testify to the incredible variety of human structures developed to organize, control and give meaning to life. All the humanist disciplines challenge the present: some, like history, by digging into the past; others, like sociology, by exposing the structures of thought and power that produce an illusion of permanence in the present.

There is a problem in using the word *deviance* that relates to the humanist challenge. The word in itself suggests that there must be a permanence, an order of accepted, 'proper' thought and behaviour which acts as a standard. Movements away from the standard are, by definition, *deviant*. There is a danger, if we discuss deviance in terms of individual *deviants* that we may ignore the other form of deviance—broader social movements that vary from or challenge the dominant culture. If *deviance* is personalized and *deviants* are seen as odd or dangerous individuals, attention may be diverted from the social construction of competing realities. In particular, our media have aided and abetted this sort of social understanding of *deviance* by their treatment of *deviants*.

Another problem is that modern society virtually *requires* that multiple realities exist side by side. The division of labour is so complex, contains so many forms of specialized knowledge, and so stratifies access to alternate 'worlds' (at home, in schools, in occupations), that no consensus can cover every aspect of social organization and cultural life. If our social roles and life concerns differ, so must our values, attitudes, expectations, norms and typifications—our worlds taken-for-granted. Does *deviance* then encompass every form of straying from those areas of common agreement that *do* exist, from the *recipe knowledge* imposed by the powerful? Clearly, it does not, for some forms of 'straying' (like being a Catholic in a 'Protestant' country) are not seen as *deviant*.

The Causes of Deviance

Unless people have no realistic choice (as under a dictatorship) they only conform to rules that serve (or seem to serve) their own interests. If people are convinced that their interests lie in behaving *normally*, that is how they will behave. So we may not lightly dismiss consensus theories that explain deviance in terms of faulty socialization. Dennis Wrong (1961) rightly pointed out that sociologists had gone too far in their portrayal of *oversocialized man*. But we would not be able to talk of society or social conflict without the cultural acquisition of shared norms and values.

Where conflict theory helps, is in the emphasis it places on the values and interests of competing groups and on the unequal distribution of resources that makes it possible for some groups to emerge as dominant and to impose their views on others.

What every sociologist has to say about social order and deviance reflects his or her political interests. But for all of them, there is an assumption that human behaviour is ordered, orderly and predictable in patterned ways. Even the most extreme exponent of humanistic free will or the most radical of conflict theorists does not deny that we make our individual choices and decisions within a context of rules that we share more or less with other individuals. To say there are social rules is not to deny individual freedom. As we have seen, man only becomes human within the social limits imposed upon him. Without language, labels, types, categories and rules for linking ideas and regulating behaviour, we would be asocial: we would have no idea of ourselves as we appear in 'the looking-glass' of others; we would have no way of projecting our thoughts into predictable social expectations. So we should not be dismayed at social pressures for conformity. Conformity makes life meaningful and therefore controllable.

Every word or symbol that we use 'stands for' something whose existence we take for granted. The person whose symbols do not match our own and who behaves in strange and unpredictable ways is out of our control. Goffman shows how central are the presentation of self, the negotiation of meaning and the imposition of *normal* rules whenever we interact with others. So many of the rules are taken-for-granted that we hardly know when we are following them, but if we cannot assume that others *know* rules, we have no way of using a situation to suit our own purposes. For example, a teacher who walks into a classroom assumes that his definition of the situation is shared by his students and that certain rules can be taken-for-granted.

Notice that there remains the problem of assuming one all-pervasive set of social values against which human behaviour is measured. It is here that Robert K. Merton (1938) used Durkheim's ideas of normative consensus and *anomie* to explain deviance. *Anomie* refers to a state of society where there is a 'lack of rules' (*normlessness*), and where people drift individually, not strongly bound by shared communal bonds. Merton broadened this meaning to suggest that *anomie* also exists where the means for achieving desired social goals are unevenly distributed. Thus, while it may be that cultural values and desirable goals for life are accepted widely, the social structure may prevent some groups and individuals from reaching them. Expressed another way: deviance arises from disjunctions between cultural life concerns and the structure of social organization. 'Everyone' aims at success. When success equals money and status, people work to earn money and work earns success and status. But if an individual, despite his hard work, still fails to achieve money and status he may turn to less legitimate ways of achieving those ends.

Table 12 – 1 Merton's typology of deviance

Cultural Goals	Legitimate Structural Means	Response	Type
Accepts	Has access Accepts	⟶ Conformity	Non-deviant conformist
Accepts as desirable	No access Rejects	⟶ Innovation	Deviant Criminal
Rejects or forgets	Accepts	⟶ Ritualism	Rule-bound conformist
Abandons	No access Abandons	⟶ Retreatism	Social Drop-out
Rejects Creates new goals	Rejects Develops new means	⟶ Rebellion	Rebel

(Based on Merton, 1938)

While this is clearly more of a sociological, structural theory than a psychological one, it still fails to explain why people accept or reject the dominant cultural goals or why some without access to legitimate means continue to conform rather than turn to crime. Nor does it offer any explanation for the way in which legitimate means of achieving desired goals come to be socially distributed. To obtain such an explanation we would have to consider the processes of socialization and the structures of domination that define the parameters of normality and legitimacy.

It is, of course, through socialization that we learn the symbols and the rules of our social groups. We say that rules are *internalized* when we have accepted the rules as part of ourselves and habitually behave according to the rules because it is *normal* to do so. We learn what is normal from, and with, others whose valuation of the standard knowledge is revealed in their approval or disapproval of our conduct.

Social sharing and this sort of predictability make social interaction work. We fit together, and patterns of relationships become stable over time; our conduct becomes *institutionalized*. We may conflict with others but our conflict usually takes place against the background of a shared framework of ideas. The *roles* we play may be accepted or rejected, but if we are *in* them, people expect certain patterns of behaviour and not others. If we drop out or die, someone else can step in to play our roles and perform our functions, so social *continuity* is assured.

It follows, therefore, that if we become *competent* at playing our roles, at reading the signs and intentions of others and at negotiating the process of meaning, then we are likely to be accepted as *normal* members of society. People who give 'wrong' responses or react strangely, are likely to be regarded as incompetent or *deviant*.

All of the evidence we have so far brought to bear suggests that competence is socially distributed; it is neither an accident of birth nor the result of personal effort. We have also seen that competence is socially defined and that different forms of competence are valued differently. So our starting point for studying deviance and social order must be the notions of power and of conflicts over power. A person who does not fit in with our definition of a situation, our assertions of what constitutes *reality*, is a potential threat to our control. That is why babies are so hard to manage: they fail to understand; they insist on having their own way; they have strong lungs to coerce us into meeting their needs. But with babies, we have the upper hand. We may also suspend our anger because we do not expect them to behave *normally* in adult terms. They are ignorant, uncivilized and untrained, and must be controlled with patience until they become competent as *normal* adults.

We are less tolerant, however, of older children and of adults 'who ought to know better'. Their power to interfere with our plans and to damage our vested interests is more threatening. If they refuse to behave competently, then something must be wrong and must be put right. Since one of our strongest *master symbols* is that of the individual with individual responsibility for action, what is wrong must necessarily lie within the individual. We may reason that his parents have been too lax with discipline or his family ignorant; but if he is now 'old enough to know better' he must be 'brought into line'. If people are allowed to continue being homosexuals, drug addicts, thieves or thugs, they not only challenge our sense of identity but may also interfere with our property, lives or future plans.

What is *normal* is what serves the interests of dominant groups. Obviously every group's and every individual's interests are served by rules against murder. However other sets of rules work to the advantage of some groups and the disadvantage of others. There are rules against drugs but not against alcohol; against de facto relationships but not against marriage; against unauthorized wage increases but not against price increases. In wartime, homicide may not only be legitimate, but even heroic. And crimes which used to be regarded as serious (like stealing a loaf of bread) are these days no longer punished so severely.

As the balance of power alters, new definitions of the normal will take over; reality is redefined in terms of new interests. Valuations change too, along with shifts in needs, resources and life situations. At one time salt was more valuable than gold; the Church's definitions of morality were once more powerful than they are now. Since individuals are born into different social and moral communities, they are socialized into different views of reality. Deviance is not simply the result of 'faulty' socialization. The child of a professional thief may be faultlessly socialized—to become a thief. What is taught as normal to one group may not be normal to another; so ethnic groups may experience severe culture clashes and problems of identity.

So if *deviance* is behaviour contrary to what is considered to be *normal*, it may be seen to result from several conditions. It will reflect the structure of dominance relations in society or within a social group. Those in positions of authority will be the major definers of deviance. And because they possess their authority by virtue of the fact that other people see their power as legitimate, their definitions will be shared by others. The debate about 'private' deviance (such as homosexuality, transvestitism, devil worship, and so on), only makes sense in a social context. In modern society the main definers of deviance are professionals who act as guardians of the major institutional values. Teachers, police, doctors, lawyers, social workers and public servants administer the master rules, seek out offenders and bring these offenders to judgement as 'incompetents' who are unable to control themselves and who may thus legitimately be placed under the supervision of others. Particular contexts, of course, will alter both the definers and the definitions of deviance. Drunken behaviour may be seen as 'normal' for young males at a buck's night or after the football; it is a little more deviant at a mixed party; it is certainly deviant during working hours.

Deviance may be *ascribed* to whole groups of people (Goffman, 1963). Skin colour, age, odd dress or appearance, deeply held beliefs and patterns of sexual behaviour can respectively stigmatize negroes, old men who marry, hippies, Jews and homosexuals. This form of labelling—amounting to stereotyping —can have both silly and drastic social consequences. On the less consequential side we may see how deviance can be ascribed according to hairstyle. During the 1950s short hair, a 'crew cut', was the sign of loutish American behaviour; by the late '50s long greasy hair was the sign of a 'bodgie'; by the 1960s long hair of any kind revealed a 'hippy', drug-smoking non-conformist (Braithwaite and Barker, 1979). More serious, however, may be the consequences for women whose doctors stereotype them as 'neurotic' and prescribe drugs to cure conditions which are socially rather than psychologically caused. The real problems may be forever ignored in the easy acceptance of the label.

In most cases, however, there is some objective behaviour that triggers the label *deviant*. For that reason there is not a clear distinction between *ascribed* and *achieved* deviance (Edwards & Wilson, 1975). What is meant, though, is that *achieved* deviance follows from an individual's doing something wrong, rather than from merely being 'typical' of a group of people regarded as deviants. There will have been some overt act (like theft or assault or mental breakdown), outside the bounds of socially approved expected behaviour.

Labelling

Even these overt acts of deviance may be labelled and treated differently. For example, consider the case of a group of young middle-class youths, getting drunk from a parent's liquor cupboard and stoning passing cars. If they are caught, police may consider their action to be seriously 'deviant'. But if their parents define it as just 'youthful boisterousness', promise to exercise more parental control, and carry some social status, punishment may not take the 'normal' course. In contrast, police often do harass youths in lower socio-economic areas simply because they are 'on the streets', or constantly suspected of being up to mischief (Windshuttle, 1978). An overt act from them will imply 'Go directly to jail. Do not pass Go'.

The notion of labelling carries with it several corollaries. The first is that when a label is attached the 'deviant' is treated accordingly. His rights are curtailed; he is stigmatized by the label as a criminal. But the second implication is that the individual *feels* stigmatized, *feels* his identity spoiled from within as well as without. (The second stage of the process, however, may not be inevitable. Goffman's study, *Stigma* (1963) reveals some remarkably skilful techniques used by the inmates of mental hospitals in the 'management of spoiled identity', and the brilliant novel *One Flew Over the Cuckoo's Nest* suggests how even the most vicious institutional efforts to destroy self-respect may be resisted.)

Labelling may also be a *political* theory when it is used to explain how rule-makers successfully attach the notion of deviance to those who break the rules (see Hiller, 1974, p.520). Most of us violate norms and most of us will admit to having actually broken the law even though we have not been caught. But we are not considered to be deviant. So the dividing line between normal and deviant is not between norms and behaviour, or between those who have acted 'deviantly' and those who have not. Rather, it is the line drawn by being caught, publicly labelled and processed as a deviant. Research interest here shifts from trying to explain the social causes of deviance to explaining the symbolic interaction processes that lead to the label being applied, and to the 'effects this has on the deviant individual's self-conception, group affiliations and whole future career' (Hiller, 1974, p.522; see also Rubington and Weinberg, 1968). Howard Becker (1963) uses the notion of the *deviant career* to analyze the steps by which labels are attached. There can be no assumption (as there is in law) that deviants are motivated to commit crime, that they are 'people who want to violate norms' (McGee, 1972, p.126). Most of us feel the urge to violate norms at times; however only some of us follow through. Becker holds that as we mature our *commitment* to norms, social institutions and a standard web of relationships grows. The longer we have survived by conforming, the harder it becomes to violate social rules. Those who have few commitments, who have either cut loose from standard institutions or have grown up with different subcultural values, feel less committed and less guilty if they deviate. The committed conformist can 'neutralize' an occasional lapse into deviant behaviour by self-justification (Sykes and Matza, 1957).

Being caught and labelled may damage one's self-image; it will certainly damage one's public identity and social status. Furthermore the nature of the deviant act now becomes irrelevant. The deviant now becomes loaded with a 'diffuse status characteristic' and is regarded as untrustworthy in every way: embezzlers may be seen to be potentially violent. As Nisbet puts it, the 'social bond' has been violated, and a whole new set of symbolic expectations comes into operation. Becker suggests that these expectations trigger a 'self-fulfilling prophecy'. The ex-prisoner cannot find an employer willing to take him on; furthermore his degraded self-image may lead him to distrust himself. He is therefore forced into a deviant group which extends the 'career' by offering support, new means for deviant action and a new setting for a positive self-image. Only in a few cases can group support help de-label the deviant individual, as with Alcoholics Anonymous or drug rehabilitation programmes (Trice and Rowan, 1970, pp.538—46).

The processing of labelled deviants is also affected, of course, by other structural factors. If you arrest too many 'criminals' the jails may become overcrowded and the courts back-logged with cases. For that reason sociologists look somewhat sceptically at the criminologists' figures on 'crime rates' (for some Australian figures, see Biles, 1974, pp.548—57). Cicourel and Kitsuse (1963, p.137) argue that official statistics about deviant behaviour must 'be viewed as indices of organizational processes rather than as indices of the incidence of certain forms of behaviour'. Jack Douglas (1970, pp.49—56 and p.59) likewise delivers a blast at the 'pigeon-hole perspective on man' which fails to see that official statistics represent the control attempts of 'official morality'; David Sudnow (1965, pp.255—76) gives an interesting *ethno-methodological* account of how the police 'normalize' crimes by charging offenders with less serious offences so that they can be processed more quickly.

It must be stressed that being caught, labelled and processed as deviant need not necessarily produce a 'spoilt identity' for the individual. This is where social theory must take account of both structural factors and the meanings developed in symbolic interaction processes. If individuals have been socialized into *deviant* forms of behaviour, they are less likely to accept society's labels as relevant or damaging to them. Recent work by Geoff Asher on reactions of inmates at Turana Boys' Home in Melbourne suggests that many of them come from homes where theft, being in trouble with police and even being in jail, are part of everyday reality. Getting caught is the only fault; being in Turana is not stigmatizing because the boys' social audience—both their membership group and the reference group to which they will return—do not see being in jail as something disgraceful. The possibility is, then, that so-called *labelling theory* is once again the creation of middle-class professionals, this time anti-punitive institutional ones, but nonetheless people who, if *they* were caught *would* feel stigmatized. The fascinating work of Jeff Lachmund (1979) on the social networks of professional thieves in Melbourne indicates that some solid rethinking is needed. His acceptance into their families for research purposes is a unique triumph of technique and trust and has produced one of the rare studies of 'crime as the criminal sees it'.

Deviance can also be associated with social conformity. Drinking alcohol is part of the Australian culture (as it is in many other societies); for some Australians it is even a matter of national pride. Peer pressures to 'show you're a man' by getting drunk, and to prove that you can drive after drinking, or that you can 'hold your liquor', are very strong for males. Yet such social norms of acceptability lead to a great deal of anti-social and *deviant* behaviour. The Senate Standing Committee on Social Welfare's report on Drug Problems in Australia (1979) says that alcohol has caused 30 000 deaths in the past ten years (mainly through car accidents). It has cost $1000 million a year through absenteeism and accidents in industry. Alcohol is associated with 50 per cent of all fatal road accidents, between 20 and 30 per cent of hospital admissions, 73 per cent of violent crimes, 40 per cent of adult drownings, 45 per cent of mixed drug poisonings, 40 per cent of divorces and separations, 20 per cent of baby bashings and 66 per cent of all household and industrial accidents. Senator Peter Baume comments that:

> There is nothing wrong with alcohol. The drug is not at fault. The drug is merely an instrument. When we are talking about the alcohol problem we are really talking about society and social conditions ... If I were an Aboriginal, if I had been brought up with no education, no job opportunities, no tradition of coping and no hope that anyone really cared, then I might see alcohol as a very important part of my life. And who could blame me? (*Australian*, 26–27 May 1979, p.13).

The point to be emphasized is that *deviance* is produced by society; it is not merely some sort of personal defect or aberration. This is a different point from the major and more obvious one—that what is *deviant* is by definition produced by what is seen as *normal*. We are now suggesting that the structural life chances distributed by dominant groups push some people into *deviant* behaviour patterns regardless of any cultural values that they may or may not have acquired.

Some examples from the field of work may be cited. Shiftwork is linked with irritability, stress and conflict in family life (Rogers, 1976). Giving shiftworkers rights of flexitime arrangements improves their family life, but only if the employers trust them and do not monitor their movements (Gibbons, 1977). Where workers are treated with genuine respect, they are more likely to treat spouse and children with respect (Emery et al, 1974). Marital breakdown is most at risk in jobs which either involve frequent travel or which require a high degree of preoccupation with intellectual demands (Harvey, 1978).

One can easily point to more dramatic illustrations of the link between deviance and *social problems* on the one hand and structured social relations and cultural values on the other. Social values reflect agreements about what constitutes desirable behaviour and what constitutes desirable institutional arrangements. As we have seen, institutions and their associated norms represent the outcome of conflicts and power struggles; the groups who 'lose' then come to be seen as deviant. Crime can only exist if we place values on certain objects. A society which values personal property will *produce* different crimes from a society (like that of the Aborigines) where property is communal. Sexual promiscuity is only a social problem in societies where Christian or other beliefs require that sex should be confined to marriage. Divorce would not be deviant individually or regarded as a social problem if marriage and the family were not valued so highly. (Given current trends, then, divorce may become the norm.) Institutions in this light are forms of legitimated violence through which one set of values is imposed on the whole society. While normative consensus gives a degree of legitimacy to those social arrangements, we should not assume that agreement is always widespread: much *deviance* is a deliberate refusal to conform, not merely a failure to do what is expected.

While it makes some sense to construct *punishments* for deviance according to how *harmful* the deviant act has been to society, such an approach clearly contains anomalies. *Private* acts may be deviant yet not do harm, even to the actors. So 'harm' or 'damage' must be seen in terms of whose interests are challenged. Society builds powerful norms around the sanctity of sex in marriage. Homosexuality may therefore challenge not only the 'normality' of heterosexuality, but also the power of men over women, the vested property interests that lie in monogamous marriage, and the security of lasting marital contracts. Even female homosexuality is viewed differently from male homosexuality.

Further, whole areas of rule-breaking may go unpunished. As Braithwaite and Wilson point out, doctors flaunt hospital regulations, business-men fiddle the books, whole companies go bankrupt and harm thousands of shareholders, yet most go unpunished. Drawing on the seminal work of E. H. Sutherland on *White Collar Crime* in 1949, they claim that the very term *deviance* supports the status quo. To the man in the street, deviance means *malevolent abnormality*, while for the sociologist it means *rule-breaking*. They call for less talk of *deviance* and more of *exploitation*. They contrast *crimes of the powerless* with *crimes of the powerful*, and argue that:

> the rule makers are the most flagrant rule breakers in Australian society. But . . . we do not simply want to say that the powerful are more deviant than the powerless, rather than vice versa; we want to suggest in the process that exploitation and domination may often be more fruitful categories of analysis than deviance itself for understanding phenomena normally subsumed under the deviance rubric (Braithwaite & Wilson, 1978b, p.5).

The treatment of deviance, like the treatment of ethnicity, thus has a double meaning. Society has punished some forms of harmful action and some forms of rule-breaking but has condoned other forms. Sociological definitions have also reflected that inequity. In addition, the actual treatment of *deviants* has shifted from one of punishment to one of treatment, or as Baldock (1978, p.149) puts it, from a legal model to a medical model of deviance.

In effect this reflects the shift Durkheim noted long ago from *repressive* to *restitutive* justice. As society became more complex and its normative agreements less binding, so it became impossible to punish in a *mechanical* way. Alcoholics, the mentally ill and even criminals are now imprisoned not merely for punishment, but also for *rehabilitation*. Treatment centres, some of which are outside the usual penal institutions, aim at re-educating, training people for jobs and restoring a sense of self-respect and social responsibility. Notice, however, how each of these terms echoes the assumptions of stigma, of faulty socialization, of individual blame. Indeed this approach reflects the 'organic' model of society because it aims at restoring what is seen as an underlying natural harmony. Very few efforts have been made to restructure the social structures which prisoners and patients must re-enter when they leave the 'corrective' institution. Again the master symbols suggest a vocabulary of motives and a host of assumptions.

Order and Social Change

C. Wright Mills long ago pointed out that all theoretical explanations are associated with historically situated actions. He argued, for example, that Freudian theory, with its terminology of *ego*, *id*, *superego*, *repression* and the *subconscious* was the product of 'an upper bourgeois patriarchal group with a strong sexual and individualistic orientation' (Horton, 1966; Mills, 1942). Until 1940 the vocabulary of American sociology was based on the 'motives of small town bias'; after the 1950s, however, it came to reflect an increasingly bureaucratized life experience.

Most sociological theories, as Horton puts it, portray an image of society through a vocabulary either of *order* or of *conflict*. Order theories have an image of society as a structured system of shared norms and values, with social problems resulting from *anomie*—a breakdown in social organization. Conflict theories, on the other hand, see society as a 'continually contested political struggle between groups with opposing goals and world views'. For conflict theorists, social change represents not deviant behaviour, but new behaviour by people in response to their alienation; to challenges to their meaning systems; and to the social structures that limit their powers of expression. As we suggested in the first chapter, a dichotomy of theoretical views is useful provided that we do not feel impelled to select one view to the total exclusion of the others. In this book sociology has been presented as a discipline which seeks to reveal the tentative nature of social *agreements*. Because humans have symbolic abilities, their meanings, world views, and social orders are not only created but also open to reconstruction.

The *normative* model directs attention to certain processes by which social actors operate.

Figure 12–1   The Normative Model

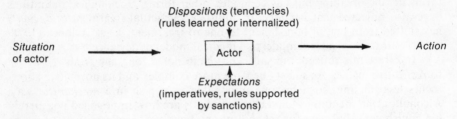

Explanations based on the notion of agreed norms suggest stability and order because the actor either brings a set of learned dispositions to bear on each new social situation, or reacts to the expectations that apply to action in that setting. This is a Skinnerian, *behaviouristic*, model, which assumes that we can predict the behaviour of people as we can the behaviour of rats subjected to various forms of conditioning. But as Wilson (1971) insists, such a model wrongly assumes that there is consensus among the various actors about the rules that operate in a given situation. Garfinkel's (1967) experiments in challenging typical definitions of a situation show how dubious such assumptions are. Act as a boarder in your own home, or redefine a classroom situation as a party between friends and the other people around you are likely to show considerable surprise.

Wilson suggests that an interpretive model comes closer to the facts of life.

Figure 12–2   Interpretive Model

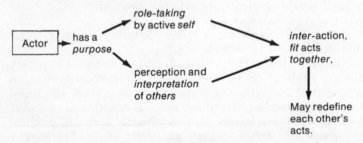

Without necessarily having many prior agreements, people enter situations with their own purposes in mind (for example, to learn, to have a party or to make money). Their intentions then lead them to assume appropriate roles, and to make active choices of appropriate norms. Rather than assume agreement, they actively observe others who may help or hinder the achievement of their purposes, and interpret how these people define the situation. As a result there is a fitting together, a negotiation which produces agreed upon norms and definitions.

The interpretive model is more useful than the normative one. It takes account of the facts of unequal power derived from unequal resources and of man's capacity to symbolize. It is also a more dynamic model than one which assumes consensus and an almost automatic acting out of pre-defined roles. But in our view it is too idealistic in its humanistic assumption of free will and intentionality. People do not enter social situations as equals. Some of us have purposes which can never be fulfilled because both our resources and our ability to bargain with others and redefine their view of the world are inferior. What is implied in Wilson's interpretive model, but not spelled out sufficiently, is the relative power of individuals and groups to negotiate meanings in social contexts to suit their own purposes. Too much stress on the ways in which meanings are interpreted and redefined in a given context (what is called the *indexicality* of meaning) may lead to the conclusion that prediction in sociology is impossible. It also ignores the fact that the power to define meaning is socially distributed; that people have unequal equipment for competence and unequal images of *the competent self*; that social structures limit the range for action and negotiation available to unequal social groups; and that the very sharedness of meanings which allows people even to begin negotiating with others limits what is possible in any cultural situation.

Figure 12–3 Competence Model

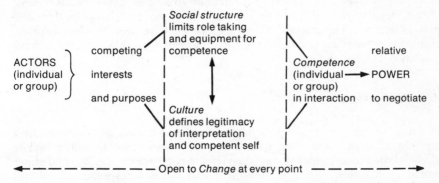

In accord with the model of social structure and culture presented in this book, we can use the social distribution of competence as a link between the normative and interpretive models. As we have suggested, our social structure not only limits access to valued resources (money, language and cultural capital), but also limits our cultural horizons (Holzner, 1968), the very nature of whatever life concerns we are likely to develop. Through the family, education and the media, the structures of work and the groups with which we associate, dominant groups manage to reproduce their dominance while the dominated struggle to wrest some control from their hands. Since cultural meanings (whether in the form of religions, political ideologies or secular preoccupations) give us a sense of control over our environment, we will be more or less effective depending upon how successful we are in imposing *our* meanings upon others. Having others confirm our views is reassuring and makes life more predictable, more manageable in terms of our own particular purposes. So group support will be vital in having our views accepted as legitimate rather than *deviant*. But as we have emphasized, the social structure limits life chances and distributes access to both individual competences and group capacities. In consequence, the outcome of struggles to re-interpret and re-negotiate cultural values and the social structures through which they can be realized, will be predictable to some extent.

Just as we may not assume normative consensus in a complex world, neither may we ignore trans-situational meanings, the master symbols that cover all social groups, the vocabularies of motive that set the limits for all cultural concerns. While every new situation offers a context in which meanings may be revamped and in which the balance of power may change, we should not overplay the notion of situational effects. People are symbol makers and users and their symbols go beyond specific situations. People *do* behave in absolutist ways as though rules were unalterable. We give absolute, 'rational' accounts of everyday life—'It's a matter of principle', 'I have no choice', 'It's God's will'. We create *as if* practices to preserve a professional image of rationality; and we resort to force to impose our view of the world when all else fails (Wilson, 1971).

Social change is therefore an integral part of every social *order*. At every point there are possibilities for new thoughts, new symbols, new interests and purposes, new roles, new institutional rules and structures, new versions of what is 'true', 'legitimate' and 'real'. So the scales of power can always be tipped or upset altogether. The notion of *balance*, as we have seen, is inappropriate because it assumes an equal chance for groups in a pluralist society to have some say.

Social Movements

The rather vague term *social movement* refers to an organized movement by a large number of people to change some aspect of a society and its culture. While individual dissatisfactions and counter-views may be seen as *deviant* and either ignored or punished, a social movement is a more widespread, united and lasting attempt to assert an alternate point of view. Once people realize that others share their views, they gain confidence in expressing them. Groups may form, meetings be held, campaigns mounted and enthusiasm build. At the start, a social movement is usually diverse and not well organized, its goals may be vague and its methods diffuse. But the people who comprise the movement share a social situation that calls out for change, a viewpoint or ideology around which their enthusiasm clusters, and a preparedness to translate their beliefs into action.

Examples abound in every society and age. Early Christianity grew as a social movement. Its new and radical ideology inspired its adherents to face persecution together. The socialist movement worked through pamphlets, newspapers, the Fabian society, trade unions and political parties. As with all such movements its fortunes rose and fell depending on the appeal of the ideology in different times.

It is important to note that a movement's chances of achieving its aims depend, among other things, on the extent to which its aims and ideologies correspond to the felt needs of large numbers of people. If there is such a correspondence the dominant group can never totally control a social movement. The media may portray the movement's ideology as immoral, communist or a threat to law and order but no amount of hostile propaganda can remove the real social problems that give rise to a social movement. Furthermore, if the movement is not only vocal but also active—through street marches, meetings and other forms of community action—it will be even more difficult to silence or suppress.

One of the largest social movements of recent times has been the *Women's Liberation* movement. Its ideology is by no means new; the earlier Suffragette movement made remarkable political gains for women at the beginning of this century. Nevertheless it seemed, in the 1960s and 1970s, to challenge the whole structure of modern society. Nor was Germaine Greer's *The Female Eunuch* the first feminist book (Simone de Beauvoir's *The Second Sex* had been published 17 years earlier) but it captured the public imagination and fuelled counter-attacks from male chauvinists and female preservers-of-the-home. Though its members were often labelled as 'bra-burners', 'radicals' and 'lesbians', this social movement nevertheless managed to secure legislative changes for equal opportunities in work, education and other fields, and to restructure radically the world views of most people. Social movements develop out of real social conditions; they do not 'just happen'. Radical leaders emerge because there is someone to be led somewhere, because the current state of things fails to meet the interests of large numbers of people. Real changes in the conditions of life for women, such as safe methods of contraception, rising affluence and new work opportunities, all helped to make a renewed attack on sexual inequality possible and more likely to succeed than ever before. Just as the Black Liberation movement in the United States challenged the racist world view, so the women's movement has managed to penetrate both the cultural awareness and some of the structured limits to life chances for women in western societies. Radical action, careful political lobbying, screaming polemics and academic research went hand in hand. Although divided (like all social movements) over aims and about the best methods to use, the women's movement has still managed to challenge the image of *deviance*, and to lead both women and men to question their assumptions about traditional sex roles. Obviously there are groups and individuals who disapprove, who mock, who still believe that 'woman's place is in the home'. That kind of rejection typifies every social movement. The point is that changes have taken place and that each change provides new conditions for social action. Despite unequal resources, despite both their inferior access to equipment for competence and their inferior self-image and social status, women have managed to restructure their place in the world (Mercer, 1977).

A similar movement seems to be taking place in the advanced societies in relation to forms of social organization. Disillusionment has grown with big bureaucracies, big government, big schools and the impersonality of 'rational-legal' forms of 'efficient' management. There is nothing new in the yearning for a return to closer relationships in small-scale communities, but modern conditions give the call a new edge. Not yet articulated under any clear ideology, it takes various contradictory forms. In California, *Proposition 13* rejected greater taxation and thereby seriously threatened social welfare and education programmes. Yet it echoed the more humanely oriented arguments of Schumacher (1973) in his book *Small is Beautiful*, as well as David Tyack's call (1974) to demolish *The One Best System* in American schools. There is growing criticism of large business organizations, at a time when multi-national corporations are getting bigger and bigger. In Australia there are growing moves towards community participation in the schools, in welfare and in local development. What the movement will achieve will depend upon the extent to which competing interest groups can use the movement to serve their diverse purposes. It is too early to predict the outcomes. While the government's reduction of the size of the public service has been inspired by a concern to reduce expenditure, the results of this reduction may come to include increased self-reliance, group competence and power sharing. The movement may then have a favourable environment in which to work.

Social Restructuring

The theory of capitalist hegemony does not go so far as to suggest that such institutions as the family, the school, work and the mass media are so dominated by one world-view that no change is possible. Gramsci's (1974 [1926]) notion of hegemonic control does not imply that people need actually espouse or accept the dominant values, but rather that they bow to them. Their sense of competence never totally denies the self, but it may inhibit their action against the structures of domination.

A recent review of the Bowles and Gintis book (Beneria, 1977), has suggested that 'the potential rebelliousness of rule-oriented people is under-estimated by Bowles and Gintis—insofar as the studies on which they base their analysis show the external rather than the true attitudes of those who have been compelled to follow rules in order to survive in the wage labor system'. Beneria defines as *true attitudes* 'those that surface when the contradictions generated by the circumstances in which people live become extreme or when the consciousness of oppression becomes generalised'. This is the crux of Gramsci's view of hegemony. The task of a new sociology of competence is to spell out the varying conditions that give rise to those contradictions and that produce forms of consciousness and action.

Gramsci's notion of hegemony is that it does not obliterate working-class consciousness but, rather, involves 'the co-existence of two conceptions of the world, one affirmed in words and the other displayed in effective action' (Gramsci, 1971, p.327). Thus though people may affirm the words of the master symbols, 'for reasons of submission and intellectual subordination', their desire to take *effective action* may grow as their social conditions change. Unemployment, poverty and objective economic and social relations may begin to contradict and undermine the dominant rhetoric.

As Dreier (1979) and Gorz (1973) suggest, changes take place at such times through *transitional reforms*. They are transitional in that they heighten awareness of the contradictions within capitalism and produce strains that threaten the status quo. For example, governmental health and safety laws may reduce production, revealing the contradiction between decent working conditions and the search for profits. Better and wider education may make people more aware of their abilities and stimulate their desire to do creative work within a system that degrades both blue-collar and white-collar work. Such reforms may also help people see personal problems as social ones, and to assign the blame to the system rather than to the individual. When that happens ideological controls break down because the official world view of those in power is challenged and with it the legitimacy of their authority.

Individual alienation and cynicism about one's limited effectiveness may decrease; group confidence may increase through group action. The old union catch-cry 'United we stand, divided we fall', is more than a mere slogan. It is a recognition of the social power of groups, of the divided nature of labour and of the victimizing effects of the ideology of individualism on which capitalism rests. Too great a stress on individual competence keeps people apart, in competition, and in ignorance of their interdependence. A new emphasis on *cooperative competence* which under-lies moves towards 'worker control', 'production units', community organizations and the growing movement for citizen participation, may indicate a future with vastly changed social class relations (see Toffler, 1979). As Dreier puts it,

> Transitional reforms break down the fragmented roles inherent in voluntary associations and other social institutions. They weaken the divisions within the working class—sex, race, income, authority, geography. Transitional reforms are based on collective action, not individual victories but attainments by a group of people working together. Transitional reforms build indigenous leadership in a class or other group; they are not carried out on behalf of a group (e.g. advocacy planning) but by a group (Dreier, 1979, p.10).

This somewhat optimistic view of the future of work and its associated social relations, however, needs to be seen against the backdrop of the stark power of capitalism and of governments acting in the interests of the owners of the means of production. As Garner (1975) comments, the economics of crisis in advanced capitalist societies produces a shrinkage in profits and a slowdown in capital accumulation as labour costs increase (through wage rises, fringe benefits, corporate taxation for social services, etc.). The capitalist defence comprises not only opposition to wage increases and attacks on 'union irresponsibility' but also the closing down of plants and the withdrawal or withholding of capital investment. The consequent increased unemployment leads to popular support for (or at least acquiescence in) limitations both to wage demands and to expenditure on social welfare. In Australia the call by A.C.T.U. President Hawke in May 1978 for a re-thinking of trade union wages policy and his acceptance of the impossibility of full employment is a telling example of such acquiescence: too much reform and the system may collapse. Garner thus insists that in looking at the future structure of work, class relations and the role of the State, we must take account of particular national and international historical and social conditions.

Is transition a euphemism for social-democratic gradualism, for a process involving elections, socialist education, cooperative institutions, economic democracy, and the continued existence of multiple parties—a process in which socialism crowds out capitalism? In short, is it a process by which we can find the socialist pot of gold at the end of a social democratic rainbow? Or is transition a euphemism for a storm, a revolution, a conflict that results in a dictatorship of the proletariat? (Garner, 1975, pp.17—18).

Prevailing social structures of domination, even in the form of very subtle ideological controls, are always subject to challenge, renegotiation and change. The study of sociology is an attempt to isolate and analyze the nature of that structuring and restructuring process; it enables us to see why what was deviant yesterday is normal or legitimate today. Students of sociology should therefore try to avoid the two extremes: of assuming either that society is monolithic and that power structures are too entrenched to change or that individual free will enables people to solve their problems.

Society only becomes a *thing* out of control when people lose their symbolic ability to construct and when they forget that what is, is there only because people have put it there. The human being becomes social within society. But society only becomes human through the action of human beings. Social structures are made by people to serve their human purposes. When those purposes change, new structures have to be built. If sociological analysis helps us to understand and enhance our capacity to reconstruct society in more humane ways, it may be a worthwhile pursuit.

Ah Love! could thou and I with Fate conspire
To grasp this sorry Scheme of Things entire,
Would not we shatter it to bits—and then
Re-mould it nearer to the Heart's Desire!

The Rubaiyat of Omar Khayyam.

Readings and References

a. Australian Society:

ALTMAN, D. (1972) *Homosexual Oppression and Liberation*, Angus & Robertson, Sydney.

ALTMAN, D. E. (1975) 'Deviance, Society and Sociology', in A. R. Edwards & P. R. Wilson (eds), *Social Deviance in Australia*, Cheshire, Melbourne, pp.264-77.

BALDOCK, C. V. (1978) *Australia and Social Change Theory*, Novak, Sydney.

BILES, D. (1974) 'Who Goes to Prison?' in Edgar, D. E. (ed.), *Social Change in Australia*, Cheshire, Melbourne, pp.548-60.

BILES, D. & B. McCOY (1973) 'Police Attitudes to Deviance in Victoria', *ANZJS*, Vol. 9, No. 2, pp.67-70.

BRAITHWAITE, J. & M. BARKER (1978) 'Bodgies and Widgies: Folk Devils of the Fifties', in J. Braithwaite & P. R. Wilson, (eds), *Two Faces of Deviance*, University of Queensland Press, Brisbane, pp.26-45.

BRAITHWAITE, J. & P. R. WILSON (eds) (1978a) *Two Faces of Deviance*, University of Queensland Press, Brisbane.

BRAITHWAITE, J. & P. R. WILSON (1978b) 'Introduction: Pervs, Pimps, and Powerbrokers', in J. Braithwaite & P. R. Wilson (eds), *Two Faces of Deviance*, University of Queensland Press, Brisbane, pp.1-14.

BURNLEY, I. H. (1978) 'The Ecology of Suicide in an Australian Metropolis: The Case of Sydney', *Aust. J. of Social Issues*, Vol. 13, No. 2, pp.91-103.

CHAPPEL, D. & P. R. WILSON (1969) *The Police and the Public, in Australia and New Zealand*, University of Queensland Press, Brisbane.

COCK, P. (1974) 'Alternative Life-Styles: Theory and Practice', in Edgar, D. E. (ed.), *Social Change in Australia*, Cheshire, Melbourne, pp.630-42.

CRAWFORD REPORT (1979) *Study Group on Structural Adjustment*, A.G.P.S., Canberra.

de HOOG, J. (1972) *Skid Row Dossier*, Sun Books, Melbourne.

EDGAR, D. E. (1974) 'Reality Construction—Micro Processes and Macro Change', in D. E. Edgar (ed.), *Social Change in Australia*, Cheshire, Melbourne, pp.669-76.

EDGAR, D. E. (1975) 'The Schools Commission and Rural Disadvantage', *Collected Papers on Rural Education*, La Trobe Sociology Papers, No. 49, 1979.

EDGAR, D. E. (1976) 'Preparing Teachers for Change', *La Trobe Sociology Papers*, No. 32, La Trobe University, Melbourne.

EDWARDS, A. R. & P. R. WILSON (eds) (1975) *Social Deviance in Australia*, Cheshire, Melbourne.

EMERY, F. et al (1974) *Futures We're In*, Centre for Continuing Education, A.N.U., Canberra.

GIBBONS, A. R. (1977) 'Extending Flexi-time to Shiftworkers', *Work and People*, 3(1), pp.10-12.

GORRING, P. (1978) 'Multinationals or Mafia: Who Really Pushes Drugs?', in J. Braithwaite & P. R. Wilson (eds), *Two Faces of Deviance*, University of

Queensland Press, Brisbane, pp.81-100.

GRABOSKY, P. N. (1977) *Sydney in Ferment. Crime, Dissent and Official Reaction, 1788-1973*, A.N.U. Press, Canberra.

GRAYCAR, A. (1976) *Social Policy: An Australian Introduction*, Macmillan, Melbourne.

HAMPTON, R. (1975) 'Labelling Theory and the Police Decision to Prosecute Juveniles', *ANZJS*, Vol. 11, No. 3, pp.64-6.

HARVEY, L. V. (1978) 'Work and Family—Interacting Environments', *Work and People*, 4(1/2), pp.33-6.

HAY, C. G. (1979) 'Capitalism and Growth: The Environmental Cleavage', *La Trobe Sociology Papers*, No. 3 (new series), La Trobe University, Melbourne.

HEADLAM, F. (1978) 'Deviance Research: Bibliography of Australian Studies from 1960 to Date', *Bibliographies in Social Research*, No. 3, La Trobe University, Melbourne.

HILL, S. (1974) 'Science, Technology and Industry in Modern Society', A.I.P.S., *Industrial Australia 1975-2000*, Australia & N.Z. Book Co, Sydney, pp.1-23.

HILLER, A. (1974) 'Deviance in Australia', in Edgar, D. E. (ed.), *Social Change in Australia*, Cheshire, Melbourne, pp.515-34.

HODGE, P. (1978) 'Medibank Fraud', in J. Braithwaite & P. R. Wilson (eds), *Two Faces of Deviance*, University of Queensland Press, Brisbane, pp.123-31.

JORDAN, A. (1974a) 'Living Death in the Social Policy Section' in D. E. Edgar (ed.) (1974) *Social Change in Australia*, Cheshire, Melbourne, pp.409-25.

JORDAN, A. (1974b) 'Why These People? Why Skid Row?', in Edgar, D. E. (ed.), *Social Change in Australia*, Cheshire, Melbourne, pp.535-47.

KEMP, D. (1978) *Society and Electoral Behaviour in Australia: a Study of Three Decades*, University of Queensland Press, Brisbane.

KIRSNER, D. (1972) 'Domination and the Flight from Being', in J. Playford and D. Kirsner (eds), *Australian Capitalism: Towards a Socialist Critique*, Penguin, Melbourne.

LACHMUND, J. (1979) *Ideology of Working Class Systematic Thieves*, unpublished MA thesis, La Trobe University.

O'BRIEN, L. (1973) 'Some Defining Characteristics of the Hare Krishna Movement', *ANZJS*, Vol. 9, No. 2, pp.72-3.

PATIENCE, A. & B. HEAD (eds) (1979) *From Whitlam to Fraser*, Oxford University Press, Melbourne.

PETTMAN, J. (1975) 'Development Through Self Reliance', *ANZJS*, Vol. II, No. 1, pp.42-3.

PLAYFORD, J. (1969) *Neo-Capitalism in Australia*, Arena Publications, Melbourne.

ROGERS, P. H. (1976) 'Shiftwork: How Acceptable is it?', *Work and People*, 2(1), pp.20-6.

SAX, S. (ed.) (1970) *The Aged in Australian Society*, Angus & Robertson, Sydney.

SMITH, M. & D. CROSSLEY (eds) (1975) *The Way Out*, Lansdowne Press, Melbourne.

TELECOM 2000 (1975) Australian Telecommunications Commission.

TRAHAIR, R. C. S. (1978) 'A Contribution to the Psychoanalytic Study of the Modern Hero: The Case of James Bond', *La Trobe Sociology Papers*, No. 28, La Trobe University, Melbourne.

WHITROD, R. (1979) 'The Organization of Police Forces', in Edgar, D. E. (ed.) *Australia's Changing Future*, Monograph, La Trobe University, Department of Sociology.

WINDSHUTTLE, K. (1978) 'Granny Versus the Hooligans', in J. Braithwaite & P. R. Wilson (eds), *Two Faces of Deviance*, University of Queensland Press, Brisbane, pp.15-25.

b. General:

BAR-HILLEL, Y. (1954) 'Indexical Expressions', *Mind*, Vol. 63, pp.359-79.

BECKER, H. (1963) *Outsiders: Studies in the Sociology of Deviance*, Free Press, N.Y.

BELL, D. (1973) *The Coming of the Post-Industrial Society*, Basic Books, N.Y.

BENERIA, L. (1977) Book Review of Schooling for Socialist America, *Social Policy*, March/April, pp.51-5.

BIRNBAUM, N. (1970) *The Crisis of Industrial Society*, Oxford University Press, N.Y.

BOURDIEU, P. and J. C. PASSERON (1977) *Reproduction in Education, Society and Culture*, Sage, N.Y.

BOWLES, S. and H. GINTIS (1976) *Schooling in Capitalist America*, Basic Books, N.Y.

BURKETT, S. R. (1972) 'Self-Other Systems and Deviant Career Patterns', *Pacific Sociological Review*, Vol. 15, No. 2, pp.169-83.

BURNS, T. & G. STALKER (1961) *The Management of Innovation*, Tavistock, London.

CAMERON, W. B. (1966) *Modern Social Movements: A Sociological Outline*, Random House, N.Y.

CICOUREL, A. V. and J. I. KITSUSE (1963) *The Educational Decision-Makers*, Bobbs Merrill Inc., reprinted in J. Karabel & A. H. Halsey (eds), *Power and Ideology in Education*, (1977) pp.282-92.

COHEN, A. K. (1966) *Deviance and Control*, Prentice-Hall, New Jersey.

DENZIN, N. K. (1970) 'Rules of Conduct and the Study of Deviant Behavior: Some Notes on the Social Relationship', in J. D. Douglas (ed.), *Deviance and Respectability*, Basic Books, N.Y.

DENZIN, N. K. (1974) 'The Methodological Implications of Symbolic Interactionism for the Study of Deviance', *British Journal of Sociology*, 25, pp.269-82.

DOUGLAS, J. D. (ed.) (1970) *Deviance and Respectability*, Basic Books, N.Y.

DREIER, P. (1979) 'The Case for Transitional Reform', *Social Policy*, Vol. 9, No. 4, pp.5-17.

DRUCKER, P. F. (1971) *The Age of Discontinuity*, Pan Books, London.

EISENSTADT, S. N. (1966) *Modernization: Protest and Change*, Prentice-Hall, New Jersey.

ETZIONI, A. & E. ETZIONI-HALEVY (eds) (1973) *Social Change* (2nd ed.), Basic Books, N.Y.

GALT, A. H. & L. J. SMITH (1976) *Models and the Study of Social Change*, Halstead, N.Y.

GARFINKEL, H. (1967) *Studies in Ethnomethodology*, Prentice-Hall, New Jersey.

GARNER R. (1975) unpublished manuscript referred to in Dreier, P. 1979.

GOFFMAN, E. (1963) *Stigma*, Prentice-Hall, New Jersey.

GOFFMAN, E. (1968) *Asylums*, Penguin, U.K.

GORZ, A. (1973) *Socialism and Revolution*, Anchor Books, N.Y.

GRAMSCI, A. (1971) *Selections from the Prison Notebooks*, Lawrence & Wishart, London.

GRAMSCI, A. (1974 [1926]) 'Letters From Prison', *New Edinburgh Review*, special double issue, translated by Hamish Henderson, Edinburgh.

GUSFIELD, J. R. (ed.) (1970) *Protest, Reform and Revolt: A Reader in Social Movements*, John Wiley, N.Y.

HOLZNER, B. (1968) *Reality Construction in Society*, Schenkman, Cambridge, Mass.

HORTON, J. (1966) 'Order and Conflict Theories of Social Problems as Competing Ideologies', *American Journal of Sociology*, 71, pp.701-14.

JENCKS, (1972) *Inequality: A Reassessment of the Effect of Family and Schooling in America*, Basic Books, N.Y.

KAHN, H. & B. BRUCE-BIGGS (1972) *Things to Come*, Macmillan, N.Y.

KIRSNER, D. (1972) 'Domination and the Flight from Being' in J. Playford and D. Kirsner (eds) *Australian Capitalism*, Penguin, Melbourne.

LAING, R. D. (1965) *The Divided Self*, Pelican, U.K.

LAING, R. D. (1967) *The Politics of Experience*, Penguin, U.K.

LEMERT, E. M. (1967) *Human Deviance, Social Problems and Social Control*, Prentice-Hall, New Jersey.

LERNER, M. P. (1979) 'Surplus Powerlessness', *Social Policy*, Vol. 9, No. 4, pp.18-27.

LOFLAND, J. (1969) *Deviance and Identity*, Prentice-Hall, New Jersey.

McGEE, R. (1972) *Points of Departure*, Dryden Press, Ill.

McHUGH, P. (1969) 'A Common-sense Perception of Deviance', in Douglas, J. D., *Deviance and Respectability*, Basic Books, N.Y.; and in H. P. Dreitzel (ed.), *Recent Sociology No. 2*, Macmillan, London.

MATZA, D. (1969) *Becoming Deviant*, Prentice-Hall, New Jersey.

MERCER, J. (1977) *The Other Half*, Penguin, Melbourne.

MERTON, R. K. (1938) 'Social Structure and Anomie', *American Sociological Review*, 3, pp.672-82.

MERTON, R. K. (1956) *Social Theory and Social Structure*, Free Press, N.Y., especially pp.131-60.

MILLS, C. W. (1942) Referred to in Horton, 1966.

NISBET, R. A. (1969) *Social Change and History, Aspects of the Western Theory of Development*, Oxford University Press, N.Y.

PEIRCE, C. S. (1952) *Peirce and Pragmatism*, W. G. Gallic (ed.), Penguin, U.K.

RIST, R. C. (1977) 'On Understanding the Processes of Schooling: The Contributions of Labelling Theory', in J. Karabel & A. H. Halsey (eds), *Power and Ideology in Education*, Oxford University Press, Oxford, pp.292-306.

RUBINGTON, E. & M. S. WEINBERG (eds) (1968) *Deviance: The Interactionist Perspective*, Macmillan, N.Y.

SACKS, H. (1972) 'Notes on Police Assessment of Moral Character', in D. Sudnow (ed.), *Studies in Social Interaction*, Free Press, N.Y., pp.280-93.

SCHROYER, T. (1970) 'Toward a Critical Theory for Advanced Industrial Society', in H. P. Dreitzel (ed.), *Recent Sociology No. 2*, Macmillan, London, pp.210-34.

SCHUMACHER, E. F. (1973) *Small is Beautiful, a Study of Economics as if People Mattered*, Blond & Briggs, London.

SCHUR, E. M. (1971) *Labelling Deviant Behavior*, Harper & Row, N.Y.

SCHUTZ, A. (1971) 'Concept and Theory. Formation in the Social Sciences', in K. Thompson & J. Tunstall (eds), *Sociological Perspectives*, Penguin, U.K.

SLATER, P. (1970) *The Pursuit of Loneliness, American Culture at the Breaking Point*, Beacon Press, Boston.

SMITH, A. (1973) *The Concept of Social Change*, Routledge & Kegan Paul, London.

SUDNOW, D. (1965) 'Normal Crimes: Sociological Features of the Penal Code in a Public Defender Office', *Social Problems*, Vol. 12, No. 3, pp.255-76.

SUTHERLAND, E. H. (1949) *White Collar Crime*, Dryden, N.Y.

SYKES, G. and D. MATZA (1957) 'Techniques of naturalization', *American Sociological Review*, 22, December, pp.664-70.

TOFFLER, A. (1979) 'No Allocation Without Representation', *Social Policy*, Vol. 9, No. 4, pp.2-4.

TOURAINE, A. (1971) *The Post-Industrial Society*, Random House, N.Y.

TRICE, H. M. & P. M. ROMAN (1970) 'Delabelling, Relabelling, and Alcoholics Anonymous', *Social Problems*, Vol. 17, No. 4, pp.538-46.

TYACK, D. B. (1974) *The One Best System: a History of American Urban Education*, Harvard University Press, Cambridge, Mass.

WEINBERG, (1968) *The English Public Schools: The Sociology of Elite Education*, Atherton, N.Y.

WILSON, T. P. (1971) 'Normative and Interpretive Paradigms in Sociology', in J. D. Douglas (ed.), *Understanding Everyday Life*, Routledge and Kegan Paul, London.

WRONG, D. H. (1961) 'The Oversocialized Conception of Man', *American Sociological Review*, 26, 2, pp.183-93; reprinted in P. I. Rose (ed.), *The Study of Society*, 1970 (2nd ed.) Random House, N.Y., pp.132-43.

YINGER, M. J. (1960) 'Contraculture and Subculture', *American Sociological Review* (Oct.), pp.625-35.

ZIJDERVELD, A. C. (1971) *The Abstract Society, A Cultural Analysis of Our Time*, Doubleday Anchor, N.Y.

Appendix

Table A   College Plans of High School Students, by Intelligence and Family Social Status

		Family Socio-Economic Status (SES)					
		Hi				Lo	
		5	4	3	2	1	
Hi	5	85%	80%	75%	60%	45%	69%
	4	80%	76%	62%	53%	40%	62%
Intelligence	3	70%	68%	49%	44%	30%	52%
	2	65%	60%	50%	24%	20%	44%
Lo	1	60%	45%	25%	15%	10%	31%
		72%	66%	52%	39%	27%	
						(N = 1204)	

How to Read a Table

1. Don't panic. Numbers are not as frightening as they may appear. You do not have to be a mathematician to understand the tables that occur in this book. Tables, graphs, charts and diagrams are simply more concise ways of showing relationships between one aspect of social life and another. Our example here *cross-tabulates* two variables (intelligence and social status) to show how one dependent variable (college plans) is affected by them.

2. Read the *table headings*. They should tell you what is being explained (the *dependent variable*, usually shown by the figures *inside* the cells); and what influences are suggested as 'causes' (the *independent variable(s)*), usually listed as column (down) headings and row (across) headings. In our example, the rows split the sample of high school students into five intelligence groups, ranging from high (5) to low (1) and the columns split them into five family status groups, again ranging from high (5) to low (1).

3. Look at the figures in the *margins*, for each row and each column. They tell you the average effect of one independent variable on what is being explained. For the first row across, the 'marginal' figure is 69 per cent, whereas for the bottom row it is only 31 per cent. That tells us intelligence affects college-going plans quite drastically. In other words, the lower your intelligence, the lower your plans to attend college. Similarly, the first column of high family status students averages 72 per cent, whereas those from low status homes include only 27 per cent who plan to go to college. From the table, then, we may say that both lower status and lower intelligence reduce college-going aspirations.

4. Look at the figures *inside* the cells of the table. Each cell represents a group of people within the total sample. The figure inside tells you how many of that group plan to go to college (or whatever the *dependent* variable happens to be). In our table example, the top left-hand cell tells you that 85 per cent of those in the highest intelligence group, who are also from the highest family SES, plan to go to college once they've left school. Compare that figure with the bottom right-hand cell, where only 10 per cent of the least intelligent students from the poorest homes plan to go to college.

5. Now you can start *interpreting* the table. Notice that the reduction in college plans in column one (from 85 to 60 per cent) is not as great as the reduction in row one (from 60 to 10 per cent). Perhaps, then, low intelligence has less effect on college aspirations than does coming from a low status family background. In other words, comparing cells shows us the *interaction effects* of one variable on another. What other conclusions can you draw from comparing figures in the table?

6. Read what the author claims the table shows. Remember, there are 'lies, damned lies, and statistics'; it's very easy to select some figures for emphasis and ignore those that don't support your argument.

7. Overall, be critical and inquisitive. Ask what is the *sample*? How big is it? (usually shown as N= and preferably also shown for each cell). How representative is it, and how far can we generalize to the wider *population*? Should other factors have been taken into account? For example, sex, school type, parental pressure, religion, might all have had an effect on college-going plans, but this table looks only at intelligence and social status. How were these measured, anyway? The measures may have been unreliable, or may distort the usually accepted meanings of those terms.

8. When measures of *association* and/or *significance* are given they indicate the *strength* of the relationship between the independent and dependent variables. That is, how much greater than *chance* it is that these findings have occurred. If they could have happened by chance, then we would have explained nothing. A probability of 0.05, for example, means that there are *fewer than five chances in a hundred* that these effects could have occurred by chance. If that were the case, we could be confident that we had 'explained' the social relationship in a significant way.

9. Always look at the table *first*. It saves time then in reading the text and assessing what the author claims has been 'shown'.

Author Index

Subject Index